SOCIAL ORIGINS OF THE IRANIAN REVOLUTION

Studies in Political Economy
A series edited by Michael Schwartz

SOCIAL ORIGINS OF THE IRANIAN REVOLUTION

Misagh Parsa

RUTGERS UNIVERSITY PRESS
New Brunswick and London

Library of Congress Cataloging-in-Publication Data

Parsa, Misagh, 1945–
  Social origins of the Iranian revolution / Misagh Parsa.
    p.   cm.—(Studies in political economy)
  Bibliography: p.
  Includes index.
  ISBN 0-8135-1411-8 (cloth) ISBN 0-8135-1412-6 (pbk.)
    1. Iran—Politics and government—1941–1979.   2. Iran—Politics
  and government—1979–   3. Revolutions—Iran.   4. Revolutions—Case
  studies.   5. Revolutions—Social aspects—Iran.   I. Title.
  II. Series.
  DS316.6.P37   1989
  955'.053—dc19   88-31285
                                                                                              CIP

British Cataloging-in-Publication information available

For Susan and Arlen Kian

Contents

Preface

In this book I attempt to explain the social causes of the Iranian revolution. In many ways, the revolution and its outcome have appeared unusual and, undoubtedly, very complex. Over the years, I became skeptical of the prevailing explanations of the revolution offered by other scholars. Some explained the revolutionary conflicts in Iran in terms of reactions to modernization, which, they argued, undermined traditional social structures and created normlessness. This explanation was not convincing because many participants in the conflicts insisted on political freedom, social justice, and the elimination of foreign domination. Iranians had fought for these goals long before the 1979 revolution. Hence, normlessness and confusion could not account for the revolution. Other scholars explained the revolutionary conflicts in terms of socioeconomic development and the rise of new social classes that demanded political participation. Once again, this analysis was unconvincing because Iranians had held the ideals of political freedom and participation long before the recent socioeconomic development. Still other analysts explained the revolutionary conflicts in terms of the rise of Islamic fundamentalism. This explanation also seemed unconvincing because the vast majority of participants in the revolutionary uprising did not indicate in any way that they wanted to establish a society based on fundamentalist principles. Moreover, the establishment of the Islamic Republic did not put an end to the social and political conflicts, as might have been expected had a consensus existed. Finally, these theories were entirely too sketchy to explain the very complex processes that led to the downfall of the monarchy.

To explain this revolution, I concluded that a broad theory of revolution and political conflict was needed that could be applied to contemporary Third World countries, Iran among them, From the mid-1970s, I had been working on developing such a theory. The Iranian revolution spurred me to put together the elements of this theory, which is intended to illuminate political conflicts and revolution in the Third World. This book presents a structural theory of collective action and revolution. Specifically, the research analyzes Iranian social structure as a framework within which to understand how and why social conflicts emerged and were directed against the state.

To avoid explaining the revolution in terms of its outcome, I have focused on the actions and interactions of all the major participants in the revolutionary conflicts, in depth and over time. To my knowledge, no previous study of the Iranian revolution has undertaken a detailed investigation of the mobilization and collective actions of various groups and classes prior to, during, and after the overthrow of the monarchy. The present work represents just such an undertaking, focusing on specific events of collective action initiated by the major groups throughout the country that participated in the revolution. The most important sources of data on mobilization and collective action were official newspapers, although I also interviewed a number of individuals, particularly bazaaris, who were active in the political mobilization. In addition, I used government documents and scholarly sources to gather evidence on the pattern of economic development of Iran. Thus, this book contains both a new theoretical framework and new data on the collective actions that comprised the revolution.

Chapter 1 opens with a critique of previous explanations of the Iranian revolution and presents my alternative structural theory of economic development and social conflict. Chapter 2 presents an outline of the political conflicts of Iran during the twentieth century, particularly the period prior to the overthrow of the monarchy. Chapter 3 analyzes the regime's economic policies, which set the stage for the revolutionary conflicts. Chapters 4 through 7 examine the attacks against the state mounted by merchants, artisans, industrial and white-collar workers, secular organizations, and the clergy. The role played by each group or class in the political conflicts is evaluated in depth. Chapter 8 reviews the final confrontation between opposition groups and the regime and details the disintegration of the state. Chapter 9 examines the post-revolutionary conflicts and collective actions within the Islamic Republic and analyzes the political outcome of the revolution. Finally, chapter 10 presents the conclusions derived from this research.

A number of scholars read an earlier version of the manuscript and provided valuable comments. They include Ervand Abrahamian, William Gamson, Jeffery Paige, Charles Tilly, and Thomas Weisskopf. I also discussed various ideas in the manuscript with Howard Kimeldorf, Aldon Morris, Marc Steinberg, and Mayer Zald, and benefited from their comments. I owe a great debt of appreciation to Michael Schwartz, whose comments and questions significantly enriched the manuscript and helped me clarify many of the difficult and puzzling issues in the work. I also wish to thank Gernot Windfuhr for his assistance in preparing the English transliteration of Persian names. John Downey at the University of Michigan Library obtained and generously made available many government documents and official newspapers. I am grateful to all of the above-mentioned individuals for their interest and for their suggestions. My thanks go also to Marlie Wasserman, Kate Harrie, and the editorial staff of Rutgers University Press for their assistance in preparing the manuscript.

Several other individuals generously encourged and supported me in various ways, including my brother, Shoa Parsa, and Paula Nelson. My wife, Susan Rosales Nelson, not only provided support, patience, and love throughout the preparation of the book, she also read the entire manuscript and raised a number of critical issues. Many people helped to gather leaflets and statements published by various groups during the years 1977 to 1981. Others helped locate unusual publications and specific individuals in Europe and the United States for interviews. Finally, a number of individuals agreed to be interviewed for this research and provided invaluable information. For a variety of reasons, they wish to remain anonymous. Although I have thanked them privately, I would like to take this opportunity to express my deepest appreciation to them.

SOCIAL ORIGINS OF THE IRANIAN REVOLUTION

Part One

Introduction and
background

Chapter 1

Explanations of the Revolution

> Collective action of ordinary people exposes the fallacy of treating "violence," "protest," or "disorder" as a world apart, as a phenomenon distinct from high politics, as a mere reaction to stress. There lies the most important teaching of popular collective action: it is not an epiphenomenon. It connects directly and solidly with the great political questions. By the actions that authorities call disorder, ordinary people fight injustice, challenge exploitation, and claim their own place in the structure of power. (Tilly 1986:403)

In the spring of 1977, the Shah of Iran faced challenges from separate segments of the population that gradually became consolidated and culminated in the overthrow of the Pahlavi dynasty in February 1979. The revolutionary struggle was largely carried out by a coalition of classes and political groups, each mobilized by separate interests and conflicts. Eventually, political power was transferred to a religious faction led by Ayatollah Ruhollah Khomeini, who by that time had garnered overwhelming popular support.

The emergence of the opposition movement and its revolutionary outcome came as a surprise to many experts and observers. Iran had been one of the most rapidly industrializing Third World nations and gave the impression of having brought prosperity to its citizens. Furthermore, the Pahlavi regime was supported by a powerful, loyal army and by a network of demands for popular participation. The Shah's unwillingness to permit greater participation led to societal instability and eventual breakdown. More recently, Green added additional factors to explain the revolution (1986). These included the Shah's declining coercive will to repress middle-class professionals who demanded political liberalization. Another factor was the polarization of the population against the regime, particularly by the thousands of mullahs who, through mosque networks, politicized recent urban migrants. Amin Saikal (1980:203–204) and Nasser Momayezi (1986) explained the revolution in terms of rapid socioeconomic development, which generated new factors, such as a new middle class that demanded political participation, incompatible with a centralized monarchy. Iran's lack of political development gave rise to instability and conflict. Gary Sick (1985:159) argued that the revolution resulted from a long period of economic growth, which was not accompanied by political development as most social groups were still excluded from the political process. As a result, once discontent began to seethe in reaction to a halt in the economic boom, Iranians attacked the political system. Nikki Keddie's (1983) application of a "Marxist formula," which predicted that revolutions occur when there is a disjunction between economic and political structures, also falls within this analytic category. According to her analysis, the rise of new classes and the monarch's increasing arbitrariness explain the conflict and revolution.

A number of analysts have invoked the theory of rising expectations and Davies' J-curve to explain the Iranian revolution. John Stempel (1981:9) maintained that the government's rapid development policy encouraged Iranians to expect a better quality of life. Improved economic conditions, however, did not reach most Iranians. The shortfall between expectations and results produced the political conflicts. Nikki Keddie (1983) applied Davies' J-curve to explain the revolution. She maintained that Iran's pre-revolutionary experience fit neatly into Davies' J-curve: rapid economic improvements followed by a sharp downswing, which prepared conditions for the revolution. The economic decline especially affected recent urban migrants and the clergy; these groups, along with intellectuals and a large educated class, provided the backbone of the conflicts.

There are both theoretical and empirical weaknesses in these analyses. One variation of breakdown theories emphasizes the disruptive impact of large-scale transformations that generate disorientation and anomie. Analysts often point to the politicization of populations, such as recent urban migrants, who have been uprooted from their social institutions.

Chapter 1

Explanations of the Revolution

Collective action of ordinary people exposes the fallacy of treating "violence," "protest," or "disorder" as a world apart, as a phenomenon distinct from high politics, as a mere reaction to stress. There lies the most important teaching of popular collective action: it is not an epiphenomenon. It connects directly and solidly with the great political questions. By the actions that authorities call disorder, ordinary people fight injustice, challenge exploitation, and claim their own place in the structure of power. (Tilly 1986:403)

In the spring of 1977, the Shah of Iran faced challenges from separate segments of the population that gradually became consolidated and culminated in the overthrow of the Pahlavi dynasty in February 1979. The revolutionary struggle was largely carried out by a coalition of classes and political groups, each mobilized by separate interests and conflicts. Eventually, political power was transferred to a religious faction led by Ayatollah Ruhollah Khomeini, who by that time had garnered overwhelming popular support.

The emergence of the opposition movement and its revolutionary outcome came as a surprise to many experts and observers. Iran had been one of the most rapidly industrializing Third World nations and gave the impression of having brought prosperity to its citizens. Furthermore, the Pahlavi regime was supported by a powerful, loyal army and by a network of secret police. The army guaranteed stability within Iran as well as in the entire Persian Gulf region, while the secret police demonstrated considerable competence in repressing internal dissent. Finally, no division, conflict, or defection had taken place within the dominant class or the armed forces prior to the revolutionary conflicts that might have left a state susceptible to collapse, as Skocpol (1979) theorized in her analysis of the French, Russian, and Chinese revolutions.

The Iranian revolution was distinct from most other twentieth-century revolutions in several ways. First, the collective actions that emerged and became the basis of the revolution were primarily urban. In contrast to the Russian, Chinese, and Vietnamese revolutions, which had a strong rural component, the Iranian revolution lacked peasant participation until the final stage; even then, peasants were never essential to the downfall of the regime. Second, the conflicts were manifested primarily through massive, unprecedented demonstrations and prolonged workers' strikes with no large-scale guerrilla attacks launched against government security forces, as occurred in China, Cuba, and Nicaragua. Third, mobilization of the regime's opponents and their collective actions were carried out in part through the institution of the mosque. Consequently, a segment of the Islamic clergy gained ascendancy within the opposition and was eventually able to establish a theocracy. This outcome contrasts sharply with other modern revolutionary movements, which have been fought in the name of socialism and/or nationalism and have concluded with the transfer of power to a secular, modernizing intelligentsia.

In other ways, the collective actions that overthrew the monarchy bore certain resemblances to other twentieth-century revolutions, thereby allowing us to regard it as a revolution. To begin with, the collective actions were initiated by social classes and groups that had been excluded from the power structure. The vast majority of those who participated in the demonstrations and strikes opposed the system's repressive nature and demanded political freedom, democracy, social equality, and economic justice. They also rejected foreign domination and vowed to put an end to external exploitation. Finally, the conflicts culminated in the transfer of power to a new group of leaders who envisioned fundamental economic and social changes in the structure of Iranian society. Specifically, Ayatollah Khomeini consistently promised independence and freedom; after the revolution he also emphasized that the Islamic Republic would be an egalitarian social and economic system in which the interests of the *mostazafin*, the deprived and the oppressed, would be served.

Theoretical explanations of the conflicts and collective actions that led to the overthrow of the monarchy in Iran fall into two general types: models of social breakdown and models of social movement.[1] The social breakdown model emphasizes the processes that result in the dissolution of traditional social structure, norms, and values. Large-scale social transformations such as industrialization, commercialization, and urbanization are hypothesized to generate social disorganization and its accompanying strains, frustrations, and grievances, which may explode in collective violence and civil disorder (Johnson 1966; Smelser 1962, 1966). One variation of this model emphasizes social mobilization and the resultant rise of new needs and demands, which in turn may engender political tension (Deutsch 1961). Another variation stresses the destabilizing effects of rapid social and economic change and the resultant disjunction between political and economic development, which may produce disorder and violence (Huntington 1968). In contrast, the social movement model follows Weber's emphasis on ideational factors and authority figures. Social movements are founded upon "the conscious volition, normative commitment to . . . aims or beliefs, and active participation on the part of followers or members" (Wilkinson 1971:27). According to this view, groups develop new collective definitions of the world and of themselves that elaborate new goals, norms of behavior, and justifications for the power of authorities. The collective actions of any group follow from its initial commitment to such a particular belief system.

BREAKDOWN THEORIES

Most scholars who have attempted to explain the Iranian revolution have used some form of the social breakdown model.[2] Majid Tehranian, for example, argued that modernization entailed a triple curse for Iran (1980). It reduced the cohesion of a traditional society by uprooting the indigenous social institutions; at the same time, it created a new elite whose culture differed from the rest of society, thereby creating deep social divisions; and finally, modernization generated an acquisitive consumption culture. The social system was not able to absorb the disintegrating effects of these forces.

Another aspect of the breakdown model was emphasized by Jerrold Green (1980), who focused on the emerging disjunction between economic and political development: rapid socioeconomic development gave rise to demands for popular participation. The Shah's unwillingness to permit greater participation led to societal instability and eventual breakdown. More recently, Green added additional factors to explain the revolution (1986). These included the Shah's declining coercive will to repress middle-class professionals who demanded political liberalization. Another factor was the polarization of the population against the regime, particularly by the thousands of mullahs who, through mosque networks, politicized recent urban migrants. Amin Saikal (1980:203–204) and Nasser Momayezi (1986) explained the revolution in terms of rapid socioeconomic development, which generated new factors, such as a new middle class that demanded political participation, incompatible with a centralized monarchy. Iran's lack of political development gave rise to instability and conflict. Gary Sick (1985:159) argued that the revolution resulted from a long period of economic growth, which was not accompanied by political development as most social groups were still excluded from the political process. As a result, once discontent began to seethe in reaction to a halt in the economic boom, Iranians attacked the political system. Nikki Keddie's (1983) application of a "Marxist formula," which predicted that revolutions occur when there is a disjunction between economic and political structures, also falls within this analytic category. According to her analysis, the rise of new classes and the monarch's increasing arbitrariness explain the conflict and revolution.

A number of analysts have invoked the theory of rising expectations and Davies' J-curve to explain the Iranian revolution. John Stempel (1981:9) maintained that the government's rapid development policy encouraged Iranians to expect a better quality of life. Improved economic conditions, however, did not reach most Iranians. The shortfall between expectations and results produced the political conflicts. Nikki Keddie (1983) applied Davies' J-curve to explain the revolution. She maintained that Iran's pre-revolutionary experience fit neatly into Davies' J-curve: rapid economic improvements followed by a sharp downswing, which prepared conditions for the revolution. The economic decline especially affected recent urban migrants and the clergy; these groups, along with intellectuals and a large educated class, provided the backbone of the conflicts.

There are both theoretical and empirical weaknesses in these analyses. One variation of breakdown theories emphasizes the disruptive impact of large-scale transformations that generate disorientation and anomie. Analysts often point to the politicization of populations, such as recent urban migrants, who have been uprooted from their social institutions.

The theoretical problem with this analysis is that uprooted individuals rarely possess the necessary resources, solidarities, and organizations for mobilization and collective action. The very experience of being uprooted is likely to reduce their capacity for collective action by dissolving preexisting solidarity structures (Tilly, Tilly, and Tilly 1975). Second, even if uprooted populations were to engage in collective action, they would be more likely to attack other social groups such as landlords or merchants through rent strikes or food riots rather than the state. After all, why should uprooted individuals suddenly become politicized and attack the government, which possesses great resources to repress the unruly?

Although Iran's economic development created a large group of urban migrants, available data, though sparse, does not support the breakdown model. Evidence indicates that in the summer of 1977 when the regime began demolishing shantytowns around Tehran, recent migrants who lived in those areas were the last to organize and act collectively against the government (OIPFG 1978a:4–5). Later, during the revolutionary uprising, squatters' mobilization was far from complete (Kazemi 1980:95). As late as December 4, 1978, one squatter told a *New York Times* reporter that he was obliged to work from 6:00 A.M. to 7:00 P.M. and had no time to demonstrate, but he knew that "things will get better once the king goes." On January 14, 1979, less than a month before the monarchy fell, the *Washington Post* quoted another squatter as saying, "The demonstrations are all crap. No one has done anything for us except when we stopped a car heading elsewhere that was distributing clothes in Khomeini's name. We have heard about the demonstrations, but we don't take part; to demonstrate you have to have a full stomach." The man added, "Whoever gives us bread and work, we will be with him."

In the more formal industrial sector, recent migrants appear to have been the least inclined to join strikes. For example, recent migrants employed at Isfahan Steel lacked the politicization of urbanized workers and partly caused the failure of the steelworkers' strike in the fall of 1978 (*Zobe-Ahan* 1978:16–17). Their politicization was inhibited because some migrants worked only part-time in the city to supplement their agrarian income. They also had the option of returning to their villages if urban employment proved unsatisfactory. It is worth noting that, with the exception of villagers in Varamin, most peasants did not take part in the 1963 uprising led by the clergy.

During the final weeks of the revolution, some urban migrants, like a segment of the peasantry, became politicized and joined antigovernment demonstrations. By this time, however, the regime was already unstable. Recent migrants and some peasants were mobilized after the revolution and supported the clergy once they came to power, but these groups did not play a crucial role in overthrowing the monarchy. In sum, one cannot conclude that migrants were crucial in initiating the conflicts or were essential to the overthrow of the government.

Another version of the breakdown theory emphasizes the disjunction between socioeconomic and political development. According to this perspective, the Shah's development policies generated a new middle class that demanded political freedom and democracy. Some theorists point to the National Front, the Lawyers' Association, and the Writers' Association as examples of middle-class organizations that began demanding political freedom in the summer of 1977. Without a doubt, the new middle class expanded during Iran's rapid economic development of the 1960s and 1970s. This theory fails, however, to account for the earlier emergence of vigorous political conflicts in Iran in the absence of a sizable new middle class during the Constitutional Revolution of 1905–1911 or during the 1940s and the 1950s. It should be noted, though, that most of the leading figures in these organizations had been politically active since the 1950s and early 1960s, before Iran had yet experienced much socioeconomic development. Even if we assume that these organizations represented the new middle class, this class did not respond to attempts by these organizations to mount opposition against the government. The new middle class had little capacity for political action, lacking the requisite solidarity structures and organizations to act collectively. White-collar employees and professionals refrained from entering the conflict for more than one year after reformist political organizations had initiated opposition activities. When they finally joined the conflict, most initially demanded economic rather than political changes. In short, the new middle class cannot be said to have instigated collective action against the state; rather, they joined in struggles that had been launched by others.

Theoretical explanations that invoke rising expectations or Davies' J-curve argue that when oil revenues suddenly dropped, satisfaction, which had risen along with expectations as Iran's economic condition improved, rapidly diminished, leading to collective action and revolution. These theories ignore several important components of collective action, including the differential effects of economic development, the capacity of actors, and the targets of action. First, although higher oil revenues undoubtedly improved the satisfaction of some social groups, that experience cannot be generalized to the country as a whole. In highly stratified societies, economic improvements are unlikely to benefit all social classes or to benefit them equally. Although land reform raised peasants' expectations and temporarily improved conditions for some of them, the economic growth of the 1970s had a negative impact on the income and expectations of the vast majority of the rural population. In urban areas, although Iranian industrialists accumulated huge sums of capital, most industrial workers were adversely affected by higher oil revenues, which boosted inflation. Second, in order for groups to respond with collective action when their established rights and interests are violated, they must possess sufficient solidarity structures and resources. The J-curve and the theory of rising expectations assume the existence of both solidarity and organization, a dubious assumption, and hence are inadequate to explain mobilization and collective action. Despite deteriorating agricultural conditions, peasants took little part in the collective actions of revolutionary conflicts. Not until the final days of the revolution did a segment of the peasantry join in the antigovernment protests, and their actions were inconsequential. Similarly, industrial workers lacked the capacity and organization to mobilize and initiate collective action to obtain a greater share of the increased national resources. Thus they did not engage in any political action in the early stage of the conflicts, despite declining satisfaction, or "frustration" of their "expectations."

Nor, finally, do these theories specify the target of collective action. Reduced satisfaction does not necessarily lead to an assault on the state. A natural disaster, for example, might drastically reduce human satisfaction but may not generate collective action, let alone a challenge to the state. Even when reduced satisfaction is attributed to social causes, adversely affected groups may turn upon a class or group deemed responsible. In such cases the dominant class or a minority group, rather than the state, may become the target of attack. During the 1930s, the Great Depression in the United States did not prompt an offensive against the state. Instead, industrial workers confronted their employers and achieved certain rights, including the recognition of labor unions for collective bargaining (Parsa 1985). In contrast, Iranian bazaaris acted against the state, which they identified as the source of conflict and injustice. Had the Iranian economic decline been perpetrated by the market mechanism, bazaaris might have ended up blaming themselves, as did some American businessmen during the depression. For all these reasons, the J-curve and the theory of rising expectations provide at best only a partial explanation of the Iranian revolution.

THE SOCIAL MOVEMENT MODEL

A second line of explanation for the Iranian revolution follows the social movement model. In contrast to breakdown theories, which identify the erosion of traditional values and structures as the fundamental cause of the revolution, the social movement model assigns primary importance to religious values and the legitimate authority of the clergy. Said Arjomand (1981, 1986) has presented an analysis combining elements of both breakdown and social movement models, but with greater emphasis upon the latter. He assigns only a minor role to class interests in the revolution (1986:400; 1988:200), stressing instead ideology, tradition, and legitimacy. According to Arjomand, rapid social change led to dislocation, "normative disturbance," and disorientation (1986:383). To reintegrate themselves into the community and reaffirm their collective cultural identity (Arjomand 1981:312), dislocated individuals and groups—specifically recent migrants, the urban poor, and the new middle class—embraced an Islamic revival from the mid-1960s onward. The clergy opposed the Shah because his policies had systematically undermined their position. During the revolution, the entire clergy rose against the state (Arjomand 1988:192). With the disintegration of central authority, the clergy extended their legitimate authority from the religious sphere to the political sphere and assumed leadership. Finally, specific features of Shiite Islam such as the Shiite theodicy of suffering, the martyrdom of Imam Husayn, and Shiite millenarianism enabled the clergy to harness traditional religious sentiments in the struggle against the regime (Arjomand 1981; 1988:99–101).

Although Theda Skocpol is not a social movement theorist, her analysis of the Iranian collective actions falls within this category. In her 1982 discussion of Iran, Skocpol departed from her earlier structural theory of revolution in which she had refuted a model of revolution based on ideological causation (1979). The Iranian case, she later argued, was unique and did follow a model of purposive action. More specifically, she elaborated on the possible role of ideas and culture in shaping political action (Skocpol 1982:268). Although the Iranian monarchy was fundamentally weak, lacking a strong class base, and the Shah's program of crash industrialization and military modernization generated universal resentment against him, the Shah, according to Skocpol, should have been able to retain power due to the enormous wealth and ominous repressive power at his disposal. Ultimately, the force behind the Shah's downfall lay in "traditional centers of urban communal life and in networks of Islamic communication and leadership" (Skocpol 1982:271), that is, in bazaars and mosques. In Skocpol's view, the clergy were the leaders of the bazaar. By the mid-1970s, "the Shah seemed determined to attack the traditional aspects of bazaar life" (Skocpol 1982:272), which also coincided with the Shah's steady efforts to exclude the Islamic clergy from educational, legal, and welfare activities. The clergy, who, trained to interpret Islamic law for believers, could claim, "as well or better than the monarchs, to represent authentically the will of the Hidden Imam" (Skocpol 1982:273), provided leadership, networks, and symbols of communication against the Shah during the revolution. Even more important in sustaining the struggles, Skocpol argues, was the Shiite belief system. In particular, the story of Husayn's willing martyrdom in the just cause of resisting the usurper caliph, Yazid, inspired devout Shiites to continue their opposition against the Shah in the face of repression and death.

Although Arjomand and Skocpol differ on major theoretical issues, their explanations of the determinants of political conflicts are very similar. Both focus on the importance of specific Shiite beliefs and on the clergy's legitimate authority in mobilizing the Iranian people, overthrowing the monarchy, and seizing power. In short, they stress the role of ideas, symbols, and legitimacy. Perhaps cultural and religious symbols do play a role in political mobilization; however, their part must be considered within the larger social and economic framework. Current explanations that use the social movement model tend to be circular accounts beginning with the outcome of the revolution, that is, clerical victory or the establishment of the Islamic Republic, and working backward to rationalize it. Such analyses obscure the process that led to those outcomes. In this connection, it is important to note that in 1963, when most clergy opposed the government reforms as anti-Islamic, clerical authority and appeals to Shiite martyrdom were insufficient to mobilize industrial workers, white-collar employees and professionals, and the peasantry. Protests of segments of the population in a few major cities lasted for a short time, after which government repression brought them to an end. Thus, by themselves these variables are not sufficient to explain the collapse of the monarchy in the 1979 revolution. Furthermore, Arjomand's hypothesis that the political conflicts stemmed from religious revival brought about by modernization is faulty. The political protests of 1963 assumed a religious character just as religious processions of Muharram assumed a political character. However, in 1963, Iran had not yet experienced any significant modernization; rapid modernization supposedly came only after the Shah's White Revolution and reforms. In addition, the conflicts of 1977–1979 were too complex, both in terms of actors and of their grievances, to be explained simply as a social-psychological variable of anomie resulting from dislocation.

Skocpol's analysis is also misleading because it portrays urban Iranians as constituting traditional communities that always followed their religious leaders. That urban Iranians all ultimately opposed the monarchy does not prove that they were composed of such communities. Indeed, Iranian society was divided along class lines long before the 1979 revolution. Even bazaaris did not form communities because, as I will show, they were economically and politically diverse. More importantly, the different groups and classes that opposed the government had different resources and solidarities, as well as different conflicts and grievances, and therefore entered into active opposition at different times (Abrahamian 1982:496–524; Ashraf and Banuazizi 1985).

Both Arjomand and Skocpol stress the significance of the clergy and their legitimacy as leaders. They tend to portray the clergy as a homogeneous social stratum pursuing a united politics. In fact, the clergy were far from unified in the 1970s. Religious authorities represented a spectrum of political views, and generalizations about their political contribution are misleading. Finally, explanations that emphasize the role of legitimate authority and reintegration cannot explain why the establishment of the Islamic Republic and clerical rule did not put an end to the political conflicts. There seem to be other variables and factors involved that must be taken into account.

In the remainder of this chapter, I shall offer a structural theory of collective action and revolution to explain the Iranian revolution in the context of the revolutionary movements in the Third World. This structural theory will illuminate the importance of the state and social classes in generating social revolutions. Thus, I shall analyze the relation between state economic policies and social conflict. Furthermore, this theory will also focus on the capacity of social groups to undertake collective action and the likelihood of social classes to form coalitions and consolidate their opposition against the government.

A STRUCTURAL MODEL

Recent theories of social revolution have analyzed structural factors such as international pressures and the political economies of states (Goldstone 1986). In contrast to earlier works, which focused on determinants of political violence, these theories have attempted to explain not only revolutionary conflicts but also their possible outcomes. The following analysis is inspired by Jeffery Paige's 1975 structural theory of revolution, as well as by the contributions of various resource-mobilization theorists (Gamson 1975; Schwartz 1976; Tilly 1978; McCarthy and Zald 1977).

Although conflicts characterize all social orders, the natures and outcomes of conflicts vary widely. Under some social conditions, conflicts may have reformist consequences; in others, they may lead to revolutions. These two alternative experiences have characterized political developments in developed and developing countries in the twentieth century. While core capitalist countries have experienced reformist social movements, many Third World societies have undergone revolutionary upheavals. To some extent, reforms in the core and revolutions in the periphery are interrelated as both are parts of a single world system. Economic exploitation of the periphery by core countries makes possible higher standards of living, social reforms, and reduction of internal conflicts in the core. At the same time, foreign domination and extraction of resources from peripheral countries undermine attempts by these societies to industrialize, thus generating conflicts that may have revolutionary outcomes. Because the world system renders some states politically and economically vulnerable, an understanding of the location of different societies within the world system is necessary to analyze the relationship between social conflict and political development.

However, the world system only sets the stage; it does not determine the actors and the nature of the action. Thus, we must also pay close attention to concrete social structures and the sources of their vulnerability, both internal and external. A social structural explanation will enable us to specify the circumstances under which fundamental change occurs and the conditions that generate alternative possibilities in the absence of revolution. Social revolution is but one outcome of social conflict, and a comprehensive theory must specify situations that generate other results as well. Under what conditions do human beings join together to bring about partial or fundamental changes? Alternatively, at what point do aggrieved groups grant inevitability to their situation or blame themselves or other victims for their suffering? In the theory presented below, we shall examine the interaction among state, economy, and capacity for collective action, as well as international dependence. By focusing on these structural factors, we can better analyze social conflicts and their possible outcomes: inaction, repression, reform, or revolution.

The likelihood that collective action will occur, its targets, and its outcome are all influenced by social structure. In particular, two structural factors are of central importance: the link between political and economic structures, and the level of solidarity and consolidation among adversely affected groups. The variable of state intervention represents the extent to which the state, rather than market forces, determines the forms and nature of allocation and accumulation of capital. Measures of state intervention include the following: the degree of ownership and investment in the economy, especially in the key sectors; the amount of control over financial resources; the extent to which the government's allocation of capital excludes major social groups below the narrow ruling bloc; the degree to which the government creates and protects monopolies through limited licensing and rationing of foreign exchange; and the extent of government repression used to extract surplus from the working classes. Consolidation refers to the extent of social cohesion. By levels of consolidation, I mean the proportion of population that is both disadvantaged and organized in a bloc. Thus, a high level of consolidation implies the formation of coalitions. In the theory presented below, I shall focus on collective actions that are directed against major centers of political and economic power. This theory can best be used to explain social conflicts in societies characterized by both public and private spheres, although aspects may be applicable to other types of social orders as well. Table 1.1 presents a schematic view of the relationship between levels of state intervention in capital accumulation and levels of consolidation of adversely affected groups, as well as expected outcomes of social conflict.

I shall argue that segmented class conflict is likely when the level of state intervention in capital allocation and accumulation and the level of consolidation are both low. Under such conditions, disadvantaged groups or classes with strong solidarity structures engage in collective action against the dominant class for economic gain. Because state intervention is low, the government does not become the target of attack and consequently remains intact. In contrast, where state intervention is high and consolida-

Table 1.1. Interaction between State Intervention and Consolidation, and Likely Outcome

	LEVELS OF STATE INTERVENTION	
CONSOLIDATION LEVELS	Low	High
Low	Segmented class conflict	Segmented conflict against the state
High	Popular struggles for social reforms	Popular struggles to seize state power

tion is low, segmented conflict develops and may be directed against the state. Because these conflicts are segmented, they can be suppressed or rendered ineffective. A third possibility, reformist conflict, may occur when the level of consolidation is high and intervention is low. Under such conditions, conflict tends to remain restricted to the civil society, thus increasing the likelihood that political structures will remain unchallenged. Although the state may be drawn into class conflict, it is unlikely to become the target of attack. Instead, disadvantaged classes often attempt to use the state against their adversaries, which is usually the dominant class. The result may be social reform. Finally, the likelihood of revolutionary conflicts is greatest when levels of state intervention and consolidation are both high. State intervention in capital accumulation limits and politicizes the market and economic issues, rendering the state vulnerable to attack. Adversely affected classes and groups that have consolidated their forces will attack the state and may be able to seize state power.

To clarify the logic of this theory, the relationship between various forms of political-economic structure will be presented along with their implications for collective action. The theoretical discussion will be illustrated with some brief examples. The effect of solidarity structures and consolidation on collective action will also be analyzed.

SOCIAL STRUCTURE AND THE NATURE OF COLLECTIVE ACTION

Collective action results from the pursuit of common interests by adversely affected collectivities and has often occurred in response to violations of established rights. But aggrieved classes or groups do not automatically initiate collective action. Human suffering and pain by themselves do not generate sufficient cause for insurgency, let alone attempts to transform society. For collective action to take place, victimized collectivities must at least identify a concrete social or human entity responsible for their suffering. As Barrington Moore observed, "It is not the objective suffering that is the main cause of moral anger; it is the apparent social cause. To perceive the causes as human is a necessary first step towards doing something about human misery and injustice" (1978:455). Blaming fate, the gods, other victims, or one's self inhibits the development of a sense of injustice and impedes collective action, even in the face of extreme misery.

Thus, it is essential that disadvantaged groups first identify a concrete target for collective action. Targets can vary widely, ranging from the dominant class to machines, competing groups, or tax collectors. These targets are often chosen because of conflicts of interests and the constraints they impose on the life experiences of disadvantaged classes. Depending on the target, collective action will have different outcomes. When directed against targets in the private sphere such as landlords and merchants, the result may be land reform or changes in commodity prices. When the state apparatus comes under attack as the source of injustice and suffering, however, the entire social structure may experience revolutionary transformation.

The target of collective action, and consequently the nature of social conflict, is largely conditioned by social structure and, as we shall see, the capacity of disadvantaged groups and classes for collective action. Whether a society will experience segmented conflict, reform, or revolution depends on the character of that social order. Different social structures may obscure or reveal the connection between the suffering of victimized groups and the human or social causes of that suffering. In general, a low level of state intervention in capital allocation and accumulation reduces the likelihood that the state will become the target of collective action, which in turn reduces the likelihood of revolutionary conflicts. Under such conditions, an abstract, depoliticized, and "self-regulating" market system determines the processes of capital allocation and accumulation. Because it is abstract and depoliticized, the market cannot be attacked and overthrown. Due to the nature of its operation, even conflicts deriving from the market's operation cannot easily be articulated into political issues. In market economies, buyers and sellers of all commodities, including human labor, are considered legally free and equal and, as such, enter "voluntarily" into contracts of their own choosing. For such economic actors, the market appears to be a set of conditions within which they must work. Furthermore, actors in markets are numerous and highly decentralized and thus difficult to attack and challenge. Of course, disadvantaged groups could under extreme conditions intervene directly or indirectly through the state to control the prices or supply of certain commodities. But such acts are often short-lived and, even when successful, fall short of radically changing the system. Finally, the market regularly causes misfortune for certain capitalists, adding to the illusion that the system itself is impartial and that individual decisions and actions determine one's life chances. Hence, market systems may obscure the social origins of human suffering and injustice. As a result, adversely affected groups and individuals may end up blaming themselves or other victims for their misfortune and suffering.

In addition, where state intervention in capital allocation and accumulation is low, the state tends to appear autonomous, serving general societal interests. The state reproduces the general and external conditions of production that cannot be created by individual capitalists (Hirsch 1978:66). It reproduces the system as a whole without directly intervening in the accumulation process except when the market is threatened or undermined. In such conditions, the state can claim to stand above all social classes, serving no particular interest but that of the nation. Once the state evokes an image of neutrality, it may serve as an integrative rather than a divisive force. All social strata can be given formal representation in the political arena without threat of revolutionary challenge. Formal democracy, in turn, creates an illusion of equal political power among all social classes. Political conflicts will be institutionalized and confined to matters that are permitted within the existing social structure. As a result, a low level of state intervention in capital accumulation reduces the likelihood of revolutionary conflicts and challenge by insulating the state from attack.

Class and social conflicts in market economies may be articulated in reformist movements because such conflicts tend to remain confined within the economic sphere or, at best, restricted to the civil society. In essence, actors in such movements attempt to alter some aspects of the social order rather than to transform the entire state and social structure. Consequently, conflicts are absorbed away from the state. Protest groups, however, attempt to draw the state into their struggle and act against their adversaries. In other words, they attempt to use state power to settle the conflicts in their interests. Because they stop short of challenging the state, they remain reformist.

An example of reformist conflict in the context of low state intervention in capital accumulation occurred in the United States during the 1930s. Despite intense crisis and conflicts between labor and capital, the Great Depression did not result in revolution for reasons that were rooted in the American social structure. Economic transformations in the United States after the Civil War were largely independent of the state, taking place instead in a free-market economy. The state did not intervene in capital accumulation; it did not allocate resources in the industrial or financial sectors. Direct state intervention in the economy was limited to a few regulative activities that maintained the general conditions of accumulation. In addition, formal democracy in the political sphere allowed the middle and working classes to vote during elections, which gave the impression that the state represented the general societal interests. In the absence of state intervention in capital accumulation, economic development was promoted by a powerful industrial-commercial class through the market system. Because of the predominance of a depoliticized market, social conflicts during the Great Depression remained in the civil society and were absorbed away from the state.

The economic crisis of the 1930s adversely affected major social groups and provided a favorable condition for industrial workers to engage in collective action. American workers had fought against the industrial upper class for much of the nineteenth century without success. During the depression, they engaged in numerous strikes and collective actions that disrupted industrial production. Working-class conflicts were directed principally against private corporations, not against the state or the social structure as a whole (Parsa 1985). Workers pressured the state and politicians to force corporations to recognize unions and collective bargaining. Their collective actions, combined with middle-class sympathy and the efforts of politicians such as Robert Wagner, enabled workers to obtain the right to bargain collectively. The result was reform rather than revolution.[3]

In the contemporary capitalist world, no true market economy exists because all states intervene to varying degrees in their economies, influencing capital allocation and accumulation. The crisis of the 1930s generated political processes that led to a restructuring of economic systems from a laissez-faire approach to Keynesian demand-management and social welfare policies designed to stabilize the macroeconomy and enhance the economic security of firms and individuals. Subsequent state policies have generally consisted of attempts to maintain full employment, control inflation, provide welfare programs and unemployment or accident insurance for the underclass, and assist ailing industries. In most Western states, such defensive intervention was limited to those periods during which market mechanisms were weakened or actually failed. Labor legislation and fiscal-monetary policy influenced the conditions of accumulation, but the state did not assume primary responsibility for capital allocation and accumulation. Following World War II, some European states intervened still further in the economy in response to international competition and working-class struggles. These states rank in the intermediate level of intervention. Inefficient, uncompetitive industries were nationalized as a result of pressure from workers, while capitalist demands led to broad, long-term economic planning to balance payment deficits and prevent declining growth rates. In other cases, states intervened to provide subsidies for certain sectors of the economy or depressed regions. Greater state intervention in capital allocation and accumulation increased the likelihood of politicization of conflicts, and as a result the states were drawn into social and economic conflicts. However, in most European countries, state intervention has not reached a high level. In fact, many state activities, such as welfare and social security, have been redistributive rather than accumulative. The normal operations of the economy are still predominantly determined by the market mechanism.

The likelihood of revolutionary conflicts tends to rise where state intervention in capital allocation and accumulation increases to a high level, thus rendering the entire state apparatus vulnerable to challenge and attack. High state intervention undermines the depoliticized, abstract, and invisible hand of the market by centralizing capital allocation and accumulation. The state often becomes a major investor and owner of economic assets; it may control financial resources and allocate them to other investors. Such high intervention tends to politicize the economy, thereby making the state susceptible to attack. In addition, the interventionist state may be unable to sustain its claim to be autonomous and serve the national interest, but may instead become enmeshed in a continual round of contradictions: simultaneously representing general societal interest and particular dominant-class interests and capital accumulation. State investment in joint ventures with private and foreign capital, combined with allocation of capital to large corporations, limited licensing, and rationing of foreign exchange, is particularly damaging to state claims of autonomy. Finally, state mediation of class conflict on behalf of the dominant class always has the potential to politicize conflicts. These factors in combination increase the likelihood that collective action may be directed against the state, generating a revolutionary conflict. These arguments are illustrated in figure 1.1.

In contrast to the United States, many Third World governments have actively intervened in the allocation and accumulation of capital. In the past few decades, intervention has reached a high level in some Third World countries. Several factors explain the high levels of intervention. For complex social and historical reasons, partly deriving from the colonial experience, a strong commercial-industrial class did not develop in these societies prior to the twentieth century. In the present century, the entrepreneurial class in these countries has remained small and weak in resources. Major obstacles continue to impede its development, including powerful international competition, rising costs of capital in the world market, declining terms of trade, and varying degrees of protectionism in advanced industrial countries. The weakness of the entrepreneurial class has led the state to undertake ventures that require massive amounts of capital or represent high risk. A second reason for high levels of state intervention in capital accumulation has been the nationalization of foreign assets, which occurred as colonies became independent. Finally, these states have been the recipients of foreign aid and development loans, which have converted them into principal economic actors in the twentieth century.

As a consequence, Third World states have become highly interventionist, initiating industrial development and providing favorable conditions for the rise of an industrial class. Many governments invest extensively in heavy industries and own and control vast economic resources such as banking, financial institutions, and crucial sources of raw material. In some countries, state investments account for as much as 60 percent of the national investment. To prevent market misallocations and wasted resources, many Third World governments practice economic planning. Some states also enter into joint ventures with private businesses and multinational corporations. Industrial development is encouraged through allocation of state funds and capital at subsidized interest rates, credit rationing, quotas, limited licensing, tax concessions, wage-price controls, high tariff walls, and overvalued foreign exchange rates that favor the industrial sector.

Although sometimes successful in general economic terms, these policies have often proved to be detrimental to various social classes and interests in Third World countries. Frequently, insufficient resources, credit, and machinery are allotted to the agrarian sector, resulting in the deterioration of agriculture. Overvalued currency, designed to facilitate the pur-

Fig. 1.1. Levels of State Intervention in Capital Accumulation and the Nature of Collective Action

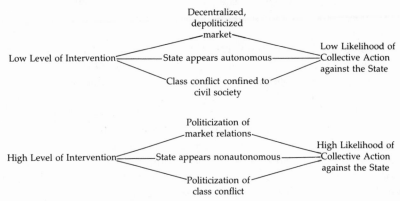

chase of capital goods and machinery, reduces the value of agricultural exports. Food-pricing policies combined with government-subsidized food imports often undermine food producers. In some cases, government intervention to improve the agrarian sector has benefited large, rich producers at the expense of small cultivators. These policies have widened income gaps in rural areas as well as disparities between rural and urban sectors. As a result, peasants have often been important political actors in the twentieth century. In the absence of political options, however, peasants have chosen urban migration, intensifying social problems in the cities.

In urban areas, state intervention has often adversely affected the working class and sometimes the middle class. Government emphasis on capital-intensive industry has impeded the absorption of the expanding labor force, generating a large reserve army of unemployed. The presence of this army of unemployed, along with government repression of labor organizations, has adversely affected the economic position of the working class. Nor have small and medium-sized firms been served by state capital allocation and price controls. Limited licensing, quotas, and tariff walls have encouraged the growth of inefficient monopolies at the expense of small businesses and consumers. High state intervention has generated a bureaucratic bourgeoisie that is often greatly privileged at the expense of the rest of the bureaucracy. Finally, the need for rapid accumulation has often impelled the state and the private sector to invest in relatively developed regions. Such investment policies have widened the gap between regions, adversely affecting ethnic and racial minorities residing in less developed areas. The overall result has been a high level of economic polarization. The beneficiaries have often been a tiny upper class consisting of the state bourgeoisie and an industrial-financial class often tied to multinational corporations.

The high level of state intervention in capital allocation and accumulation in developing societies has significant political consequences, such as political instability and collective action, which may culminate in revolution. High state intervention in these societies undermines the invisible hand of the market, politicizing capital accumulation. With the politicization of the market, victimized collectivities can more readily identify the state as the source of their suffering. A second consequence is the polarization of society. State accumulation policies in Third World countries often exclude important segments of society such as small and medium-sized capital, the working class, and the peasantry. Once the state enters into a direct and visible alliance with large capital, it can no longer claim to represent society and the general, national interests, for its concrete actions violate such claims. As a result, social support for the state is eroded, rendering it vulnerable to attack.

The Russian Revolution of February 1917 provides an example of how extensive state intervention in capital allocation and accumulation can lead to politicized class conflict directed against the state. In contrast to the United States, where industrial development was initiated by a strong industrial bourgeoisie, in Tsarist Russia the bourgeoisie remained weak and dependent on the state. As a result, the state took the initiative to industrialize Russia during the years between the Crimean War and World War I. To finance industrial development, the state heavily taxed the working classes and borrowed vast sums of money from Western European countries. The government's role in the economy progressively expanded to the point where, by 1914, the Russian state was the largest landowner, banker, and capitalist in the world. The state rejected laissez-faire development and instead assisted the private sector directly in rapid industrialization. Domestic heavy industries such as iron, steel, machinery, and petroleum were protected by high tariffs, limited licensing, loans, and exclusion of foreign bidders on state contracts for railroad and port construction. This state intervention resulted in rapid economic development and capital accumulation.[4]

However, development was highly uneven. Small firms producing consumer goods and traditional light manufacturing received little of the preferential treatment extended to large enterprises. State intervention on behalf of the capitalist class proved detrimental for workers because the government directly intervened in factories to prevent the formation of strong labor organizations. National minorities also suffered because industrialization was concentrated in relatively few regions of the country, thus widening regional disparities. Economic development was paid for in part by a declining standard of living among the peasantry. The state failed to improve the conditions of the vast majority of peasants who lived in communes, nor did it extend to them economic subsidies handed out to the landed upper class. Instead, the state used agricultural surplus to subsidize industrial projects.

Eventually, the high level of state intervention in capital allocation and accumulation undermined market forces and politicized social and economic conflicts. The state, rather than the market, mediated between workers and capitalists. The narrow alliance between the state and the upper class precluded any claim of state autonomy. State-sponsored development policies adversely affected the working classes and eventually polarized the population. The state was rendered vulnerable to challenge and attack from below, and ultimately succumbed to popular action.

Another example of the effect of high state intervention in capital accumulation on social and economic conflicts is illustrated by the case of Nicaragua. Like the Russian Revolution, the Nicaraguan Revolution of 1979 took place within the context of state-sponsored economic development. Following World War II, the Nicaraguan government actively undertook the promotion of economic development (Biderman 1983). The state received substantial foreign aid, enabling it to expand the nation's infrastructure by building highways and rail systems, extending electric power, and allocating capital for economic investment. Industrial development was promoted through state policies of import substitution, favorable exchange rates, tax holidays, subsidized credit, and limited licensing. The state also encouraged agricultural diversification, subsidized credit, constructed irrigation projects, and built storage, processing, and marketing facilities.

These economic policies generated sustained economic growth, which was very unevenly distributed. State allocation of capital was biased in favor of large, modern firms and industries, leading to further concentration and severely jeopardizing small and medium-sized businesses. Workers' wages were kept low by means of state repression, thereby preventing the formation of strong, autonomous labor organizations and permitting rapid accumulation of capital. Similarly, state intervention in agriculture benefited only large enterprises, which received most of the state resources. For example, small farmers received less than 4 percent of the credit and consequently became rapidly proletarianized. Distribution of agrarian land grew increasingly skewed, and wealth became more unequally distributed.

As occurred in Tsarist Russia, state intervention in capital accumulation undermined market forces and rendered the state vulnerable to attack. The state was unable to claim autonomy in the face of a clear alliance with a fraction of the bourgeoisie. When Managua was devastated by an earthquake in 1972, state intervention increased through major reconstruction projects. The state also became the vehicle for the expenditure of massive foreign loans, which were used to enrich the Somoza family and the National Guard. As a result of high intervention in capital accumulation, the state became the visible target of attack and was successfully overthrown by a coalition of disadvantaged collectivities.

As we have seen, certain social structures are more vulnerable to challenge and attack than others. In the United States in the early twentieth century, state intervention in accumulation was low, and politicization of economic conflicts was low also. Consequently, workers' conflicts were directed against corporate, rather than state, structures, and the result was reform, not revolution. In contrast, in Russia and Nicaragua, a high level of state intervention in capital allocation and accumulation undermined market forces and politicized social and economic conflicts. As a result, the state became the target of disadvantaged collectivities, and the outcome in both cases was revolution.

SOLIDARITY STRUCTURES AND CONSOLIDATION

Thus far, I have argued that a high level of state intervention in capital accumulation increases the likelihood of politicization of social conflicts by undermining the market mechanism, revealing the social origins of injustice, and providing the target for collective action. Conflicts of interests, however, do not necessarily lead to social conflict. It is also necessary to specify those conditions that generate collective action. To be able to act upon their condition of oppression, victimized classes or collectivities must mobilize their resources, develop solidarity structures, and overcome the impression that suffering and injustice are inevitable. Solidarity theorists such as C. Tilly, Gamson, and McCarthy and Zald maintain that the mobilization process is facilitated by social solidarity; that is, the integration of individuals into community life, which establishes a common set of interests, communication networks, resources, and authority structures with leadership to minimize factionalism. The greater these solidarity structures, the greater the community's capacity to claim resources from individual members, at the same time reducing disloyalty and resignation. More specifically, autonomous organizations and resources, communication networks, and favorable opportunities play crucial roles in generating collective action. For collective action to lead to revolution, major social classes and groups must form coalitions, consolidate their forces, and disrupt the social order. In combination, these factors may undermine the repressive power of the state, paving the way for a transfer of power.

Social structures influence solidarity and the capacity of different groups and classes to mobilize for collective action. Groups and classes possessing independent organizations and economic resources are usually in an advantageous position to mobilize and act collectively. Autonomous organizations are necessary to mobilize resources for collective action. As Schwartz has pointed out, these organizations must be independent of the structure under attack, otherwise the structure's power will block the effectiveness of the challenge (1976:171–177). In addition, autonomous organizations have the potential for providing leadership, an independent financial base, and meeting places to articulate group interests and plan tactics and strategy (Morris 1985). Moreover, when such organizations are already in existence, they can provide ready-made networks and channels of communication to coordinate various protest activities. Groups lacking preexisting organizations by necessity must "borrow" the structure, space, and networks of other institutions and convert them into protest organizations in times of conflict (Schwartz 1976:197). If preexisting organizations are unavailable, mobilization may be severely restricted. Independent economic resources enable groups to endure hardship during periods of conflict without fear of losing their livelihood due to their adversaries' actions. Powerful groups have accumulated resources that can be allocated for mobilization in times of conflict and are often able to anticipate and prepare for conflicts. In contrast, groups without resources tend to act defensively, inasmuch as they are unable to commit their resources in advance. Spatial concentration can provide a population with the networks and ties essential for mobilization. Egalitarian distribution of resources enhances cohesion, while high levels of stratification increase factionalism and reduce the likelihood of discovering common interests and demands.

Another key variable affecting mobilization and collective action, especially by groups with few resources, is the structure of opportunities, or balance of power, among contenders (Tilly 1978:98). In general, as the balance of power changes in favor of aggrieved groups over their adversaries, it increases the likelihood that such groups will instigate conflicts (Korpi 1974). On the basis of this principle, the likelihood of insurgency by aggrieved but weakly organized groups increases under the following conditions: when weakly organized groups anticipate a favorable response from government authorities or are able to form alliances with more powerful groups, such as a segment of the dominant class. Such situations arise especially when a reformist government comes to power, promising social change, or when the dominant class is divided. Under such conditions, weak aggrieved groups will benefit from the resources and support of others to mobilize for action.

Repression is a key factor affecting opportunities for action. In general, reduced repression increases the likelihood of insurgency, while an upsurge in repression reduces the likelihood of protest by raising the cost of mobilization and collective action. Under repressive situations, victims of social processes find themselves incapable of overcoming their adversaries, not because they cannot conceive of alternative possibilities, but because they are unable to maintain their resources, networks, and solidarity structures in the face of repression. In fact, the very persistence of repression indicates the vitality of alternative possibilities. Unable to change their circumstances, victimized and powerless groups may demobilize and abandon their struggle at least temporarily. In addition to reducing the likelihood of mobilization, repression may also alter the nature of protest tactics. More importantly, repressive measures may discourage certain types and channels of mobilization and collective action, while encouraging others that appear less threatening to the power structure. Thus, repression may limit options for mobilization and, as a result, fundamentally affect the nature of the conflicts.

Repression may backfire, however, and become counterproductive. It may fail under conditions of crisis when its application against one group leads to an escalation of conflicts, instigating others to join in the antigovernment protests. Such escalations of conflicts are likely when a social group has appropriate resources for broadcasting the government's use of violence and sustaining mobilization and collective action. Escalation of conflicts or its likelihood is especially threatening to governments that have a narrow base of support. Although regimes with a weak social base are obliged to use repression to remain in power, their repressive measures may lead to destabilization resulting from the escalation of conflicts.

The likelihood that repression will fail increases when major social groups and classes form coalitions and consolidate their forces into a single bloc against the state. Without consolidation, fragmented collectivities at best may become mired in protracted conflicts and achieve little in the way of fundamental change. Most importantly, to succeed, the consolidated opposition must effectively disrupt the social structure by withdrawing their resources and services. The paralysis of the social structure may destabilize the government and generate a revolutionary situation by creating alternative bases of power. To regain control and eliminate the emerging bases of power, the state must use the armed forces on a broader scale to repress ever-greater numbers of people. This may, however, reduce the reliability of the army, especially one composed primarily of conscripts, resulting in insubordination and defection and facilitating a transfer of power. The greater the level of consolidation and disruption of the social structure, the greater the probability that insurgents will succeed in disrupting the repressive apparatus and will gain power.

Consolidation, however, is neither easily nor frequently achieved. Economic crises often set the stage for conflict and consolidation, disrupting modern social systems and threatening established rights and interests. Worsening conditions create multiple grievances, eliminate previously plausible solutions, and force people actively to seek methods of redress (Schwartz 1976:195). In the meantime, during economic crises, alternative strategies for survival and action become more restricted. Individuals increasingly have difficulty resolving their troubles. As a result, they are forced to promote collective attempts to find ways out of the crisis. Crisis situations diminish state resources as well, limiting the government's ability to carry out its economic programs. As a result, states and dominant classes may attempt to shift the cost of the crisis onto subordinate classes. If such costs are heavy and the victimized classes or groups possess sufficient resources and can develop solidarity structures to oppose the government, intense conflicts may erupt. Thus, economic crises tend to facilitate consolidation by adversely affecting major blocs of the population.

High levels of social and economic inequalities also increase the likelihood of consolidation. In situations of high economic polarization, where a minority of the population controls the bulk of wealth and income, the vast majority tends to experience a common condition of exploitation and injustice. Such adversely affected collectivities can easily form alliances and consolidate against the ruling minority. Finally, low levels of social and occupational differentiation also increase the likelihood of consolidation. In contrast, the appearance of new occupational and status groups that widen divisions within each social class reduces the likelihood of consolidation by generating differential experiences and interests.

Based on this analysis, we can see that the likelihood of consolidation is low in developed societies. These societies are characterized by differentiated economic structures, which reduce the likelihood and frequency of severe economic crisis. High levels of economic surplus provide developed societies with a cushion during periods of recession and depression and therefore some resilience, reducing the intensity of economic crisis. In addition, industrial societies are marked by low or moderate levels of economic polarization. The advent of parliamentary democracies, successful industrialization, and working-class mobilization have reduced the inequality that characterized these countries during the early stages of capital accumulation. Finally, these societies have a highly differentiated occupational structure, with the result that various social groups and classes tend to experience economic crisis somewhat differently. In combination, these factors reduce the likelihood of consolidation. These arguments are illustrated in figure 1.2.

In contrast, the likelihood of consolidation is high in developing societies. These societies are greatly dependent on the world market and, hence, are vulnerable to frequent and severe economic crisis. As a result of their history of colonialism, most Third World societies rely heavily on a single crop for foreign trade and are at the mercy of fluctuations in the world market. This extreme dependence on the world market makes them also susceptible to inflation, recession, depression, and other economic cycles that beset more advanced countries. Because they are characterized by low levels of accumulation, they lack the resilience to recover from economic crises and difficulties. These countries are also politically dependent on more developed countries, which renders them even more vulnerable to decisions made abroad. In addition, the economic structures of these societies are highly polarized. The dominant class is very small but appropriates the lion's share of the national income. Its small size renders it socially weak and therefore susceptible to attack. Finally, Third World societies are characterized by minimal social and occupational differentiation, with the result that economic crises generate similar experiences among large blocs of the population, thereby facilitating consolidation. Thus, Third World societies are more prone to consolidation.

A consolidated opposition that can effectively disrupt the social structure may be able to generate a revolutionary situation by supporting an alternative basis of power and may in time be able to seize state power and install

Fig. 1.2. Levels of Development and Likelihood of Consolidation of Disadvantaged Collectivities

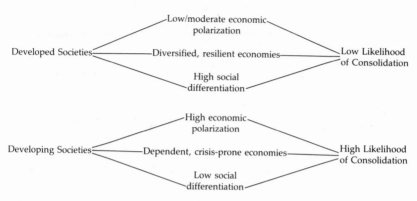

a new government. The new power holders often represent a coalition of the forces and interests that participated in the revolutionary conflicts, provided that each insurgent group possessed a strong solidarity structure and an autonomous organization for mobilization. However, if the coalition partners lacked strong solidarity structures and independent organizations and merely "borrowed" a preexisting organization in order to mobilize, then those who control that organization may attain great power in the new government. In such a situation, if the new power holders have interests that diverge from those of the rest of the coalition, then groups and classes without solidarity structures and autonomous organizations are in trouble. Conflicting interests inevitably lead to the collapse of the coalition, and new conflicts may erupt. The outcome of these postrevolutionary conflicts is influenced by many factors, including each group's capacity for collective action, their opportunities for mobilization, the extent of consolidation of the opposition and formation of new coalitions, and the means of coercion at the government's disposal. The breakdown of the coalition may result in loss of resources for some social groups. In addition, once the short-term goal of overthrowing the government has been achieved, the various groups and classes that coalesced in the earlier conflicts may not be able to form a coalition again because of divergent interests. As a result, no consolidation may be reached. In the absence of consolidation, the government may easily succeed in repressing or eliminating its rivals. One can conclude that although a wide coalition is essential to overthrow a regime, a narrower coalition buttressed by a strong repressive apparatus may be sufficient to keep a regime in power.

To sum up the argument thus far, I have suggested that low levels of state intervention in capital allocation and accumulation combined with a low level of consolidation generate segmented class conflict but do not give rise to struggles that challenge the entire social order. In the presence of low state intervention, abstract, depoliticized, decentralized market forces predominate, which cannot be attacked or overthrown as a government might be. Where a market economy operates in conjunction with formal democracy, an illusion of equal political power among all social classes is created, and the state appears to serve societal interests. Thus, the likelihood of attacks against the state is further reduced. Instead, conflicts remain confined to the civil society and directed against the upper class. Those groups that possess strong solidarity structures and resources may organize and demand economic benefits; but their conflicts are handled through economic structures and hence fall short of politicization. Groups possessing weak solidarity structures and few resources are likely to remain inactive. They may even blame fate, the market, themselves, or other victims for their situation.

High state intervention and low levels of consolidation are likely to generate segmented conflict against the state. Although disadvantaged groups frequently target the state for attack, the low level of consolidation among these groups renders them vulnerable to repression. In contrast, low levels of intervention and a high level of consolidation may generate reformist conflict. Coalitions among adversely affected groups such as workers, farmers, and small capitalists tend to be directed against owners of large capital and specific aspects of class relations. Although the state may be drawn into the arena of conflict, it does not become the target of attack. Thus, it is most likely that the conflicts may only bring about social reforms.

Finally, high levels of state intervention in capital allocation and accumulation in combination with a high level of consolidation are likely to generate revolutionary conflict. High state intervention politicizes accumulation, reduces the scope of market operations, makes the state a centralized, visible actor, and consequently renders it vulnerable to challenge and attack. Neither market forces nor fate can be blamed for social problems or the erosion of established rights and interests. High state intervention, particularly in Third World countries, often polarizes society, thus discrediting the government's claim to serve societal interests. In the process, class conflict becomes politicized and is directed against the state. Twentieth-century revolutions such as those in Russia and Nicaragua fit this model well, as does the Iranian revolution.

Before concluding, I will briefly recapitulate the structural changes and the mobilization of the major social classes that formed the backbone of the antigovernment struggles in Iran. As Iranian oil revenues increased, state intervention in capital allocation and accumulation expanded, reaching a peak in the mid-1970s. This process undermined market forces, politicizing capital accumulation. At the same time, by controlling the main sources of wealth, the state became the most significant economic actor. State allocation of capital favored large, modern enterprises to the disadvantage of small, traditional businesses and industries. Government development policies systematically repressed the working classes in the interest of the industrial upper class. In combination, these policies clearly revealed that the state's economic policies served particular, rather than societal, interests, contradicting the government's claims to the contrary. As a result, the state was rendered structurally vulnerable to challenge and attack. Concurrently, the economy became totally dependent on oil revenues and the world market. The oil sector's uneven development led to a crisis of revenue absorption, which in turn resulted in a high rate of inflation. The state attempted to check rising inflation through a number of policies that had an adverse effect on bazaaris. These policies set the stage for intense conflicts between the state and the bazaaris, a class deeply divided both economically and politically. The policies reduced divisions in the bazaar and, combined with a slight reduction in repression, allowed mobilization to occur. Bazaari mobilization began in 1977 when legal changes reduced the cost of repression and provided an opportunity for collective action. The struggles of bazaaris were soon channeled through the mosque because government repression left no other option for mobilization. Mosques provided a national network for mobilization and a safe place for gathering and communication. Several cycles of mourning ceremonies held in mosques effectively broadcasted the government's killings and violence. The sustained mobilization and struggles forced the government to proclaim a brief period of liberalization and reforms toward the end of summer of 1978.

The proclamation of reforms provided an opportunity for other collectivities that lacked autonomous resources and had weak solidarity structures to engage in collective action against the state. These groups included industrial workers, white-collar employees, and professionals, all of whom had been adversely affected by the government's accumulation policies. Initially, most workers and white-collar employees demanded economic rather than political concessions. But, as we shall see, they were soon politicized through a complicated process and called for the overthrow of the monarchy. Toward the end of 1978, all major opposition social classes formed a coalition and consolidated their forces; they then disrupted production, trade, distribution, and services throughout the country. They all recognized the leadership of Ayatollah Khomeini and supported the formation of an Islamic Republic. Eventually, a combination of social disruption, defections in the military, and assaults on the armed forces paralyzed the government and led to the rise of dual sovereignty. The monarchy was overthrown in February 1979.

Because collective action was the fundamental instrument of struggle in the Iranian revolution, I shall focus on collective struggles in order to illuminate the dynamics of the revolutionary process. To date, there has been no thorough analysis of the collective actions that so vividly characterized the Iranian revolution. Systematic presentation of these events will direct attention to the conflicts and concerns of the participants and clarify some of the misconceptions about the Iranian revolution. In conjunction with the study of collective actions during the 1977–1979 period, I shall examine the actions of various classes and groups in historical context. Such an analysis will illuminate the nature and timing of the collective actions of each group and class. This in turn will enable us to construct a theory of collective action and revolution.

Chapter 2

The Politics of Power
An Overview of the Conflicts

As a result of actions taken by the former Company and the British Government, the Iranian nation is now facing great economic and political difficulties. . . . The standard of living of the Iranian people has been very low as a result of century-old imperialistic policies, and it will be impossible to raise it without extensive programs of development and rehabilitation. (Letter from Dr. M. Mosaddegh to President Eisenhower, May 28, 1953, quoted in Alexander and Nanes 1980)

There is a strong feeling in the United States . . . that it would not be fair to the American taxpayers for the United States Government to extend any considerable amount of economic aid to Iran so long as Iran could have access to funds derived from the sale of its oil and oil products if a reasonable agreement were reached. . . . Similarly, many American citizens would be deeply opposed to the purchase by the United States Government of Iranian oil in the absence of an oil settlement. (Letter from President Eisenhower to Prime Minister Mosaddegh, June 29, 1953, quoted in Alexander and Nanes 1980)

Many of the social and political conflicts that have rocked the Third World in the twentieth century were conditioned by the rise and expansion of Western capitalism, imperialism, and parliamentary democracy. On the one hand, Western industrialization and parliamentary systems inspired people in other parts of the world to attain economic development and formal political rights. At the same time, Western domination generated nationalist and socialist movements aimed at breaking free from the world system and pursuing independent routes of economic development. Iranians in the twentieth century fought against unjust and arbitrary authority and for democracy, against foreign exploitation and for nationalism, and against social inequality and class domination and for socialism.

Iranian society in the decades prior to the revolution was characterized by significant political events, which set the stage for the contradictions and conflicts that impelled various classes and political actors into the revolutionary struggles. The outcome of earlier conflicts limited and conditioned the options available during subsequent confrontations. To understand the revolution of 1979 it is necessary to examine prior critical events. In this chapter, I shall briefly review some of the major conflicts in order to shed light on the history of British and American involvement in and influence on economic development and political events in Iran. Since my aim is only to highlight the crucial events rather than to write a comprehensive history of Iranian political development, I shall rely on previous original scholarship in conjunction with newspaper accounts from 1950 to the present.[1]

The territory of Iran extends some 628,000 square miles, or 1,648,000 square kilometers. In size, Iran equals the combined area of Texas, New Mexico, Arizona, and California and is roughly six times the size of France, the largest country in Western Europe. Iran's geographical location has made it the communication bridge linking Far Eastern Asia, the Mediterranean, and Europe. Lying between the Caspian Sea and the Persian Gulf, Iran shares extensive borders with the Soviet Union to the north and Iraq to the west. In addition, Iran has a common frontier with Turkey to the northwest, Afghanistan to the east, and Pakistan to the southeast.

Iran entered the twentieth century with a revolution and civil war lasting from 1905 to 1911 that formally terminated the traditional political system under which kings ruled arbitrarily and without institutional restrictions as the Shadow of God on Earth. The weak, inefficient, and corrupt Qajar dynasty was brought down by a combination of military defeats; granting concessions, monopolies, and privileges to foreign powers; and failure to protect commerce and industry against European capital (Abrahamian 1968). Other decisive factors included the absence of a modern state bureaucracy and a standing army. The Constitutional Revolution, initiated by merchants, clergy, and intellectuals, deposed the Shah in favor of his twelve-year-old son. However, despite the entrusting of formal power to a popularly elected parliament, the Majles, the royal family soon regained power.

With the cessation of civil war in 1911, external alliances and foreign dependency became significant political issues as the imperial powers of England and Russia attempted to enlarge their spheres of influence in Iran. When the Bolsheviks seized power in Russia the Russian army was withdrawn from Iran, shifting the balance of political forces. The departure of the Russians weakened an Iranian government highly dependent on the Tsar and his forces, leaving the British in a better position to attempt to reduce Iran to a vassal state. The 1919 Anglo-Persian Agreement drawn up by Lord Curzon set off an intense political conflict within Iran that lasted twenty months, during which time the premiership changed hands nine times (Abrahamian 1968). The populace became increasingly politicized. Leftist movements, partly inspired by the Russian Revolution, gathered momentum in northern Iran, alarming the British and the Iranian upper class, who were increasingly threatened by the Left. Both groups welcomed alternative political arrangements that might stabilize the situation and prevent the spread of socialist movements.

In 1921, in the midst of this uncertain political climate, an unknown colonel named Reza Khan entered Tehran with his troops and carried out a coup d'etat; while preserving the monarchy, he became the real power behind the king. Three years later, he introduced a bill to abolish the monarchy and establish a republic. This move was opposed by both the Majles and religious leaders, eventually leading Reza Khan to withdraw the bill. Instead he announced that the "institution of constitutional monarchy was the best bulwark against Bolshevism" (Abrahamian 1982:134). Soon a group of conservative Majles deputies, high-ranking clergy, and Tabriz bazaaris, who were encouraged by the local army commander, pressured for the dissolution of the Qajar dynasty. In the autumn of 1925, a bill was introduced to formally depose the Qajar and entrust the state to Reza Khan until a Constituent Assembly could be convened. Eighty deputies voted in favor of the proposal, thirty abstained, and five opposed it. One of those opposed was Dr. Mohammad Mosaddegh, who was to become prime minister a quarter of a century later (April 1951–July 16, 1952, and July 1952–August 1953). Although Mosaddegh praised Reza Khan for bringing about law, order, and security for property owners, he objected to the proposed system under which Reza Khan would simultaneously head the government and the armed forces. Mosaddegh argued that such a concentration of power was unconstitutional, recidivistic, and likely to result in absolute autocracy. When the Constituent Assembly was convened, Reza Khan packed it with his supporters by using the Ministries of War and Interior. Not surprisingly, of the 260 deputies to the assembly, only 3 socialists abstained from the decision to install Reza Khan upon the throne (Abrahamian 1982:135). In 1925, Reza Khan took over the reins of government and inaugurated a new dynasty, the Pahlavi.

Reza Shah, as he became known, ruled Iran until 1941. During this period, Iranian society underwent considerable change as the new monarch embarked upon a policy of rapid capital accumulation and industrialization. Although the vast majority of the population, especially the working classes, paid a heavy cost, Reza Shah's policies succeeded in building some basic infrastructure and initiating capital accumulation. State accumulation policies benefited only a fraction of the upper class and the royal family. The government established a national bank, Bank Melli of Iran, in 1928, which instigated the establishment of four other state-owned banks, including the Agricultural and Industrial Bank in 1933 (Bharier 1971:241). The deposits of these banks grew rapidly from 560 million rials in 1936 to 1,320 million in 1939 and 2,000 million in 1941 (Issawi 1978:132). Although most of the banks' capital came from taxes paid largely by the poor, the banks served large estate owners (Bharier 1971:242), wealthy private individuals, and government officials. The banks provided reasonable credit to the upper classes, while smaller bazaaris, artisans, and working-class people were subject to high interest rates (Keddie 1981:102). In addition to finance, the government expanded its commercial activities by monopolizing the sale of a number of items, such as tea, sugar, opium, and tobacco products, beginning in 1925. In 1931, the government monopolized foreign trade and the sale of some twenty-seven items.[2] In some cases, the government established joint trading monopolies with large merchants at the expense of smaller merchants and consumers (Keddie 1981:107).

To facilitate accumulation, the state expanded Iran's infrastructure by extending roads and railroads in many parts of the country. The government pursued a number of policies that favored the nascent industrial bourgeoisie. It encouraged private industry by issuing exemptions from custom duties and other taxes, by arranging a cheap credit supply through the Agricultural and Industrial Bank, and by instituting protective measures including tariffs, quotas, and exchange control (Issawi 1978:131). The government reduced the cost of freight transportation by subsidizing fuel prices (Bharier 1971:87) and expanded the market for the textile industry by requiring all civil servants to wear Iranian-made clothes. More significantly, government repression of the working classes boosted capital accumulation by keeping wages down. These efforts paid off. Between 1933 and 1940 the number of registered industrial and commercial companies multiplied from 92 to 1,725, while their capital jumped from 143 million rials to 1.1 billion rials. The share of Iran's national income owned by industry nearly doubled between 1937 and 1941, from 9.8 to 18.4 percent. Reza Shah himself owned several large factories (Ivanov n.d.:76). At the same time, state intervention in capital allocation and accumulation ignored small handicraft industries. These industries were adversely affected by the rise of modern manufacturing and a lack of cheap capital, which the government made available to the modern sector. For example, many small textile producers went bankrupt.[3]

The state itself became an important wealth holder, benefiting the royal family and the upper echelon of the bureaucracy. Government taxes, tariffs, duties, and monopolies of a number of essential goods enriched the state at the expense of the poorest segments of the population. Oil revenues also increased sevenfold during the 1925–1941 period. In 1937–1938, oil accounted for 13 percent of the total government receipts. Overall, the government's revenues expanded from 229 million rials in 1922 to 400 million in 1931 and 3,200 million in 1941 (Issawi 1978:132).

These resources enabled the state to become the most powerful industrial owner in the country. During the 1930s, partly in response to the Great Depression, which reduced the prices of Iranian exports and increased the cost of Iran's imports, the government pursued a vigorous policy of industrial expansion in manufacturing. Between 1934 and 1938, fifty-three large factories, hiring ten or more workers, were built. Many were government owned. The number of workers employed in large factories increased by 250 percent (Bharier 1971:172–173). By 1941, approximately thirty-thousand workers, excluding oil workers, were employed in large factories. By the end of the decade, the government was spending approximately 20 percent of its budget on industry (Bharier 1971:176). In the interest of capital accumulation, the government outlawed strikes and labor unions. As a result, workers' wages were kept low, and they suffered from long working hours and harsh exploitation.

Government development policies largely ignored the agricultural sector. No attempt was made to change the agrarian structure because landowners were the largest single bloc in government ministries and the

Majles during Reza Shah's rule. In the mid-1930s, large landlords owned one-half of the land, while 95 to 98 percent of the agrarian population owned no land at all (Keddie 1981:103). According to one report, entire villages, including for all practical purposes the peasants themselves, were owned by landlords (Overseas Consultants 1949, 3:8). The average area of land cultivated by peasants under the sharecropping system was approximately three hectares. The net income from this small amount of land was insufficient to furnish a satisfactory level of living for a peasant family, even without the landlord's share (Overseas Consultants 1949, 3:9). Nevertheless, the government did not proceed with any land reform. The major change in agriculture was Reza Shah's expropriation of land belonging to landlords who had fallen into royal disfavor. Reza Shah, himself from a family of small landowners, became the largest landowner in the country, with personal estates estimated to encompass two thousand villages or parts thereof in 1941 (Lambton 1969:49–50).

State accumulation policies served the interests of large landlords, industrial owners, the bureaucratic bourgeoisie, and large merchants. These policies increased economic polarization throughout the country. Government intervention in trade and the formation of monopolies and joint ventures with large merchants adversely affected the interests of small shopkeepers. The working class, constituting the vast majority of the population, paid a heavy price for Reza Shah's accumulation policies. The Trans-Iranian Railways, for example, were financed entirely by special taxes levied upon tea and sugar. In this way, the working class bore the major portion of this project. The interests of the royal family were best served as their economic position rose dramatically. In 1930, Reza Shah's personal account in the National Bank (Bank Melli) totaled one hundred thousand tomans. By 1941, it had risen to sixty-eight million tomans, the equivalent of three million pounds (Wilber 1975:243–244).

In the political sphere, Reza Shah's policies reduced the political power of traditional groups such as the clergy. The percentage of clerics serving as deputies in parliament declined from 40 percent in the sixth Majles to 30 percent in the seventh Majles to zero in the eleventh Majles, which met in 1937 (Wilber 1975:263). At the same time, Reza Shah favored greater participation by women in social life. He ordered that the chador, or traditional women's veil, be abandoned in favor of Western clothing. The Majles even passed a "uniform dress law" instituting compulsory Western dress for men (Wilber 1975:128).

As Abrahamian has noted, under Reza Shah's dictatorial rule, Western modernization was gradually introduced into Iran in the form of "oriental despotism," reducing the likelihood of opposition and challenge. Increasing revenues enabled the monarch to create a large, well-equipped army with which to bring every part of the country under direct government control, repressing protests and rebellion. Reza Shah wielded absolute control over the political system. The government dominated not only ministers and deputies, but the press as well. In the sixteen years of his rule, Reza Shah determined the outcome of every Majles election (Abrahamian 1982:137–138). Mosaddegh was booted from his position as deputy and did not attempt to return to politics until Reza Shah's rule came to an end. The government even killed a few opposition leaders who criticized the monarch, such as Mir-Zadeh Eshqi, Sayyed Hasan Modarres (Keddie 1981:93–94), and Farrokhi-Yazdi. Reza Shah pursued a vigorous antilabor policy, severely repressing leftist revolutionaries, writers, teachers, and labor leaders. Upon assuming power, he arrested eight hundred labor union activists and leftists and forced many others underground or abroad (Tabari 1977:87). There were a number of labor strikes and peasant rebellions in the early 1930s due to worsening economic conditions. They were mostly unsuccessful because of repression. Between July and December 1932, over 150 peasants were executed, and a large number were sentenced to long prison terms or exiled to distant regions (Ivanov n.d.:84). Repression prevented the formation of broad-based movements to overthrow the state. Mass demonstrations, which had played a major role in the events of the earlier Constitutional Revolution, ceased to exercise much influence in Iranian politics (Abrahamian 1968). Nor was any significant opposition mounted by religious elements in response to reduced clerical influence or changes in dress and women's participation. The monarch's use of repression effectively weakened mobilization and political opposition.

Reza Shah's eventual downfall was brought about by external forces, specifically by the shifting international situation brought on by World War II. Although Iran declared its neutrality when war broke out, the Allies, especially the British, objected when Germany became Iran's major trading partner. British dependence upon Iranian oil, coupled with the need to supply the Soviets against the Germans, finally led the Allies to advance upon Iran. In 1941, the British invaded from the west and south, while the Soviets entered Iran from the north. After being a major force in Iranian politics for two decades, Reza Shah was forced to abdicate in favor of his eldest son, Mohammad Reza Pahlavi.

ROYALISTS VERSUS MODERNIZERS, 1941–1953

The departure of an extremely repressive ruler paved the way for the articulation of intense social conflicts. The new monarch's relative weakness provided an opportunity for various groups and classes to mobilize. Over 1,250 political prisoners were released (Abrahamian 1981:214), and political organizations were permitted to operate. The Majles was strong, and the young Shah was not yet able to impose authoritarian rule. The clergy regained many of their rights and privileges. After the war, Kurdish and Azerbaijani national minorities succeeded in establishing separate autonomous republics under Soviet auspices, which endured roughly one year before being crushed by the Shah's army. Most important was the oil crisis of the early 1950s, which deepened divisions within the dominant class and led to the formation of opposing coalitions. Intense conflicts and controversy erupted over issues such as control of the state apparatus and the army, the power of the royal family and the landed upper class, nationalization of oil, economic inequality, land reform, uneven regional development, and election laws.

The social structure remained virtually the same during the next few years, but a number of developments generated an economic crisis that worsened conditions for major social classes and intensified political conflict, which eventually led to the coup d'etat of 1953. State intervention in capital allocation and accumulation continued. As before, state policies served the interests of the landed upper class, industrialists, and the bureaucratic bourgeoisie. Bureaucratic capitalists and landlords with business interests pressed the Majles to continue the government's subsidy to businesses (Keddie 1981:114). The state remained the largest industrial owner in an economic sector that was growing but still small. By 1948, there were over 240 large factories in the country, together employing over fifty-three thousand workers (not including some sixty thousand oil workers). The state employed roughly twenty thousand workers in the manufacturing sector.[4] Although labor unions were allowed to form, leftist unions representing the vast majority of workers in the still small industrial work force were repressed before the end of the decade. Harsh labor exploitation continued, despite passage of laws reducing working hours, establishing a

minimum wage, and prohibiting children under ten from working in factories. Indirect taxes on items of mass consumption increased during and after the war, jeopardizing the working classes.

State policies also adversely affected bazaaris and domestic industries.
During the war, Allied troops spent large sums of money in Iran; this
increased the number of bazaaris, some of whom were able to profit. However, after the war, the government's import policies reversed their situation dramatically. In the absence of government protection, cheap Western
goods flooded the Iranian market, causing bankruptcies among artisans
and bazaar shopkeepers. The import policies also caused an industrial recession between 1947 and 1952. Importation of goods led to the closure of
many factories. A number of textile, weaving, and leather factories and
workshops were closed down in Tehran, Isfahan, and Yazd. Not surprisingly, bazaaris, who constituted about 25 percent of the Tehran work force
by the end of the 1940s,[5] formed the backbone of the nationalist movement during the next few years.

Finally, as oil revenues increased from 1944 to 1950, Iran's dependence
on oil and, consequently, on the world market increased, rendering the
country more vulnerable to fluctuations in the international economy. Oil
provided one-third of Iran's overall budget and financed 60 percent of all
visible imports between 1946 and 1950 (Bharier 1971:159). The country's
first development plan, 1949–1956, was to have received more than 37 percent of its budget from oil revenues. However, a conflict between Iran and
England drastically reduced Iran's oil sales on the world market. Revenues
from oil exports fell from more than $400 million in 1950 to less than $2 million between July 1951 and August 1953 (Blair 1976:79). Oil fields and
refineries were closed for almost three years. The state faced a severe shortage of capital, and the first development plan collapsed due to inadequate
financing. These conditions generated massive political conflicts toward
the end of the 1940s and early 1950s.

Both the liberal National Front, founded by Dr. Mosaddegh, and the
Tudeh party grew rapidly. The National Front, formed in 1949, was a coalition of several nationalist, liberal, and conservative political parties and a
fraction of the Majles. It was never a political party per se with an independent structure and network of members and activists. Leaders of the
National Front believed that Iran's development should proceed independently and by means of Iranian resources, particularly oil. They also
advocated an independent foreign policy. The National Front pressed for
social changes such as the nationalization of oil, changes in the agrarian

structure, curbing the Shah's power through a reinterpretation of revised Article 48 of the constitution (which granted the Shah the right to dissolve the Majles), a change of martial law to prevent army interference in politics, changes in the electoral laws to grant the franchise to women, and liberal new press laws (Bashiriyeh 1984:17).

In contrast, the Tudeh party was a relatively well-organized political party, more radical than the National Front; it had become the official communist organization in 1949. The Tudeh party numbered approximately twenty-five thousand members, of whom 23 percent were intellectuals, 75 percent were workers, and 2 percent were peasants (Bashiriyeh 1984: 15). The Tudeh party organized a branch within the army that included roughly six hundred officers and thousands of rank-and-file supporters and sympathizers. In the early 1940s, six Tudeh members were elected to the Majles. In 1946, three Tudeh members were appointed to the cabinet of conservative prime minister Ahmad Ghavam for a brief period. Tudeh organized the United Central Council of Unified Trade Unions, which drew its major support from students and the urban working class. The Tudeh party was declared illegal following an attempted assassination of the Shah in 1949, however, and was forced underground. Although still illegal in the early 1950s, Tudeh resumed relatively open activity, especially during Mosaddegh's tenure as prime minister. By 1953 the Tudeh party had attained substantial influence and become the nation's most powerful political organization (Abrahamian 1968).

The social conflicts of this period culminated in the early 1950s in a struggle against the British-owned Anglo-Iranian Oil Company, which had a monopoly over the most important Iranian asset. Iranian nationalists regarded the company's 1933 operating agreement as unfair because since its inception the company had paid fixed royalties to Iran while its revenues had increased dramatically. In addition, the company paid more taxes to the British government for importing Iranian oil than it paid in royalties to Iran. In 1949, as a result of the nationalist movement, the Iranian government demanded that the British accept a fifty-fifty profit-sharing arrangement on oil, similar to terms conceded to Venezuela and Saudi Arabia by American firms. The British rejected the demand, offering instead to increase oil royalties from twenty-two cents to thirty-three cents a barrel. This offer was completely unacceptable to the Iranian public, which by this time was thoroughly incensed by British domination and exploitation. Most Iranian politicians were unwilling to commit political suicide for British interests. In the midst of public protests and a general strike by oil workers,

Mosaddegh, who had led the nationalist opposition, was appointed prime minister at the end of April 1951. He agreed to accept the position provided the nationalization bill was passed, which it soon was.

When England filed suit in the International Court of Justice protesting Iran's nationalization of oil, Iran countered that the court lacked jurisdiction over the dispute. The court agreed, in effect rejecting England's claim. The British then organized a boycott of Iranian oil by major oil companies, arguing that until the Anglo-Iranian Oil Company received adequate compensation for its losses, the oil still belonged to them. Legal proceedings were filed in Italian and Japanese courts, which ruled that Iranian oil was free and unencumbered. Nevertheless, England continued to bring lawsuits against companies that purchased Iranian oil, causing great hardships for Iran in marketing its main source of foreign exchange. Although the prime minister maintained that Iran's claims against the Anglo-Iranian Oil Company and the British government were legitimate, he indicated a willingness to pay compensation for property owned by the company in an effort to solve the nation's economic dilemma.

Mosaddegh attempted to gain the support of the United States in his battle against the British. In a letter to President Eisenhower, he accused the Anglo-Iranian Oil Company of imperialism and the British government of harboring a desire to regain its former position. At first, the United States took a neutral position in the dispute, calling for negotiation and compromise between the two countries. Soon, however, the United States sided with England. Eisenhower refused to purchase Iranian oil on the grounds that public opinion in the United States opposed it "in the absence of an oil settlement." When Mosaddegh asked the United States government for economic and technical assistance to develop Iran's other resources, Eisenhower declined again, stating that Iran should first settle its dispute with England and then resume marketing its oil.

Severely reduced oil revenues plunged Mosaddegh's government into an economic crisis so deep that at times the government was scarcely able to pay salaries. Shortages were widespread, and prices rose steadily. The worsening economic crisis intensified existing divisions within Iranian society and reduced Mosaddegh's support among the fraction of the dominant class that was traditional and conservative. At the same time, however, Mosaddegh's nationalist economic policies, combined with decreased imports and the drop in oil revenues, stimulated the Iranian economy, especially small industries in the bazaar. Bazaaris who benefited from the expansion of domestic production and markets formed the core of

Mosaddegh's support, which enabled Mosaddegh to push for fundamental changes. In early 1951, Mosaddegh dissolved the Senate, which had been formed by the Shah two years before under a condition of martial law (Jami 1976:486–487; Abrahamian 1982:250). In so doing, he threatened both conservative politicians and the royal court. Mosaddegh also antagonized the landed upper class by issuing two decrees instituting agrarian reforms. The first stipulated that 20 percent of the landlord's share of a crop should remain in the village, with one-half going to the peasants and the other half allocated for village developmental projects. In addition, this decree called for the establishment of village councils to operate as local governments. The second decree abolished free service and all other dues ordinarily imposed by landlords on their peasants (Hooglund 1982:43–44). Because of these reforms, most landlords, who constituted the largest single bloc in the Majles, remained steadfastly behind the monarchy. Mosaddegh also antagonized powerful elements in the army by purging more than 130 officers, including 15 generals. His policies and outlook also threatened the clergy. Most prominent religious leaders eventually ended up opposing the prime minister, including Ayatollah Sayyed Abolghasem Kashani, speaker of the Majles, and Ayatollah Mohammad Behbahani, who reportedly was influential among the poor and illiterate in South Tehran (Cottam 1979:154–55).

In July 1952, the prime minister threatened to resign if the Shah did not relinquish his practice of illegally appointing the heads of the armed forces and the minister of defense. When the Shah did not respond, Mosaddegh made good his threat and resigned on July 16. In his resignation he stated, "Under the present situation, it is not possible to bring the struggles initiated by the Iranian people to a victorious conclusion" (*Ettelaat,* July 17, 1952). In his place, the Shah appointed Ahmad Ghavam, who had been prime minister in 1946 during a major oil workers' strike. Despite Ghavam's warning that "anarchy and disorder" would be broken up by repressive measures, the National Front, and later the Tudeh party, called for a demonstration against the Shah on July 21. A *Kayhan* newspaper reporter described the events of July 21 in the following way:

In addition to the closure of bazaars and shops, drivers of city buses and workers in factories stopped work and joined the demonstrators. Attempts by the police to prevent the closure of government offices failed after 9:00 A.M. Trains stopped due to workers' strikes in the railways. Around noon, street fighting intensified in the Baharestan Plaza and the bazaar. . . . In Mashhad, Abadan, Kerman, Shiraz, Tabriz, Isfahan, Rasht . . . people intensified their struggles. . . . On Ekbatan Avenue, a young man who had been wounded rose to his feet and with his blood wrote on the wall: "This is the blood of the toiling people of Iran; long live Mosaddegh." He died thereafter. At the height of the struggles, signs of insubordination appeared among army officers and soldiers. Approximately eight hundred people were killed or injured in Tehran. Around 4:00 P.M., the Shah ordered the army to retreat to its barracks. Immediately, Ghavam resigned and went into hiding. . . . Around 7:00 P.M. thousands of people marched towards Mosaddegh's house. Mosaddegh appeared and said, while crying, "I wish I were dead rather than seeing the Iranian people in mourning." He added, "Oh, people, with certainty I know that the independence of Iran had been lost, but with your bravery, you have recovered."[6]

The consolidation of major social classes, including bazaaris, workers, and white-collar employees, disrupted major cities and instigated insubordination in the armed forces, and finally forced the Shah to back down and reappoint Mosaddegh.

Stiff opposition from the royal court and in the Majles continued to plague Mosaddegh. The prime minister's foes, led by Abolghasem Khan Bakhtiari, instigated a rebellion to give the impression of instability throughout the country. Right-wing elements engineered the kidnapping and murder of Afshar Tus, chief of the Tehran police, who had been appointed by Mosaddegh. Eventually, most of the members of the parliament who had initially backed Mosaddegh in the nationalization conflict withdrew their support, in part out of disagreement with his plan to print 300 million tomans to bolster the government's money supply. In turn, Mosaddegh's remaining supporters, a small minority, resigned from the Majles. The prime minister temporarily recessed the parliament and ordered a plebiscite to dissolve it completely. Popular support for Mosaddegh on this issue was overwhelming. In Tehran, the vote to dissolve the parliament was 155,544 in favor and only 115 against (*Ettelaat,* August 4, 1953). Nationwide, 2,043,380 voted to dismiss the parliament, while only 1,207 voted to retain it (*Ettelaat,* August 15, 1953). In a radio message the prime minister declared:

A Majles that is unwilling to carry out the goals of the people in their anti-imperialist struggles must be eliminated. Imperialists want to imply that the Iranian people have aims other than overthrowing foreign domination. Imperialists are afraid of being cut off. The Iranian people say that for a long time they have been under imperialist domination that has exploited the fruits of their labor. (*Ettelaat*, August 15, 1953)

Mosaddegh ended his message with the hope that a nationalist Majles would be elected to solve the country's problems and continue the nationalist movement. The Shah was obliged to dissolve the Majles and order new parliamentary elections on August 15, 1953.

The following day, a group of royalist officers attempted a coup d'etat against the prime minister, who reacted by ordering their arrest. The group included Colonel Ne'matollah Nasiri, who was arrested that evening, and Generals Batmanghelich and Shaybani, who were arrested the following day. General Fazlollah Zahedi, who had been named the new prime minister by the Shah, went into hiding. With the coup d'etat a failure, the Shah fled the country. Popular demonstrations against the royal family erupted everywhere. In several places in Tehran, crowds tore down statues of the Shah and his father. In other large cities, such as Tabriz, Isfahan, and Ahvaz, people stopped working and demonstrated against the Shah, demanding that the government take action against those who had attempted to overthrow Mosaddegh. In some cities, people held sit-ins in telegraph offices and sent telegrams to the prime minister urging that the instigators of the abortive coup d'etat be punished immediately (*Ettelaat*, August 16, 1953).

Throughout these events, the United States consistently supported the Shah, who represented conservatism, against the liberal, reformist Mosaddegh. Iran's oil resources, the strained international climate, and Iran's proximity to the Soviet Union were critical factors influencing the United States government's preference for the monarch. Had the United States agreed to Iran's nationalization of oil, it would have set an unfavorable precedent that might have jeopardized other Western capitalist interests. Nor was the United States about to antagonize England, its most important ally. Moreover, President Eisenhower and Secretary of State Dulles claimed that Mosaddegh was ready to open the door to communist influence; this claim was based on the Tudeh party's open support of Mosaddegh's government during the final months of his premiership. Finally, the United States had maintained a military mission in Iran since 1942 and provided the Shah's regime with economic aid, political backing, and support for the armed forces (Halliday 1979:24). As a consequence, the United States had the capacity as well as the interest to intervene in Iran.

In the midst of the anti-Shah demonstrations and protests, the American ambassador returned to Iran from Washington and informed Dr. Mosaddegh that before the United States would extend aid to Iran, the streets must be cleared and law and order reestablished (Abrahamian 1982:280). In response to this request, the prime minister ordered the army into the streets to bring about calm in the wake of the failed coup d'etat. However, once the military was in control it promptly carried out another coup d'etat, which was successful. The overthrow of the government was engineered in part by Kermit Roosevelt, a CIA officer who later became vice-president of Gulf Oil. Mosaddegh was removed from office through the joint efforts of high-ranking Iranian officers and a fraction of the clergy, along with well-paid thugs, all of whom were financed, equipped, and supported by the United States government. The initiative of the United States was crucial because the Shah's departure and the arrests of some of the officers involved in the first, abortive coup d'etat had weakened and demoralized his supporters. Without external intervention the conservative opposition would have been unable to remove Mosaddegh.

Harsh repression followed Mosaddegh's ouster. When the Shah returned to power, most of the leaders of the National Front received prison sentences of up to five years. Mosaddegh himself was imprisoned for three years, and after his release he was confined to his home and forbidden to meet with anyone outside his immediate family. Mosaddegh's foreign minister, Hossein Fatemi, who had taken refuge in the Tudeh underground, was executed. The political organization that suffered most after the monarchy's reinstatement was the Tudeh party. Over the next four years, Tudeh leaders and members were systematically eliminated. When their underground hideouts were discovered, forty party officials were executed and another fourteen tortured to death by security forces. More than three thousand rank-and- file members were arrested, and some two hundred were sentenced to life imprisonment (Abrahamian 1982:280). Many others fled the country. Iran remained under martial law until 1957.

Thus, the forces supporting the status quo were triumphant, and Iran's "democratic" experiment, which had been accompanied by great popular mobilization and struggle, came to an abrupt end. Many factors were responsible for the movement's failure. In the first place, not one but two movements proceeded side by side for most of the period of conflict: the nationalist movement led by Dr. Mosaddegh, and the socialist movement advanced by the Tudeh party. The National Front faced an organizational problem. The masses strongly supported the prime minister; yet with the exception of bazaaris, they had never been organized by the National

Front, which depended instead on Mosaddegh's considerable popularity. Mosaddegh had always used his influence in the parliament and the media to mobilize the populace. This method worked; but when he was denied access to those channels, he was unable to reach large segments of his constituency. In addition, as a loose coalition of several individual political parties, the National Front was weakened by the departure of conservative groups such as the Mojahedeen party, under the leadership of Ayatollah Kashani; the Toilers' party, led by Mozaffar Bagha'i; and the Third Force, led by Khalil Maleki.

A more fundamental dilemma stemmed from the division within the opposition, which prevented a consolidation of forces. The National Front, representing privileged social groups, sought to control the state apparatus and weaken royalist and traditional segments of society for nationalist and reformist ends. Mosaddegh, himself from an aristocratic background, did not intend to abolish the monarchy, despite the wishes of the vast majority of the Iranian people.[7] In contrast, the Tudeh party sought state power in order to restructure Iranian society along socialist lines. Throughout most of the struggles, the Tudeh party characterized the National Front as the "Imperialist Front" (Jami 1976:525). The two organizations did not hold joint rallies or demonstrations. For example, in June 1953, when the National Front called for a mass meeting, the marchers supporting the Tudeh party were not allowed to participate in the event, but were forced to hold their own meeting elsewhere (Jami 1976:601). On the anniversary of the July 21, 1952, rebellion, the two organizations held separate rallies. Even more telling, during the three days between the failed coup d'etat and the second, successful one, supporters of the two organizations shouted different slogans and fought against each other in the streets.[8] Mosaddegh's order to the army to clear the streets paved the way for the coup d'etat by removing the Tudeh protesters. Finally, the Tudeh party's failure to use its networks inside and outside the army insured the success of the royalists and their Western allies.

With the liberal National Front and the leftist Tudeh party neutralized as effective political organizations, the United States assisted the Shah in consolidating his power. The United States increased economic and military aid as well as technical assistance for Iran's development and stability. Between 1946 and 1952, the United States had extended $33 million in grants, half of which went to the armed forces. Immediately following the coup d'etat, the United States granted a $45 million emergency loan to the Iranian government. Between 1953 and 1957, the United States provided

Iran with $501 million in loans and grants, more than 26 percent of which was earmarked for the military (Bharier 1971:119). When the oil dispute was finally settled in 1954, American oil companies reaped substantial benefits, ending up with 40 percent of Iran's oil, which formerly had been a British monopoly. A consortium composed of the United States, England, France, and Holland signed an agreement fixing royalties based on a fifty-fifty division of profits. After the agreement was reached, President Eisenhower personally thanked the Shah for arriving at an oil settlement so favorable to North American oil companies:

> Your Majesty must take great satisfaction at the success of this significant phase in the negotiations to which you personally have made a valuable contribution. I am confident that implementation of this agreement, under Your Majesty's leadership, will mark the beginning of a new era of economic progress and stability for your country. (Alexander and Nanes 1980:235)

The United States maintained its support for the Shah throughout the next quarter of a century. The United States continued to equip and train the Iranian army, which was transformed into one of the most sophisticated military organizations in the world and the mainstay of the Shah's regime. From 1946 to 1970, nearly one-half of all American aid to Iran was military aid. In addition, the Central Intelligence Agency (CIA) helped establish the Savak, the Shah's secret police, in 1957 to silence all opposition.

THE WHITE REVOLUTION AND REPRESSION

With the elimination or weakening of the opposition and a strengthened repressive apparatus, the Shah's position seemed secure. However, a number of unanticipated factors undermined the stability of the system, impelling the Shah to introduce a series of reforms that eventually fundamentally transformed the Iranian social structure. The main factor was an economic crisis in the late 1950s that derived from rapidly expanding domestic and international credit as well as government expenditures on the Second Seven-Year Development Plan (1955–1962). As a result of increased resources, monetary and fiscal controls were relaxed, the government increased its spending, extensive import permits were issued, and massive amounts of foreign goods were imported. Despite increases in oil revenues in 1959, Iran's imports multiplied to more than six times their level in 1954 (Katouzian 1981:206). These policies, combined with repayments of foreign loans, reduced foreign exchange to nothing, forcing the government to impose a stabilization program recommended by the International Monetary Fund (IMF) and supported by the World Bank. The new program, put into effect in September 1961, forbade the importation of expensive luxury items, increased import duties on nonessential goods, and limited bank credit and the sale of foreign exchange. As a consequence, the economy was forced into nearly three years of complete stagnation, which provided a favorable setting for conflict (Bharier 1971:95).

Another possible factor was political pressure exerted by the United States State Department in late 1959 and early 1960 encouraging the Shah to liberalize his policies. Although the State Department denied an allegation advanced by the *Christian Science Monitor* that the United States was considering encouraging opposition elements against the Shah, it is highly possible pressure was put on the Shah to open up the political sphere and allow moderate opposition.[9] Finally, rising inflation, combined with the lifting of martial law in 1957, led to a number of strikes, despite a government ban against them. Between 1957 and 1960, workers struck on at least fourteen separate occasions (Ivanov n.d.:205–207).

To resolve the crisis and satisfy the United States, in the summer of 1960 the Shah announced that the upcoming elections would be open to all political groups. He then initiated a series of reforms that led to a realignment within the dominant class and undermined the position of the clergy. Land reform was an important feature of this realignment. Up to this point, the landed upper class had remained the backbone of the Shah's support. With Mosaddegh eliminated, the landed upper class had regained its domination of the political sphere. In elections for the nineteenth Majles, held in 1959, 61 percent of the representatives were from the landed upper class; and 58 percent of the representatives were from the landed upper class in the twentieth Majles, held in 1961 (Shaji'i 1965:173). The Shah's reforms in the 1960s shifted the basis of the state from this class to the industrial bourgeoisie by transferring capital from the agrarian to the industrial sector. Land reform took away a portion of the land belonging to the upper class. In compensation, the state turned over to them some government-owned industries and encouraged industrial growth.

External as well as internal political and economic considerations may well have affected the Shah's decision to inaugurate land reform.[10] After World War II, the United States government established a large-scale agricultural extension program in Iran to promote economic development. The Agency for International Development (AID) mission drafted a land reform law in September of 1959 at the request of the minister of agriculture (A. Tabari 1983). In the early 1960s, the Kennedy administration advised Third World countries to introduce land reform, partly as a means of reducing the likelihood of peasant uprisings and communist revolution such as those that had taken place in China, Cuba, and Vietnam. In the case of Iran, greater economic development, rather than a military buildup, was recommended. Accordingly, the United States administration offered a $35 million loan to Iran, contingent on the implementation of land reform.

For the Shah, the prospect of land reform involved several serious drawbacks. In the first place, the royal family itself was one of the largest landholders in the country. In addition, the parliament was dominated by large landlords who constituted a considerable portion of the monarch's base of support. Land reform was also likely to antagonize powerful segments of the clergy who possessed extensive landholdings. On the other hand, there were distinct advantages to be gained from implementing land reform. Such a program would strengthen the Shah's relationship with the United States, his primary ally, and would guarantee increased economic assistance, which was vital to counteract an economic recession in Iran. In addition, land reform would boost the monarch's popularity among the peasantry, the main beneficiaries of reform, and thereby reduce the likelihood of peasant revolt. Finally, it would substantiate the Shah's claim to be as progressive as Mosaddegh, who had first suggested land reform several years previously. This claim would, the Shah perhaps expected, reduce criticism and challenge by the opposition (Hooglund 1982:50).

The initial land reform bill was modified by the landlord-dominated Majles to such a degree that it became very difficult to implement, due in part to requisite time-consuming surveys that would have lasted for years. In May 1961, in the midst of a growing economic crisis and a nationwide teachers' strike, the Shah dissolved the Majles and, under American pressure, appointed Ali Amini as prime minister (1961–1962). Amini named Hassan Arsanjani, an intellectual with socialistic views, to formulate a land reform program. Arsanjani presented a radical design, which, if fully implemented, would have fundamentally changed the agrarian class structure. Eventually, Arsanjani was dismissed and the reforms diluted. The Shah introduced other reform measures, however, including a six-point reform package, and called for ratification by nationwide referendum. According to the government's figures the plebiscite, held on January 26,

1963, endorsed the reforms. The six points were: (1) land reform, (2) nationalization of forests and pastures, (3) public sale of state-owned factories to finance land reform, (4) profit sharing in industry, (5) reform of electoral laws to enfranchise women, and (6) establishment of a literacy corps.

Despite the government's claim of popular support for the Shah, his policies provoked opposition from several quarters. The context of this opposition was an economic crisis that had been caused by state policies. The government's stabilization program, recommended by the IMF, had brought a recession that adversely affected most social groups and classes. The government reduced credit to bazaaris, who had been experiencing bankruptcy on an ever- widening scale. These government policies, combined with attacks on the landed upper class and the clergy, provided favorable conditions for conflict.

The Shia mourning month of Muharram in June 1963 took on a highly political character. The religious mourning ceremonies held during Muharram were used for openly political purposes and became opportunities to condemn the Shah's regime. The day after the peak of the mourning period, Ayatollah Khomeini was arrested. His arrest sparked three days of conflict between June 5 and June 7, 1963. In the previous months, Khomeini had become popular among segments of the population because he was the only religious or political leader who strongly opposed the Shah and actually called for the overthrow of the government in March 1963 (see chapter 7). The rebellion lasted for three days but failed to overthrow the regime.

In part, its failure can be attributed to the weakening of all opposition organizations in the repression following the 1953 coup. The Tudeh party had been virtually eliminated. Before the rebellion, most leaders of the National Front had been jailed for organizing opposition against the government five months earlier, just before the plebiscite. The second National Front, which surfaced after the Shah's gesture of liberalization and gained massive support in the bazaar and in the universities, opposed the Shah's growing arbitrariness and authoritarianism but was badly divided over their response to the reforms, which they had advocated before the Shah did.

Participants in the collective action consisted primarily of segments of the bazaars and the urban poor in a few major cities. University students opposed the regime, but did not join the demonstrators. Instead, they stayed on the university campus and hung a banner from the front gate that proclaimed, "The murderer and bloodthirsty Shah spills the blood of the people." Students shouted slogans against dictatorship and in favor of Mosaddegh (Jazani 1979:130–131). More critical than the students' absence was that white-collar employees and professionals and industrial workers did not join the demonstrators, nor did they go on strike. Without a consolidated opposition, repression succeeded in crushing the uprising and demobilizing the regime's opponents. The defeat of this rebellion marked the cessation of popular collective action until the revolutionary period of 1977–1979.

The United States government welcomed the Shah's reforms and continued to praise him as a progressive leader and a Western ally. In 1967, on the occasion of the Shah's visit to the United States, President Johnson declared:

> The changes in Iran represent very genuine progress. So far as economic growth rates tell the story of a nation's achievements, Iran's recent record—an annual growth of about 10 percent—is surpassed by very few countries on this earth. In the five years since we visited Iran, 6,500 village schools have been established by your new Literacy Corps. In 1962, only 8 percent of the rural population went to elementary schools. Now, a short five years later, under your leadership the figure is more than 20 percent and still rising. . . . Iran is a different country now from the one that we saw in 1962. The difference has sprung from Your Majesty's dedicated inspirational and progressive leadership. (quoted in Alexander and Nanes 1980:362)

At the same time that Iran was undergoing economic development, the nation's strategic importance was attracting more attention from the United States. The British government announced the withdrawal of its armed forces from the Persian Gulf region by the end of the 1960s. Meanwhile, in response to the trajectory of events in Vietnam, the foreign policies initiated by President Nixon and Secretary of State Kissinger placed an emphasis on regional security, rather than on reliance on direct intervention. A stable Iran became ever more desirable to Western Europe and the United States, which needed secure access to Middle Eastern oil. To build regional security, President Nixon, who as vice-president in 1953 had played a part in restoring the Shah to power, favored a buildup of the Iranian armed forces. In 1972, Nixon and Kissinger went so far as to recommend that the United States sell Iran any weapon it wanted.

The Shah was quick to volunteer for the task of maintaining regional security and, in the process, became the largest single purchaser of American arms. Sales of military hardware to Iran jumped from $524 million in 1972 to $3.91 billion in 1974. Different branches of the United States armed services competed to sell arms to Iran, while some American corporations paid bribes in the form of "commissions" to Iranian military officials to secure their orders for equipment. Between 1970 and 1978, the Shah ordered $20 billion worth of arms, which accounted for 25 percent of all United States arms sales. By 1978, half of the order had been delivered. The weapons were technologically advanced equipment, including the F-14 Tomcat Fighter, the DD993 modified Spruance-Class Destroyer, and AWACS aircraft. With the assistance of United States arms manufacturing companies, the Shah planned to create a modern military industry in Iran. Westinghouse and Hughes Aircraft were invited to build a missile assembly and repair plant in Shiraz, while Bell Helicopter was asked to develop an entire helicopter industry in Isfahan (Klare 1979).

Because Iranian military personnel lacked the training and expertise to operate such sophisticated equipment, thousands of Americans were hired to operate the weapons and instruct Iranian soldiers in their use. In 1972, approximately fifteen thousand Americans worked in Iran, most of them military personnel. By 1976, the number of Americans had risen to twenty-four thousand and was expected to climb to over fifty thousand by the end of the decade. The expenditures associated with maintaining such a large corps of foreign advisors were staggering for a nonindustrial country like Iran. In addition to the high cost of purchasing advanced military equipment, enormous salaries were paid to American military advisors; some personnel received monthly salaries in excess of one hundred thousand tomans, or roughly fifteen thousand dollars. In all, the Shah's military expenditures, excluding the Savak, absorbed roughly 30 percent of the total national budget. By the mid-1970s, Iran was spending seventy-three dollars per capita on defense and a mere twenty-nine dollars per capita on education and health.

After oil revenues began to rise, the United States government promoted corporate economic interests in Iran. In November 1974, the two countries established the United States–Iran Joint Commission, headed by United States Secretary of State Henry Kissinger and Iranian Minister of Economic Affairs and Finance Houshang Ansari, to broaden and intensify economic cooperation and consultation on economic policies. The following March, at the second meeting of the commission, the two countries agreed to cooperate on an ambitious construction agenda that included a series of large nuclear plants totaling eight thousand electrical megawatts; one hundred thousand apartments and other housing units; five hospitals with a total of three thousand beds; twenty factories to manufacture prefabricated housing; a major port to handle agricultural imports; and other joint ventures to produce fertilizers, pesticides, farm machinery, superhighways, and processed foods. The cost of these projects was estimated to reach $12 billion. At the next session of the joint commission, in 1976, the representatives expressed optimism that trade between their two countries would expand even more during the years to come (Alexander and Nanes 1980:386).

As Iran became more and more dependent on the United States for military and economic assistance, an important opportunity was created for the American government to influence the Shah's domestic policies, especially regarding human rights. For a long time, however, the United States did not invoive itself in such matters, and when the issue of human rights was finally raised it was not addressed seriously. In a visit to Iran in 1972, President Nixon noted that students protesting his presence were beaten and arrested. He remarked to the Shah, "I envy the way you deal with your students. . . . Pay no attention to our liberals' griping" (Hoveyda 1980:54). In testimony before the House Subcommittee on International Organizations on September 8, 1976, Alfred Atherton, assistant secretary for Near Eastern and South Asian affairs, noted that although between 2,800 and 3,500 prisoners were being held in the Shah's jails, the vast majority were terrorists who had committed acts of violence against government officials. Only 100 to 150 inmates, he claimed, could be described as political prisoners detained for their beliefs. Atherton also maintained that most of the charges of torture he had heard were at least two or three years old, and that recent complaints concerned terrorists who were allegedly killed or maimed under torture. Finally, he noted that the United States government considered these matters to be internal affairs of a sovereign government and that Iran had made great progress in the area of human rights.[11]

CAPITAL ACCUMULATION, CRISIS, CHALLENGE, AND COLLAPSE

Following the reforms of the early 1960s, the Shah's regime embarked upon a policy of rapid economic development. Boosted by rising oil revenues, state intervention in capital allocation and accumulation reached its peak by the mid-1970s. State intervention in accumulation served the interests of the dominant class, consisting of the royal family, upper-level government officials, bureaucrats including heads of the army, and a group of entrepreneurs engaged in large-scale industry, finance, and commerce. This intervention, however, adversely affected broad segments of the population, as we shall see in chapter 3. Political parties and formal democracy, which might have absorbed some of the conflict away from the state, briefly reemerged in the early 1960s, but were quickly repressed. At the same time, the state had become ever more dependent on oil revenues, which meant that the entire economy and society became increasingly vulnerable to the fluctuations of the world market. When oil revenues began to decline in the mid-1970s, the result was an economic crisis. Thus, a combination of high state intervention in capital accumulation, undermining market mechanisms, the negative effects of government intervention on major social groups, the elimination of formal democracy, and growing dependence on the world market rendered the state susceptible to challenge and attack.

In the political arena, the Shah was pressured to liberalize and to reduce repression. Amnesty International and the International Commission of Jurists began to expose the government's violations of human rights. More important, Jimmy Carter, during the final stages of the 1976 United States presidential campaign, singled out Iran as a country where human rights had been violated (Abrahamian 1982:498–505). As we shall see later, however, Carter's administration did not seriously pressure the Shah to change his human rights policies. As many observers have noted, the Shah understood that he had to make some effort to show that human rights in Iran were improving in order to obtain arms and support from the United States. Hence, the Shah initiated some changes that were intended to reduce the criticism. In March 1977 he released 256 political prisoners, and in May he permitted the International Red Cross to visit political prisoners. The Shah also introduced legal changes that provided civilian trial for political opponents who criticized the government.

The pressures and the limited changes provided an opportunity for voicing criticism of the government. Iranian intellectuals responded by writing open letters criticizing the government and demanding broader changes and the opening of the political sphere. A number of groups such as the National Front, the Writers' Association, and the Lawyers' Association were formed and pressed for political freedom, nonintervention in legal affairs, and freedom of expression and the press. At the same time, broader social groups such as students and bazaaris mobilized and engaged in collective action. In early 1978, segments of the clergy that had been silent for many years began criticizing the government for harsh repression and violence against protesters. Several rounds of mourning ceremonies held through the mosques resulted in repeated cycles of violence and deaths at the hands of government troops.

Opponents of the regime effectively used the mosque network to mobilize and broadcast the government's use of violence. Conflicts and mobilization continued until the end of summer 1978, when the Shah decided to reduce repression and introduce political reforms. The timing of the Shah's decision was prompted by several incidents. In early August the Moslem month of fasting, Ramadan, began with increased mosque attendance, which had significant consequences. Every night following prayers in the mosques, students and youths demonstrated in the streets, shouting antigovernment slogans, attacking government buildings, and smashing bank windows. In this way, the advent of Ramadan enhanced mobilization and collective action. Then, on August 20, 430 persons died in a fire in a movie theater in Abadan. Although the government blamed "Islamic Marxists" for the fire, opposition groups held the government responsible. The burials of the victims, held between August 22 and August 25, became highly political events during which mourners shouted "Death to the Shah." On August 26, the Shah, afraid that the conflicts might spread to the Abadan oil refinery and disrupt work in the oil fields, dismissed Prime Minister Jamshid Amuzegar (1977–August 26, 1978) and appointed Ja'far Sharif-Emami to the post (August 26, 1978–November 5, 1978; Sharif-Emami was also prime minister from 1960 to May 1961).

Sharif-Emami designated his administration a government of national reconciliation, formed a new cabinet, and announced that his most important task would be to establish communication with opposition groups. Almost immediately, he contacted top religious leaders and reintroduced the Islamic calendar. He promised a number of reforms, including full freedom of the press, permission for all political parties—except the Communist party—to organize, reinstatement of expelled students, and prosecution of those responsible for recent violent incidents. Other promises included (1) establishing appropriate conditions for free elections, (2) reducing taxes for lower-income classes, (3) making salaries of government employees more equitable, (4) abolishing inappropriate laws, and (5) reconciling government programs with national and religious traditions (*Ettelaat*, September 10, 1978). Through these promises, Sharif-Emami attempted to satisfy both the liberal and the religious opposition. His administration received a strong vote of confidence from the Majles; 176 representatives voted yes, 16 no, 2 abstained, and 1 turned in a blank ballot.

The new prime minister took steps to restrict relatives and associates of the Shah. Members of the royal family were forbidden to interfere in governmental and economic affairs. Sharif-Emami dissolved the Shah's Rastakhiz party and declared that the government would no longer have its own party. He dismissed more than thirty notorious, high-ranking Savak officials, prohibited two thousand government functionaries from traveling abroad, and jailed several prominent figures. One was former prime minister Abbas Hoveyda, who had served as head of state for thirteen years (1965–1977). Others who were imprisoned included several ministers, high-ranking government officials, and a few wealthy importers and industrialists who were accused of speculation and profiteering. Sharif-Emami announced that a people's tribunal consisting of representatives of bazaaris, lawyers, and supporters of human rights would be formed to carry out trials (*Ettelaat*, October 21, 1978).

As a result of student demonstrations and protests by faculty in the fall of 1978, the new government guaranteed independence and political freedom for universities and promised to dissolve the university guard and release jailed students. The number of freed political prisoners gradually increased until by the end of October some two thousand had been released. Among them were Ayatollahs Mahmoud Taleghani and Hossein Ali Montazeri, who had been in jail for roughly three years. Seven members of the military wing of the Tudeh party were also freed, as was a Kurdish political leader, Ghani Bolourian, who had been in jail for twenty-five years. Most noteworthy was the release of Safar Ghahremani, who had the distinction of having served the longest jail sentence—more than thirty years—of any political prisoner in the country.

In the volatile ambience generated by months of conflict, Sharif-Emami's policies generated new conflict. Sharif-Emami's own cabinet and administration were beset by internal disagreement and dissension. Several ministers and governors resigned to protest various administration policies. At the end of October, six provinces, including the Central Province where Tehran is located, were without governors (*Kayhan*, October 31, 1978). The Majles was also divided over Sharif-Emami's policies. Within two weeks of taking office, the prime minister was facing opposition from eighty-three members of the Majles on conservative as well as liberal grounds (*Ettelaat*, September 3, 1978). The period of reform had a decided impact on wealthy segments of the upper class, who were alarmed by the growing instability. Since the beginning of the year, they had been sending money out of the country. With the advent of a reformist government, they became even more apprehensive and intensified their flight preparations. By the end of October, reportedly $50 million was leaving the country every day. In the first two months of fall 1978, some 150 individuals sent most of their money abroad. Of these individuals, all major segments of the dominant class were represented: twenty-seven from the royal family, twenty-one from the army and Savak, seventeen industrialists, eight bankers, thirty-two high-level bureaucrats, thirty-two government ministers and deputies, and fourteen Majles representatives (The Freedom Movement 1983, 9:150).

Of even more consequence was the popular response to Sharif-Emami's government. Despite coming from a clerical family, Sharif-Emami was unable to gain the trust of the opposition. Sharif-Emami was accused of having participated in the corruption of the previous several decades; his reforms were attacked as spurious and intended to deceive the public. The prime minister's protests that he was no longer the same Sharif-Emami of the preceding twenty years (*Ettelaat*, September 16, 1978) were of little avail. A new wave of strikes, demonstrations, rallies, and marches swept the country. Prior to Sharif-Emami's appointment, some seventy cities had experienced political protests. During Sharif-Emami's reform government an additional one hundred cities experienced political protests and demonstrations. In addition, demonstrations grew in size in major cities. On September 4, during the religious holiday of Aid-e Fetr, a large antigovernment march was spontaneously organized after the prayer. Three days later an even bigger rally and march was organized by the opposition. The next day the government imposed martial law in twelve cities and killed a large number of people in Tehran.

More important, Sharif-Emami's promise of reforms and liberalization provided an opportunity for workers and white-collar employees to mobilize and engage in collective action. Toward the end of October, some strikers began making political demands in addition to their initial economic demands. In response, the Shah suspended the nascent reforms and returned to his previous course of repression. On November 5, any possibility of a compromise between the opposition and the regime was precluded by the Shah's appointment of a law-and-order military government headed by General Gholam-Reza Azhari (November 5, 1978–December 28, 1978). Initially, the military administration succeeded in bringing about some degree of order as a number of strikers resumed work. But the military was unable to repress the popular struggles altogether because the escalation of conflict had mobilized all major social classes and groups against the government. Although strikes and demonstrations declined somewhat during the early days of the military administration, they soon resumed with even greater impact. Furthermore, as the use of armed force became more widespread, segments of the military increasingly manifested signs of insubordination. Finally, when oil workers struck for the third time, most productive activities were disrupted and state revenues were quickly reduced to nearly zero.

In response to the worsening of the crisis, the Shah decided to pursue another attempt at reform. This time, he nominated Shahpour Bakhtiar (December 29, 1978–February 11, 1979) as his fourth prime minister in six months. Bakhtiar, a member of the National Front, had served under Mosaddegh and been jailed by the Shah several times. Nevertheless, on December 29 he accepted the Shah's invitation to form a new cabinet, and three days later he was confirmed by the Majles in a vote of 140 to 25. His new cabinet was installed a week later.

The new prime minister clearly stated his intention to be independent. He declared, "The Shah will reign, and [Bakhtiar] will rule." He also announced that although the monarchy would be preserved, those who had committed treasonous offenses since 1953 would be punished. Bakhtiar promised freedom of the press, leading the national newspapers, which had been on strike for two months, to resume publication. He was successful in passing a bill to dissolve the Savak. Many political prisoners committed to leftist ideologies were released, such as Shokrollah Paknejad, a Marxist intellectual; Masoud Rajavi, one of the leaders of the Islamic Mojahedeen; and many members of the Marxist Fedayee guerrillas. Regarding international matters, Bakhtiar announced that the government would no longer sell oil to South Africa and Israel. He also pledged that under his administration Iran would not become the gendarme of the Persian Gulf.

In contrast to previous governments, Bakhtiar introduced fundamental reforms that might have had far-reaching consequences had they been adopted earlier. But against the backdrop of widespread violence and bloodshed, they had little effect in quelling the opposition. Although several demonstrations attracting approximately one hundred thousand people were held in support of the new prime minister, he was unable to reconcile the people with the monarch. To most of those who opposed the regime, the Shah was the guilty party who deserved punishment for treason committed since 1953. They rejected Bakhtiar's compromise with the monarch. The opposition forced the United States government, which had consistently supported the Shah throughout months of crisis, to announce on January 12, 1979, that the Shah could have no role in the political future of Iran and must leave the country. Four days later the monarch departed, and the government closed the airport to prevent the return of Ayatollah Khomeini, who had been exiled by the Shah for more than fourteen years. However, the people forced the airport to reopen, and on February 1, Khomeini returned to Iran and was given a tumultuous welcome by millions.

To summarize, Iranian politics since 1900 have been characterized by repressive, autocratic rulers and powerful foreign influences, predominantly Russia, England, and the United States. During the first decade of the twentieth century, Iranians struggled to obtain political rights and a constitution to curb the arbitrary power of their rulers. With the elimination of Russian influence after 1917, the anti-imperialist struggle was focused against the British. In the decades following World War I, political opposition declined due to the authoritarian rule of Reza Shah. His removal during World War II opened the political arena to social movements, including nationalism, socialism, and regional autonomy. In the 1950s, the movement to nationalize oil was successful in expelling the British from Iran; but this movement ended abruptly with a coup d'etat against Prime Minister Mosaddegh. Throughout the following decades, the United States assumed a major role in Iranian politics. In the 1960s the monarchy introduced a number of reforms, which resulted in rapid economic development and weakened the landed upper class and the clergy as well as political opposition groups. Finally, in the late 1970s, conflict against the Shah reemerged and extended to his principal supporter, the United States. In 1979 the monarchy was overthrown and relations with the United States ceased.

Over the past thirty years, the policies of the United States and the Shah successively decreased the alternative directions Iranian politics might have followed. Although Dr. Mosaddegh was successful in ousting the British from Iran, the United States quickly stepped in as the major foreign power. The overthrow of Mosaddegh engineered by the United States reduced the likelihood of a progressive, liberal option that might have pursued independent development and modernization. The repression of the Tudeh party and independent leftist intellectuals, combined with land reform in the 1960s, decisively eliminated the possibility of a leftist revolution such as those that occurred in other Third World countries. Finally, the United States's growing involvement in Iranian affairs and consistent support for the Shah made it inevitable that any attack on the Shah would be directed against the United States as well.

This brief review of Iranian history over the past few decades indicates the significance of a number of variables. The state's dependence on external economic and political powers rendered it vulnerable to crisis and conflicts. For example, growing oil revenues in the 1940s made the government dependent on external revenues. The conflicts of the 1950s were brought about in part by the decline in oil revenues resulting from a Western boycott of Iranian oil. External political decisions played a major role in shaping the outcome of domestic conflicts at that time. These variables were also important during subsequent conflicts. Political pressures in the early 1960s, combined with the IMF stabilization program and President Kennedy's emphasis on economic and political reforms provided opportunities for social conflict. Finally, as we shall see, the economic crisis of the 1970s was partly conditioned by reduced oil prices, and the mobilization of opposition was partly the result of the Shah's response to allegations that Iran violated human rights.

A more critical variable is the state's role in capital allocation and accumulation. Increased state intervention in accumulation limited the scope of the market and rendered the state vulnerable to challenge and attack. When state intervention adversely affected the interests of the major social classes, conflicts erupted and the state became the direct focus of attack. During the 1930s and 1940s, the state began intervening in capital accumulation. Throughout the 1950s, all political conflicts centered around state control. In the 1960s and 1970s, state intervention in capital accumulation reached its peak. State intervention jeopardized the interests of major classes. As a result, the state became the direct target during the conflicts of 1977–1979.

Finally, the analysis indicates that the formation of coalitions and the consolidation of opposition was important for a successful transfer of power. When the opposition was divided, as in August 1953, the contenders failed to make any gains and were crushed by the repressive forces. The absence of consolidation likewise led to the failure of the struggles of the 1960s, when the industrial working class, the peasantry, and white-collar employees did not join the opposition. In contrast, the consolidation of all social classes and opposition groups in the 1977–1979 period led to the revolution.

To understand the processes that led to this eventual confrontation and consolidation, our analysis must transcend broad historical events and examine the specific transformations and conflicts that emerged from Iran's economic development during the one and one-half decades that followed the Shah's reform and repression in 1963.

Chapter 3

State Accumulation Policies
The Setting of Social Conflicts

The source of current turmoil is Iran's rush into the 20th century, engineered by the Shah over the past 15 years. In 1963, a decade after the United States helped him seize power, he began his effort to bring Iran's feudalistic society into the modern world. . . . But modernization has collided with ancient social and religious traditions, whose proponents refused to budge. (Associated Press, September 4, 1978)

Beginning with the 1960s, Iranian society experienced rapid economic growth and industrial development. However, the popular wisdom expressed in the above quotation is only partially accurate. Although some industrial development did take place, it proceeded very unevenly and was dependent on the state, oil revenues, and external technology. An important characteristic of Iranian economic development was the extraordinary role of the state, as opposed to market forces, in promoting industrial development. State accumulation policies led to uneven development, with rapid expansion of the oil and large, modern manufacturing sectors, accompanied by a decline in small industry and agriculture. The oil sector expanded primarily in response to the world market rather than to domestic demands. As a result, the state and the entire economy became dependent on international economic forces. Finally, these developments rapidly generated massive social problems and inequalities among major social classes. Iran's experience exemplified rushed, dependent development with insufficient deliberate planning and a lack of long-range policies that might have minimized the adverse effects of the transition. This course of economic development, rather than traditionalism, generated the structural basis of the conflicts of the 1977–1979 period.

The Shah's White Revolution of 1963 expanded state intervention in the economy. In contrast to Western states, which derived their income from taxes, the Shah's state relied heavily on a single major resource: oil. Revenues from oil exports provided the state with a high level of independence, for it no longer relied significantly on internal sources of revenue. Rising oil revenues allowed the state to enlarge its own economic activities, becoming the most prominent agent of economic development and totally dominating Iranian society and the economy. By the end of the Shah's rule, the state had become the largest wealth holder, industrialist, and banker in the country. In addition, the state interfered in commerce and the distribution of goods, and regulated prices in the private sector. Such a high level of intervention limited the market's operation and politicized capital allocation and accumulation.

State development policies clearly served particular rather than general societal interests, as claimed by the government. These policies gave rise to widening economic inequality and burgeoning inflation. In industry, agriculture, and commerce, the government's development strategies consistently favored the upper class over the working classes, urban over rural, and large, modern enterprises over small, traditional ones. These policies enriched a minority of the population. Because the state's economic policies promoted accumulation within a narrow circle, it came to be regarded by many as a regime bent on serving particular rather than general interests. Government policies also resulted in the deterioration of the country's agriculture, widespread peasant migrations, and urban housing shortages, which adversely affected the working and middle classes.

The high level of state intervention in capital allocation and accumulation limited the market mechanism and rendered the government vulnerable to challenge and attack. The state's policy of direct, visible support for the upper class against the working classes polarized the economic structure and eventually directed the conflicts against the government. Since many of these developments were affected by the growth of the oil industry, we must examine fluctuations in oil revenues to understand the structural transformations that occurred in Iranian society. The following analysis uses the Iranian government's own documents and statistics in an attempt to minimize bias in assessing the situation.

THE STATE, OIL, AND CAPITAL ACCUMULATION

State intervention in capital allocation and accumulation was made possible by the government's control of oil. The share of oil in the government's total revenues increased from 45 percent in 1963 to 56 percent in 1971. In 1977, despite some decline from the mid-1970s, oil's share increased to 77 percent. The increased dependence on oil can also be seen in the government's development plans. Oil revenues financed approximately one-third of the first development plan, but 62 percent of the Third Five-Year Plan (1962–1967) was financed by oil revenues. By the Fifth Five-Year Plan (1973–1978), oil revenues accounted for more than 80 percent of the financing (Graham 1979:38). All this was made possible by increases in oil revenues, which rose from 73.9 billion rials (constant prices) in 1963–1964, representing less than 20 percent of the GNP, to 1,333.3 billion rials in 1972–1973, which represented 50 percent of the GNP. In 1973–1974, they jumped even further to 1,450.6 billion rials. Although by 1977–1978 they declined to 1,284.9 billion rials, oil revenues still represented over 34 percent of the GNP (Bank Markazi Iran [hereafter BMI] 1978:94–95).

As a result of the oil boom, the economy embarked upon a period of unprecedented growth that lasted for two years. Increased oil revenues enabled the government to spend $22 billion from March 1974 to March 1975, a sum almost equal to the total expenditures during the three previous years. Consequently, the GNP, which had risen by 8 percent per annum in the 1960s, increased by 14.2 percent in 1972–1973, 30.3 percent in 1973–1974, and 42 percent in 1974–1975. Between 1972 and 1978, the GNP grew from $17.3 billion to an estimated $54.6 billion, while the GNP per capita rose from $450 in 1972 to over $2,400 in 1978 (Halliday 1979:138).

The significance of the oil sector in the economy can be understood by its effect on the share of production sectors in the Gross Domestic Product (GDP). For example, table 3.1 shows that the share of agriculture in the GDP steadily declined from 25.8 percent in 1963–1964 to 9.4 percent in 1977–1978. The share of industry grew from 17.7 percent in 1963–1964 to 19.1 percent in 1977–1978. The share of manufacturing in the GDP grew from 9 percent in 1963–1964 to 13.1 percent in 1977–1978. The share of construction rose from 4 percent in 1963–1964 to only 5 percent in 1977–1978.

Table 3.1. Distribution of Iran's GDP by Sector, Selected Years (by percentage)

SECTOR	1963–1964	1968–1969	1972–1973	1977–1978
Oil	21.2	25.1	51.9	35.8
Agriculture	25.8	20.6	10.6	9.4
Industry[a]	17.7	20.7	13.0	19.1
manufacturing and				
mining	9.0	13.6	8.8	13.1
construction	4.0	4.4	3.6	5.0
water and power	1.2	2.0	0.6	1.0
Services	35.2	34.1	24.5	35.7
state services	7.8	9.7	8.1	11.2
Total GDP[b]	348.1	578.9	2,567.1	3,589.1

Sources: BMI 1971:116; and 1978:94–95.

[a]Some industries not listed here.

[b]GDP in constant prices (billion rials).

The most important consequence of increased oil revenues was the domination of the entire economy by the state. The state owned all of the principal sources of wealth, including oil, all other minerals and energy sources, all large modern industries, most of the finance, a sizable number of farms and agribusinesses, most of the transportation and communications facilities, and insurance firms. In contrast, the entire private sector seems to have received less than 20 percent of the national income (Katouzian 1980:370).

As oil revenues grew, state expenditures for fixed capital formation expanded rapidly, exceeding private investments. In 1962–1963 before the oil boom, the state invested only 18,000 billion rials, compared to private investments of 31,000 billion rials. In 1967–1968 the state almost caught up, investing 55,000 billion rials, in comparison to 58,000 billion rials by the private sector (BMI 1972:145). State investment exceeded that of the private sector before the oil boom, reaching 189.1 billion rials in 1972–1973, compared to 150.6 billion rials (BMI 1973:139). Eventually, state investment reached 647.2 billion rials in 1977–1978, while private sector investments totaled 505.4 billion rials (BMI 1977:96).

The oil boom of the last quarter of 1973 quadrupled the country's financial resources, enabling the government to increase its expenditures and industrial investment. Shortly afterwards, the government set aside its Fifth Five-Year Plan, which was less than one year old, and introduced instead a new set of objectives costing $69 billion, or twice the original cost. Under this revised plan, the government allocated additional resources to industrial development. Fixed investments were to be distributed in the following proportions: industries and mines, 18 percent; agriculture and natural resources, 6.6 percent; transportation and communication, 10.5 percent; housing, 19.7 percent; oil and gas, 16.8 percent; other activities, 28.4 percent. In short, nearly 35 percent of all fixed investments were allocated to industries, mines, oil, and gas (BMI 1975:34). The rate of fixed capital formation in industry jumped from 44.6 in 1973 to 239.4 in 1974 (BMI 1975:146). Nearly 42 percent of fixed capital formation went into metal and metallurgical industries. Petrochemicals received the next highest allocation, 17 percent. This distribution was maintained over the next two years.

The state's efforts produced some spectacular results, including exceptional industrial development and one of the highest rates of growth in GNP among Third World nations. Manufacturing grew at an average of 12.3 percent per annum for the 1963–1972 period. Industrial growth for the decade of 1965–1975 was 15.2 percent per annum, almost twice as high as the average growth of this sector in other developing countries. Iran's production of industrial goods increased. In 1968, the country manufactured 20,222 automobiles and jeeps, 1,879 trucks and vans, and 141,000 refrigerators. By 1976, production had increased to 102,000 automobiles and jeeps, 55,322 trucks and vans, and 513,000 refrigerators. Most manufacturing industries experienced similar high rates of growth (BMI 1971:147; BMI 1976:140–141).

The state, investing in a variety of capital-intensive industries, became the largest industrialist in the country. In 1976, the state owned 130 large factories and workshops, with an additional 55 joint ventures with private domestic and foreign corporations (Statistical Center of Iran [hereafter SCI] 1981a:30). The state owned and operated all petroleum plants and four large petrochemical plants, as well as all oil refineries in Abadan, Tehran, Shiraz, and Kermanshah. The state also owned other large factories such as machine-tool plants in Tabriz and Arak, a tractor assembly plant in Tabriz, steel refineries in Isfahan and Bandar Abbas, an aluminum factory in Arak, and a copper mill in Sarcheshmeh. Other significant government-owned plants were several cement and textile factories and sugar mills. Even the tobacco-cigarette company was a government monopoly. The government not only invested in heavy industry, where lots of capital was required and the private sector was weak; it also operated in some light industries like the rug sector, in which the private sector was historically strong and successful. The state owned the National Iranian Carpet Company, which had a number of workshops throughout the country.

The state's economic influence extended far beyond the manufacturing sector. The government also owned the entire railway transportation system, approximately forty-four hundred kilometers; air transport; the main sea transport, National Arya Shipping; and all communication facilities. Fisheries on the Caspian Sea and the Persian Gulf were government monopolies. Many utilities, all major dams, and insurance companies were government owned, as were a sizable number of agribusinesses. Furthermore, the state ventured into the distribution sector, setting up the Urban and Rural Consumer Cooperatives with hundreds of outlets throughout the country. To avoid intermediaries these supermarkets bought directly from producers and import agents and sold to urban consumers. Finally, the government itself became an intermediary for certain essential goods by either importing them or buying them from producers and selling to private retailers for distribution. Items distributed in this manner included meat, wheat, flour, sugar, and tea.

Another key area of state domination was the financial sector, through which the government channeled the allocation of capital in desired directions. A government survey indicated that of thirty-one banks in 1974, nine were completely government owned, ten were private—with five established in 1973 and 1974—and twelve were joint ventures between the government and the private sector. More significantly, nearly 69 percent of all banking capital in the country was owned by the state (SCI 1976b:1, 8).

With increasing resources, the government also pursued policies to promote accumulation in the private sector. Following the 1963 White Revolution, the government encouraged industrial development within the private sector through tariffs as high as 200 to 300 percent for many imported goods, limited industrial licensing to reduce competition in developing branches, easily accessible low-interest loans for investment in modern industries, tax holidays, and export incentives. Between 1971 and 1975, loans to the private sector increased by 289 percent (Bashiriyeh 1984:87). These policies created favorable opportunities for companies in the private sector to develop and accumulate capital, and their performance was indeed spectacular. From 1972 to 1973, the number of registered companies in large cities multiplied from 1,517 to 2,208, an increase of

46 percent. Their capital grew more than threefold, from 14.2 to 52.8 billion rials. In 1974, private companies increased to 3,322 and their capital to 72.3 billion rials (BMI 1975:202). Despite falling behind the state, investments in the private sector nevertheless rose dramatically, by 250 percent from 1962 to 1978. This impressive rate of growth was due primarily to state capital allocation policies in the form of gifts, grants, subsidies, and low-interest loans provided to the private sector, especially in the 1970s.

The oil boom and government policies also attracted foreign corporations. The government encouraged multinational corporations to invest in Iran by offering tax exemptions and guaranteed profit repatriation. The results were again impressive. Between 1956 and 1969, before the oil boom, 86 multinational corporations had investments in Iran. From 1970 to 1974, 97 additional companies invested, bringing the total to 183. In 1974 alone, 32 additional foreign corporations invested in Iran, including nine American firms representing the largest number from a single country (Ghoreyshi and Elahi 1976:379). Investments by multinational corporations totaled 1,336 million rials in 1972. By 1976, they had reached 6,537 million rials, accounting for almost 5 percent of all investments. Foreign investments were usually joint ventures with Iranian private or public capital in basic and heavy industries such as petrochemicals and metallurgy, which were capital and skill intensive. In 1976, for example, petrochemicals accounted for 35.3 percent of all foreign investment, followed by metallurgy with 26.5 percent (BMI 1976:145).

THE WEAKNESSES OF STATE-SPONSORED DEVELOPMENT

Although economic and industrial growth was dramatic, Iranian development was marred by numerous weaknesses. Despite increases in production, Iranian industry failed to compete in the world market. In 1976, non-oil products totaled less than 3 percent of all exports.[1] In 1977, industrial products, predominantly textiles, detergents, and soap, represented only 27.5 percent of all non-oil exports; while traditional and agricultural goods totaled 72.3 percent. More than one-fifth of traditional exports were carpets, long a major export. The principal agricultural products to reach the world market were cotton and fruit (BMI 1977:152).

The government's policy of imposing high tariffs on imported goods created a monopolistic condition, shielding modern domestic industries from competition, encouraging inefficiency, and boosting prices of Iranian goods. In 1976, twenty-one modern manufacturing industries employed less than 11 percent of the total manufacturing labor force, while the value of their products accounted for more than 55 percent of the value of all manufactured products (BMI 1976:139, 142). According to a 1972 estimate, goods manufactured in Iran were 25 to 35 percent more expensive than the average world prices. In part, this was due to high profits in the monopoly conditions of the modern manufacturing sector. Profits commonly ranged from 30 to 50 percent, although there were cases of 100 percent returns and more. Inefficient management was also a factor. For example, in 1976 a GM Chevrolet required forty-five hours to be assembled in Iran, in contrast to twenty-five hours in West Germany (Halliday 1978a). Moreover, many new plants produced at only a fraction of their actual capacities.

The industrial upper class was greatly dependent on the state and the bureaucratic bourgeoisie. The royal family dominated this fraction of the population, and no group within it enjoyed an independent power base. No one could launch a major economic undertaking without including the royal family, if only indirectly. Very few individuals could have spectacular economic success without links to the royal family and the bureaucratic bourgeoisie.

The state's capital allocation policies failed to broaden the industrial base within the upper class, leading instead to a high level of industrial and economic concentration. In 1966, the manufacturing industry consisted of approximately forty thousand employers. By 1976, this figure had increased to fifty thousand, which still represented only slightly more than 1 percent of the total urban work force. Two-thirds of these employers were located in the traditional sectors of food and textile manufacturing. Fewer than nine thousand employers owned most of the modern private factories (Ladjevardian 1982:3).[2] The upper echelon of industrial owners remained extremely small and was composed of roughly 150 families who owned 67 percent of all industries and financial institutions (Bashiriyeh 1984:40). In 1974, 47 wealthy families controlled 85 percent of all firms with turnovers of more than 10 million rials (Halliday 1979:151). Not surprisingly, the royal family itself was the wealthiest family in the country, owning 137 of the 527 largest corporations and financial institutions. Their investments included 18 banks and insurance companies; 29 factories; 11 industries; 45 construction firms; 43 corporations involved in food, agriculture, and husbandry; 10 commercial businesses; 39 service companies; and 8 mining firms. In addition, the Pahlavi Foundation maintained investments in more than 18 corporations. In this way, the royal family controlled a major segment of the economy through their private assets. Elite families who owned approximately 390 of the largest corporations included the Farmanfarmayan family, which owned 74 enterprises; Khosrow-Shahy, 67; Ladjevardi, 61; Reza'i, 38; Sabet, 33; Akhavan, 22; Vahab Zadeh, 21; and the Elghanian, Taymor Tash, and Khayami families, with 17, 16, and 10 corporations respectively (Ravasani 1978:109–117).

While the upper class succeeded in amassing fortunes, the state's accumulation policies totally ignored small, traditional manufacturing, which represented approximately 98 percent of all manufacturing establishments in 1976 and employed over two-thirds of the urban industrial labor force. Traditional manufacturing concerns did not benefit from the grants, subsidies, and interest-free loans extended to the modern sector. In 1973, traditional handicrafts received only .2 percent of all government payments allocated for industrial development. In 1974, payments to handicrafts increased only slightly to .7 percent (BMI 1975:184). By 1976, the amount had increased to 5.2 percent, still very low given the predominance of the traditional sector (BMI 1976:144). Unlike modern industries, traditional industries such as carpets, shoes, copperware, and silverworking were not protected. Throughout the 1970s, machine-made goods flooded domestic markets, subjecting these industries to stiff competition.

These traditional sectors that were ignored by the state employed much of the manufacturing work force because the modern, industrial enclaves failed to absorb the growing urban labor force. Despite its economic precedence, the oil sector remained an enclave with few backward or forward linkages to the rest of the economy. The oil sector was extremely dependent on Western countries for its modern, highly sophisticated technology. It employed only approximately thirty thousand skilled and semi-skilled industrial workers and thus neither drew from nor contributed to the general labor pool. In contrast, in 1976, the carpet industry employed nearly half of the country's manufacturing labor force in roughly 135,000 small workshops.[3]

Although the economy experienced rapid growth and some industrial development, Iran did not become an independent industrialized nation. By the end of the Pahlavi era, Iran had established a number of modern, technologically advanced plants and factories, but they remained disconnected from the rest of the economy. While the government promoted this pattern of industrialization, it paid insufficient attention to the small, traditional manufacturing sectors. Still worse, the government virtually ignored agriculture, which resulted in the failure of land reform.

ECONOMIC DEVELOPMENT AND AGRICULTURE

One of the most serious consequences of uneven development was in the agrarian sector. Although agricultural production rose between 1963 and 1976, it could not keep pace with the demand for foodstuffs and other agrarian commodities. Faced with a population growth of 3 percent, accompanied by increases in urbanization and the rapidly rising income of some social groups, the agricultural sector was hard-pressed to meet the needs of the populace. Inadequate supplies led the government to import foodstuffs, further reducing agricultural growth.

Although the agrarian sector employed over 50 percent of the population, real investment in agricultural machinery and equipment from 1963 to 1971 grew by only 6.7 percent per annum, while the total real investment increased by 20 percent. The contribution of agriculture to total capital formation declined throughout the 1970s. In 1976, capital formation in agriculture amounted to some 71 billion rials at current prices, a drop of nearly 22 percent from the previous year. Although more than 50 percent of the population was employed in agriculture, the share of agricultural output in the GNP dropped from 10.6 percent in 1971–1972 to 9.4 percent in 1977–1978 (BMI 1978:95).

According to government statistics, which should be interpreted with caution, between 1960 and 1970 the average annual growth rate of the value of all agricultural products (defined as farming, animal husbandry, forestry, and fishery) was less than 3.8 percent (in constant prices). From 1972 to 1977, it rose to approximately 4.5 percent. However, the growth of the value of farming products alone rose by only 3.25 percent per year during the same period. For example, the value of wheat increased by less than 3.9 percent, and the value of rice by 3.1 percent (in constant prices). Despite some government attempts to expand agricultural productivity, both cultivated land and the production of important agrarian products had decreased by 1977. Specifically, wheat, rice, and barley production declined by 8, 13, and 18 percent respectively (BMI 1977:17). For example, in Dezful, where some of the best rice in the country was produced, 130,000 hectares of land had been allocated for rice cultivation, which fed the entire population of the province of Khuzestan. By 1978, only 6,000 hectares of land were allocated to rice production. Most farmers simply migrated to cities in search of other jobs (*Kayhan*, January 10, 1978). The government, however, blamed reduced cultivation and productivity on bad weather, the high cost of agricultural workers, and crop loss due to pests.

Although data on agricultural productivity are scarce, some figures are available for land productivity for wheat and barley, which together account for three-quarters of the cultivated area. The best evidence suggests that between 1963 and 1974 the average rate of growth of land productivity for wheat was zero, while that of barley was negative (Katouzian 1978). No data are available for labor productivity. However, because total agricultural output increased, labor productivity also must have risen despite stagnating land productivity and a drop in both the labor force and the area under cultivation. Increased labor productivity may have been due to substantial investments in machinery, fertilizer, and irrigation, which were limited to a small portion of agrarian producers, namely agribusinesses and wealthy farmers.

Rising urban income heightened the demand for agricultural commodities. The agrarian sector was unable to meet this demand, in part because of technical and structural constraints, and in part because of the deliberate neglect of agriculture by the government's development strategy (Katouzian, 1978).

The structural constraints were rooted in the nature of the Shah's land reform, which began in 1963 and lasted until 1971. The reforms exempted all mechanized agricultural holdings and orchards. This excluded thousands of acres of the best land held by wealthy landlords and members of the royal family throughout the country, especially in the Turkoman region of Gonbad Kavous. Absentee landlords were allowed to keep one-half of their holdings. Although absentee landlords accounted for only 2 percent of all landowners in 1960, they owned 55 percent of the arable land. As a result, twenty million acres out of a total of forty-two million acres were exempted from land reform. In addition, the government permitted absentee landlords to select that portion of their land to be sold to peasants (Hooglund 1981:15). Consequently, roughly half of the best land was never subject to redistribution at all, while most of the land that was distributed was of poor quality and in insufficient allotments barely adequate for cultivation. Furthermore, land reform excluded one-half of all village families from receiving land because they lacked formal sharecropping agreements with landowners. This group was quickly transformed into a rural proletariat living in extreme poverty without any resources. Finally, because those who received land included army generals and government officials, even less land was available for the peasantry. Of those peasants who obtained land, over 72 percent acquired less than six hectares; in all, approximately three-quarters of the peasantry received less than the seven hectares necessary for subsistence (Hooglund 1982:90).

Thus, despite land reform, land distribution remained highly unequal (see table 3.2). The last agrarian survey by the Shah's regime, carried out in 1975, indicates that 1 percent of all landowners, or approximately twenty-five thousand persons, owned more than 20 percent of the land. In contrast, more than 65 percent of landowners held only 15 percent of the land. Finally, 82 percent of landowners owned less than 34 percent of the land. In some regions, such as Mazanderan, Khorasan, and Kurdestan, the distribution of land was even more concentrated. In Mazanderan (near the Caspian Sea), with plentiful rainfall and some of the best agrarian land in the country, .26 percent of the landlords owned roughly 19 percent of the land (SCI 1980). In this region, large tracts of land were owned by members of the royal family, their associates, and high-ranking army officials.

The government's capital-allocation strategy following land reform largely ignored the technical needs of the agricultural sector. Most absentee landlords cultivated their arable land in the traditional way by means of peasant sharecroppers. Only a minority whose holdings averaged 250 acres or more practiced capitalist agriculture, using wage laborers, machinery, and production inputs such as fertilizers. The government did not encourage modern production techniques. In 1975, in the entire agrarian

Table 3.2. Land Distribution in Iran, 1975

Size in Hectares	Percentage of Owners
Less than 1	31.11
1–1.99	13.84
2–4.99	20.41
5–9.99	16.84
10–49.99	16.75
50–99.99	.63
100 or more	.36

Source: SCI 1980.

sector there were approximately 41,000 tractors and 2,633 combines, which were very unequally distributed. One-fourth of all tractors and nearly 28 percent of all combines were located in the provinces of Mazanderan and Khorasan. Most peasants were left to their own devices, as if the formal transfer of land titles would miraculously increase agricultural productivity. On the whole, government aid to agriculture was sparse, and with the reduction of oil revenues it was further reduced. The government's decision in the 1970s to pay greater attention to the agricultural sector came too late. In 1976, as a result of reduced oil revenues, government disbursements to this sector declined by 5.1 percent. It is important to note that wherever extensive state investment brought about land improvement and the use of machinery, tractors, leveling, irrigation, fertilizers, and so on, the results were satisfactory (Burn and Dumont 1978). But these resources were unavailable to most agricultural producers because the government extended low-interest credit to big producers only. Rich landlords paid less than 5 percent interest on loans, while others were charged in excess of 14 percent.

Faced with growing shortages, the government began to import large quantities of foodstuffs. In 1972, imports of food and live animals amounted to $206 million. By 1977, imports had increased more than 621 percent, to $1,485 million (BMI 1977:154). High international prices forced the government to subsidize the sale of imported food, a practice that proved enormously costly. In 1973, for example, the government spent 19 billion rials to reduce the prices of cereals, meat, and sugar (BMI 1974:42). Whereas prior to land reform Iran had imported very few food products, afterwards it became one of the leading importers of food and agricultural products in the Middle East. By 1978, food imports were increasing by 14 percent per annum.[4] At this rate, Iran would have been importing half of its food by 1985.

Government food imports further undermined agricultural production. By 1977, the cost to farmers to produce a ton of wheat or rice was greater than the prices these products could fetch in the urban retail market. Consequently, poor peasants became more indebted to the government, banks, and moneylenders; some were obliged to relinquish their land to wealthier farmers and migrate to cities in search of jobs. From the mid-1960s on, approximately one-quarter of a million peasants left for urban areas every year, further worsening conditions in the rural sector. With the departure of the young from the countryside, many traditional irrigation canals, or *ghanats*, dried up because of neglect or because the water table was sinking as a result of uncontrolled pumping by machines belonging to rich farmers, agribusiness, or state-run farm cooperatives. Deprived of the younger generation, its most active and able members, agrarian society was unable to use its resources. In an unprecedented occurrence, agrarian land was left fallow in many parts of the country, with no one to tend it or even fight over rights of possession.

The comparison with other countries is instructive. In Russia and China, adverse peasant conditions led to massive rebellions, violence, and revolutions. In Iran, however, the peasantry did not mobilize to combat worsening conditions or to acquire land. In England, peasants were forced off the land; while in Iran, they voluntarily left for the cities to find jobs in the growing construction sector. In England, according to Thomas More, "sheep ate men" during the enclosure movement; whereas in Iran, the state's development policies eliminated both sheep and people. In England, a process of primitive accumulation violently separated producers from their means of production, resulting in rapid capital accumulation and economic development. The separation of producers from their means of production in Iran was nonviolent and was carried out through a combination of impersonal market forces and government inaction, which were characterized by neither bloodshed nor development but were replete with suffering nonetheless.

ECONOMIC DEVELOPMENT AND SOCIAL INEQUALITY

During the 1960s and 1970s, Iranian society was characterized by housing shortages, land speculation, and considerable social and economic inequality. The government's rushed development policy and its strategy of serving the interests of the upper class and wealthier groups were largely responsible for these problems.

The nation's population grew from roughly 19 million in 1956 to 25.8 million in 1966 and 33.6 million in 1976. By 1976, there were 6.7 million households, with a mean number of inhabitants of five.[5] In 1956, 31 percent of the population lived in urban areas. This figure rose to 39 percent in 1966 and 47 percent in 1976. In 1976 the Central Province had the highest concentration with 6.9 million, or over one-fifth of the total population. Tehran alone had approximately 4.5 million inhabitants. Tehran's population had increased at a rate of 4.2 percent per year since 1966 (SCI 1976a). Urbanization multiplied the number of large cities. In 1966, there were 249 cities of more than 5,000 persons, while 29 cities had over 50,000 people. In 1976, 373 cities had populations greater than 5,000, and 45 cities were larger than 50,000. Tehran was the only city with over 1 million residents. Isfahan, Mashhad, and Tabriz each had over 500,000; while Shiraz, Ahvaz, Abadan, and Kermanshah had more than 250,000 people each. There were 22 cities with populations over 100,000.

Urban population growth was due in part to peasant migration, which exacerbated existing urban problems such as land speculation, housing shortages, and growing inflation. The price of urban land rose daily. Between 1967 and 1977, urban land prices increased by an estimated 2,000 percent (*Ettelaat*, August 23, 1977). In 1975, in an attempt to control land speculation, the government forbade selling vacant land. One government minister estimated that in each city some five hundred individuals owned the urban land, while the rest had to settle for "envying" them.[6] It appears that only the wealthy could afford to own land in the central zones of large cities.

The state itself became one of the largest holders of urban land (*Ettelaat*, May 11, 1977). The government purchased 33.8 billion square meters of land near large cities, including more than 15 billion square meters near Tehran. Approximately one-third of the government-owned land was located within large cities where land prices were highest. The government's entry into these markets as a major owner itself increased land prices. Recognizing the gravity of the situation, in 1977 the government announced that land would be offered for sale at its original cost (*Ettelaat*, September 12, 1977); but there is no evidence that such sales actually took place.

Housing presented critical problems. In 1972, urban areas were estimated to fall short of sufficient housing by at least 1.1 million units. During the Fourth Five-Year Plan (1968–1973) only 290,000 units were built. The housing shortage became so intolerable that by 1973 the government was forced to make a major adjustment in its Fifth Five-Year Plan and increased credits to the housing sector by 129 percent over previous levels. Capital investment in construction jumped from 174.5 million rials in 1972 to 890.8 million rials by 1976. The private sector share rose from 66.3 million rials to 307.8 million rials, while the government's share over the same period increased from 108.2 million rials to 583 million rials (BMI 1976:154).

Despite increased spending, the housing shortage remained unalleviated for the working classes and the poor. Part of the reason was that most government investments financed the construction of military and "national" buildings. In 1973, the government spent 45,063 million rials on construction, of which less than 30 percent went to provide housing. By 1975, government expenditures for housing had increased to 41 percent. Most housing that was constructed was allocated for white-collar employees, which increased existing inequalities. In 1973, out of a total of 13,484 million rials spent for housing, 67 percent was allocated for white-collar employees, 24 percent for workers, and the rest of the 9 percent for "low-cost" housing. Although by 1977 housing allocations had increased more than fivefold, workers received only 26 percent, while 60 percent went to white-collar employees (BMI 1977:115). Government demand for construction materials reduced the amount available for private-sector housing projects. From 1972 to 1976, the private sector completed only some 164,000 units in large cities (BMI 1976:157), falling far short of the needed targets.

By the end of 1977 in Tehran alone, an estimated thirty-five hundred families were searching daily for rooms, apartments, or houses to rent (*Ettelaat*, January 2, 1978). Nationwide, approximately 28 percent of all families lived in rented homes (SCI 1976a:151), while in Tehran roughly 37 percent occupied rented apartments or houses (SCI 1976:370). The housing shortage was accompanied by sharp increases in rents. The official newspaper of the Shah's own party estimated that rents in some parts of Tehran had risen 1,000 percent (*Rastakhiz*, September 16, 1977). As investment in housing became ever more lucrative, wealthier segments of society, including some professionals such as physicians and dentists, capitalized on this opportunity and made huge fortunes in the housing industry (*Ettelaat*, July 2, 1977). By the mid-1970s, rents had increased to the point where urban workers were spending more than one-half of their income on rent (*Ettelaat*, June 11, 1977). Even the Shah condemned the situation and promised a remedy: "For every job we must build a house. Each worker should be able to own a house by retirement. We must identify land owned by religious institutions and build houses for workers upon it" (*Ettelaat*, April 14, June 1, 1977; and *Kayhan*, February 15, 1977). In 1977 the Ministry of Labor announced a program to build homes for workers near their factories with the help of labor and industry (*Ettelaat*, July 10, 1977). Such statements were primarily empty promises that were contradicted by the government's actions, which included reducing credits to this industry. Consequently, the housing shortage did not improve for white-collar and industrial workers, who still made up 90 percent of those renting housing.

Within housing units, space was unequally distributed. In southern Tehran, for example, each one room was occupied by an average of six persons, with an average allotment of three square meters per person. In richer districts the average was thirty square meters per person. In an extreme case, one hundred persons reportedly occupied a single house (*Ettelaat*, December 30, 1970). Between 1967 and 1977, the percentage of urban families living in a single room rose from 36 to 43 (Abrahamian 1982:447). On the eve of the revolution, as many as 42 percent of the inhabitants of Tehran lived in inadequate housing.

In 1977, despite these shortages, the government ordered commercial banks to halt credit for housing on the pretext of directing capital into "productive" sectors (*Kayhan*, February 14, 1977). This ban did not affect the wealthier segments of society. Two weeks later, seven large construction firms and banks, along with several international corporations, signed a contract to construct prebuilt housing units (*Kayhan*, February 28, 1977). The housing problems of the poorest segment of the population were completely ignored by the government. Instead of expanding low-income housing, the regime instead chose to devote resources to the construction of large complexes for the upper class. The government also encouraged migrants to return to their villages and even made a point of providing grants to a small number who agreed to do so.

High rents effectively barred most people from the central zone of large cities. As a consequence, shantytowns sprang up on the outskirts of urban areas. In Tehran, at least twenty-four large shantytowns containing thousands of families had arisen on the edges of the city (*Ettelaat*, August 6, 1977; *Payam-e Mojahed* 1977, no. 51). Although there are no accurate statistics as to the number of inhabitants of Tehran's shantytowns, estimates range from five hundred thousand to more than one million people (Kazemi 1980:3). Most shantytown dwellers were unskilled workers, along with some recent migrants from rural areas, peddlers, artisans, and even some white-collar employees (OIPFG 1978a:3–5).

These shantytowns provided notoriously poor living conditions. Houses were generally erected by family members themselves, who were forced to pay exorbitant prices for black-market building materials. Drinking water was supplied by private companies at seventy times the rate within the city (*Rastakhiz*, June 25, 1978). Whereas 80 percent of the city budget was allocated to provide services for the wealthy inhabitants of northern Tehran, shantytowns lacked running water, electricity, public transportation, garbage collection, health care, education, and other services (*Washington Post*, January 14, 1979). The contrast between urban shantytowns and rich high rises was an embarrassment to a regime that had promised the advent of a

"Great Civilization." As shantytowns proliferated, the government de-clared them illegal. Eventually, in mid-1977, the government sent bull-dozers to demolish a number of shantytowns in large cities, including Tehran.[7]

Inequality also existed in the area of health care. In 1973, approximately one-half of all physicians resided in Tehran, which had one doctor for every 787 inhabitants. The ratio for the rest of the country was 1:5,011, but in remote provinces such as Ilam it reached 1:12,570. The Central Province, which included Tehran, had 160 hospitals with 23,552 hospital beds, or one hospital for every 43,256 persons. In contrast, the province of Zanjan had only 3 hospitals with 205 beds, or one hospital for every 193,000 per-sons. Two provinces, Ilam and Boyer Ahmad, had one hospital each with 50 and 60 beds, serving a population of 244,000 and 245,000 respectively (SCI 1977a:110). In the entire country, there were only 1,965 dentists, more than half of whom lived in Tehran (SCI 1977a:105, 107). By the end of the Shah's rule, the nation's population of 34 million people was provided for by only 13,428 physicians and 525 hospitals with a total of 53,944 beds.

Inadequate health care was a grave problem, especially in rural areas. According to the minister of health, infant mortality in rural areas was 120 (per 1,000 live births), one of the highest in the world (*Kayhan*, December 7, 1977). Malnutrition was prevalent in many parts of the country, and ane-mia was almost universal. Marasmus and kwashiorkor were common in shantytowns, as were goiter in the central region, rickets in Isfahan, and xerophthalmia south of the Persian Gulf (Burn and Dumont 1978:16). The creation of a national health corps helped to mitigate the situation. Even so, in the mid-1970s the health corps could send only 181 physicians, who had been conscripted into the army, to thousands of villages where millions still lived in poverty and ill health (SCI 1977a:110). The extreme shortage of health care professionals was due in part to a brain drain to advanced countries, a problem that was partly political because of the regime's au-thoritarian nature. The real problem was the regime's failure to commit sufficient resources to meet society's needs. Instead, resources were spent, or rather wasted, on military buildup.

Education expanded during the 1960s and 1970s. In 1966, 28.7 percent of the total population was literate; this included 39.2 percent of all men and 17.4 percent of the women. In 1977, 47.1 percent of the population was lit-erate, including 58.6 percent of the men and 35 percent of the women. However, literacy was unevenly distributed. In Tehran in 1973 it was esti-mated at 76 percent, while in the rest of the country it was only 38 percent.

According to Walton (1980) literacy was lowest in the provinces of Ilam (21.5 percent) and Kurdestan (22.3 percent). A national educational corps was created to reduce unequal access to education, but more than 60 percent of all schoolchildren still failed to complete primary school. In 1975, 68 percent of all adults remained illiterate. From 1963 to 1977, the absolute number of illiterate adults actually rose from thirteen million to fifteen million (Abrahamian 1982:447).

Marked regional inequalities followed the nation's pattern of economic development. In 1971–1972, according to the Statistical Center of Iran (SCI), the average household expenditure in the Central Province was 1.4 times that in Kurdestan, 2 times the expenditure in Sistan and Balouchestan, and 2.7 times the rate in Kerman. Regional industrial development was also very uneven. In 1976, the country had 7,500 large manufacturing establishments employing 10 persons or more. Of these, 2,934, or roughly 40 percent, were located in the Central Province. In contrast, only .34 percent of these establishments were located in Kurdestan. Together, the Central Province, Khorasan, East Azerbaijan, and Isfahan contained over 66 percent of the large manufacturing enterprises.[8] Regional uneven development also characterized the financial sector. A survey of banks in 1974 indicated that nearly 35 percent of all banks were located in the Central Province, while Boyer Ahmad and Kurdestan provinces had .1 and .9 percent of the banks. The ratio of banks to population was one bank for every 2,852 people for the Central Province, one per 57,000 for Boyer Ahmad, and one per 10,672 for Kurdestan (SCI 1976b:10–11).

The data clearly demonstrate a pattern of unevenness. The Central Province, which includes Tehran city, was the most developed in all dimensions and benefited from sufficient resources. In contrast, the provinces of Ilam, Kurdestan, Balouchestan, and Boyer Ahmad were the least developed in most respects. Uneven distribution of government expenditures was primarily responsible for these regional inequalities. Table 3.3 shows the percentage and per capita regional development disbursements during the Fourth Five-Year Plan. As the table indicates, Hamedan and Lurestan, Sistan, and Kurdestan were among the most disadvantaged provinces.[9]

The government's allocation and accumulation policies inevitably increased income inequalities among social groups and classes. The urban/rural income differential declined from 2.13 in 1959 to 1.91 in 1965 due to land reform. By 1972, it had risen to 3.21 (Vakil 1976:101). In a study on income distribution, the International Labor Office concluded that in 1969–1970 the Gini coefficient, a measure of income inequality, was higher

Table 3.3. Regional Development Expenditure of the Fourth Plan of the Government of Iran (1968–1973)

REGION	Percentage of Total State Expenditure	Per Capita Amount Spent[a]
Gilan, Gorgan, Mazanderan	7.9	6,230
Azerbaijan	11.8	7,735
Central	28.3	13,710
Khuzestan, Boyer Ahmad	15.9	20,366
Hamedan, Lurestan	1.2	1,321
Isfahan, Yazd	17.7	17,761
Fars	6.8	10,056
Sistan, Kerman	1.1	2,049
Khorasan	4.8	3,896
Kurdestan	2.4	2,530
Saheli	2.6	10,335

SOURCE: Adapted from Jabbari and Olson 1981:179.

[a]Figures in rials.

in Iran than in any other country in the Middle East, Southeast Asia, or Western Europe, and was as high or higher than Latin American countries for which data were available. Between 1959 and 1974, the share of expenditures of the top 20 percent of urban households increased from 52 to 56 percent, while that of the bottom 40 percent declined from 14 to 11 percent (Walton 1980). The share of expenditures of the bottom 10 percent of households decreased from 1.77 percent in 1959–1960 to 1.34 percent in 1971–1972; this trend reversed itself only slightly over the next two years, increasing by a fraction to 1.37 percent. In contrast, the share of the top 10 percent of households increased from 35.4 percent in 1959–1960 to a peak of 39.5 percent in 1972–1973, and dropped slightly to 37.99 in 1973–1974 (Pesaran 1976:268).

Many factors were responsible for rising income inequality in cities. The state's accumulation strategy consistently served the interests of the urban dominant class engaged in industry, banking, commerce, and agriculture at the expense of the vast majority of the population. The government's development policy and the oil boom intensified existing inequalities and led to uneven development. State banking policies provided the small dominant class with cheap credit while denying it to the middle and poor segments of the population. Import substitution (producing locally rather than importing) and high tariffs favored the growth of highly profitable monopolies in the industrial sector at the expense of consumers. Industrial development was capital intensive and restricted through limited licensing, thus preventing medium-sized capital from entering the most profitable sector. The capital-intensive nature of development adversely affected the working class by using primarily skilled labor, which created a labor aristocracy. The pool of unskilled labor further expanded due to the government's neglect of agriculture and the consequent peasant migration. As a result, stratification within the labor force increased. Government taxation policies worsened the inequalities. The poorest 10 percent of the population paid 11 percent of their income in taxes, whereas the richest 10 percent paid only 8 percent in taxes (*Kayhan*, October 23, 1978). Many of the wealthy did not even bother to pay taxes. Finally, rising inflation reduced the purchasing power of those living on fixed incomes, adversely affecting their standard of living.

In sum, many areas of society fell far short of the "Great Civilization" promised by the Shah. The monarch predicted that by the year 2000, Iran's progress would surpass that of Sweden. Yet by the time he was deposed, more than half of the country's population did not have access to running water (SCI 1976a:table 4-10).

THE STATE AND ECONOMIC CRISIS

As we have seen, the state, with its control over enormous oil revenues, pursued accumulation policies that widened social, economic, and regional disparities. However, the state was not able to control all the factors that affected the Iranian economy. The state's development strategy had made the economy increasingly dependent upon the world market, over which the government had no control.

The world market affected the state and the economy in two contradictory ways. In the first place, increased oil income created a crisis of revenue absorption. The rapid growth of the oil industry was not matched by expansion in other sectors, especially production sectors. Therefore, the economy could not absorb the increased oil revenues, and the result was rising prices. On the other hand, the government was unable to increase its revenues from the world market as anticipated. Continued worldwide recession, a mild European winter in 1975, and a relatively modest increase in the OPEC (Organization of Petroleum Exporting Countries) price of oil soon reduced Iranian oil production and revenues. By December 1975, oil production was running 20 percent below that of the previous year. Oil revenues fell from 1,333.3 million rials in 1973 to 1,284.9 million rials in 1977. The drop in revenues was felt throughout the economy. The production of large manufacturing firms declined, as did the value of industrial and non-oil exports (BMI 1977:111, 152). At the same time, the value of imports continued to increase. Total imports rose from $2,570 million in 1972 to $14,124 million in 1977, a jump of approximately 450 percent (BMI 1977:153). As a result of declining income, by mid-1976 government expenditures exceeded revenues. The deficit for 1976 was 37.6 billion rials, and the following year it skyrocketed to 388.5 billion rials (BMI 1977:139).

Thus, on the one hand, too much money and income in the system caused rising prices; while on the other hand, there were inadequate revenues to finance ambitious government projects. To solve the second problem and meet its financial needs, the government raised taxes on public corporations and the self-employed, excluding domestic producers (*Kayhan*, February 1 and 23, 1977), and began borrowing funds from international sources. A shortage of funds had already led some commercial banks to turn to the international market for short-term loans. Despite financial shortfalls, commercial banks during this period were allowed to maintain a liberal credit policy as the money supply kept increasing at a rate of 60 percent per annum. This policy exacerbated the first problem of rising prices and high inflation. To remedy this situation, the IMF mission advised the government to reduce expenditures. Government officials ignored this advice and instead blamed the rapid price increases on imported inflation. To curb inflation, the government sought to bring prices under control and encourage imports by lifting tariffs. However, ports lacked the facilities and infrastructure to handle increased imports and satisfy the demands of a suddenly hyperactive economy. Inadequate transportation created bottlenecks of up to two hundred ships waiting an average of five to six months to unload their cargo. As a result, resources and imported goods were wasted on a massive scale.

In an attempt to control prices, the government implemented a campaign against "profiteering." In August 1975, prices of sixteen thousand items were rolled back to their levels of January 1974. The profit rate was officially set at 14 percent, despite an inflation rate of at least twice that amount according to the government's own figures. The government reported that thousands of people joined a consumer protection agency created to inspect prices and detect profiteers. Anyone who violated the price controls was subject to arrest. As we shall see in the next chapter, thousands were fined and imprisoned as a result of this policy. In at least one case in Tabriz, a customer took the law into his own hands and killed a butcher who had allegedly raised meat prices slightly from the previous week (*Kayhan*, February 7, 1977). Price controls were instituted at the level of retail markets where merchants, shopkeepers, and artisans operated. No serious control was imposed on factories where commodities were produced and priced; nor were controls placed on the few giant import firms. Because the antiprofiteering campaign was unevenly enforced, few industrialists were arrested. Those who were prosecuted were outsiders, such as Elghanian, a Jewish industrialist, or Habib Sabet, a Baha'i who refused to return from Paris after being charged with profiteering.

None of the solutions the government pursued were adequate to resolve the dual problems facing the Iranian economy, in part because the solutions were contradictory. After two years of futile measures, the Shah decided to address the problems through a major political change. In mid-1977, he dismissed Prime Minister Abbas Hoveyda, who had held office for thirteen years, and appointed instead Amuzegar. Upon assuming office, Amuzegar reduced government expenditures and abandoned the more ambitious projects that had been planned by the government but not yet begun. To control inflation, he restricted access to bank credits (*Ettelaat*, August 23 and 29, 1977) while continuing the antiprofiteering campaign. The new policies reduced all economic activities. Shortages of funds and electricity slowed industrial production, causing workers to be laid off. Tens of thousands of private housing projects in Tehran alone were halted by lack of capital and construction materials (*Ettelaat*, November 16, 1977). An economic crisis was underway. The superheated economy had not only cooled down, but was close to freezing completely.

In summary, Iranian society experienced fundamental changes in the years following the White Revolution of 1963. As oil revenues increased, the state became more integrated into the economy and expanded its intervention in capital allocation and accumulation. The state became the most visible actor, playing a central role in the country's economic development. State intervention undermined the abstract market mechanism, thus politicizing the accumulation of capital. Linkage to the state and to the government bureaucracy, rather than to the market, was the main source of accumulation. During this period, the state was not only the primary vehicle for distributing the new wealth, but itself became the major wealth holder. With increased resources and increased intervention, the state affected all aspects of social and economic life. The high level of state intervention in capital allocation and accumulation combined with adverse policies made the state potentially susceptible to crisis, challenge, and attack. Given the subordination of the market forces and the entire private sector to the state, the government could not avoid being blamed for adverse policies.

Government policies failed to strengthen the country's social structure to the point where it could become independent of oil and the world market and, in fact, by the mid-1970s, interdependence of the state and the economy had increased. Iran's oil revenues were necessary to purchase food and technology. The increased dependence rendered both the state and the economy vulnerable to fluctuations in the world market. By the end of the Shah's rule, Iranian society had not really succeeded in becoming industrialized. Genuine, independent economic development, industrialization, or modernization had not taken hold. Instead, rapid economic growth enabled the government to establish some enclave industrial structures that were highly dependent on the world market and lacked adequate backward or forward linkages to the rest of the economy.

This pattern of rushed development created massive social problems and generated unevenness and inequalities in all aspects of society. Agriculture was neglected, resulting in a deterioration of conditions for the peasantry. Although more than one-half the population still depended on agriculture for its livelihood, this sector accounted for less than 10 percent of the national income. The upper class represented a very small fraction of the population, but possessed a disproportionate share of the nation's wealth. The state systematically strengthened upper-echelon bureaucrats and big capital at the expense of other classes and interests, especially the holders of medium- and small-sized capital. These policies widened social and economic inequalities. Inflation threatened those portions of the working and middle classes dependent on fixed income. Housing policies jeopardized or ignored the working class and shantytown dwellers. State capital-allocation policies paid little attention to less developed regions; as a result, regional inequalities were magnified. In all, the state's development policies adversely affected large segments of society, generating a diverse set of potential opponents.

The stage for conflict was set when the government attempted to confront its economic problems in the mid-1970s. The uneven expansion of the oil sector relative to other sectors generated new income, causing a crisis of revenue absorption. A developed economy would have been able to capitalize on such resources and generate greater prosperity. In Iran, the uneven development resulted in demand-pull inflation. Thus, on the one hand, the state needed to reduce the supply of money and economic activities. At the same time, however, the government had initiated a number of ambitious projects that required additional income. To address the first problem, the government attempted to check rising inflation and speculation through price controls and an antiprofiteering campaign. As for the second problem, when oil revenues declined the government borrowed capital from the international market. These two solutions were contradictory and, not surprisingly, failed to solve Iran's economic woes. Ultimately, the government shifted its policy and cooled down the hyperactive economy by bringing about a recession. Together, these policies had fatal consequences for the regime.

Beginning in the fall of 1977, groups of urban Iranians began to mobilize and engage in collective action against the government. Gradually, all major social classes and groups, including bazaaris, the industrial working class, white-collar and professional employees, clergy, and intellectuals joined the antigovernment struggles. These groups and classes had different interests, conflicts, resources, and solidarity structures, which determined their contributions to the overall struggle. In coalition they were able to disrupt the social structure and bring about a revolutionary situation that in February 1979 culminated in the overthrow of the state. The process by which these groups and classes mobilized and consolidated their forces is crucial in understanding how the revolution took place and its outcome. Let us now examine the nature and timing of various conflicts and the mobilization of each of these groups and social classes.

Part Two

Mobilization and Revolution

The next four chapters will examine the conflicts between the state and particular social classes and political organizations whose mobilization generated a revolutionary situation. To understand the causes and nature of the conflicts, I will examine state policies and their impact upon various classes and groups. I will also analyze the collective actions of these groups and classes during the crucial political conflicts of the past few decades, including the revolutionary period of 1977–1979. My goal is not to provide a historical account, but rather to delineate those factors that determined the nature and timing of the earlier collective actions of these classes and their political orientations. The specific variables that determine mobilization and collective action include interest, organization, resources, opportunity structures, and the likelihood of coalition formation with other groups and classes. The combination of these factors will enable us to develop a coherent analysis of the mobilization of various classes and groups in the Iranian revolution.

By interest, I mean the shared advantages or disadvantages that are likely to accrue to these various classes as a result of their interaction with other groups (C. Tilly 1978:54). Given the significance of state intervention in capital allocation and accumulation in most developing countries, the conflicting units will consist of classes and the state. I have focused both on the objective interests of various classes and groups and on their stated demands, whenever such statements have been available. By organization, I mean the existence of a constituency that represents a group or class and possesses a communication network to mobilize the group and coordinate its action. Obviously, such an organization would have to be autonomous of the structure under attack in order to be effective (Schwartz 1976:171–177). If repression or lack of resources has prevented a group from forming an autonomous organization, its options will be limited. Such a group may have to "borrow" a preexisting organization and use its space and communication network to mobilize. If such a channel is unavailable, mobilization might suffer from serious weaknesses.

Resources are also critical in times of conflicts. A major problem is that disadvantaged groups often do not have resources available for mobilization. Resources include such things as independent economic assets and safe, designated places for gathering, communication, planning, and broadcasting the disadvantageous and unfavorable actions of the group's adversaries. Opportunity for action is also crucial because it provides favorable conditions for mobilization by reducing or neutralizing repression and thus reducing the cost of action. Periods of crisis often provide favorable conditions for collective action by generating multiple conflicts, by blocking previously used methods of redressing grievances, and by forcing large groups of people to search for alternative solutions and courses of action (Schwartz 1976:195). Crisis situations may also provide favorable opportunities for action by giving rise to conflict and divisions within the dominant class or the government. Under such conditions, disadvantaged classes may be able to coalesce with one segment of the government against the other, using their resources and shielding themselves against repression. Although such coalitions might impede fundamental change, they are conducive to mobilization and collective action. Liberalization of the political system or collapse of repressive forces provides highly favorable conditions for mobilization by reducing the cost of collective action. Finally, formation of broad coalitions and consolidation of opposition groups and classes may be the most effective means by which challengers can overcome repression. The sustained mobilization of a major social class possessing appropriate resources to mobilize and broadcast government's adverse policies is often crucial in providing opportunity for weakly organized classes to mobilize. In time, this may lead to escalation of conflicts and consolidation of all major social forces into a single bloc. A consolidated opposition that is able to disrupt the social structure may succeed in generating a revolutionary situation by creating alternative bases of power, or what is often called dual sovereignty. If, as a result of structural weaknesses within the army, disruptions spread to the armed forces, a revolution becomes highly likely. I will use these variables to examine the mobilization of various groups and classes in the Iranian revolution.

In contrast to explanations based on ideological consensus, these variables better illuminate and predict the conflicts that unfolded before, during, and after the downfall of the monarchy. Ideological explanations are too broad to account for the mobilization and political actions of various groups and classes located differently in the social structure and with different sets of grievances, interests, solidarities, and resources. They fail to explain both differences in the timing of the actions of various groups and the diversity of their demands. An examination of values or cultural orientation cannot systematically explain these differences. My analysis does not deny that some segments of Iranian society are and have been traditional. Individual values or attitudes are not at issue here. The point I wish to stress is that for collective action to occur, certain structural requisites must be met. The focus of analysis should be placed on the options available to the actors, rather than their cultural beliefs. Under highly repressive conditions, victimized social groups and classes often have severely limited options for mobilization, regardless of their values. Moreover, the role and impact of cultural symbols must be understood within the broader political and economic framework. Individuals or groups may hold certain ideas over long periods of time but never act upon them. More importantly, certain social groups or classes may hold traditional social views but follow liberal or nontraditional political programs or leaders in their collective actions. For these reasons, I have focused on variables that have been developed by resource mobilization theorists.

In the chapter that follows, I will examine the struggle between bazaaris and the state. Their conflict was crucial in providing an opportunity for other social groups to attack the government. Chapter 5 will examine the conflicts and mobilization of workers and white-collar professionals, whose participation in antigovernment struggles disrupted production and services and generated a revolutionary situation. Chapter 6 will discuss the organization of secular contenders and their role in antigovernment mobilization and protests. Chapter 7 analyzes the relation between clergy and the state. The condition, politics, and resources of the clergy are examined. Chapter 8 will examine the final assaults on the government organized by students and the younger generation in the last months, which led to the paralysis of the armed forces and the overthrow of the monarchy. In Chapter 9 I will discuss the conflicts within the Islamic Republic that culminated in the establishment of a theocracy. These conflicts provide another test of my analysis of mobilization and collective action. Finally, Chapter 10 will provide a summary of the research.

Chapter 4

The Bazaar
The Eye of the Storm

Is our only aim the destruction of autocracy? . . . Or is it the construction of a free and developed Iran, with a government based on justice, law, and progress? We, the shopkeepers and artisans of Tehran, strongly believe that with solidarity, the courageous Iranian people will destroy injustice and despotism . . . and with unity of heart and intention, will move toward the establishment of a just and genuine democracy, building a proud Iran on the ruins of corruption. Solidarity guarantees our victory! (*Guilds* newsletter, January 1979, no. 2)

In every social revolution certain established classes with embedded solidarity structures have played important roles in the overthrow of the government, paving the way for the rise of a new social structure. For example, in Russia, a coalition of peasants and industrial workers was crucial in the conflicts against Tsarist rule. In China and many other developing countries the peasantry has played central parts in the political conflicts. The Iranian political conflicts and revolution of 1979 cannot be understood without an analysis of the struggles of bazaaris, a term that encompasses merchants, shopkeepers, and artisans. Bazaaris were among the principal actors in the Constitutional Revolution of 1905–1911. They also played a significant role in the conflicts against royalists and the British during the nationalization of oil in the 1950s. More recently, they were in the forefront of the conflicts against the Shah from 1977 to 1979. Bazaari mobilization and collective action quickly emerged as the most significant features of the revolutionary conflicts and were of primary importance in bringing down the Pahlavi regime. The following analysis differs sharply from the works of other theorists, such as Green and Saikal, who emphasize the role of the emergent middle class, spawned by rapid economic development, as the most significant actor in the Iranian revolution. Furthermore, this analysis also differs from analyses, like Arjomand's, that emphasize the unsettling and uprooting impact of rapid modernization and the consequent normlessness and anomie.

An important part of the explanation of the significance of bazaaris in the political conflicts lies in the particular structure of the central bazaar. This structure can generate a strong capacity for mobilization and collective action in times of conflict. In most major cities, the central bazaars are concentrated in a single location, in narrow alleys under covered roofs. The concentration and proximity of shops facilitate communications. All bazaaris, meaning both merchants and shopkeepers who distribute goods and artisans who produce goods on a small scale, deal in very specialized commodities. They buy, sell, or produce a single line of goods only. Furthermore, all those who deal in that specific product work in the same street or alley. As a result, different bazaars are located in different streets, although the entire bazaar is interconnected. Closeness and dependence on single commodities can generate intense competition for customers. At the same time, however, proximity and dependence on similar commodities for livelihood can also create a common fate with respect to market conditions, changes in technology, rise of new competitors, and external factors of production such as the role of the state in business. These conditions can generate strong solidarity during periods of crisis and conflict, especially when various segments of the bazaaris are faced with a common enemy.

Another significant factor enabling bazaaris to play an important role in political conflicts has been their resources. By the time of the revolution, Tehran's central bazaar, the heart of the nation's trade, numbered close to forty thousand shops and workshops, one-half of which were located within the covered bazaar and the remainder in the immediate vicinity.[1] Shopkeepers outside the covered bazaar followed bazaari politics, even though their shops were not part of the bazaar proper. Despite a relative decline, bazaaris controlled most of the national trade in the 1970s, including more than two-thirds of the nation's domestic wholesale trade and more than 30 percent of all imports (Graham 1979:221). Bazaar moneylenders, comprising several hundred individuals, controlled approximately 15 percent of the private-sector credit (Graham 1979:221).[2] Their independent economic resources enabled them to engage in collective action without losing their jobs or immediate livelihood. Finally, bazaaris sold goods to shopkeepers throughout the country on the basis of extended credit. This practice created a dependent relationship in which bazaaris exerted additional influence over the commercial sector outside the bazaar. In 1976, this sector numbered more than half a million (SCI 1976a).

An additional feature of bazaari mobilization is that their collective actions often have broader consequences, going beyond their own sector. For example, bazaari strikes and shutdowns disrupt a major part of the national trade and, consequently, the economy. The disruption of trade, in turn, affects consumers' livelihood. In combination, such disruptions increase the likelihood that conflicts will escalate under favorable conditions. Bazaar closings are additionally important because they signal to other groups in society that some sort of conflict is underway. This is critical if the media and other avenues of communication are unavailable or restricted due to repression and censorship. Consequently, bazaar conflicts can create opportunities for other adversely affected classes and groups to act collectively as well. For these reasons, bazaari mobilization has been crucial for groups that oppose the government.

It is often maintained that bazaaris constitute a traditional social group who view Western mores with horror (Keddie 1981:245). This traditionalism is demonstrated by the fact that bazaaris always follow the leadership of the clergy in politics.[3] According to this view, the bazaaris and the clergy constitute traditional communities. This interpretation of bazaari collective action rests on a homogeneous view of both bazaaris and Shia clergy. As we shall see, however, both of these social groups were composed of distinct segments and characterized by diverse orientations and interests, which conditioned their actions. Undeniably, broad segments of the bazaar were traditional and greatly respected their religious leaders. This does not, however, mean that bazaari mobilization and collective action always follow their traditional values or their religious leaders.

To determine the validity of this analysis, we shall examine bazaari politics during the three decades prior to the revolution. We will demonstrate that the mobilization and collective actions of bazaaris are explainable historically in terms of their response to state policies that adversely affected their economic interests, their organizational capacity to act collectively, and the existing opportunity structure. When bazaaris possessed a strong, autonomous organization, they were able to mobilize and act collectively to defend their interests. When this avenue was not available, they attempted to mobilize through other channels, forging alliances with other groups. By the end of the Shah's rule, the mosque was the only remaining avenue through which they could mobilize. An analysis of bazaari conflicts and mobilization from 1950 to 1979 indicates the significance of these variables. The conflicts of the early 1950s were grounded in economic crisis, which, combined with specific state policies, adversely affected bazaari interests. Reduced repression and liberalization of the political arena in the 1940s after Reza Shah's downfall enabled bazaaris to organize and form an independent guild, which played an important role in the mobilization process. During the conflicts between nationalists and royalists in the early 1950s, bazaaris supported the nationalists against the royalists. It is important to note that in these conflicts bazaaris did not follow the clergy, most of whom supported the monarchy.

The context of the conflicts of the early 1960s was again an economic crisis, combined with government policies that had an adverse impact on the interests of bazaaris. The repression that followed the coup d'etat had dissolved the independent merchant guild, severely hampering mobilization. In the early part of this period, bazaaris fully cooperated with the second National Front, which had just been formed as a result of a brief period of liberalization; but the Front was soon repressed. Clerical opposition in early 1963 provided an opportunity for bazaaris to oppose the government. In June 1975, during the anniversary of the 1963 uprising, clerical students revolted against the government, calling on Iranians to rise up against the tyrannical regime. Ayatollah Khomeini endorsed this rebellion, but bazaaris failed to join the rebels. Although the interests of segments of the bazaar had been jeopardized by the state, the government had not yet imposed extremely damaging policies on bazaaris. In addition, this was a period of economic prosperity for the bazaar, with no signs of the economic crisis to come.

Bazaari collective actions from 1977 to 1979 were in protest against the political economy of the Shah's state. Bazaaris opposed the state authoritarianism that emerged following the 1953 coup d'etat and intensified after the White Revolution. Lack of political freedom, therefore, was partly responsible for the bazaaris' conflict with the state. By itself, however, lack of political freedom was insufficient to provoke the collective actions of this period. In fact, state repression had restricted the bazaaris' capacity for mobilization against the government. Once again, the context of bazaari mobilization was an economic crisis, combined with government policies that adversely affected their interests. As mentioned in the previous chapter, the government initiated a price-control policy and an antiprofiteering campaign in August 1975. In so doing, state intervention replaced the market mechanism, rendering the government vulnerable to challenge and attack. This intervention had an extremely negative impact on bazaaris. In the initial stages, bazaaris mobilized outside the mosque, but were hampered by repression. In the absence of other channels through which to mobilize, bazaaris pressured and encouraged the clergy to oppose the government. Bazaari mobilization through the mosque led the government to proclaim a policy of reform in the summer of 1978. The promise of reform in turn provided an opportunity for other social classes to mobilize for collective action. Their mobilization prompted the government to reverse the reforms and resort to military repression. In response, bazaaris initiated a series of long strikes that paralyzed the national trade, signaling instability and providing further opportunities for other groups to resume collective action. In combination, they created a revolutionary situation.

To demonstrate the usefulness of this analysis, I will now examine the actions of bazaaris during the conflicts of the 1950s, 1960s, and 1970s leading to the revolution.

THE BAZAAR AND THE NATIONALIST MOVEMENT

In the early 1950s, Iranian society was marked by intense controversy over issues such as the power of the royal family and the landed upper class, nationalization of oil, land reform, political freedom, and judicial and educational reforms. The most important conflicts emerged following the nationalization of oil. Major segments of society, including some politicized clerical leaders as well as the middle and working classes, lined up behind Prime Minister Mosaddegh in favor of nationalization. The Western boycott of Iranian oil, however, brought about a severe political and economic crisis that led to the collapse of the coalition. Political confrontation between royalists and nationalists intensified in 1952 and 1953 with other social groups joining sides. Eventually, an alliance of the landed upper class and the monarchy, combined with CIA intervention, resulted not in a revolution, but in a coup d'etat that removed Mosaddegh from office.

Bazaari interests were adversely affected by the government's trading policies, which had permitted massive importation of cheap American goods into Iran toward the end of the 1940s and in the early 1950s. This brought about an economic crisis, which led to widespread bankruptcies. In one month alone in early 1950, two hundred merchants with a considerable amount of capital went bankrupt (Ivanov n.d.:138). During this period, the vast majority of bazaaris supported Mosaddegh, who advocated nationalist and independent economic development emphasizing domestic production against foreign imports, curbing the monarchy's power, and other social reforms to modernize the country. But, as we shall see in the chapter on the clergy, the vast majority of the clergy, especially the highest-ranking clerics, supported the monarchy and opposed the prime minister. Only a small minority of the clergy who acted independently of the religious network backed Mosaddegh against the Shah. Bazaaris had established the independent Society of Merchants, Guilds, and Artisans (SMGA), which mobilized bazaaris for collective action against the Shah. They repeatedly demonstrated their support for the prime minister by closing down the bazaar on at least fifty different occasions (Lebaschi 1983, tape 1:9). When Mosaddegh's government lacked sufficient revenue to pay salaries to government employees, merchants and shopkeepers lined up to buy special government bonds issued to ease the financial crisis.

Mosaddegh recognized that to modernize the country he would need the backing of the military and the police. Mosaddegh's liberal policies contradicted the violence imposed on street demonstrators by the armed forces, which were controlled unconstitutionally by the Shah. In July 1952, Mosaddegh demanded control over the military. The Shah refused, and Mosaddegh resigned. As the news spread, on July 16, 1952, Tehran bazaaris were the first group to take to the streets in anti-Shah strikes and protests. A few days later, on July 21, shopkeepers and merchants across the country closed their shops in response to a call by the National Front to demonstrate support for the prime minister against the Shah. On that historic day, hundreds were killed or injured in antimonarchy protests. The Shah was obliged to reinstate Mosaddegh immediately.

When Ayatollah Kashani and other clerics broke with Mosaddegh's National Front, the SMGA continued to back the prime minister. On April 14, 1953, they published a statement in *Ettelaat* newspaper condemning Mosaddegh's opponents and demanding passage of a bill to curb the Shah's power that would have prevented him from interfering in civil and military affairs. Two days later they demonstrated in overwhelming numbers (*New York Times*, April 16, 1953). On June 18, when leaders of the National Front in the Majles called for a rally to tell the "truth" about conditions in the Majles and the refusal by most deputies to pass a bill limiting the Shah's powers according to the constitution, the SMGA endorsed the rally (*Ettelaat*, June 18, 1953). On the first anniversary of the July 21 massacre, bazaaris throughout the country again closed down to attend pro-Mosaddegh rallies (*Ettelaat*, July 23, 1953). Even in the religious center of Qom, shopkeepers and merchants struck in support of the prime minister (*Ettelaat*, July 14, 1953). Bazaaris went so far as to propose that a golden statue of Mosaddegh be erected in Tehran. They eventually dropped this proposal because Mosaddegh himself opposed it.

When Mosaddegh temporarily recessed the Majles and called for a national referendum to dissolve it, shopkeepers shut down again and voted with the prime minister, despite Ayatollah Kashani's call for a boycott. When a group of royalist officers attempted a coup d'etat against the prime minister on August 16, 1953, merchants and shopkeepers rallied in large numbers to condemn the Shah, who was obliged to flee the country. With the second, successful coup d'etat three days later, bazaaris struck in protest (*New York Times*, August 21 and 22, 1953). Despite assurances by the government that their shops would not be attacked and that they would not be arrested, bazaaris refused to reopen out of loyalty to the prime minister. Colonel Dadsetan, military governor of Tehran, publicly complained that merchants declined to resume business (*Ettelaat*, August 23, 1953). Finally, the government forced them to reopen under duress (*New York Times*, August 25, 1953).

Despite support by the preeminent clerics for the Shah's return, bazaaris continued to oppose the Shah's regime.[4] Following Mosaddegh's arrest, bazaaris struck twice in his support. On October 8, a few days after the prosecutor demanded the prime minister's execution, the Tehran bazaar struck in support of Mosaddegh. This protest was called by the National Resistance Movement, which had been organized by a few leaders of the National Front who had not yet been arrested. According to government reports, some 100 people were arrested during the strike and demonstrations (*Ettelaat*, October 8, 1953). A few of the detainees, including Mahmoud Maniyan, a National Front leader and prominent bazaari, were exiled to distant areas that had a "bad climate" (*Ettelaat*, October 18, 1953). Four days after Mosaddegh's trial began, the National Resistance Movement again called for a demonstration on his behalf. In response, the bazaar struck on November 12 (*Ettelaat*, November 12, 1953). According to the government's figures, more than 300 people, mostly bazaaris and students, were arrested. Of these, 218 were exiled to Khark Island in the south (*Ettelaat*, November 14, 1953). At the same time, the government destroyed the bazaar's roof in several places. After the strike, the new prime minister, General Fazlollah Zahedi (1953–1955), threatened to destroy the entire roof of the bazaar if the strikes were repeated (*Ettelaat*, November 14, 1953; Binder 1962:295). Only threats to their livelihood and severe repression convinced the bazaaris to end their strikes in support of Mosaddegh, even though most clergy supported the Shah. Thus, evidence presented above does not support the argument that bazaaris always followed clerical leadership. Rather, the data indicate that bazaari collective actions were determined by a combination of their interests, organizational capacity for action, and opportunity structures.

THE BAZAAR AND THE CONFLICTS OF THE EARLY 1960s

Toward the end of the 1950s and the early 1960s, another economic crisis set the stage for a new round of conflicts. Government policies designed to deal with the crisis adversely affected the interests of bazaaris. At roughly the same time, the reduction of repression and partial liberalization of the early 1960s provided an opportunity for bazaari mobilization. The second National Front, formed during this period, received the complete support of bazaaris (Lebaschi 1983, tape 2:7).

In 1960, the government imposed a stabilization program that led to a recession, which lasted for three years. As part of this program, the government reduced loans to bazaaris, claiming that they had borrowed money from banks and lent it to others at higher rates. The government also imposed stiff restrictions on certain imports, which resulted in disapproval by importers within the bazaar (*Ettelaat*, May 20, 1963). The recession and government policies led to growing bankruptcies among bazaaris (*Ettelaat*, May 7, 1961), who complained that the government did nothing to promote commerce (*Ettelaat*, May 21, 1963). In 1961, the government, assisted by the progovernment merchants' guilds, devised a new rate of taxation for the bazaar, which was met with protests by rank-and-file bazaaris. Shopkeepers and artisans objected that the taxation burden was shifted to poorer segments of the bazaar, while guild leaders paid little in taxes themselves (*Ettelaat*, April 30, 1961). In protest, they refused to pay taxes for more than three years.

Government policies and growing bankruptcies among bazaaris generated conditions ripe for conflict. Organizationally, however, the bazaar was in a weak position to mobilize itself for collective action, lacking both leadership and autonomous organizations. The SMGA, which had been central to the mobilization against the monarchy in the 1950s, had been dissolved; and the new merchants' guild, founded after the coup d'etat with the help of Ayatollah Behbahani, was controlled by the government and was not an autonomous bazaar organization. Because the bazaar was organizationally weak, bazaaris had to wait for favorable opportunities before they could act. When they did act between February and May 1961, the remaining bazaar leadership was crippled by the sporadic jailing from May 1961 to January 1963 of the leaders and activists of the second National Front (*Ettelaat*, January 24, 1963), which bazaaris had supported in the 1950s. In February 1961, several dozen leaders of the second National Front organized a sit-in at the Majles, demanding guarantees for free Majles elections. As the sit-in began, students at Tehran University organized demonstrations for free elections. Bazaaris closed down in support of this mounting political opposition (Jazani 1979:118). They also supported the teachers' strike of May 1961, which became political and led to the dismissal of Prime Minister Sharif-Emami's government (1960–1961).

The next collective action by bazaaris occurred in January 1963 during the referendum on the Shah's reforms. Both the National Front and the clergy boycotted the referendum, while the bazaar closed down to protest the voting. The protest led to the arrest of thirty-two individuals, the entire leadership of the National Front and most bazaari activists, including Maniyan and Mohammad Shanehchi (*Ettelaat*, January 24, 1963). With the National Front leadership in jail, bazaari supporters cooperated with the clergy who also opposed the government. For example, Abolghasem Lebaschi, a bazaari supporter of the National Front who had been living underground, went to Qom to pick up antigovernment leaflets issued by the clergy for distribution in Tehran (Lebaschi 1983, tape 2:9).

The government soon launched new attacks on bazaaris. In May 1963, the government announced an investigation of those who had not paid taxes. Three hundred thousand cases of refusal to pay taxes were uncovered in Tehran alone, most of which involved merchants, small shopkeepers, and artisans (*Ettelaat*, May 19, 1963). In addition, as inflation continued to rise, the government threatened to embark upon an antiprofiteering campaign to punish those who refused to lower prices (*Ettelaat*, April 21 and 23, 1963). At the end of April and again in mid-May, the government imposed price controls on bakers and butchers (*Ettelaat,* April 29 and May 16, 1963). These policies further threatened and antagonized bazaaris.

The advent of Muharram, the Shia month of mourning, provided a favorable opportunity for the expression of political opposition. During this period, large public religious ceremonies are held, involving mourning processions of men marching through the streets clapping their arms to their chests and chanting. Many of these processions in 1963 were politicized, and anti-Shah slogans were shouted. The day after the peak of the mourning ceremonies, on June 5, the government arrested Ayatollah Khomeini and a number of other clerics in different parts of the country. Within a few hours, protests erupted in Tehran, Qom, Mashhad, Isfahan, Shiraz, Tabriz, and Kashan.[5]

Bazaaris were not organized and did not respond to these events as a unified bloc. While shopkeepers and artisans participated extensively in the actions, merchants did not. In a sample of 579 individuals arrested or killed in the protests, only one was a merchant; while shopkeepers and artisans constituted the largest bloc (Moaddel 1986:544). Those bazaaris who participated in the demonstrations retreated very rapidly once shooting began (Jazani 1979:144). Finally, some shopkeepers outside the central bazaar did not participate in the actions at all, and as a result their shops were smashed and even looted.[6]

In sum, bazaari mobilization and collective action during this period can be explained in terms of a combination of their economic interests, an organizational vacuum or weakness, and the opportunity for collective action. Government policies directly challenged the interests of bazaaris. With reduced repression, bazaaris mobilized against the government; but soon government repression hampered their mobilization. Eventually, clerical opposition provided a brief opportunity for bazaaris to oppose the government, but heavy repression quickly put an end to their mobilization and collective action.

THE BAZAAR AND THE REBELLION OF CLERICAL STUDENTS, JUNE 1975

In 1975, an uprising of clerical students challenged the Shah's regime, providing a potential opportunity for opponents of the Shah to mobilize. On June 5, more than one thousand clerical students, known as *tullab*, seized control of the Madraseh-e Faizieh-e Qom, the most important educational establishment for training clerics. The timing and place were well chosen. The date was the twelfth anniversary of the arrest of Ayatollah Khomeini in 1963 and the subsequent massacre of protesters. The Madraseh-e Faizieh-e Qom was located near the shrine of Fatima, a pilgrimage site for Shia Moslems from all over the country. The rebellion lasted for three consecutive days and nights until it was finally put down by several units of army commandos dispatched from Tehran. Dozens of students were killed or injured, and more than five hundred were arrested.[7] Following the collapse of the insurrection the Savak shut down the school, which remained closed throughout the rest of the Shah's rule. After the rebellion, clerical students in Mashhad also mobilized and demonstrated against the government. The government promptly arrested two clerics and approximately thirty clerical students.

Ayatollah Khomeini also swiftly rose to endorse the clerical students' cause. Three days after the death of students in Qom, he sent a message of condolence to the Iranian people, congratulating them for the "dawn of freedom" and the elimination of imperialism and its "dirty agents." Khomeini's message noted that forty-five students had been killed by the second day and that the government had refused the injured admission to Qom hospitals (Khomeini 1983:215–216).

During this rebellion, bazaaris did not initiate a single shutdown, protest, or mourning ceremony anywhere in the country. This significant event seems to have passed completely unnoticed by shopkeepers and merchants. The reason was that the context of the rebellion was not ripe for bazaari mobilization. The economy was still functioning in June 1975, and no economic crisis had emerged to threaten bazaaris as a whole. State development strategies had generated competitive pressures that only affected some segments of the bazaar. For example, the rise of department stores produced unequal competition and posed a threat to some shopkeepers. Similarly, artisans in traditional occupations such as blacksmithing, coppersmithing, and shoe industries were somewhat affected by the development of modern sectors. On the other hand, the oil boom had created a unique occasion for shopkeepers and merchants to increase their assets, and many did so. The sudden increase in national investment and consumption boosted domestic trade, which was still controlled largely through the bazaar. As a result, bazaaris in various sectors were in an advantageous position to benefit from the boom, and many improved their economic position.[8] Some bazaaris even transferred a portion of their capital into the burgeoning construction sector and reaped additional profits.

Finally, prior to June 1975 the government had not yet initiated any confrontation with the vast majority of bazaaris. To understand bazaaris' eventual opposition to the state two years later, we must analyze the changes in government policy that generated intense conflict.

BAZAARIS AND THE STATE AFTER 1975

After 1975, broad segments of the bazaar faced severe economic pressures. For example, small artisans and shopkeepers in the carpet sector were adversely affected by rising costs due to inflation and higher prices for imported wool to replace declining domestic supplies. The prohibition of child labor, historically the main source of labor for Persian rugs, added to the cost of production. In combination these factors made Persian rugs less competitive on the world market. On the domestic side, growing importation of machine-made carpets reduced the sale of rugs within the country. Many bazaaris in the rug business were forced to change to other sectors. Eighty shops sold Persian rugs in 1976 in Ahvaz, capital of the oil-rich province of Khuzestan. During the last nine months of 1977, thirty-six of these shops closed down (*Kayhan*, December 24, 1977). Recognizing the negative impact of the lack of protection on this important traditional sector, the government imposed import restrictions on machine-made carpets at the end of September 1978 (*Kayhan International*, September 27, 1978). As was often the case with such government policies, the restrictions arrived too late for many producers and distributors of Persian rugs.

The government also pursued policies that adversely affected the interests of most bazaaris. In addition to interfering directly in the importation and distribution of wheat, meat, sugar, cement, and steel (Graham 1979: 221), the government instituted in 1976 hundreds of Urban and Rural Consumer Cooperatives, which purchased goods from producers or importers and sold them directly to consumers. Still worse, from bazaaris' point of view, were allegations that the bazaar was unsanitary, constituted a fire hazard, and was plagued with traffic problems. In 1976, suggestions were made to demolish the bazaar and build a new market along the lines of London's new Covent Garden. As one merchant summarized the concerns of most bazaaris, "If we would let him, the Shah would destroy us. . . . The banks are taking over. The big stores will be given most of our business. The bazaar will be flattened so new buildings can go up" (quoted by Kandell, *New York Times*, November 7, 1978).

As declining oil revenues brought on an economic crisis, the government sought to balance the budget and finance unfinished projects by imposing new demands and restrictions on the bazaar. Higher taxes were levied on bazaaris, and bank loans to shopkeepers were cut back (*Ettelaat*, August 23 and 29, 1977). Toward the end of 1977, the state further extended its control over the bazaar by making shopkeepers' operating licenses contingent on two new conditions: first, that merchants' guilds guarantee that licensees would not violate the law; and second, that landlords who rented space to shopkeepers write a formal letter of consent to the government on their behalf. These restrictions severely constrained license-seekers, for the guilds were unwilling to police their membership. Furthermore, license-seekers who had disagreements with landlords over rents or other matters were automatically at a severe disadvantage. The passage of this law sharply reduced the number of licenses issued (*Ettelaat*, December 3, 1977).

Of all the state policies affecting shopkeepers, the most damaging were price controls and the antiprofiteering campaign. In August 1975, prices of sixteen thousand items officially reverted to their January levels. The government set the profit rate at 14 percent even though inflation, according to the regime's own reports, was at least twice that figure. Prices were fixed at the retail market level where merchants and shopkeepers operated, but no serious controls were imposed on factories that produced and priced commodities; nor were restrictions placed on the small number of large importers. Throughout this uneven campaign, very few big industrialists were arrested for violating price restrictions.

The impact of price controls on bazaaris, however, was staggering. In the first few days of the campaign, 7,750 shopkeepers were arrested (*Kayhan International*, August 8, 1975). By October 1977, approximately 109,800 Tehran shopkeepers, out of a total of 200,000, had been investigated for price-control violations (*Ettelaat*, October 27, 1977). In the month of April 1977 alone, the government imposed 600 million rials in fines for profiteering, mostly against shopkeepers in the bazaar (Bashiriyeh 1984:103). According to the Ministry of Interior, 20,000 shopkeepers had been jailed by the end of 1977. By fall 1978, the nationwide total of shopkeepers in violation of the controls was 220,000 (*Ettelaat*, September 26, 1978). The manner in which the regime carried out its campaign was especially humiliating. When special courts handed down a guilty verdict, the individual's shop was shut down, a fine levied, and the owner was subject to arrest or exile. A large banner was hung from the doorway of the shop proclaiming that the store would remain closed for a period of time because the owner had been fined for profiteering. The names and localities of those shopkeepers who were arrested or fined were published daily in the national newspapers.

Shopkeepers in tightly controlled sectors of the economy such as food and groceries expressed extreme anxiety about their businesses. Some felt that each customer who entered their store might be an agent of the Otagh-e Asnaf, or Chamber of Guilds (*Ettelaat*, April 4, 1977), the organization in charge of price control. Inspectors sent by the Chamber of Guilds visited not only urban shops but also rural towns in distant areas of the country. One team, for example, was sent to the small town of Kalisa Kandy to inspect prices in shops. News of their presence quickly spread among shopkeepers; within minutes, the entire bazaar closed down and shopkeepers took the day off (*Ettelaat*, April 5, 1978).

The state's price-control campaign made it extremely difficult for most shopkeepers in the bazaar to do business without violating the new regulations. Traditionally, the bazaar placed great emphasis on honesty and honoring agreements. These traits are important occupational requisites in a society where bargaining is still widespread. At the same time, because many items in the bazaar changed hands eight to ten times, prices inevitably did go up. Bazaaris considered such profits to be their prerogative in a free market economy. The antiprofiteering campaign, however, made them appear greedy, dishonest, disobedient, and responsible for rising inflation, the major social ill. Overnight the government had created a class of criminals to be arrested, fined, and exiled to different parts of the country. Without doubt, the government was attempting, by means of the campaign, to direct popular resentment away from the state and against bazaaris instead.

To circumvent the onerous regulations, some shopkeepers initially sought individual solutions for their situation. For example, in 1977 approximately 500 Tehran food retailers, out of a total of 7,000, applied for new licenses in other sectors. Their requests were denied by the government on the grounds that their neighborhoods might suffer from their departure (*Ettelaat*, April 21, 1977). Nonetheless, some hard-pressed shopkeepers simply shut down. As an example, 130 Tehran bakers closed their bakeries in a matter of a few months in 1977 and could not be located by the government (*Ettelaat*, October 24, 1977). Some rich merchants and commercial enterprises resorted to bribery to circumvent the constraints and were thereby able to violate price controls without sanctions (*Ettelaat*, September 26, 1978). Others with ties to rich, influential customers used their connections to avoid sanctions. For example, eight shopkeepers with such connections were summoned 194 times for profiteering, but the Chamber of Guilds complained that they were unable to close down the shops because of their owners' connections (*Kayhan*, January 3, 1978). Many shopkeepers and artisans, however, had neither connections, nor large sums for bribery, nor the possibility of changing their jobs, especially once the economic crisis worsened.

In short, the government's policies radically changed the situation for bazaaris beginning in August 1975. Several months of widespread arrests and sanctions generated conditions for unprecedented conflict between the bazaar and the state. Never before had so many bazaaris experienced so many fines and arrests. By the end of summer 1977, Tehran's bazaar merchants had met at least twice with officials of the Rastakhiz party, the country's only legal political party, to express their dissatisfaction with the Chamber of Guilds, the government's credit policy, and the new taxation scheme (*Ettelaat*, August 23 and 29, 1977). As usual, the government was unresponsive and changed none of its policies. The regime's refusal to satisfy at least some of the bazaar's demands eliminated the option of compromise, leaving the door open for conflict and confrontation.

BAZAARI MOBILIZATION AGAINST THE STATE, 1977–1979

Conflicts of interests and the absence of viable options are not, of course, sufficient for mobilization and collective action. If adverse economic policies sufficed to bring on collective action we should observe continuous collective action in all societies. Instead, such violence and social disruption is hardly the norm. Additional factors are therefore necessary for collective action to occur. One such additional factor is the ability of disadvantaged groups to develop solidarity structures, mobilize resources, and build alliances in order to challenge the state. These processes do not emerge automatically, especially under highly repressive conditions where the state permits no opposition, as occurred in Iran under the Shah.

During the 1960s and 1970s, the capacity of the bazaar and the rest of the commercial sector to mobilize and act collectively was undermined by a number of factors. In the years prior to the revolution, the commercial sector was a diminishing social category despite its economic significance. In

1966, merchants and shopkeepers represented approximately 16 percent of the urban work force (see table 4.1). Ten years later, their proportion had declined to roughly 13 percent. Similarly, artisans, defined as self-employed producers of manufactured goods, accounted for 5.62 percent of the urban work force in 1966.[9] In 1976, they represented only 4.31 percent. Neither of these groups had kept pace with the general expansion of the work force. In addition to relative decline, their capacity for collective action was undermined by economic diversification and political differences. Although the vast majority of those in the commercial sector were not wealthy but possessed instead medium- or small-sized capital, economic development diversified and increased stratification within the bazaar.

A number of developments had also undermined the collective capacity of the central bazaar, the most important source of political mobilization. In the 1950s, the bazaar played a significant role in the mobilization of the commercial sector outside the bazaar. By the late 1970s, however, the commercial sector outside the bazaar had grown to several times the size of the central bazaar. A new commercial sector dealing in luxury goods had emerged outside of the central bazaar along with import-export firms and department stores, none of which followed the bazaaris' politics. Hundreds of successful merchants whose operations grew too large for the bazaar left to deal in luxury goods or joined the industrial sector.[10] Because they benefited from state policies and were unaffected by the antiprofiteering campaign, they did not oppose the regime. Even among those who stayed in the bazaar, a minority of wealthy merchants supported the government. This was true even in the most traditional sector of the bazaar; namely, rug dealers.[11]

The divisions that characterized the bazaar were also evident in the politics of merchants and shopkeepers. In contrast to the 1950s, when the vast majority of bazaaris were united behind Mosaddegh, bazaaris were not politically unified in the 1970s. Disagreements approaching hostility existed between wealthy bazaaris and those who were less well off, as well as between bazaar employers and employees (Shanehchi 1983, tape 3:18). Some shopkeepers apparently supported the regime, including wealthy bazaaris, leaders of various merchant guilds, and shopkeepers who dealt in luxury imports. When strikes were called for June 5, 1978, to commemorate the 1963 rebellion, leaders of 145 guilds announced that shops would remain open (*Kayhan,* June 5, 1978). In particular, shopkeepers dealing in luxury goods kept their stores open, especially in the northern boulevards of Tehran such as Jordan, Elizabeth, and Bukharest streets where imported

Table 4.1. Work Force Employed in Urban Commerce and Handicraft

CATEGORY	1966	% Total	1976	% Total
Total urban work force	2,610,294	100.00	4,112,636	100.00
Employed in commerce	420,206	16.09	540,289	13.13
Self-employed in manufacturing	146,736	5.62	177,401	4.31

SOURCE: SCI 1966a and 1976a.

luxury goods were sold (*Zamimeh* 1978, no. 16:52). Guild leaders refused to go along with the announced strikes because they benefited from government favors. Similarly, shopkeepers who dealt in luxury imports did not experience the severe price controls and sanctions imposed by the government upon other segments of this class. On October 1, 1978, when Ayatollah Khomeini was expelled from Iraq, the clerical community called a one-day general strike. Although this protest assumed a genuinely national character, in some places such as Ghazvin approximately one-half of all shopkeepers did not go on strike (*Zamimeh* 1978, no. 21:69).

At times progovernment guild leaders and wealthy merchants who did not favor closure were attacked during the revolutionary conflict. On the evening of June 4, Mrs. Afshar, head of the Tailors' Guild, received an anonymous warning that her store would be set afire if it did not close down the next day. She opened her shop as usual, but with a police guard and fire truck to protect it. Around midday, a terrified person entered the shop and requested help in extinguishing a fire in a nearby publishing house. The police and firefighters rushed to the scene of the reported fire, leaving Mrs. Afshar's shop unguarded. Shortly after they left, the tailor's shop was torched. In a similar manner, a store owned by the head of the Rug Dealers' Guild in Ghazvin was set ablaze because of his support for the regime. In Shiraz, the store of a well-known merchant in the central bazaar remained open throughout December 1978, although most shopkeepers had closed down. In early January, a bomb demolished his shop (*Kayhan*, January 7, 1979).

The small segment of the bazaar that opposed the government in the 1970s was divided and lacked strong, autonomous organizations. The merchants' guild was reduced to a mere formal structure after the coup d'etat of 1953 and never regained its independence. Most of its leaders supported the government. Some merchants and shopkeepers remained loyal to Mosaddegh's National Front and in October 1977 illegally reestablished the Society of Merchants, Guilds, and Artisans of the Tehran Bazaar (SMGATB), an organization affiliated with the National Front and outlawed since the 1953 coup d'etat.[12] The SMGATB was the most resourceful opposition organization within the bazaar. In 1977 and the first eight months of 1978, the SMGATB was largely responsible for organizing bazaar shutdowns and strikes. The SMGATB encouraged religious bazaaris to mobilize and printed their leaflets (Lebaschi 1983, tape 3:5, 15). However, this organization did not have the support of the entire bazaar. Religious bazaaris, too, were marked by divergent political orientations and lacked organization. The upper echelon paid religious taxes to Ayatollahs Khonsari, Sayyed Mohammad Kazem Shariat-Madari, and Sayyed Abolghasem Khoie, while some middle- and lower-level shopkeepers paid taxes to Ayatollah Khomeini.[13] None of these tiny elements of the bazaar were organized at the outset. Still other bazaaris supported the Freedom Movement, a liberal-religious organization led by Mehdi Bazargan, a supporter of Mosaddegh. Some less-well-to-do shopkeepers and artisans supported the Mojahedeen, an organization founded in the 1960s that advocated Islamic socialism. As for the vast majority of shopkeepers throughout the country, they had become nonpolitical after years of repression and had withdrawn from ideological movements. When well-known bazaari activists from the SMGATB began to mobilize and to distribute leaflets opposing the government, many bazaaris initially distrusted them, believing them to be Savak agents because they dared to act so openly against the regime without apparent fear of reprisal (Lebaschi 1983, tape 3:19).

These divisions within bazaari opposition were at least partially and temporarily offset by the government's antiprofiteering campaign and price-control policy, which adversely affected most segments of the bazaaris, politicizing and impelling them to mobilize. The struggle against the government, rather than ideological concerns, became the most urgent issue. Given their organizational weaknesses, bazaaris searched for appropriate opportunities to act. In early 1977, an opening for action was created by a law declaring that all political detainees had to be charged or released within twenty-four hours and that trials for political opponents were to be held in civilian rather than military courts. In response, bazaari activists such as Lebaschi and Maniyan began political activities and mobilized against the government. At this time, the clergy had not yet become involved in the conflicts. Ayatollah Khomeini commented on the slow pace of clerical mobilization at the end of December 1977 and encouraged clergy to take advantage of the opportunity and oppose the government (Khomeini 1983, 1:265).

In the initial stages, bazaaris mobilized along with modern, secular groups who were demonstrating against the government. In Tehran, location of the largest bazaar in terms of capital, number of bazaaris, and volume of trade, bazaaris' first opportunity to mobilize occurred in March 1977. Bazaaris initially indicated their opposition to the government by supporting striking university professors and students who were protesting the government's decision to move their campus from Tehran to Isfahan. In retaliation against the strike, the government cut faculty salaries. Bazaaris, along with university students, quickly established funds to pay faculty salaries in full (Nategh, January 1982). Bazaari politics had clearly changed toward the regime since the clerical students' uprising in June 1975 when the bazaar had not reacted; now bazaaris were quick to mobilize against the government. In July 1977, bazaaris publicly denounced the government's Rastakhiz party for "strangling" them through the price-control campaign. As mentioned above, bazaaris met twice in August with officials of the Rastakhiz party to express their opposition to a number of government policies, particularly the price controls and taxation.

The death of Ayatollah Khomeini's son in Iraq provided bazaaris with an opportunity to express their opposition to the Shah as well as respect for Khomeini. Bazaaris with such diverse political views as Maniyan, Lebaschi, and Shanehchi from the SMGATB; Habibollah Asgar-Oladi and Javad Rafigh-Doust, who were bazaari supporters of Khomeini; and a number of political leaders from the National Front and Freedom Movement signed statements calling for a mourning ceremony on October 29 to mark the seventh day of his death. In Tehran, bazaaris closed their shops to attend the ceremony at the Ark Mosque. That this was a political rather than a purely religious act was evident: only a few days earlier, another mourning ceremony for a religious leader of similar ranking had been held but had attracted far less attention and participation (Bazargan 1983b:13). Bazaaris in Isfahan also held a mourning ceremony on the seventh day of Khomeini's son's death. They closed their shops and sat on the floor of the bazaar, praying and occasionally shouting political slogans. Bazaaris in Qom did not close on the seventh day, but held mourning ceremonies on the fortieth day after the death.

On November 16, an overnight sit-in took place following a poetry night during which leftist poet Saeed Soltanpour spoke of repression and read revolutionary poems. The next day, students at the sit-in took their protest to the streets; nearby shopkeepers joined in and shouted anti-Shah slogans. After one student was killed during the demonstration, Tehran University students called for a national day of mourning on November 21. The Tehran bazaar responded by shutting down almost completely to support the protest (*Zamimeh* 1978, no. 8:12–13). The following day, bazaaris and leaders of the National Front gathered in an orchard in Karvansara Sangi to celebrate Aid-e Ghorban, a religious holiday. The Savak, knowing that the event was an incipient political mobilization, dispatched 750 agents to break up the gathering. Many participants were injured, including Maniyan, a supporter of Mosaddegh who had been an activist since the 1950s and was one of the founders of the SMGATB. This event brought home the difficulties of mobilizing against the government. A safer place was needed, and thereafter bazaaris increasingly turned to mosques for mobilization. They had to borrow this preexisting organization to be able to broaden and sustain their mobilization and launch larger attacks against the government.

In January 1978, troops attacked a student demonstration in the important religious center of Qom led by clerical students who were protesting the publication of an anti-Khomeini newspaper article. As mentioned above, these clerical students had rebelled in June 1975, but received no support from bazaaris at the time. The situation was very different in 1978. Qom bazaaris independently closed their shops on the second day of protest to support the students before anyone had been killed or arrested. Protesters, encouraged by bazaar closings, demanded that the preeminent clerics call for a national strike. The leading clergy met, but failed to agree upon a joint statement. One of the preeminent clerics argued that the bazaar should reopen. This angered bazaaris, who countered that they were willing to pay the 150 toman fine for each day they remained closed (The Freedom Movement [Abroad] 1978, 1:54). They remained closed for four days despite the refusal of the preeminent ayatollahs in Qom to endorse their strike. On the second day of the strike, several bazaaris who were instrumental in the bazaar shutdown and had assisted families of the victims of the demonstration were arrested and exiled to different parts of the country (*Kayhan*, October 26, 1978). Bazaaris in Isfahan, the third largest city and most important center of handicraft industries in the country, also closed their shops to protest the massacre of students in Qom. They were forced by the Savak to reopen after a week.

Bazaaris in Tehran did not act immediately. Instead, they decided to shut down the bazaar ten days after the massacre occurred. This day coincided with the last day of a week of mourning observed by Ayatollah Khomeini during which he canceled his classes in Iraq. The SMGATB and three other groupings of bazaaris from Azerbaijan, Shiraz, and Isfahan within Tehran bazaar called for a strike. In particular, Azerbaijani bazaaris published a statement accepting the invitation of SMGATB to strike in protest against the massacre. However, Ayatollah Khonsari, the highest religious leader in Tehran and one of the most prominent ayatollahs in the country, advised bazaaris against the strike. Defying their religious leader, Tehran bazaaris closed down their shops on January 19, 1978. Following the strike, Ayatollah Khonsari had to protect himself with police bodyguards whenever he went to prayer (The Freedom Movement [Abroad] 1978, 1:139). In response to the strike, the government arrested twelve bazaaris in Tehran. The massacre of clerical students was protested by bazaar closings in several other cities, including Mashhad, Shiraz, Abadan, and Khoramshahr.

Forty days after the massacre, on February 18, shopkeepers in more than thirty cities shut down and joined the mourning ceremonies. On this day, many people were killed in new protests. The most dramatic events of this mourning cycle occurred in Tabriz, the fourth largest city with the second largest artisanal sector. Many Tabriz residents followed the moderate, nonpolitical Ayatollah Shariat-Madari in religious matters. Shortly before the mourning ceremonies, Shariat-Madari called for a nationwide mourning ceremony for the student martyrs. He closed the Madraseh-e Elmieh in Qom and urged participants in the ceremonies to remain calm (*Payam-e Mojahed* 1978, no. 54:8). Four preeminent clerics in Tabriz followed his lead and invited people to assemble at a mosque in the bazaar for the mourning ceremonies. On the designated day, bazaaris closed their shops and went to the mosque to pay tribute to the blood of the Qom martyrs. In front of the mosque, mourners confronted police, who had locked the doors and asked them to disperse. When they refused the police fired into the air, but the crowd did not yield. When a policeman shot someone in the leg, angry mourners set upon the officer, severely beating him. In the ensuing battle, several people were killed and 125 persons injured, including 12 police officers (*Kayhan*, February 20, 1978). The mourners completely ignored Shariat-Madari's exhortation to act calmly. They first routed police, then selectively attacked and burned some seventy-three banks, nine movie theaters, and many government buildings and cars. Damages were estimated in millions of dollars; broken windows alone accounted for nearly one hundred thousand dollars (*Kayhan*, February 19 and 21, 1978). The government imposed martial law in Tabriz and arrested several well-known merchants and shopkeepers (*Kayhan*, March 1, 1978).

Although the mourning ceremony was a religious event, the inhabitants of Tabriz transformed it into a political occasion by shouting slogans such as: "Death to the Shah! We do not want the Shah!" and "Long live Khomeini!" In the heat of the demonstration, it was reported that some twenty dogs, each wrapped in a white cloth, were turned loose in the central city. On each was affixed the name of one of the members of the royal family. The dogs ran wildly about, evading capture, making mockery of the royal family (*Payam-e Mojahed* 1978, no. 54:8). The significance of this event was unmistakable. In a single dramatic act, the people of Tabriz symbolically eliminated the entire royal family.

Forty days later, on March 30, a mourning ceremony was held to honor the martyrs of Tabriz. In over fifty cities, bazaaris closed their shops and took part. On this day, more people were killed in Yazd, Qom, and Ahvaz. In retaliation, a few days later the Savak bombed the house of Maniyan (*Zamimeh* 1978, no. 14:33). The next round of conflicts occurred in May during the mourning ceremonies held for those killed in March. Bazaaris in more than thirty cities once again closed their businesses to participate in mourning ceremonies.

In June the anniversary of the uprising of June 5, 1963, was widely observed. In Tehran, opposition sources reported that 70 percent of all shops were closed. In most large and medium-size cities, the vast majority of bazaaris closed down (*Zamimeh* 1978, no. 16:52). This contrasts sharply with the original protests in 1963, which occurred in only a few cities, and 1975, which went unnoticed. In retaliation against the bazaar closures, the government arrested a number of bazaaris in several cities. In Tehran, the government jailed seven activist bazaaris. The Chamber of Guilds and the police harassed merchants still further. They prohibited shopkeepers from displaying goods outside their shops near the doors, as was their custom. Next, they forbade peddlers from spreading their wares on the bazaar floor. Trucks were prohibited from entering the bazaar to load and unload except between midnight and 6 A.M., a most inconvenient time (*Zamimeh* 1978, no. 16:49, 51). In some cities more extensive measures were taken. In Mashhad, the second largest city, on the anniversary of the June 1963 uprising the police marked doors and smashed locks of many shops that had closed for the strike. The next day, the governor of Khorasan ordered water and electricity shut off for all bazaaris in Mashhad. Despite complaints, he refused to rescind his order, thereby provoking shopkeepers to strike once again (*Zamimeh* 1978, no. 16:53). In mid-August, many protesters were killed in Isfahan and Shiraz. The government imposed martial law in those cities. The preeminent clerics in Qom avoided calling for mourning ceremonies expressly because previous mourning observances had led to additional deaths. Bazaaris, however, shut down their shops in Tehran, Isfahan, Shiraz, and Mashhad for several days to protest those killings.

Repression did not have its usual impact on bazaaris. By this time bazaari mobilization had assumed a national character, making government repression difficult. Second, because the government had arrested large numbers of bazaaris between August 1975 and 1977 for violating price controls, the mere fact of being arrested had become a commonplace experience for shopkeepers and merchants. The only novelty of these later arrests during 1978 was that they were in response to political protests that were, from bazaaris' viewpoint, on behalf of a just cause against a tyrannical regime. Had the government escalated its usual level of repression at this point, arresting and executing specific activists and leaders, the opposition might have been derailed. A policy of making examples out of particular individuals might have made repression more effective. The government, however, chose not to do this. Finally, the forty-day cycles of mourning ceremonies and the existence of mosque networks enabled bazaaris to broadcast and confront each successive brutality by the government. Without the means of publicizing the regime's repressive nature, the opposition movement would soon have been snuffed out.

In response to these cycles of mourning ceremonies, to reduce the conflicts and prevent their escalation to the oil fields, the government decided to soften repression toward the end of August following the deaths of several hundred persons in a fire in the Rex Cinema in Abadan. On August 26, the Shah replaced Prime Minister Amuzegar with Sharif-Emami, who introduced a number of reforms. To appease shopkeepers and merchants, the government embarked upon a new strategy. Fifteen regional heads of the Chamber of Guilds were dismissed and some of them were arrested. The government even filed charges against the chamber's deputy, who promptly fled (*Ettelaat*, September 20 and 21, 1978). To mitigate conflicts with bazaaris even further, the new prime minister announced that charges would be dropped against thousands of shopkeepers who had files pending court investigation, provided they promised to observe price controls. This position was unacceptable to bazaaris because a major part of their conflicts stemmed from the price controls that had been imposed in 1975.

Conflicts soon resumed. Following the Tehran massacre on September 8, bazaars closed down in Tehran, Qom, Kashan, Abadan, Ahvaz, Hamedan, Shahr-e Ray, Mashhad, Rasht, Tabriz, Ilam, Ghazvin, and Isfahan. Bazaar shutdowns in Tehran, Tabriz, and Isfahan lasted several days, causing the government to issue warnings to shopkeepers to reopen their businesses. In Tehran, Maniyan and a number of other bazaaris were arrested and jailed. The Tehran bazaar finally reopened on September 21.

Early in the fall of 1978, Ayatollah Khomeini was expelled to France from Iraq for inciting opposition to the Shah. On October 1, in an unprecedented protest, shopkeepers in more than one hundred cities went on strike. No comparable action had taken place when Khomeini was initially exiled from his homeland fourteen years earlier. Shortly thereafter, Tehran bazaaris threatened to boycott French goods if restrictions placed on Khomeini's political activities in France were not lifted. Bazaari support for Khomeini had a clear political origin. He was the only political or religious leader who refused any compromise with the Shah and who consistently called for the regime's overthrow. For most bazaaris who were in bitter conflict with the Shah's regime, Khomeini was the single most important political leader, and they would not accept any restrictions placed upon him.

Throughout these conflicts, bazaaris engaged in various other actions in addition to closing their shops. Bazaaris financed many mosque activities, and some shopkeepers actively promoted ceremonies and other gatherings held in the mosques, which in some cities caused them to be arrested.[14] Bazaaris also supported antigovernment actions by clergy and protested the arrests of activist clerics (*Zamimeh* 1978, no. 18:48; Abouzar 1978, Pt. 3:143–44, 203). In Isfahan, for example, shopkeepers closed down in August to protest the arrest of Ayatollah Sayyed Jalal Taheri. When Ayatollah Taleghani was released from prison in Tehran, bazaaris from the SMGATB organized an enormous march to his home to welcome him. When the universities announced a week-long strike, bazaaris closed their shops in solidarity. Bazaaris also supported and expressed solidarity with other groups who opposed the government. In early November, bazaaris closed down and joined a large demonstration at Tehran University to support students and faculty who had called for a week of solidarity against the government (*Kayhan*, November 5, 1978). When worker strikes spread, bazaaris collected money for their support. On October 10, when employees of the three national newspapers walked off the job for the first time ever to protest government censorship, bazaaris sent them flowers and publicly endorsed their strike. Maniyan, head of the SMGATB, telephoned representatives of the press and promised assistance (*Ettelaat*, October 15, 1978). Later, during extended bazaar strikes, a group of Tehran bazaaris helped finance twenty-five Islamic cooperatives to provide basic goods for low-income individuals and families. These cooperatives sent out fourteen trucks to distribute goods at low prices to various parts of the city (*Ayandegan*, January 10, 1979).

In October the government, recognizing that bazaaris were a crucial group in the conflicts, decided to meet with bazaar representatives in an attempt to bring about a reconciliation. Twenty merchants met to discuss their concerns with Manouchehr Azmoun, a government minister. They demanded that the Chamber of Guilds be dissolved and that a Council of Guilds composed of bazaaris be formed instead to deal with profiteering in a more appropriate manner. They agreed to price controls on a few basic items, but suggested all other goods be sold according to supply and demand. Finally, they asked the government to extend running water into the bazaar. Azmoun promised to convey the concerns of these bazaar representatives to Prime Minister Sharif-Emami (*Kayhan*, October 10, 1978).

The identities of these merchants were never revealed by the government. Their concerns, as published by the regime, did not include any political demands. By this we may safely conclude that they were neither followers of Ayatollah Khomeini nor of the National Front. Had merchant supporters of Khomeini or the National Front been willing to meet with government representatives at all, which was unlikely, at the very least they would have demanded political reforms. It is possible that they were instead leaders of the merchants' guild who had been appointed by the regime. If this was the case, the meeting was little more than part of the government's propaganda campaign.

The regime made no attempt to resolve the issues. Instead, greater repressive measures were adopted that generated an unprecedented anarchic situation. Shortly after the meeting, the Savak hired hooligans to attack, loot, and burn stores and shops. As these attacks spread, bazaaris in some cities began transferring their goods to safe locations. In Kermanshah, for example, many stores were burned and half a million tomans stolen. The next day, bazaaris removed their wares from their shops and closed down (*Kayhan*, October 29, 1978). When bazaaris in Sar-e Pol-e

Zahab, another Kurdish city, heard that hooligans had threatened to show up, some took their goods out of town, while others simply closed their shops and went home. When the hooligans arrived, they removed the doors completely in order to loot shops (*Kayhan*, October 31, 1978). In Tehran and Shiraz, rumors of hooligan attacks led bazaaris to arm themselves. Tehran merchants turned off the bazaar lights and waited for an attack that never took place. In Khorram Abad, talk of hooligan attacks led shopkeepers to evacuate their stores (*Kayhan*, October 31, 1978).

By the end of Sharif- Emami's government in the first week of November 1978, hooligans had attacked more than forty cities, in many cases burning and looting shops. During the subsequent military government these attacks against bazaaris intensified. In Ardestan, club wielders from a neighboring village attacked shops, but fled when confronted by residents of the city. In other cities, attacks were more severe. Approximately two thousand hooligans from five villages attacked the city of Arak, burning and looting many shops and houses. In a village near Najaf Abad, a pro-government cleric asserted in his sermon that if an Islamic Republic were established, lands that had formerly been given to villagers as part of the Shah's land reform would be returned to their previous owners. He then suggested that the villagers migrate from their town. The next day, the angry villagers attacked Najaf Abad in protest against the idea of an Islamic Republic, destroying many shops and demolishing parts of the bazaar. In the attack and subsequent police intervention, more than one hundred people were killed (*Hambastegi* 1978, no. 5; also *Akhbar* 1978, no. 8).

In Garmsar, approximately two hundred hooligans attacked shops and damaged considerable property. Forty-three of the thugs, some of whom were known government employees, were recognized by witnesses to the attack, but the witnesses were able to arrest only six of them. Although the police attempted to obtain their release, judges in Garmsar refused. Several days later, hooligans attacked the judges' homes, causing many to flee to Tehran, where they went into hiding (*Kayhan*, January 7, 1979). In Sanandaj, hooligans looted and torched dozens of shops (*Kayhan*, January 28, 1979). Shops in Ardabil were regularly set on fire, causing shopkeepers to complain that known agents were responsible for the fires (*Kayhan*, January 10, 1979). In Nahavand, thugs sacked shops and set them on fire. The next day they returned to loot and destroy those items too heavy to carry away (*Akhbar* 1979, no. 10). Following an antigovernment demonstration in Astaneh Ashrafiyeh, 122 shops were burned (*Akhbar* 1979, no. 10). In Ghazvin, a list of places to be attacked was published anonymously. Several days later, 12 stores mentioned on the list were attacked by hooligans (*Hambastegi* 1979, no. 10). During the last days of the military administration, several shops in Sari were set fire, while in Chalous 57 shops were burned by government agents (*Kayhan*, January 6, 1979).

In some cities, shops were regularly robbed at night. In Lahijan, for example, many shops were robbed repeatedly after hours, but the police refused to assign guards to patrol city streets and plazas despite merchants' requests (*Kayhan*, January 22, 1979). When one shopkeeper's rugs were stolen in Kashan he complained to police, who told him to ask Ayatollah Khomeini for his rugs (*Akhbar* 1978, no. 2). In Ahvaz and Behbahan, store owners who had been robbed at night discovered items belonging to police at the scene of the crime (*Akhbar* 1978, no. 9). In Dezful, some shops were robbed several nights in a row (*Kayhan*, January 11, 1979), and in Bandar Abbas 14 shops were robbed in one night (*Kayhan*, January 13, 1979). Similar reports of robbery appeared in other cities, including Birjand.

In response to these attacks, bazaaris in several cities closed down and organized demonstrations to demand that hooligans and their organizers be punished. Elsewhere, shopkeepers organized their own defenses to protect their stores. In Amol, bazaaris mounted guards to watch over the business area. At night they stood guard over their own shops, armed with clubs (*Kayhan*, October 30, 1978). In Zanjan, thugs attacked the Ghaisarieh bazaar, injuring five shopkeepers who were guarding the bazaar. In Ardabil, fifty young men assumed responsibility for guarding shops at night. Similar measures were taken in Bandar Abbas, Hamedan, and Meshkin-Shahr. In Dameghan, shopkeepers decided to guard their own shops and warned that if government officials were discovered violating life or property they would be punished (*Kayhan*, January 15, 1979).

In many other cities, shopkeepers and merchants shut down the bazaars for long periods of time in response to violence by hooligans. With the imposition of the military administration, bazaar closings intensified. The bazaar in Yazd went on strike for three weeks; at the end of the second week, residents of the city began to raise funds for the shopkeepers' support (*Akhbar* 1978, no. 1; and 1978 no. 3). The Isfahan bazaar closed for more than seventy-five days, and the central bazaar in Shiraz was closed for over two months. Bazaars in Zanjan, Arak, and Qom shut down for more than forty-five days. Shortly after the military came to power on November 6, merchants in the central bazaar in Kashan went on strike; on January 13, they announced that they would not reopen their shops until the final victory (*Kayhan*, January 13, 1979). The central bazaars in Ghazvin and

Kazroun were closed for more than fifty days, while the Abadan bazaar was closed for weeks in December and January (*Ayandegan*, January 7, 1979). In Tabriz, the central bazaar closed two weeks before the military administration took over and remained on strike for more than four months. Shops throughout Khomein, birthplace of Ayatollah Khomeini, also were closed for more than four months. In that city, a committee supervised by the clergy distributed basic goods (*Kayhan*, January 17, 1979). The central bazaar in Tehran also struck for more than four months, finally reopening on February 17, six days after the collapse of the regime.

Hooligan attacks and robberies continued after the military government was replaced by Prime Minister Bakhtiar. In Loshan a number of shops were attacked. The next day, 16 shops in Rasht were set on fire. In Zahedan, two hundred Balouchis attacked several shops. Several days later, some one thousand hooligans gathered in the Fouzieh Plaza in Tehran and smashed windows of shops displaying Khomeini's pictures. In Meshkin Shahr and Hashtpar, hooligans sacked and burned several shops (*Kayhan*, January 21, 1979). All shops located along one street in Andimeshk were set on fire by hooligans backed up by army tanks (*Kayhan*, January 22, 1979). Hooligans also attacked shops in Rezaieh, Langeroud, and Rezvan-Shahr. In Zabol, fifteen hundred hooligans attacked the bazaar and looted 250 shops (*Kayhan*, January 28, 1979). During the final week of Bakhtiar's administration, hooligans attacked shops in Sar-e Pol-e Zahab, Manjil, and Harsin; in Harsin, 80 shops were sacked (*Kayhan*, February 10, 1979).

The regime's accumulation policies had served the interests of modern industrial and financial capital, not those of the bazaaris. The government's unprecedented price controls and antiprofiteering campaign had generated intense conflicts with shopkeepers and artisans. In the last few months of its rule, the regime added a new type of attack to the repertoire of repression; namely, hooligan attacks on property. Bazaaris were a primary target of hooligans' informal repression. These anarchic tactics resorted to by the regime in an attempt to repress bazaaris and other opposition violated the state's basic promise to protect private property from hooligan attacks, looting, or theft. In response to such unprecedented policies, bazaaris resorted to various defensive measures, one of which was closing down for long periods. Bazaar shutdowns disrupted trade and distribution of goods throughout the country, causing hardships for all consumers. At the same time, the lengthy disruptions signaled instability and thus created an opportunity for collective action by others against the government.

BAZAARIS AND THE ARTICULATION OF CONFLICTS

Throughout 1978, and especially in the second half of that year, bazaaris portrayed their movement as Islamic. The sociological questions are why they chose such a label and what exactly their movement opposed. A conventional explanation might hold that Iran's rapid modernization uprooted the population, generating anomie, normlessness, and the desire of individuals for integration into the community. Such desires, in turn, found expression in the revival of Islam to bring about reintegration. This explanation is both misleading and insufficient. In the first place, bazaaris were not an uprooted social category who had just arrived from rural areas. By and large, the vast majority were established members of the bazaar. Azerbaijanis, the largest single bloc within the Tehran bazaar, had come to Tehran during and immediately after World War II out of fear that under the short-lived Azerbaijan Republic private property would be socialized. They were staunch supporters of Prime Minister Mosaddegh in the 1950s. Second, most bazaaris were already and are now religious, and many paid religious taxes. In fact, the Tehran bazaar is the site of several large mosques. Finally, many bazaar activists and leaders during the conflicts of 1977–1979 had been politically active during the 1950s and 1960s, prior to the rapid modernization. Some, like Maniyan, Lebaschi, Shanehchi, and Asgar-Oladi, had been arrested in these earlier struggles. Hence, neither bazaaris' religiosity nor their political activity can be attributed to rapid modernization per se.

Such a conventional explanation fails to examine the nature of the Islamic movement from bazaaris' point of view. By calling their movement Islamic, bazaaris clearly did not intend to renounce worldly affairs or establish an authoritarian state. Instead, their intent was to break with the existing order in hopes of restructuring it to overcome what they considered injustice and oppression. An analysis of statements made by bazaaris during the revolutionary conflicts is very revealing. The bazaaris in large cities issued a number of statements in which they expressed the nature of their opposition. I have chosen a few representative statements made by bazaaris in the three largest cities of Tehran, Mashhad, and Isfahan. Tehran has the largest bazaar in the country, with the largest number of shopkeepers, artisans and merchants, and capital. Its reactivated SMGATB issued a number of statements during the revolutionary conflicts attacking the Shah's dictatorship and autocracy and advocating the establishment of an independent, nationalist government that would grant political freedom. In a special call for a march on the religious holiday of Tasoua during the military rule in December 1978, the SMGATB invited people to participate in a long march against the "numerous oppressions and betrayals of the usurpers of the national rights." They labeled the Shah's regime a lawbreaking government and puppet of "international looters" that barbarously violated basic human rights. They declared that their long march on Tasoua would be the sign of their increasing organization and absolute determination to overthrow the usurpers of power and participate ever increasingly in the governing of the nation. The statement concluded by recognizing Ayatollah Khomeini's leadership of the movement and vowed that the Iranian people would continue their struggles against dictatorship, corruption, and plunder until the final victory.

At the end of the Shah's rule, Tehran bazaaris published the *Guilds* newsletter in which they advocated social justice, democracy, economic development, and the elimination of corruption. In the third edition of the newsletter, they condemned the press during the Shah's era and the policies of fifty years of dictatorship that had forced the press to laud the Pahlavis. Due to such policies, people had turned away from the newspapers, radio, and television. The newsletter praised the strikes by journalists and urged the press to reflect, objectively and without bias, the views of all social groups because various groups did not yet have their own publications (*Ayandegan*, February 1, 1979).

In Mashhad, the second largest city and a major religious center, bazaaris opposed the Shah for a series of basic problems and policies. In a statement published in early 1978, they labeled the Shah's government the "servant of America and chained dog of international imperialism." They condemned mass killings by the government in Qom and Tabriz and the lack of freedom of expression, association, and the press. They also criticized the regime for high taxes, arbitrary fines, shortages of housing, and for not solving the problems of deprived groups in society who experienced hardships due to the rising cost of basic necessities. It is clear, they stated, that "where people are deprived of their basic rights, freedom and human dignity, their wealth and potentialities will be plundered by a gang of rabble and rascals" (The Freedom Movement 1978, 3:95–97).

In Isfahan, the third largest city, with the most important handicraft center in the country, bazaaris made the following statement during a two-week sit-in protesting the arrest of Ayatollah Taheri, a pro-Khomeini cleric, in the summer of 1978:

> Immediately following the arrest of Ayatollah Taheri, the Isfahan bazaar was shut down, and people went to the house of Ayatollah Khademi to initiate a sit-in. The people of Isfahan have been subjected to the severest class inequality and repression. They have seen with their own eyes how their mineral resources and material and spiritual wealth have been plundered by a minority of dirty foreigners with the cooperation of internal servants; they have also seen how corruption and decadence have spread in the country. . . . Their actions have been responsible for poverty and moral decay. The kidnapping of Ayatollah Taheri fueled the outrage of the people who began numerous attacks on banks in protest against usury and the concentration of wealth, which caused class inequality. They attacked hotels and cinemas, which are responsible for the spread of moral decay and weakening of Islamic morality among the young generation. . . . And they attacked and burned municipal buildings in various parts of the city because of their part in stealing, bribery, and plundering the people. (Organization of Iranian Moslem Students 1978:43– 44)

These statements clearly indicate the bazaaris' concern with the major social, economic, and political problems that adversely affected them and other social classes and groups. They condemned the dictatorship for usurping power and repressing all democratic freedoms; for the concentration of wealth, rise of inequality and social problems; for the Shah's obedience to foreign powers; and for the plunder of Iranian resources. These attacks on dictatorship resulted from the government's intervention in the market through price controls and the antiprofiteering campaign. Of course, the Shah's regime had been dictatorial ever since the coup d'etat of 1953 that dissolved the SMGA. But with the imposition of price controls, the regime replaced the market and became the arbiter of prices and profits. With political freedom, independent merchant guilds could exist along with a free market economy in which the bazaar could prosper. The concentration of wealth and rise of inequalities resulted from government policies of capital allocation that favored large industries and commercial houses instead of the bazaar. Because usury had existed in Iran long before the Shah and because, in fact, bazaaris were the main usurers in the country, attacks on banks were expressions of outrage against these policies. Independence from external powers would provide protection from competition by powerful foreign capital and industry, allowing the growth of domestic sectors and markets.

All this does not mean that bazaaris were not concerned with moral issues and the spread of corruption. On the contrary, as mentioned above, most bazaaris have always been religious and concerned with moral issues. With the exception of a small minority, however, the bazaaris never pursued religion as a political ideology (Lebaschi 1983, tape 3:15). Furthermore, in the context of the mid-1970s, bazaaris' concern with moral issues and corruption cannot be isolated from their concrete experiences. With the imposition of price controls, corruption spread rapidly to replace the market mechanism. In order to survive, bazaaris had to resort to bribery to avoid arrests and fines by the Chamber of Guilds. In this connection, it is relevant to mention that the chief of the Chamber of Guilds was among the 150 individuals who, in the fall of 1978, transferred large sums of money abroad (The Freedom Movement 1983, 9:152). For wealthy bazaaris who could afford them, bribes were a burden that interfered with their established right to set their own prices for their goods in a free market economy. Less wealthy bazaaris and especially artisans could not afford to bribe. For them, bribery was an unfair practice that penalized the less prosperous. Not surprisingly, less wealthy bazaaris, shopkeepers, artisans, and apprentices opposed the Shah's government more vigorously than the wealthy ones.[15]

Bazaaris supported Ayatollah Khomeini and respected him as the revolution's leader for several important reasons. They considered Khomeini an indomitable fighter against "despotism." As we shall see later, Khomeini was the only religious or political leader who continuously called for the overthrow of the Shah and refused to compromise with him. Bazaaris also supported Khomeini because he consistently condemned the Shah's dictatorial rule as well as the moral decadence and corruption of the Pahlavi dynasty. Throughout the revolutionary period, he promised political freedom to all social groups under an Islamic government. Khomeini also advocated social justice, which bazaaris found lacking under the Shah's regime. Finally, Khomeini attacked imperialist plundering of Iranian wealth. These statements were widely supported within the bazaar because they reflected bazaaris' own central concerns. Leading members of the SMGATB, including Maniyan and Lebaschi, visited Khomeini in Paris in the fall of 1978 and were favorably impressed with his political ideas. At that time, Khomeini asked them to resist pressures to reopen the bazaar.[16]

CONCLUSION

This analysis demonstrates that over the last several years of the Shah's rule the mobilization and collective action of bazaaris was determined by a combination of their responses to government policies that adversely affected their economic interests, organizational structures and capacity for mobilization, and opportunity for action. The importance of economic grievances and the existence of divisions within the bazaar render insufficient an ideological explanation of bazaaris politics. Toward the end of the 1940s and early 1950s, the government's economic policies adversely affected the interests of bazaaris. At the same time, a short period of political liberalization and reduction of repression enabled bazaaris to establish their own independent guild, which played an important role in the mobilization. The economic crisis during the nationalization of oil led to massive political conflicts in which bazaaris participated. During these conflicts, they supported Dr. Mosaddegh, a progressive modernizer, even though most clerics backed the royalists.

In the early 1960s, government policies again led to an economic crisis, which resulted in widespread bankruptcies among bazaaris. Again a brief period of liberalization provided an opportunity for bazaaris to mobilize and oppose the government. However, the repression that ensued hampered the bazaaris' capacity for mobilization and collective action. Toward the end of 1962, the clergy withdrew their support from the Shah and opposed the reforms of his White Revolution. Bazaaris in major cities joined the clerical opposition and transformed religious processions into political events. However, their movement failed because it was unable to consolidate other major social groups and classes behind it.

In June 1975, during a period of favorable economic opportunity, shopkeepers and merchants throughout the country ignored the uprising of clerical students, which was supported by Ayatollah Khomeini. Not until the government initiated an antiprofiteering campaign in August did merchants and shopkeepers respond to oppose the government. The economic crisis led the government to pursue a set of unprecedented policies that adversely affected the bazaaris' interests. Government intervention and regulation of prices replaced the market and rendered the government vulnerable to challenge and attacks. An opportunity for action was provided when limited changes were introduced in the legal sphere regarding trial procedures for political opponents. Adversely affected by government price controls, various segments of the bazaar soon began mobilizing against the government. Bazaari mobilization began before that of any faction of the clergy, and in the initial stages they supported various struggles against the government. Lacking strong, autonomous organizations and hampered by repression, bazaaris used every opportunity to engage in collective action. Repression made it very difficult to mobilize, however, and bazaaris increasingly turned to the mosque for mobilization. Bazaari mobilization pressured the divided and indecisive preeminent clerics in Qom to condemn government killings by calling for cycles of mourning ceremonies.

Our data demonstrate that in the 1977–1979 period, bazaaris effectively used the cultural tradition of mourning for the dead in forty days and mobilized their opposition against the government through the mosque. In the initial stages, mourning ceremonies were the only occasions for political processions and activities. The mosques were most appropriate locations for these ceremonies because consistent repression by the government had left no alternative structure through which people could mobilize. In fact, religious centers were the only organizations that retained some measure of autonomy from state supervision and control. Mosques therefore provided a relatively secure location for bazaaris to gather, broadcast government repression, and oppose the regime. In addition, the elimination of all other organizations and political groups except religious ones signaled that the articulation of conflicts by means of any other framework would have reduced the chances of success.

The vast resources of this class—its sheer size, concentration, extensive trading network, economic assets, and ties to the mosque—made it possible to respond vigorously to the state's adverse economic policies. Their concentration and networks enabled bazaaris to shut down as a sign of protest against the government and disrupt the national trade. Their independent economic assets enabled them to remain on strike for long periods of time and to finance other strikers and the mosques.

In sum, bazaaris' conflicts with the government resulted from growing state intervention in capital allocation and accumulation and the increasing limitations and regulations of the market system. The state's development policies systematically favored the industrial and modern sectors of the economy. Government capital-allocation policies and lack of protection for small, traditional industries jeopardized artisans, while government intervention in the commercial sector adversely affected bazaaris. A crisis of revenue absorption during the mid-1970s led the government to pursue policies designed to control inflation. These policies replaced the market mechanism and violated the rights of merchants, shopkeepers, and artisans, forcing them to engage in collective action in order to defend their socioeconomic and political interests. The sustained struggles of bazaaris, in turn, provided an opportunity for other social classes and political groups to confront the Shah's regime. By themselves, however, bazaaris and clergy could not have overthrown the government, just as they were unable to do so in 1963. The participation of other social classes was essential for a political transformation. The most important classes to oppose the government were industrial workers, white-collar employees, and professionals, to whom we now turn.

Chapter 5

Autumn Allies
Industrial Workers and
White-Collar Employees

> We have struck along with other Iranians to destroy despotism and
> sever imperialist influence in our country; and to build an indepen-
> dent, free, progressive, and developed Iran. This is the imperish-
> able right of the Iranian people, and to attain it, they will not hold
> back from any sacrifice. (*Oil Workers' Newsletter*, no. 1, January 1979)

By autumn of 1978, large numbers of industrial workers, white-collar employees, and professionals had joined in the struggle against the Shah's regime. Although under other circumstances their interests might have been
quite diverse, even conflicting, these groups will be considered together
here for several reasons. First, they were not part of the struggles from the
outset, but joined in only when the conflict was already well underway.
Their delayed entry is an indication of these groups' divergent orientations, conflicts, and resources. Second, because major segments of these
classes were employed by the state, they faced similar problems and grievances in confronting a common enemy. Moreover, once they entered the
fray, industrial and white-collar workers directly targeted the state—their
employer—for attack. Third, both classes used the strike as their principle
weapon, at times joining together in walkouts at factories and workplaces.
And finally, their initial demands were largely economic in nature and defensive in orientation; only later were grievances expressed in political
terms.

It is important to note at the outset that these classes did not participate in the several rounds of mourning ceremonies during which bazaaris shut down their shops. The explanation for their absence lies in the nature of their conflicts, capacity for action, and resources. In contrast to bazaaris, who did not become targets of state repression until the mid-1970s, industrial workers had been consistently suppressed by the government since Mosaddegh's downfall in 1953. Although the state was politically and economically autonomous of the dominant class, government policies consistently repressed workers. State intervention in capital accumulation demobilized the industrial workers. After the coup d'etat of 1953, strikes were banned and independent labor unions were dissolved. New laws made it extremely difficult to form autonomous labor organizations. Similarly, white-collar employees did not have the right to form associations. As a result of repression and lack of organizational autonomy, both these classes faced severe restrictions in mobilizing.

Lacking independent organizations, workers and white-collar employees could not have initiated mobilization and collective action against the government, despite worsening economic conditions. This is evidenced by the fact that only a few days after Sharif-Emami became prime minister and announced liberal reforms, industrial workers embarked upon massive strikes. This promised retreat by the government from its previous policy of repression provided an opportunity for workers and white-collar employees to mobilize and act collectively. In the context of mounting inflation and a worsening standard of living, the initial demands of workers and white-collar employees, unlike the bazaaris' demands, were mainly economic as strikers pressed to relieve their immediate grievances.

As strikes continued, those segments of these classes that possessed greater solidarity structures issued political demands that attacked the fundamental nature of the state, which had consistently intervened in capital accumulation on behalf of the dominant class while repressing workers. By the end of Sharif-Emami's government, these politicized strikers were confronting the state directly and demanding significant changes. In the midst of growing politicization of strikers, the government reversed its promise of reforms and resorted to repression by imposing a military regime. Although repression succeeded in sending most strikers back to work, some workers remained on strike. As mentioned in the preceding chapter, in response to the imposition of military rule bazaaris initiated prolonged shutdowns in major cities. Within a few weeks industrial workers, led by oil workers, and white-collar employees resumed their walkouts, paralyzing the entire economy and the functioning of the government. Workers in strategic industries refused to obey the government and instead negotiated with Ayatollah Khomeini's representatives, thereby generating a situation of dual sovereignty. In the end, workers and white-collar employees allied themselves with bazaaris behind Khomeini as the leader of an "antidespotic and anti-imperialist" struggle. This coalition created a revolutionary situation that culminated in the overthrow of the monarchy.

Some scholars who have attempted to explain the Iranian revolution have largely ignored the contribution of the working classes to the overthrow of the monarchy. For example, Skocpol (1982) did not even mention worker mobilization or collective action. Arjomand (1988:107–108) went so far as to state that industrial workers supported the Shah because he "could successfully buy" them. According to Arjomand, with the exception of oil and tobacco workers, industrial workers did not participate in the revolutionary movement. In the following analysis, I will demonstrate that industrial workers did indeed participate in the revolution and in fact played a crucial role in creating a revolutionary situation. The data I shall present reveal that industrial workers have been central to political developments in Iran since World War II. Their mobilization in the early 1950s, despite their relatively small numbers, was critical in the struggle to nationalize oil and in Mosaddegh's confrontation with both the British and the royalists. Their subsequent absence from the political conflicts of 1963 prevented the opposition from consolidating and increased the likelihood that repression would succeed in demobilizing them. Finally, their participation in the 1978–1979 conflicts was essential in bringing about the overthrow of the monarchy.

THE WORK FORCE PRIOR TO THE REVOLUTION

The nation's economic structure underwent significant changes in the decades prior to the revolution. At the turn of the century, approximately 90 percent of the work force was engaged in agriculture. By 1946, the agrarian labor force had declined to 75 percent (Halliday 1979:173). In 1976, as shown in table 5.1, agricultural workers had dropped to 34 percent of the work force. Most of the dislocated agrarian work force was absorbed in construction, which nearly doubled between 1966 and 1976. The rest went into manufacturing and the service sector, which grew rapidly in the 1960s and 1970s.

Table 5.1. Distribution of Labor Force by Economic Sectors

ECONOMIC SECTOR	1956		1966		1976	
	N	%	N	%	N	%
Total Employment	5,907,666	100.00	7,115,787	100.00	8,799,420	100.00
Agriculture, forestry, hunting and fishing	3,325,721	56.29	3,380,023	47.50	2,991,869	34.00
Mining and quarrying	24,654	.42	26,312	.37	89,888	1.00
Manufacturing	815,699	13.80	1,298,040	18.24	1,672,059	19.00
Construction	335,754	5.68	509,778	7.16	1,188,720	13.50
Electricity, gas, water and health services	11,736	.20	52,858	.74	61,633	.70
Wholesale and retail trade	355,005	6.01	552,566	7.77	668,494	7.60
Transportation, storage and communication	208,052	3.52	224,086	3.15	431,471	4.90
Financing and insurance	—		—		100,473	1.10
Community, social and personal services	655,434	11.09	933,576	13.12	1,520,124	17.30
Activities not adequately reported	175,611	2.99	138,548	1.95	74,689	.90

SOURCE: SCI 1976a and 1966b.

During this same period, the industrial labor force expanded greatly. As illustrated in table 5.1, 815,699 workers out of a total work force of 5,907,666 were employed in manufacturing in 1956. Two decades later, the manufacturing sector employed 1,672,059 workers, an increase of over 100 percent. Nearly half a million of these workers worked in large factories that employed ten people or more.[1] Between 1956 and 1976, employment in the construction sector rose by 254 percent. Mining and quarrying, which belonged mostly to the state, employed roughly 90,000 persons in 1976; its employment had increased by 264 percent.

The occupational structure of society also changed during this period. The proportion of self-employed and wage/salary earners in the private sector declined in urban areas (table 5.2). At the same time, the number of government employees increased dramatically, especially between 1966 and 1976. By 1976, more than one-third of the urban labor force was directly employed by the state. The state bureaucracy continually expanded as more white-collar and professional employees were hired to carry out the government's growing operations, widen its narrow base of social support, and attempt to silence political discontent. Data also indicate that the state was the largest industrial employer in Iran. By 1976, the state owned 130 large factories and workshops, excluding government-owned carpet factories (SCI 1981a:30). The state was a major investor in another 55 joint ventures with the private sector and multinational corporations. The state employed 24 percent of the urban manufacturing and mining work force (SCI 1976a:85). Finally, state industries were highly sophisticated and employed large numbers of skilled and semiskilled workers in concentrated factories. The large size and extreme concentration of state-owned factories facilitated communication and increased workers' capacity to act collectively and disrupt production and accumulation.

Let us review the collective actions of workers and white-collar employees in the few decades prior to the revolution. Because oil workers have played crucial roles in the major political conflicts, the following analysis will focus on their actions.

COLLECTIVE ACTIONS OF WORKERS AND WHITE-COLLAR EMPLOYEES

During the 1940s and early 1950s, the Iranian working class achieved some degree of organization and played an important role in the the country's

Table 5.2. Occupational Structure of Urban Iran, 1956–1976

CATEGORY	1956 N	1956 %	1966 N	1966 %	1976 N	1976 %
Total Employed	1,807,325	100.00	2,602,900	100.00	4,112,636	100.00
Employers	35,381	1.95	98,200	3.77	142,213	3.45
Self-employed	473,697	26.20	634,200	24.36	915,283	22.25
Government employees	328,447	18.17	544,700	20.93	1,404,959	34.16
Private-sector wage and salary earners	858,370	47.49	1,243,300	47.76	1,545,082	37.57
Unpaid family workers	42,790	2.37	45,500	1.75	85,581	2.08
Unpaid apprentices	—	—	18,300	.70	—	—
Occupation not reported	68,640	3.80	18,700	.72	19,518	.47

SOURCES: SCI 1956, 1966a, and 1976a.

political development. A number of factors facilitated working class mobilization and collective action. Reza Shah was removed from power and more than 1,250 leftist political prisoners were released, including 53 Marxist intellectuals and many veteran labor organizers who subsequently formed the Tudeh party, which was central in organizing the working class (Abrahamian 1981:214). Although the size of the industrial labor force at that time was still quite small compared to the rest of the population, modern enterprises employed some 120,000 (United Nations 1953:40–41). Within the modern sector, worker mobilization was helped by the high concentration of workers in a number of large factories and plants. For example, the oil industry employed 52,000 workers, most of whom were concentrated in a few geographic areas. Finally, worker mobilization increased during periods of economic crisis and was facilitated by divisions among the ruling class.

The downfall of Reza Shah and the opening of the political arena allowed the Tudeh party to establish a Central Council of Trade Unions in Iran in 1942; in 1944, this organization became the United Central Council of Unified Trade Unions of Iranian Workers. By 1946, it claimed four hundred thousand members and 186 affiliated unions (Halliday 1979:199). The United Central Council was declared illegal in 1949 along with the Tudeh party following an attempt on the Shah's life. The government attempted to form another union but failed to gain much support from workers; by 1952, it had only three thousand members. During the Mosaddegh years between 1951 and 1953, the United Central Council began to revive due to reduced repression. Workers played an important role in the struggles of this period and in the nationalization of oil.

Oil workers, the single largest category of modern industrial workers, were in the forefront of workers' struggles during the nationalist movement following World War II. They were heavily concentrated in Khuzestan, which facilitated both organizing and mobilizing. Oil workers were organized by the Tudeh party in 1946, and in their collective actions pursued objectives that were anti-imperialist and antidictatorship. The first major strike of oil workers began on July 13, 1946, when they demanded that the Anglo-Iranian Oil Company observe Iranian labor laws, specifically the provision for paying wages and salaries for Fridays and holidays. The following day, all the oil workers throughout Khuzestan walked off the job without any prior warning. In addition to paid holidays, the strikers demanded that the oil company abstain from interfering in Iranian political affairs and cease instigating Arab tribes against union workers and that Fatemi, governor-general of Khuzestan, be replaced (*Ettelaat*, July 16, 1946). Fifteen hundred white-collar employees of the company also joined the strike. The government immediately imposed martial law throughout the region and arrested hundreds of strikers. In clashes between the local Arab minority and supporters of the Tudeh party, 17 people were killed and 150 injured. Government forces also killed a number of workers, increasing the number of deaths to between 40 and 60. A team of investigators, including a representative of the prime minister and a member of the Tudeh party, was dispatched from Tehran to look into the incident. After two days of strikes the company, which had originally claimed that workers' demands were strictly political and therefore irrelevant, agreed to consider all demands, including payment for days off. The military released the detained strikers, and workers withdrew their demand for the removal of Fatemi and agreed to stop making inflammatory denunciations of the company and the Arab tribes (Abrahamian 1981:229). The Tudeh party, with two of its members in Prime Minister Ghavam's cabinet, was instrumental in putting an end to the conflicts. In particular, Dr. Reza Rad-Manesh from the Tudeh party, a member of the investigative team, was central in persuading the strikers to resume work. At a meeting of thirty thousand oil workers in Abadan, he declared that Prime Minister Ghavam's government was prolabor and pledged that it would serve their interests (*Ettelaat*, July 17, 1946). After striking for three days, the workers won most of their demands and returned to their jobs.

Oil workers played an important role in the nationalization of oil. Pressured by a strong, popular nationalist movement, the Majles passed a bill authorizing the nationalization of oil in March 1951. At roughly the same time, the Anglo-Iranian Oil Company instituted a 30 percent pay reduction for three thousand oil workers in Bandar-e Ma'shoor in Khuzestan. This led to a second wave of strikes as some thirty thousand oil workers in Abadan and Ahvaz walked off their jobs out of sympathy with strikers in Bandar-e Ma'shoor. This second strike was not economic in origin, but was instead a political statement against British ownership of Iranian oil and British influence in Iran. Within a few days, oil workers in Masjed Soleyman, Khorramshahr, and Aghajari also joined the strike. In response, the government imposed martial law on the entire region and urged strikers to return to their jobs. Two weeks after the walkouts began, the Majles sent a message to the strikers urging them to resume work so that the government could insist that the company restore the pay that had been cut (*Ettelaat*, April 4, 1951). Nevertheless, the strikes continued.

All along, the company argued that the strikes were illegal and that workers must return to work. As a precaution, British naval vessels were dispatched to the Persian Gulf to defend British interests. The workers refused to back down, leading the company to reverse its position and agree to some of the strikers' demands, including paying salaries and meeting other obligations. As a result, some workers in Masjed Soleyman returned to work. In Abadan, however, where the vast majority of oil workers were concentrated, the strikes continued. When the government ordered the army to arrest some of the labor leaders, workers defied the army; and in the subsequent clashes, nine workers were killed and sixty injured. In retaliation, workers attacked British employees, killing three of them (*Ettelaat,* April 13, 1951). This led the British to evacuate women and children from Abadan, and thirty Americans working for the company also left.

Abadan oil workers held a large rally to demand the immediate nationalization of oil. The following day, another rally was held during which strikers declared that their walkout was to protest British imperialism and support other strikers in the region. They gave thanks to their supporters and vowed to fulfill their obligations to the people until "final victory" (*Ettelaat,* April 18, 1951). Workers' intransigence coupled with telephone threats against British employees led the government to reinforce martial law and send additional soldiers to Abadan. More clashes followed in which upwards of thirty workers were killed by the military. In the fifth week of the strike, the government began arresting labor leaders. Within a few days, several hundred workers had been jailed.

The Tudeh party neutralized the repression by organizing demonstrations and sympathy strikes on behalf of oil workers in major cities, including Isfahan where demonstrators were killed in a strike. These combined actions strengthened the position of those like Dr. Mosaddegh who pushed the government to cease procrastinating and implement the nationalization of oil. On April 25, a special Majles committee headed by Mosaddegh voted unanimously to proceed with nationalization. The following day Prime Minister Hossein Ala resigned, although he had been in office only a short time (1951; Ala was also prime minister in 1955–1957). He admitted having failed to deal with strikes that had spread throughout the country and noted that the committee's vote had been in violation of executive powers as well as an expression of lack of trust in his government. The Majles then offered the premiership to Mosaddegh, who agreed to accept only if parliament immediately acted to nationalize oil. After obtaining the approval of seventy of the one hundred members of the Majles, the new prime minister quickly moved to implement nationalization. Thus, oil workers were critical in bringing about the nationalization of oil as well as Mosaddegh's premiership.

After oil was nationalized, workers supported Mosaddegh during major political conflicts against the Shah despite clerical opposition to the prime minister. When Mosaddegh resigned the premiership in July 1952 because of a dispute with the Shah over control of the army, workers in major cities backed the prime minister's stand against the monarch. In Abadan, Kermanshah, and Isfahan, thousands of oil workers went on strike for several days. In Abadan fourteen people were killed in demonstrations (*Ettelaat,* July 23, 1952). In Tehran, on July 20, the day before the protests, workers in several factories held meetings and called for a strike, despite the slowness of the Tudeh party to demand a walkout (Jami 1976:574). The next day, workers in Tehran overwhelmingly participated in the demonstrations. On that historic day, some eight hundred people were injured or killed in antimonarchy protests. The next day the Shah reinstated Mosaddegh, and the strikes ceased. In April 1953, when the Majles refused to convene to pass the report of the eight-member special Majles committee to curb the power of the monarchy, workers again struck in support of Mosaddegh. On April 16, workers in large cities rallied against the Majles, demanding that the report be made into law. On the first anniversary of the July 21, 1952, massacre, workers everywhere, including the religious center of Qom, joined political rallies and demonstrations to support the prime minister against the royal court and the Majles (*Ettelaat,* July 22, 1953). When Mosaddegh called for a referendum to dissolve the Majles, workers throughout the country voted in favor despite continued clerical opposition to the prime minister.

Throughout these conflicts white-collar employees and professionals joined industrial workers in supporting Mosaddegh. Most followed either the National Front or the Tudeh party and thus pursued either liberal or leftist politics. Faced with a choice between the prime minister and the royal court, they overwhelmingly chose Mosaddegh. Even when the majority of the clergy broke with the prime minister, white-collar employees and professionals rallied and demonstrated in his favor. For example, upon hearing news of the massacre of Mosaddegh supporters on July 21, 1952, most government employees in Tehran stopped work and left their offices in protest (*Ettelaat,* July 23, 1952). Along with industrial workers, they demonstrated in April 1953 to demand passage of the bill to limit the monarch's power. On the first anniversary of the July 21 massacre, white-collar employees throughout the country took part in pro-Mosaddegh rallies (*Ettelaat,* July 23, 1953). White-collar employees also voted overwhelmingly in favor of Mosaddegh's bid to dissolve the Majles.

Following the military coup d'etat in 1953, trade unions that had been active for twelve years were crushed, never to regain their strength and independence. During the next several years, the military arrested a large number of Tudeh members and union leaders. Martial law was imposed for four years, and nonofficial trade unions were dissolved. In addition, repression against the Tudeh party, the main organization linking together industrial workers in Tehran with provincial industrial centers, fragmented the working class and made possible demobilization and repression of the workers' movement. Strikes, which had peaked at two hundred in 1951 (Kambakhsh 1972:181), declined to seventy-nine in 1953, seven in 1954, and a mere three from 1955 to 1957 (Abrahamian 1982:420).

In early April 1957, Manouchehr Eghbal became prime minister (1957–1960) and dissolved martial law, in part because the leftist opposition had been effectively repressed and the Savak had been established.[2] The lifting of martial law eased repression and enabled workers to initiate a number of strikes, despite the banning of the shadowy official unions (Halliday 1979:202). Between 1957 and 1961, workers in different factories struck at least twenty-three times (Ivanov n.d. 205–209). Although most of the strikes demanded increased wages, they were independent and uncoordinated. As a result, almost all of these walkouts were repressed by the military. Oil workers struck once during this period. At the end of June 1957, twelve hundred oil workers in Aghajari went on strike demanding higher wages. They claimed that their living expenses had increased and that the consortium of foreign oil companies had also increased oil prices. A representative of the Ministry of Labor and the head of the Savak in the province of Khuzestan went to Aghajari to persuade the strikers to return to work. When they refused, the Ministry of Labor's representative declared the strike illegal and stated that workers would not be paid for its duration. The official *Ettelaat* newspaper noted that the strike lasted for three days and ended when the head of the gendarmerie spoke to workers and promised an investigation (June 30, 1957). Other sources, however, state that strike leaders were sentenced to be executed, although it is unclear whether the sentences were actually carried out (Ivanov n.d.: 206). This was the last reported oil workers' strike until the revolutionary struggles in the fall of 1978.

In 1959 the government passed a new labor law that required every labor union to be approved by the Ministry of Labor. Each new union had to submit a copy of its proceedings, constitution, biography of its members, and pictures of its elected leaders to the Ministry of Labor. After conducting an investigation, the ministry sent the documents to the Savak for final approval. If approved, the union had to report all activities to the ministry (Ivanov n.d.:299). These unions were placed under strict limitations and were only allowed to "conclude collective agreements; to purchase, sell, and acquire movable and immovable property on condition that it is not for commercial purposes or with a view to profit; to defend the occupational rights and interests of their members; to establish cooperative societies to meet the requirements of their members; to establish unemployment funds for the purpose of assisting unemployed workers" (Halliday 1979:203). The law omitted any mention, even in theory, of workers' right to strike; a change in the law introduced in 1964 noted that in cases where disputes were not resolved by mediating organs, workers could declare a strike (Ivanov n.d.:283). Finally, the law made it clear that "syndicates, unions, and confederations shall not be entitled to interfere in political affairs. They may, however, in cases of safeguarding their trade and economic interests, express tendencies towards and cooperate with political parties" (Ghotbi 1978:14).

When union leaders were elected, the Savak insured that the unions remained under government control by electing either Savak agents or employees who could be controlled. The Savak made certain that "undesirable" or "subversive" workers were not elected to union office. If nominated, such persons were subjected to intense Savak pressure to withdraw. If they refused, they sometimes "disappeared" shortly before the elections. The regime deliberately prevented workers' organizations from becoming autonomous, keeping them highly fragmented in order to reduce their capacity for collective action. Unions were restricted to individual factories, and no industrywide unions were allowed to emerge. By 1978, there were 1,023 such unions in the country (Halliday 1979:203). Given unions' lack of autonomy and ineffective nature, workers had little interest in joining them. In 1973, a secret survey conducted by a government organization found that only 22.3 percent of factory workers were union members, and one-third of them either thought the union was of no use or else had no idea of its positive functions (Bayat 1987:62).

The government expanded and intensified its repressive activities in the

1970s as workers' strikes increased. In April 1974, the Senate passed a new law punishing "industrial saboteurs." This law authorized the government to establish the Office of Security Affairs, which supervised all activities in ten major industries, including steel, petrochemicals, gas, aluminum refining, the machine-tool factories in Tabriz and Arak, and helicopter and airplane manufacturing. Under the law, industrial saboteurs could be sentenced to fifteen years in prison or even to death (Ivanov n.d.:299). The security office was mostly staffed with ex-military officers who were in direct contact with the Savak.

Leftist and militant labor leaders who attempted to organize workers or played important roles in strikes were arrested or even disappeared. For example, bus drivers in Tabriz went on strike in the summer of 1974. During a meeting one of their leaders, Majid Charkhchi, declared that their monthly income was only sufficient to meet fifteen days of expenses for drivers and their families. He noted that if the government propaganda about defending workers' rights were true, then workers should be able to organize unions freely and their living conditions would not become increasingly difficult day by day. He demanded that international labor laws and considerations be applied to Iranian workers. Twenty-four hours after the meeting, he was hospitalized for poisoning and died (Ivanov n.d.: 301–302).

The government's tactics of controlling the unions, preventing the formation of industrywide labor organizations, banning strikes, and forbidding political activities worked in favor of capital accumulation by insuring workers' subordination and obedience to the state and to industrialists. These policies weakened the solidarity of the working class and reduced its capacity for collective action. Workers' repression and demobilization were the key to capital accumulation. Furthermore, repression resulted in the elimination of the working class from the national political scene for several years until the fall of 1978.

THE TEACHERS' STRIKE OF MAY 1961

Reduced repression, the political opening of the early 1960s, and the promise of freedom for political activities, combined with a severe economic crisis and deteriorating living conditions for low-income groups, prompted teachers in elementary and high schools to organize a nationwide strike. In their efforts to improve their living conditions, teachers were helped by a natural feature of their working conditions: a large network of students linking them to the rest of society. In times of conflict between the state and other social groups, this network could bring about an escalation of conflict by attracting other social groups into the political arena. This in turn might result in the neutralization of repression.

In the spring of 1961, teachers' complaints over their salaries mounted. The vast majority received monthly salaries ranging between forty dollars and sixty-five dollars. In mid-April, teachers in Tehran circulated leaflets and called for a nationwide strike on May 2, while the government prepared to control an anticipated wave of demonstrations and protests. On May 2, teachers throughout the country walked off the job (*Ettelaat*, May 2, 1961). In Tehran, teachers gathered in front of the Majles in Baharestan Plaza to make speeches and choose representatives to meet with the parliament. When the demonstrators began shouting their demands, the government sent in firefighters with hoses to disperse them. At the same time, the armed forces arrived and arrested many of the demonstrators. They opened fire, killing Dr. Khanali, a high-school teacher, and wounding three other teachers and a student (*Ettelaat*, May 3, 1961).

In the context of the other conflicts discussed in chapters 2 and 4, repression quickly led to the politicization and expansion of mobilization and collective action. University students struck in support of the teachers and participated in the funeral for the slain teacher on May 5. During the funeral, the teachers demanded that those responsible for Khanali's death be punished. Later that afternoon, thousands of teachers gathered at the Mehregan Club to hear a speech by Mohammad Darakhshesh, head of the Society of Teachers. On the third day of the strike, the teachers held a sit-in of thirty thousand people in front of the Majles and demanded that the government be dismissed. They sent six representatives to discuss the issues with members of parliament. To prevent further mobilization and politicization, parliament members promised to investigate the teachers' demands.

Because of the crisis of the early 1960s and the government's economic policies, the teachers received sympathy from segments of the population in Tehran. Universities closed down in support of their strike, and bazaaris and some workers also backed the walkout. Several workers' syndicates in Tehran issued statements of support.[3] Bazaaris in the Baharestan Plaza closed their shops in support of the teachers, and several demonstrations were held in front of the central bazaar. On the seventh day following Dr. Khanali's death, thousands of teachers, students, workers, and bazaaris went to the cemetery to pay tribute. The bazaar's representative declared that "bazaaris have vowed to continue their support of teachers and their demands" (*Ettelaat*, May 9, 1961).

The coordinated, nationwide strike by teachers and the sympathy expressed by other social groups forced the government into a defensive posture. As soon as the strike began, the Shah proclaimed his intention to improve conditions for teachers. The Ministry of Culture immediately announced that thirty million rials had been allocated to supplement the teachers' wages, which averaged less than six thousand rials per month. In addition, the authorities promised that teachers would be given insurance, a salary increase, a new hospital, and priority in government housing (*Ettelaat*, May 2, 1961). At the same time, however, the government proceeded to arrest many teachers and students in the provinces.

Neither arrests nor promises ended the walkout. Teachers vowed to continue their strike until all their demands had been won. On the fourth day of the strike, in the midst of growing politicization and demonstrations, Prime Minister Sharif-Emami and his government resigned. In his place, the Shah appointed Ali Amini, a liberal and favorite of the Kennedy administration. The new prime minister met several times with the teachers and finally accepted their demands, including higher salaries and punishment within six months of those responsible for Dr. Khanali's death. The government also promised to establish a bank for teachers and to provide housing loans. On May 13, thousands of teachers gathered at the Mehregan Club and voted to end their twelve-day strike.

THE UPRISINGS OF 1963

The uprisings of 1963 that followed the arrests of Ayatollah Khomeini and a number of other clergy provided an opportunity for workers and white-collar employees to oppose the regime. With some individual exceptions, however, the vast majority of industrial workers and white-collar employees did not take part in the uprising of June 1963. There was no strike or factory shutdown of any sort anywhere in the country, and white-collar employees continued their work without interruption. Teachers, who had successfully mobilized against the government and won all their demands, did not take part in the conflicts. The inaction of these classes prevented the opposition's consolidation and facilitated the success of repression.

The absence of industrial workers from these events can be explained in part by the lack of independent organizations, which reduced their capacity for collective action. Another element contributing to workers' inaction was that the Shah's reforms promised profit sharing for industrial workers. According to government claims, several industrial sectors had been covered by this plan by early 1963 (*Ettelaat,* May 20, 1963). It is possible that the promise of improved wages and income by the government was taken seriously by workers, who did not therefore see the necessity of mobilizing against the government. Finally, both workers and white-collar employees might have backed the government's policies on land reform and women's right to vote as just and progressive policies that served the interests of the working classes, especially because both the Tudeh party and the National Front had advocated these very reforms in the 1950s.

WORKERS IN THE 1970s

The promise of improving workers' conditions did not, however, materialize after the Shah's reforms and White Revolution. Instead, the state pursued policies that enhanced capital accumulation and imposed a heavy cost on the vast majority of the working class. The government's continued policy of fragmenting and controlling unions reduced workers' capacity for collective action while benefiting employers. In addition, Articles 32 and 33 of the labor laws granted employers extensive and arbitrary powers to dismiss workers. Most workers labored ten to twelve hours a day. Only 22 percent of wage earners had social insurance in 1974 (Ivanov n.d.:292).

With rising inflation, especially after 1973, workers' situation worsened. Rising rents alone consumed more than one-half of workers' income. The government promised to provide workers with housing, life insurance, higher income, and better working conditions. Data indicate that although economic development had a positive impact on the earnings of highly skilled workers, the majority could not maintain a decent livelihood in the 1970s. The gap between highly skilled and unskilled segments of the working class widened as a result of the regime's development strategy, which favored modern industries. Government figures for wage levels in large factories, defined as plants employing ten or more workers, reveal that petrochemical employees, who constituted less than 11 percent of the work force in these factories, received the highest average yearly income; textile employees, who represented the largest single category with nearly 28 percent of those employed, were among the lowest paid (SCI 1981a:11–12). A

1974 survey covering 224,000 workers in 2,779 different enterprises reported the existence of a labor aristocracy: "While more than half of the families have a weekly income per head of less than 100 rials, 34.5 percent of them receive more than 501 rials each." The report concluded that 73 percent of the working population received an income below the statutory minimum living wage.[4]

In the face of a declining standard of living, workers occasionally engaged in collective action in an attempt to improve their situation. During the early 1970s, workers in a handful of industrial units responded with wildcat strikes. One example was a walkout in April 1971 by workers in the Chit-e Jahan factory in Karaj, near Tehran. After repeated complaints about low wages, workers struck for more pay. The Savak intervened immediately in an attempt to end the strike, but were unsuccessful. On the third day, striking workers from all three shifts gathered at the factory along with their families and began a march to Tehran. Twice along the road the armed forces attempted to stop them; each time workers broke through the lines and continued their march. In Karvansara Sangi, near Tehran, a colonel and a number of gendarmes blocked the road. When an angry worker hurled a stone at the colonel, knocking off his hat, the colonel ordered the gendarmes to open fire, killing between sixty and seventy people. Workers were prevented from retrieving the bodies of their slain relatives for a long time (*Kayhan*, April 30, 1979).

The number of strikes rose from a handful between 1971 and 1973 to at least twenty in 1974–1975 (Ivanov n.d.:300–305). Three factors explain the rise of strikes. First, rising inflation reduced the standard of living for major segments of the working class. Second, increased investment led to labor shortages and provided alternative employment possibilities in the event that workers were fired for striking. Finally, greater oil revenues led the authorities to grant rare concessions in place of using repression, thereby possibly encouraging collective action in other factories.

In response to increased strikes, the Shah announced the implementation of a previously adopted policy of industrial divestiture. He stated, "We are always more steps ahead in satisfying the workers' and peasants' demands than what they would expect themselves. For this is a revolution that should always be ahead of the events of the future so that no unexpected event and no social or economic change may catch us unawares" (Bashiriyeh 1984:91). The plan for industrial divestiture ordered the sale of 49 percent of 320 private companies and 99 percent of the state-owned factories. Shares were to be offered first to the companies' employees and then to the general public. A special government-financed institute was established with $15 million in capital to facilitate the purchases. At the time, the government estimated that one million industrial workers would benefit. But by July 1977, only 72,235 industrial workers had purchased company shares.

As inflation rose, the regime replaced its positive propaganda about improvements for workers with sporadic attacks upon labor. In autumn of 1976, the Shah complained that workers did not work hard enough: "This is intolerable in contemporary Iran. We shall take those who do not work by the tails and throw them out like mice" (*Kayhan International*, October 25, 1976). Less than a month later, the *Tehran Economist* reported that some workers who had been slow to carry out their duties were dismissed and prevented from returning to work (November 20, 1976). By March 1977, the Shah could boast, "The difficulties of the West are due to lack of discipline and the way work is managed; whereas in Iran, there is not one minute of workers' strikes" (*Kayhan*, March 5, 1977). The government also attacked what it labeled the high cost of labor. In May 1977, the minister of labor complained that wages were too high in the construction sector (*Ettelaat*, May 19, 1977). *Ettelaat*, the official newspaper, reported that rising construction wages had led to a general price increase of 34 percent (June 20, 1977). Several months later, another *Ettelaat* report asserted that industrialists had no right to increase wages arbitrarily; rather, increases in wages should be directly linked to rises in productivity (October 21, 1977).

Worker response to inflation and the rising cost of living was to step up strike activities. The number of strikes grew to approximately twenty in 1977. The walkouts appear to have been independent, spontaneous manifestations of workers' protests over their declining purchasing power. A major strike broke out in the industrial city of Alborz and hundreds of workers were arrested. In Rasht, sanitation workers and firefighters walked out in a dispute over long-delayed benefits. Workers also went on strike in Bandar Shahpour, the Foor construction company, and the nuclear power plant in Boushehr, as well as several Tehran factories, including the Ferdows shoe factory, a metal factory on Karaj Road, the Tehran slaughterhouse, the Ardj factory—where most of the workers were arrested and dismissed—Ab-e Yek cement plant, Benz-e Khavar automobile plant, and Bella Jam shoe factory. It is important to stress the lack of political demands by workers at this stage of the conflict. The example of a strike at the Benz-e Khavar automobile plant is indicative. During this strike, the army was called in to take over the factory. To avoid any retaliation they might have suffered had the management attached political connotations to the strike, striking workers greeted the soldiers' arrival with shouts of "Long live the Shah!"

The following year, strike activity intensified among significant segments of the industrial labor force. During just the first three months of 1978, more than ten strikes were called. In the spring and summer of 1978, three more strikes occurred, mainly over economic issues. The most important strike during this period was initiated by twenty-seven hundred machine-tool workers in Tabriz in mid-April and was crushed. The significance of this walkout lay in the nature of the demands put forward by strikers and in the fact that the strike forecast what was soon to come from the working class as a whole. Workers stated that because of economic unevenness and the dependent nature of the state on the United States, living expenses had increased so much that their families were even deprived of a minimum living condition for survival; thus, wages must be increased. More important, they issued a number of political demands, including the prohibition of forced attendance by workers at government rallies; release of all political prisoners and return to Iran of all exiles, especially Ayatollah Khomeini; and the dissolution and expulsion of Savak agents from factories, universities, and other social institutions. Finally, they rejected a government allegation made three days before the strike that Iranian workers had participated in anti-ILO (International Labor Office) rallies (*Zamimeh* 1978, no. 20:35; Abouzar 1978:27).

The growing number of strikes and the politicization of strikers in Tabriz indicated the potential of industrial workers in times of conflict. That potential could not be realized as long as repression predominated and autonomous organizations were absent within the Iranian working class. A change in the national political sphere toward the end of summer of 1978 provided favorable opportunities for workers to act.

REFORM AND THE OPPORTUNITY FOR MOBILIZATION IN THE FALL OF 1978

The situation changed in August 1978 when bazaari mobilization led the Shah to appoint Sharif-Emami as prime minister and introduce a series of reformist measures. The new prime minister promised liberalization and reduction of repression for all political groups except communists, but he offered nothing to the working classes. The promise of reduced repression provided an opportunity for the working classes to mobilize and demand change. Workers who had previously been involved in strikes or subjected to arrests and imprisonment used their informal networks in the workplace and formed secret cells and committees with trusted co-workers, which seized the initiative and organized workers' collective actions (Bayat 1987:91).

Less than a week after the new government took office, strikes broke out across the country. Thousands of employees in large industrial establishments walked off the job. On September 2, twenty-seven hundred workers in the Tabriz machine-tool plant struck again, as did seven hundred employees of Iran Transfor in Tehran. On September 5, four thousand workers in an Ahvaz steel factory went out on strike, while a government-run union organization demanded the expulsion of unnecessary foreign workers and the development of heavy industry within the country. The next day, workers in the Arak machine-tool plant struck. Striking workers at Pars machinery factory and Foster Wheeler tore down leaflets at the local office of the Ministry of Labor, broke windows, and damaged cars. They shouted slogans such as "Unity! Struggle! Victory!" "United workers everything! Dispersed workers nothing!" and "Brother workers, believe in your power!" On September 8, employees in water installations in the province of Fars and the city of Mashhad walked out. That same day, workers in the Tehran oil refinery raised tents in front of their workplace to dramatize the plight they faced in obtaining housing. Two days later they, too, went on strike. On September 10, groups of workers and technicians in an Isfahan steel mill struck. A few days later, thousands of oil drillers went on strike. They were joined on September 24 by oil workers in Ahvaz. On October 2, two thousand workers struck a factory in Ardj. Beginning on October 6, more workers in the Isfahan steel mill began to walk off the job, and by October 9, 90 percent, or some forty-six thousand employees, had gone on strike. On October 8, railway employees in Zahedan and copper miners in Rafsanjan went on strike. The next day, workers in a Tabriz tractor factory, a steel refinery in Bafagh, and Iranit in Shahr-e Ray all left their jobs. On October 10, three thousand workers struck in Zamyad and two thousand more walked off the job at Iran General Motors.

Toward the end of September, white-collar employees and professionals began to mobilize. They complained of highly unequal salaries and the prevalence of favoritism. Most had been adversely affected by the government's policy of consistently favoring the upper echelon of the bureaucracy over the middle and lower levels. In some cases, white-collar employees resented the presence of highly paid foreign experts who occupied positions of authority. In most cities, teachers were among the first to walk out. Schools and universities reopened on September 23, but within a week teachers began to strike. By October 7 the walkout was nationwide. The next day, in retaliation, the government arrested Darakhshesh, former minister of education and then president of the Society of Teachers, for publishing the society's first newsletter.

On October 1, employees of the government-owned Bank Melli of Iran struck. A group calling itself the "Society of Government Employees" ex- in Kermanshah and employees of Jondi Shahpour University in Ahvaz struck. A group calling itself, the "Society of Government Employees" ex- horted government employees to report to their jobs on October 7, but not to work. On October 4, postal employees went on a nationwide walkout. That same day, employees struck such diverse institutions as Vanak Hospital, the Shiraz medical school, Sari regional electricity works, the Bank of E'atebarat, the state-owned tobacco monopoly, electricity installations in Tehran and smaller neighboring cities, Azarabadgan University Hospital in Tabriz, and the regional electricity works in Arak.

On October 5, 1,500 employees of Razi Hospital in Ray struck. They were joined by employees of the Development and Investment Bank, Isfahan electricity, Ahvaz water and electricity, and medical employees at Tehran University and Pahlavi University. Court clerks in Shahyad Plaza and employees in the Tehran offices of the Ministry of Economy and Finance also struck. Other strikes that same day included 2,349 electricity and water employees in Khuzestan; health care employees in Abadan; agricultural extension agents in Shemiran; employees of the Pahlavi Medical Center; hospital and electrical workers in Tabriz; employees in the Shiraz electricity installations and environmental protection organization; an organization of rural cooperatives in Rezaieh; and hospital employees in Shahr-e Ray and Kermanshah.

The number of strikes mounted daily. On October 7, close to 30 new groups struck. On October 8, 65 new strikes were reported. The next day more than 110 additional strikes were reported, and two days later there were more than 125 new strikes. On October 10 and 11, employees of the three national newspapers, *Ettelaat, Kayhan,* and *Ayandegan,* joined the strikers in protest against government censorship. That day, the *Tehran Journal* reported that some sixty thousand employees in various ministries and state agencies were on strike, awaiting a response from the new government to their demands. All this took place in a little over a month in a country where strikes were illegal.

An analysis of strikers' demands during this period reveals that with few exceptions the most important issues were economic, with job-related problems close behind. All strikers demanded increases in wages and salaries, while most also insisted on allowances or loans for housing expenses and medical insurance. Many complained of pay inequality, especially where foreign workers were employed. Some protested arbitrary promotion rules and secret "rewards" by heads of bureaucracies. In a few cases, strikers pressed for dismissal of directors of corporations or government offices. Oil workers during their second strike, striking employees of the Isfahan steel mill, a mine in central Alborz, a railway in Zahedan, and Iran General Motors in Tehran all demanded the expulsion of various department chiefs. Some, including water installation employees in Mashhad, court clerks in Shahy, Komak Hospital employees in Tehran, and postal employees throughout the country, claimed that their rights had been violated for up to eighteen years (*Ettelaat,* September 7, October 9 and 15, 1978).

To prevent issues from being further politicized, the government agreed to some demands relatively quickly. Bank employees, for example, struck for two days but resumed work on the third day when the government acceded to their demands. Telegraph workers walked out for four days, returning when their demands were met. Health employees at Firozgar in Tehran and at hospitals in Shahr-e Kord and Amol returned to work after receiving favorable promises. After a twenty-day strike, postal workers went back to work on October 24 when the government agreed to raise salaries of lower-income employees by 50 percent and 30 percent. The government also promised to change its promotion rules regarding postal workers. On October 29, employees of Iranian Radio and Television broke off their seven-day strike after the prime minister guaranteed the neutrality of their facilities. That same day, employees of the Ministry of Commerce reached agreement with the government on twenty-two demands and went back to work. Coal workers in Loshan returned to their jobs after one week once their demands were met. All factory workers in Yazd went back to work after negotiations with representatives of the Ministry of Labor (*Ayandegan,* November 5, 1978). Other strikers, including court employees in Ahvaz and teachers in Lahijan and Ghazvin, went back to work but set strike deadlines if their demands were not met. During the first oil workers' strike, some workers dragged their feet for a few days after the government had given in, but all finally returned to work.

In the private sector, a strike of 150,000 textile workers ended on October 26 after employers signed a collective contract with the union. According to the contract, employers agreed to pay monthly subsidies of three thousand rials to single workers, four thousand rials to married workers, and five thousand rials to workers with children to help defray rent and food expenses. Foreign workers were not eligible for these allowances. Employers also agreed to reconsider workers' job rankings.

In contrast to these strikes by workers and white-collar employees, a few strikes were more political in nature, though they initially demanded reforms rather than revolution or support for Ayatollah Khomeini. Workers in a machine-tool factory in Tabriz made political demands from very early on, as discussed above. In their second and third strikes, held on June 25 and August 6–10, they demanded higher wages and the dissolution of the government-run union. In their fourth strike, on September 2, they demanded a 50 percent wage raise, housing allowances, and dissolution of the union. This time, the army surrounded the factory, harassing and coercing workers for several days until they returned to work. On November 4, these workers organized a joint strike with workers in the Tabriz tractor plant to press for identical demands.

Some workers and employees were politicized in the process of their struggles. After striking for more than two weeks, employees of the Ministry of Economy and Finance augmented their initial demands by asking for the expulsion of all foreign military advisors and a boycott of trade with South Africa and Israel. Another example was the strike at the Isfahan steel mill, which employed more than thirty thousand workers. On August 19, the anniversary of Mosaddegh's overthrow in 1953, two engineering workshops stopped work and issued a list of demands. The Savak and the army were quickly brought in, and some workers were temporarily dismissed. Executives and managers promised to investigate the grievances, and workers resumed work by noon. On September 10, another strike broke out when workers in a different section of the complex shut down their machines. Shaybani, chief executive of the installations, immediately requested the intervention of General Naji, military governor of Isfahan, which was then under martial law. The army quickly surrounded the striking workers and sections. Workers and technicians held fast to their demands, which included higher wages, housing allowances, expulsion of current workers' representatives, and formation of a genuine labor syndicate. Finally, Shaybani promised to investigate these demands within two months, and workers returned to work in the afternoon. Rumors later spread throughout the complex that another strike was called for September 18; the army again surrounded the installations, but no strike occurred.

On October 4, two more sections of the complex went on strike, while in three other sections workers boycotted lunch in protest against the company. Within four days, roughly half the employees had gone on strike. By October 10, the number had grown to 98 percent. The workers' demands included dismissal of Shaybani and other "feudalists"; expulsion of the Savak from the complex; removal of current workers' representatives and selection by workers of new representatives; higher salaries; more equitable distribution of housing; provision of health care for all employees; payment of the annual profit-sharing bonus; permanent employment for all workers currently working on contract; and expulsion of military personnel from the factory. In the next few days, the government raised wages by 15 to 40 percent, and by October 25, most of the strikers had returned to work.

Students and intellectuals, active since fall 1977, were highly politicized during these early strikes. Students and teachers also were in a special position, due to their concentration, to disrupt the educational system and affect the political process. University faculty and students across the country were very active in seeking political freedoms, forming the National Organization of Universities in 1978. The faculty at the University of Arya Mehr demanded that military personnel be prohibited from entering college campuses on the grounds that they disrupted education (*Ettelaat*, October 15, 1978). University faculty in Tehran called for a "week of solidarity." To offset the effect of a boycott of classes during that week, the government declared that universities would be closed for several days that week. In response, twenty-one hundred faculty at Tehran University went on strike. They demanded an end to martial law, freedom for all political prisoners, expulsion of the university guard, and a government apology and reinstatement for all faculty who had been arbitrarily retired by the government. During the solidarity week, rallies and demonstrations were held throughout the country. On some campuses, faculty and students held sit-ins and went on hunger strikes to protest government repression and demand the release of all political prisoners. Protesting university professors and students organized antimilitary sit-ins to demand the reopening of colleges and universities. Because of similar protests elsewhere, the government was finally forced to grant political freedom to all universities (*Ettelaat*, October 23, 1978). Other intellectuals also were politically active, including journalists of the national newspapers, who walked out over the issue of freedom of the press, which they won after four days.

Teachers, who had won a political victory in 1961, made a number of demands, including higher salaries; prohibition of forced participation at government rallies (*Tehran Journal,* October 10, 1978); dissolution of parliament; release of all political prisoners; lifting of martial law (*Kayhan International,* October 22, 1978; *Ettelaat,* October 23, 1978); abolition of the office of "security" in the educational system; prohibition of police and military intervention in schools; freedom for all political parties; freedom of expression and the press; and return of all those who had been exiled. When students were arrested for reading the works of Samad Behrangi, an acclaimed Marxist writer and teacher who had perhaps been drowned by the Savak in Aras River, many teachers in Tehran refused to return to work. In their demonstrations teachers also supported the struggles of university faculty, workers, and the clergy. Some teachers protested the arrests of Darakhshesh, president of the Society of Teachers, and Beh Azin, a leftist writer and intellectual. Many schoolteachers and even university students openly supported Ayatollah Khomeini and the Islamic movement at this stage.

As the scale of strikes increased, the regime initially chose to deal with them on a national level and proceed with concessions rather than repression. The government did not use repression at the beginning because the scale of strikes was very large and growing. Thus, on October 10, the government announced that within six months, salaries of all government employees would be raised by 25 percent in two stages (*Ettelaat,* October 10, 1978). On October 15, twenty thousand government employees were promised housing loans (*Ettelaat,* October 15, 1978).

Workers' responses varied. While some returned to work, others remained skeptical about government promises. Some strikers complained that although they had been on strike for days, authorities had not even investigated their grievances. Most strikers were dissatisfied with the government's concessions, which they regarded as insufficient. Many government employees demanded 50–100 percent salary increases along with additional benefits (*Tehran Journal,* October 11, 1978). Concessions offered to industrial workers were not as favorable as those given white-collar employees. The latter were promised housing loans, while industrial workers were to be given low-rent housing by their employers, who, in turn, were subsidized through government loans. This plan meant that workers would never own their own houses and would therefore be even more dependent on their employers. Equally important, the regime only promised changes instead of actually implementing reforms. To many strikers, this regime had made many empty promises over the years. Because of all these inadequacies, major segments of the work force refused to accept the proffered settlements.

Soon a number of factors led to the growing politicization of strikers' demands and attacks on the state. Structurally, most strikers were employed by the state, which increased the potential for politicization of conflicts. Another factor was the growing solidarity among strikers, which had been made possible by the relaxation of repression and the prolongation of strikes. Previously, repression had prevented the formation of networks and solidarity among workers. Now strikers could communicate freely, express their grievances, and plan their action. Furthermore, the partial lifting of censorship in the media, especially radio and television, allowed the broadcast of most strikes and their demands. This additional means of communication also generated a sense of solidarity among different groups of strikers, especially since many groups expressed support for oil workers' strikes. Finally, by knowing that other large groups were on strike at the same time, strikers realized that the regime was vulnerable and that the cost of repression could not be very high, for pressure on any single group was reduced. All these factors increased solidarity among strikers, which, along with the mounting vulnerability of the government, led to the growing politicization of their demands.

Toward the end of Prime Minister Sharif-Emami's government, more strikers began to press for political as well as economic demands. Striking oil workers and employees of Iran Air announced their solidarity with the popular struggles and demanded the unconditional release of all political prisoners, dissolution of martial law, and expulsion of foreigners from their respective sectors, in addition to increases in their wages and salaries. Employees of the Bank Melli of Iran struck for the second time, claiming that the government had not kept its promise to raise salaries. They also added political demands, such as the release of all political prisoners and the dissolution of martial law. Three thousand employees at the Ministry of Economy and Finance held a demonstration to announce their support for striking oil workers. They asked bazaaris to withhold their taxes from the government. In retaliation, their offices were occupied by soldiers. Ministry employees then went to pay homage to two symbolic figures in the opposition movement: Ayatollah Taleghani, an important religious leader and ally of Dr. Mosaddegh, and Safar Ghahremani, a member of the Tudeh party who had been released from jail after more than thirty years (*Kayhan*, November 5, 1978).

In response to the growing politicization of protesters, the regime hired hooligans to attack demonstrators and loot and burn shops. Such attacks took place in more than thirty cities by the time Sharif-Emami's government ended on November 5, 1978. In retaliation against hooligan attacks, lawyers and judges launched protests. In Sanandaj, all the judges resigned collectively to protest the "killings of defenseless people" in their city. The next day, judges in the province of Fars unanimously resigned to protest government repression and violence. In Hamedan, Kermanshah, and Ghazvin, judges and lawyers held sit-ins to protest hooligan attacks and the burning of court buildings. Justices and attorneys in Kermanshah, Amol, and Zanjan publicly condemned burning and looting and filed suits against hooligans and those police and military officers who either organized them or failed to prevent their actions. On November 4, judges in Tehran invited the minister of justice to attend a public hearing and explain recent attacks on courts and individuals in various cities. They also demanded an apology for these attacks and other insults against the judges.

In response to the rising wave of strikes and demonstrations, the Shah suspended civilian government on November 5, 1978, and instituted military rule. For a short period of time, the military government of General Azhari succeeded in reducing the number of strikes by employing harsh methods. Almost immediately, the army tried to coerce striking workers to return to their jobs by occupying all strategic institutions, including oil installations, radio and television stations, and newspapers, which had just successfully concluded a strike. Employees of the Ministry of Post and Telegraph were forced back to work, as were employees of the State Tobacco Monopoly. The Tabriz machine-tool strike, which had just begun on November 4, was halted three days later by the arrival of soldiers at the factory.

The order imposed by the army proved illusory. The few weeks of political opening had enabled workers and white-collar employees to mobilize their resources and act collectively, form solidarities, and make demands to serve their interests. As a result, the military was unable to bring about an end to all the strikes. Some workers and employees refused to return to work and give up their demands. The imposition of the military government and repression further escalated the conflicts by leading bazaaris to initiate protracted shutdowns in major cities. These unprecedentedly lengthy shutdowns provided additional support for striking workers who refused to return to work, as well as encouraging others to resume their strikes. As a result, within a few days of the imposition of the military government, lengthy politicized strikes broke out once again in many parts of the country. Statements issued by striking workers and professionals unanimously condemned the violence and repression employed by the military government. Strike committees sprang up everywhere to coordinate strike activities and demand political change. In the end, instead of dissolving solidarity among strikers military coercion strengthened it, spreading disorder even to previously orderly sectors.

Workers in a number of factories such as the Tehran oil refinery, Arak machine-tool, and Tabriz tractor refused to work despite the military rule and coercion.[5] They were joined by the Tabriz lift-truck factory the day after the army assumed power. A few days later, workers in the Tehran cement factory joined the strikes. At the beginning of November, Tehran electrical workers threatened to cut off the electricity if their demands were not met. In late November, they regularly shut down electricity at 8:30 P.M. to prevent the broadcast of government news programs on radio and television. On December 2, oil workers in Abadan and Ahvaz began their third and final strike under the monarchy. Soon other workers joined in. In mid-December, workers in the Bandar-e Abbas steel complex walked out. They acknowledged Ayatollah Khomeini's leadership and vowed to fight for a democratic government based on the votes of the working classes (*Kayhan*, January 11, 1979). Employees of other major industries who were also on strike included more than thirty thousand workers at Isfahan Steel, coal miners, and over thirty thousand railway workers throughout the country. In mid-January, three thousand copper workers struck and announced solidarity with the struggles of oil workers and other strikers. They also demanded the dismissal of Mehdi Shaghaghi Zarghami, chief executive of the copper company, because of his ties to the royal family (*Kayhan*, January 15, 1979).

In response to the spreading strikes, the military government approved a bill on November 30 that would grant a 25 percent pay increase to public-sector employees. This measure proved too little and too late. Economically, the salary increase was not satisfactory to most strikers. More importantly, strikers had made political demands that the military government could not satisfy, demands that challenged the very nature of the state.

Strikes by industrial workers during this period were frequently lengthy as well as politicized. Machine-tool workers in Arak, who had struck three times during Sharif-Emami's regime, remained on strike throughout the subsequent military government. On January 15, 1979, after having been on strike continuously since October 9, 1978, they vowed to maintain their struggles until all political prisoners were released, all exiles returned, and imperialist influences in Iran totally severed (*Kayhan*, January 15, 1979). They also demanded the development of a nationally based technology rather than a dependent technology, higher salaries, and the expulsion from the factory of Houshang Sabeti, brother of the Savak's national spokesperson. Aluminum workers in Arak engaged in a lengthy strike, demanding that all American shares in the factory be purchased and offered to Iranian citizens for sale. After the military government assumed power, workers in the Tehran cement factory went on strike. They returned to work when Bakhtiar took office nearly two months later, but production remained at only 10 percent of capacity. In addition, the workers refused to permit the cement to be sold "until the antidespotic and anti-imperialistic struggles of the people succeeded" (*Kayhan*, January 24, 1979). On January 1, 1979, seventeen thousand coal miners in Kerman had begun their strike. Thousands of Isfahan steelworkers, on strike since November 1978, asked striking Trans-Iranian Railways workers to transport coal from Kerman so that some sections of the refinery could be heated and prevented from deteriorating (*Kayhan*, January 18, 1979). Railroad workers agreed to this request by fellow strikers. On January 31, more than five thousand civilian employees of the armed forces rallied at Tehran University and proclaimed solidarity with the popular movement. They shouted: "We are the military personnel! We are waiting for Khomeini!" and "We made machine guns to kill enemies, but overlooked the fact that they would kill brothers!" (*Kayhan*, January 31, 1979). Other factories in which workers struck and pressed political demands during this period included a pipe and machinery factory, Ardj factory, Iran National automobile factory, Benz-e Khavar automobile plant, Techno-Kar, Alyaf company, Bafandeh-Souzani knitting factory, General Factory, State Tobacco Monopoly, and the Akam construction company.

Students and university faculty also continued their struggles. More than one hundred faculty members of Tehran University who belonged to the National Organization of Universities held a sit-in at the administration building. They condemned government repression and the lack of independence within the university administration. The protesting faculty vowed to continue their sit-in until the universities were reopened and students allowed to return to classes. Immediately after their sit-in began, the army surrounded that part of the campus. Three days later, another seventy members of the National Organization of Universities held a sit-in at the Ministry of Sciences and Higher Education. That afternoon one of the participants, Dr. Nejat-Ollahy, was shot and taken to a hospital, where he died. A few minutes later, the army stormed the building and arrested the remaining sixty-nine protesters. At Azarabadgan University in Tabriz, seventy-six members of the faculty held a sit-in to protest government repression and forced closings of universities. By afternoon, the number of faculty at this protest had grown to one hundred, and they were joined by students and bazaaris. Over the next few days, faculty and students held rallies, demonstrations, and marches to pay tribute to Dr. Nejat-Ollahy's martyrdom. In a street demonstration in Mashhad another university faculty member, Saeed Neshan, was killed. The next day, faculty at the sit-in at Tehran University embarked upon a hunger strike as well. Their struggles finally succeeded on January 13, 1979, in reopening the universities which had been closed since early November by the military government. In addition, the National Organization of Universities requested all university employees to contribute one day's salary to striking oil workers.

White-collar workers and professionals also resumed strikes in large numbers during this period. By December 1978, many key institutions had been crippled by strikes, including radio and television stations; national newspapers; telegraph facilities; the Ministries of Electricity, Justice, Highways, and Economy and Finance; customs; the government's Plan Organization; Iran Air; the Central Bank; Bank Melli; and schools and universities nationwide. All these groups made political demands including at a minimum the release of all political prisoners, dissolution of the Savak, and elimination of censorship from all the media. Some strikers took additional steps to weaken the regime. In mid-December, employees of the Ministry of Foreign Affairs joined other strikers and vowed to struggle alongside them to achieve a free and democratic Iran. They published the names of Savak agents stationed in Iranian embassies and consulates who were engaged in gathering information about opponents of the government. At the Ministry of Economy and Finance, employees remained on strike to prevent the flight of foreign capital. When the government authorized the Office of Documentation to oversee this task, ministry employees exposed the policy change and provided guidelines to detect and prevent wealth from being taken out of the country.

Actions by bank employees were likewise important in disrupting the flight of capital. On the day the military government took control, employees of two government-owned banks, Bank Melli and the Central Bank, rallied at their workplaces and pulled down statues of the Shah. They were eventually forced back to work by the army. Two weeks later, Central Bank employees went on strike for twenty days, condemning government violence and military intervention in bank operations. They published a list of some 170 officials and wealthy citizens who had taken more than ten million tomans out of the country. On December 23, striking bank employees declared solidarity with the popular struggles led by Ayatollah Khomeini. A few days later, they announced that they would report to their jobs, but refused to resume work. Also on December 23, employees of Bank Melli publicly expressed solidarity with the popular struggles and announced a month-long strike to begin on December 31. The strike was announced in advance to allow people an opportunity to complete their banking transactions before the strike. They also encouraged employees in other banks to join the strikes expressly to prevent checks written by bazaaris on Bank Melli accounts from bouncing in other banks. That week they established a special account for contributions to a benefit fund for striking oil workers and allocated one day's wages from their own salaries to the fund. Following these actions, employees in other banks also walked out. On December 27, employees of the government-owned Bank of Sepah went on strike, followed by employees at the Export Bank (*Kayhan*, January 6, 1979). The syndicate of private bank employees called for the nationalization of all private banks in the interests of the people: "Through capital accumulation, bankers have exploited the Iranian people and their employees. In a genuinely democratic act, these banks should be nationalized."

The National Organization of Physicians held several meetings to denounce military attacks on hospitals in Mashhad, Isfahan, Shiraz, and several other cities. Physicians, nurses, and hospital employees were asked to stop work immediately if military personnel appeared on the hospital premises. If the soldiers refused to leave, medical staff were instructed to leave the hospital. The physicians' organization also called for the "overthrow of the illegal and oppressive regime" and passed a resolution refusing to accept insurance payments for military personnel. This resolution was put into effect by physicians in Mashhad after the army attacked a hospital in that city. In retaliation, hooligans stormed another hospital, killing two infants and wounding fifteen doctors. In Tabriz, physicians demonstrated against military attacks on the Mashhad hospital. Doctors at Jondi Shahpour University in Ahvaz went on a hunger strike and treated their patients free of charge. Physicians in Hamedan dispensed free treatments for two days and marched to protest attacks by the army on hospitals. In Babol and Shahy, physicians, dentists, and pharmacists stopped work and rallied to condemn government violence and attacks on hospitals and pharmacies. In Shiraz, two hundred physicians went on strike to protest nighttime shootings by the army and the arrest of three physicians.

OIL WORKERS AND DUAL SOVEREIGNTY

The role of oil workers' strikes during this period was distinct from that of other industrial workers because they controlled the nation's most vital economic asset. In addition, oil workers shared certain characteristics that increased their likelihood of politicization. They numbered over thirty thousand and were heavily concentrated in specific oil-producing regions, which enhanced their capacity for communication, mobilization, and collective action. Moreover, because they were state employees they had a greater potential for politicization during times of conflict. Their strikes during the nationalization of oil had provided a core of political experience. Aware that they controlled the state's primary source of revenue, oil workers rapidly became more militant and politicized. Their politicization and struggles contributed to the rise of a revolutionary situation and dual sovereignty.

Oil workers' strike committees consisted of a highly politicized leadership, 35 percent of whom were avowedly Marxist (*Washington Post*, February 26, 1979). Many oil workers were also influenced by the ideas of the Mojahedeen, an organization advocating Islamic socialism. Their strikes, however, were initiated independently of any political organization or group.[6] In fact, some friction existed between oil workers and some clergy in Ahvaz. For example, before the downfall of the monarchy the Ahvaz oil workers' first representative, who had been jailed and tortured by the Savak in previous years, resigned in protest against what he called interference by nonprogressive and "reactionary" clergy of Ahvaz who restricted strike committees' responsibilities (*Ayandegan*, February 1, 1979). This should not be taken to mean that oil workers did not support Ayatollah Khomeini. On the contrary, in the final days of the revolution they openly expressed their support for Khomeini, declaring him the leader of the "anti-imperialist, antidespotic struggles" of the Iranian people. Oil workers expected radical changes; as one oil worker told an American correspondent, "We want Khomeini. He will take power from the rich and give it to us."[7] Let us now review the collective actions of oil workers during the final months of the Pahlavi dynasty.

On September 8, 1978, oil workers in the Tehran refinery demanded government housing allowances, claiming their rents had quadrupled. They threatened to set up housekeeping at their workplace if their demands were not met. The government ignored their demands; twenty days later, workers made good their threats and erected tents in front of the refinery. The government responded by calling in troops to disband the protesters and arrest the militant leaders. The remaining oil workers went on strike in support of those who had been arrested (*Zamimeh* 1978, no. 21:64, 66). On September 24, oil extraction workers in the south walked out in a separate strike. The government quickly met their demands, and after a few days all oil workers finally returned to work.

On October 13 the Abadan oil refinery, largest in the world, went on strike. Their demands included lifting martial law; the dismissal of General Kolya'i, head of security in the refinery; prohibiting the army from entering the refinery; release of all political prisoners; expulsion of all foreign employees of Iranian oil companies; and higher wages. The strikers pledged to continue their walkout until their demands were met; if the government refused, they threatened, they would extend their strike to include the remaining workers at the company. This strike was followed by a walkout of nearly five thousand staff employees and service workers in the Ahvaz oil company on October 18. Three or four days later, production workers sent a delegation to the staff employees, pledging support for their strike. They added that they would collaborate with them provided that they "went all the way and stuck with them to the last" (Iranian Oil Worker 1980:295). Staff employees agreed. Each group produced a similar list of demands, including an end to martial law; full solidarity and cooperation with striking teachers; unconditional release of all political prisoners; "Iranianization" of the oil industry; use of the Persian language in all communication; expulsion of all foreign employees; an end to discrimination against women staff employees and workers; the implementation of a law recently passed by the Majles providing for housing for oil workers and staff employees; support for production workers' demands, including the dissolution of the Savak; punishment of corrupt high government officials and ministers; and reduced duty schedules for offshore drilling crews (Turner 1980:282).

Oil workers and service employees in Aghajari, Maroon, Gachsaran, Nafteh Safeed, Babahakim, Kazroun, Lavan, Khark Island, and Bandar Shahpour joined the strikers. As a negotiator the government sent Houshang Ansari to meet with sixty representatives from the southern oil-producing regions of Ahvaz, Abadan, Masjed Soleyman, Gachsaran, and Tehran. The government agreed to the oil workers' economic requests but rejected their political demands. In response, oil workers declared that they made no distinction between economic and political demands, and they insisted that all of them be met. The government sent office workers to run the refinery, but it was obvious that the situation could not go on for long as these employees were unable to operate the machinery. Oil workers in Tabriz, Shiraz, and Kermanshah walked off the job in support of oil workers in the south and made similar demands. In Tehran, two hundred oil extraction employees announced their solidarity with southern oil workers. On November 6, as the military assumed power, workers in the Tehran oil refinery also joined the strikers.

These strikes caused a halt in oil exports that cost the government approximately $57 million a day (*Kayhan*, November 1, 1978). Workers were issued an ultimatum to return to work in three days, but they refused to back down. On the third day of negotiations, the government broke off settlement talks and immediately sent military troops to occupy oil installations at Abadan, Tehran, and Kermanshah (*Kayhan*, November 4, 1978). When the army entered the Tehran oil refinery, workers held a sit-in for forty-eight hours. During that time, they pulled down the Shah's pictures and replaced them with ones of Khomeini. Following the sit-in, they left the refinery and stayed home for eleven days. They then resumed their strike at the refinery in order to verify each day that no one had been arrested while at home.

Because the state was almost entirely dependent on oil revenues, the military government responded to oil strikes with drastic measures. Military occupation of oil installations in the south and the use of coercion forced most oil workers back to their jobs. Many oil workers and employees were arrested, and some were reportedly tortured. One form of torture involved hanging weights from a prisoner's testicles (*Hambastegi* 1978, no. 6). Some striking workers were forced to return to their installations and offices at bayonet point. In Ahvaz, the army threatened to harm the families of oil workers who had gone into hiding (*Akhbar* 1978 no. 9). In Aghajari the government assigned naval personnel to operate the oil installations, but because they were unfamiliar with the equipment they reportedly inflicted some $3 million worth of damage. After thirty-three days of strikes and approximately two weeks of resistance, all strikes in the oil region of Khuzestan ended on November 19. Workers and employees went back, however, determined to form a national oil workers' organization to coordinate strikes and prevent their collapse.

With the formation of such an organization, strikes soon resumed. On December 2, less than a month after the military assumed power, oil workers in Abadan began what would be their final walkout. They announced that they would fight until victory, by which they meant the overthrow of dictatorship and an end to the looting of oil, the national resource. As the strike spread throughout the southern oil-producing region, oil exports dropped to zero. This time, oil workers rejected any compromise or negotiation with the regime. In an open letter to Abdollah Entezam, chief executive of the Iranian National Oil Company, they reminded him of his stint as foreign minister in General Zahedi's military government after the 1953 coup d'etat, his company's oil sales to South Africa and Israel, the dismissal of over ten thousand workers in the Abadan refinery because of mechanization, and mass firings of antigovernment employees. They concluded by saying that they were ashamed to be associated with such unsavory dealings (*Hambastegi* 1979, no. 10).

Strikes by oil workers had a profound impact on the Shah's regime. Without oil exports, the state was headed for fiscal collapse. Transportation within cities ceased as buses and cars became useless with the growing oil shortage. Lack of transportation led most government ministries to close, including the Ministries of Commerce, Industry and Mines, and Agriculture. Factories were forced to shut down for lack of fuel, and long lines formed to purchase home heating oil. The oil strikes encouraged other workers to act against the regime. Strikes by bank employees prevented capital allocation and the payment of workers' salaries. Walkouts by customs employees halted the delivery of spare parts and raw materials from abroad. Eventually, the domestic market was disrupted to the point where manufacturers were unable to sell their products. As a result, some industrial employers began dismissing their workers.

The government blamed illegal strikes for the rapidly burgeoning crisis and warned that strikers would be dismissed. Oil workers countered that the oil strike would not harm the nation, but would instead actually prevent further waste of the nation's most valuable resource. They maintained that the oil supply for domestic consumption would last up to six months if the government discontinued sales to South Africa and Israel. They pledged not to produce oil that would be used by the army to kill other Iranians. When the government threatened to dismiss the striking oil workers, they began to resign. By the end of the year, more than six thousand had quit their jobs. By December 26, all production had ceased in protest against government threats and reports of torture of oil workers.[8]

Independently and with other groups, oil workers throughout the country stepped up their political protests. In Tehran, oil refinery employees held several demonstrations during December. On December 26, they rallied at the oil company's headquarters. One speaker declared that the real leader of their movement was Ayatollah Khomeini. The demonstrators shouted political slogans such as "The dark night of the people will turn into day! Khomeini will eventually win." "Long live the champion workers! Long live our oil workers!" "Strike, strike: the school of revolution!" "Tomorrow our fists will turn into machine guns!" "The university is the barricade of freedom, not the nest of lackeys!" "Worker, worker, your fist signifies your commitment!" (*Akhbar* 1979, no. 10).

Meanwhile, at the recommendation of Ayatollah Khomeini and more than two hundred other clerics, oil workers in the south agreed to meet with Abdollah Entezam and Mehdi Bazargan, Khomeini's representative, to negotiate resumption of oil production for internal consumption. The negotiations lasted the better part of three days. Bazargan, a supporter of Mosaddegh who had played an important role in the nationalization of oil, complained that leftist oil employees did not want to resume production but preferred to continue their strike and even damage the oil facilities. Finally, the government acceded to a list of demands made by the strikers: (1) the armed forces would leave the oil installations; (2) the military would not use the oil produced by workers; (3) the export of oil was strictly prohibited; (4) protection of oil installations would be restored to the previous guards; (5) strikers who had been dismissed would be reinstated, and those who had been evicted from company housing would be allowed to return; and (6) all imprisoned workers would be released. With this agreement, oil workers resumed production for domestic consumption in early January 1979, but they vowed to fight behind Khomeini until the final victory over the Shah.

While producing for domestic needs, oil workers continued to issue political statements. On January 16 they announced, "Oil workers are a part of the Iranian working class and the greatest ally of progressive, anti-despotic, and anti-imperialistic strata." They added, "Considering the decisive role of workers, especially workers in the oil industry, throughout the antidespotic struggles, the future government is obligated to consider the interests of the working class" (*Kayhan*, January 16, 1979). Twelve days before the final collapse of the regime, a group of oil workers declared that a workers' representative should be included on the Revolutionary Council, whose membership had not yet been announced by Khomeini. They stated,

Just as workers have played a crucial role in the current revolutionary situation, they should participate the day after the revolution when it is time for the genuine construction; this is only possible by workers' participation in the political affairs of the country. The first step would be taken by the participation of a workers' representative on the revolutionary council. The coordination and organization of historic strikes in small and large factories by workers themselves indicates their political and cultural maturation. They believe that, led by Ayatollah Khomeini, they will take control of their factories in the days after the revolution and forever leave behind the exploiters and the imperialists. The revolutionary council should be composed of university members, educators, bazaaris, clergy, peasants, strike councils, and other social strata. Just as these people fight next to each other in the streets without questioning each other's political beliefs, opinions, tastes, or social class, so is their blood shed and intertwined. (*Kayhan*, January 30, 1979)

The next day, Tehran oil workers published a statement reminding the future government of the important role played by workers in the overthrow of the regime and of the necessity of considering workers' interests in the future. They demanded the dissolution of labor unions imposed upon workers and the passage of new laws to replace oppressive labor statutes. Finally, they requested changes in oil company regulations on the grounds that laws written many years previously could not satisfy present needs. For this reason, they argued, workers' representatives should participate in the creation of new laws (*Kayhan*, January 31, 1979).

The strikes deepened the country's financial crisis and led to the dismissal of thousands of workers (*Kayhan*, January 14, 1979). On January 20, the chamber of commerce announced that 3.5 million workers were out of work, including 1.5 million industrial workers. When Bakhtiar, the new prime minister, took office he declared that the first priority of his government would be to put the country's unemployed back to work (*Kayhan*, January 31, 1979). Aryana, Bakhtiar's minister of labor, pledged to provide favorable conditions for industrial workers in order that factories might resume production. He also announced that workers' organizations that had not been approved by workers should be dissolved. Immediately, a spokesman for these organizations declared that they would soon disband (*Kayhan*, January 7, 1979). When they were dissolved a short time later, the announcement also noted that workers were not separate from the rest of the Iranian people and that they, too, had participated in the popular struggles (*Kayhan*, January 20, 1979).

In the waning days of the monarchy, workers in leading industrial sectors met specifically to "strengthen their organization, increase solidarity, and promote workers' consciousness in order to serve their class interests." They charged that some officials of their own unions were Savak agents. On February 3, more than one hundred workers representing seven independent auto, oil, and electrical unions gathered at the Ghand Riz Syndicate in Tehran and denounced the dismissal of factory workers. They agreed that a workers' representative should participate in the Revolutionary Council. They also discussed the formation of a workers' solidarity council and called for independent labor organizations in factories as its basis. A representative from Iran National, an auto factory, stated that current union officials could not be part of any independent union because they had attempted to restrict his conversations with other workers about political matters (*Kayhan*, February 3, 1979). On February 11, hundreds of workers from various factories and guilds met at the Needle-knitters' Syndicate in Tehran to coordinate workers' strikes and protests. They emphasized the need to elect genuine representatives for labor unions, rather than accept those imposed by employers or the government. They concluded by visiting the General Factory to express their support for workers who had forced the chief executive to resign and taken over the factory's operations.[9] The Tailors' Syndicate in Tehran formed an independent, provisional union to defend working-class interests, cooperate with other labor unions, and participate in the struggles against despotism, imperialism, and exploitation of the working class.

In the final stage of the revolution, workers also joined other groups in organizing large rallies and demonstrations against the regime. On January 21, thousands of workers from the Ardj factory, Iran National, and Benz-e Khavar, as well as workers who had been dismissed, gathered at San'ati University in Tehran. After a speech by a representative of the dismissed workers, they began to march, chanting slogans such as "Workers' salaries must be paid; workers should not be dismissed!" "Hail to Khomeini! Unity! Unity! Unity!" "Hail to the oil workers!" "Workers, workers, we unite with each other to eliminate the basis of exploitation!" "Equality! Equality! Workers' government!" "People: we unite together to eliminate the basis of imperialism!" (*Ettelaat*, January 21, 1979). Two days later, the independent Needle-knitters' Syndicate in Tehran organized a march of thousands of workers in their industry to strengthen "the struggles against autocracy and imperialism led by Iranian workers" (*Kayhan*, January 23, 1979). Early in February, twenty-five thousand workers from 124 factories in Alborz participated in a march in Ghazvin to demonstrate their solidarity with the popular struggles.

Strikes combined with bazaar shutdowns and protests disrupted all social and economic activities and paralyzed the government. At the end of December, a central council composed of representatives from twenty-three government ministries and organizations from the private sector was organized to coordinate the strikes. Soon another twenty organizations joined the council. The council formally recognized Khomeini as leader of the people's "anti-imperialist, antidespotic" movement and simultaneously rejected any compromise with Bakhtiar, the Shah's last prime minister, who they claimed represented "imperialism and dictatorship" (*Hambastegi* 1979, nos. 9 and 10). On February 3, parliamentary employees went on strike, followed the next day by employees in the prime minister's office. They declared their solidarity with the popular struggles and denounced government violence and bloodshed (*Kayhan*, February 4, 1979). On February 7, employees of eleven government ministries announced that they would obey only the government of Bazargan, Ayatollah Khomeini's nominee. The monarchy collapsed on February 11, 1979.

CONCLUSION

Our analysis of collective action by workers and white-collar employees has revealed that these classes played crucial parts in the Iranian political conflicts prior to and during the revolution. Their mobilization and collective actions were determined by interests, solidarity structures, and opportunity for collective action. In the early 1950s, the economic crisis adversely affected the interests of workers and white collar employees, leading them to mobilize for collective action. The crisis also deepened the division within the upper class, providing an opportunity for these classes to form an alliance with the liberal modernizers against the few conservatives. The relative political opening of the early 1950s enabled the Tudeh party to reactivate its organizations, which played a role in the mobilization of the working class. The National Front and the Tudeh party were also instrumental in mobilizing white-collar employees during these conflicts. Workers and white-collar employees pursued secular and nationalist politics in their collective actions. Despite clerical opposition to the prime minister, the overwhelming majority of industrial workers supported Dr. Mosaddegh in his conflict with the Shah. Similarly, white-collar employees also backed Mosaddegh.

After 1953, government policies inhibited the rise of solidarity structures among the working classes. Repression prevented workers from forming independent labor organizations, strikes were outlawed, and independent labor leaders were arrested. Most government-run unions operated to control workers' activities and prevent collective action. During the subsequent 1963 uprising led by the clergy, industrial workers and white-collar employees did not engage in collective action. This uprising, which took place immediately following religious ceremonies, provided an opportunity for these classes to join. Perhaps industrial workers were inactive because they believed the reforms would serve their interests and those of the peasantry. White-collar employees also may have favored the reforms, including women's rights. The absence of these classes during these conflicts facilitated the opposition's defeat and the success of repression.

The reforms did not, however, fulfill their promise; the state expanded its intervention in capital accumulation, spent its resources in the interests of the dominant class, and repressed industrial workers to extract more surplus. The inflation of the 1970s adversely affected the interests of workers and white collar employees by increasing living costs. These classes, however, did not have autonomous organizations and solidarity structures to mobilize against the government. The reforms of the fall of 1978 and the government's proclamation of liberalization, initiated in response to bazaari mobilization, provided an opportunity for these classes to mobilize for collective action. The reforms enacted by Sharif-Emami's government actually paved the way for strikes. In promising to improve conditions for other social groups, the new government totally ignored the working-class and white-collar employees, who seized the opportunity to make their own demands.

These classes initially pressed for primarily economic gains. Given the nature of state intervention in capital accumulation, great potential existed for confrontation between strikers and the government and for the politicization of conflicts. Industrial workers had always experienced government repression, which was used to speed up capital accumulation. For workers, the state, rather than the market or fate, was responsible for their troubles and immiserization. They were vividly aware of the connection between their repression and capital accumulation. State intervention removed any possible illusion about the sources of capital accumulation. In addition, because many strikers in large factories were actually employees of the government, the potential for politicization was even greater. Furthermore, the upper echelon of the state bureaucracy was systematically favored with disproportionately higher salaries and special privileges, such as travels abroad and scholarships to international universities. These policies generated strife between the state and lower and middle levels of the bureaucracy. Finally, highly educated segments of the government bureaucracy such as educators and university faculty, lawyers and judges, and employees of government ministries resented the state's authoritarian nature. Therefore, as strikers' solidarity increased and as they found the government vulnerable to attack, some strikers pressed for political changes. White-collar employees and workers in advanced industrial sectors began demanding an end to martial law, the immediate release of all political prisoners, freedom of expression and the press, dissolution of the Savak, punishment of those responsible for massacres, expulsion of certain managers and heads of factories, disbandment of state-run unions, and the formation of independent workers' organizations.

The repression imposed by martial law and the military government failed because by then various segments of these classes had formed some solidarity and networks that could not all be dissolved easily or quickly. In addition, the imposition of the military government escalated the conflicts by forcing bazaaris to begin a long period of strikes. As a result, those workers and employees who had gone back to work resumed their strikes in a matter of weeks. At this stage of the conflict, freedom and independence became their main cry. Industrial workers in large factories and white-collar employees made declarations to the effect that their struggles were antidespotic and anti-imperialist. These classes acknowledged Ayatollah Khomeini's leadership of their movement. At this stage these classes brought about a situation of dual sovereignty. By supporting Ayatollah Khomeini, they laid the foundation for an alternative, competing government. In the process, oil workers played the most crucial role by disrupting the government's revenues, military transportation, industry, and most other activities. They went even further and demanded changes in foreign policy, specifically, withholding oil from South Africa and Israel. Strikes by oil workers guaranteed the collapse of the regime.

In sum, strikes by industrial workers succeeded in disrupting production in all sectors. Walkouts by white-collar employees and professionals, mostly employed by the state, interrupted all public services. The coalition of these classes with bazaaris created a revolutionary situation that eventually led to the overthrow of the monarchy. Without this coalition, it is unlikely that a revolution could have taken place. Yet, workers and white-collar employees cannot be said to have been the instigators of the revolution. Government policies had fragmented these classes. They possessed no independent organization through which to mobilize their resources against the state. Unlike bazaaris, they had no national network of communication to coordinate their activities. Finally, most of them lacked the independent economic resources of the bazaar that might have enabled them to oppose the state without being endangered. As a result, they were obliged to accept the hegemony of others who had struggled for a longer time and possessed greater resources, solidarity structures, and networks. In the next two chapters, we shall analyze the nature of organizations that attempted to gain the hegemony and leadership of these classes.

Chapter 6

The Secular Contenders

We look on the Shah, as you know, as a friend, a loyal ally, and the good relationship that Iran has had and has now with ourselves and with the other democracies in the world, the Western powers, as being very constructive and valuable. Also, having a strong and independent Iran in that area is a very stabilizing factor, and we would hate to see it disrupted by violence and the government fall with an unpredictable result. The Shah has been primarily criticized within Iran because he has tried to democratize the country and because he's instituted social reforms in a very rapid fashion. . . . But I think there's no doubt that Iran has made great social progress and has moved toward a freer expression of people. (President Jimmy Carter, November 13, 1978, quoted in Alexander and Nanes 1980: 462)

In most modern revolutions secular intellectuals have played leading roles in struggles for the establishment of just and rational societies. Because they often actively promote social change and proactive collective action, they have achieved dominant positions in most social movements.

The Iranian secular contenders for power, unlike those in other revolutions such as the Russian, Cuban, and Nicaraguan revolutions, failed to attain leadership in the revolution, although they initiated the conflicts of the revolutionary period of 1977–1979. At the time of the revolution, two secular organizations existed, each with a different political program. The first was the National Front, which had been revived in early 1977, and the second was the Organization of the Iranian People's Fedayee Guerrillas (Fedayeen), formed in 1964. Both organizations had faced repression and had been declared illegal during the 1960s and 1970s. Consequently, when the revolutionary conflicts began, both organizations had a limited membership and network, which in turn restricted their resources for mobilization. In addition, their narrow political positions did not incorporate the demands made by all the major actors in the revolutionary conflict. For example, the National Front and other liberal organizations demanded political freedom and formal democracy, but were hesitant to advocate overthrow of the monarchy. This stance did not attract segments of the bazaar, the working class, or students, who favored a more radical political course. When the National Front finally did call for the Shah's ouster, it emphasized independence and political freedom but ignored issues of economic inequality and social justice. In contrast, the Fedayeen espoused the more radical views of economic equality and social justice, which would have required a major restructuring of political and economic power. Their programs, however, were unacceptable to the vast majority of merchants and shopkeepers, for whom private property was inviolable. As a result, neither of these organizations was able to gain the leadership of the movement that overthrew the Shah.

This chapter will examine the politics of these two organizations, one liberal and the other leftist, as well as the Writers' Association, which also played a part in the political mobilization of 1977–1979. Some scholars of the social breakdown model, including Green, have placed great emphasis on the contributions of the middle class and their political organizations, such as the National Front. My analysis will demonstrate, however, that the National Front had restricted resources and pursued policies that did not win popular support. Hence, the National Front was unable to play a leading role in the political conflicts.

THE NATIONAL FRONT

The National Front was never an organized political party in the sense of possessing formal structures, networks, and a disciplined membership. During the 1950s, while in power and able to exert an influence on the media, the Front made a significant contribution by mobilizing the population against the monarchy and the British. When Mosaddegh was ousted as prime minister in 1953, however, the Front was outlawed and many of its leaders, including Mosaddegh, were imprisoned. Dr. Fatemi, Mosaddegh's foreign minister, was executed. With the imprisonment and exile of many of its leading members, the National Front was unable to maintain a strong stand against the Shah. Its capacity for mobilization and political activities was drastically reduced as a result of repression.

In 1960, during a brief period of liberalization permitted by the Shah, some of Mosaddegh's followers established the second National Front. The Front was composed of four political organizations: the Iran party, the National party, the Society of Socialists, and the Freedom Movement. They were able to acquire two designated locations to meet, plan, and coordinate their activities. The Front still had the support of the vast majority of bazaaris and the universities. In May 1961, the Front organized a rally in Tehran attended by eighty thousand people. Although the Front had decided not to attack any element of the government but to wait instead for conflict between the Shah and his prime minister to intensify, Bakhtiar violated this policy during the rally and attacked Prime Minister Amini. Bakhtiar's speech prompted government repression and led to the arrest of some of the Front's leaders. This rally was the first and last legal event held by the Front. The Front was still able to call for a few actions in which university students and bazaaris participated, but by the end of January 1963 most Front leaders and activists were imprisoned, while a few had gone underground.

By the time of the uprising of June 1963, the Front had been badly repressed. Still worse, when most of the Front's leaders were released from prison a few months after the uprising, they prevented students from holding demonstrations scheduled for early September (Jazani 1979:131–132). The Front had already expelled approximately ninety leftist students from its youth organization and thereby weakened its support among university students. For whatever reason, students called off the September demonstrations but broke away from the Front, never to follow them again. In 1965, there was an attempt to establish a third National Front. The Savak promptly arrested and jailed the organizers, who were later released when they signed statements agreeing not to engage in political activities. Their actions were perhaps due in part to the repression of the popular uprising, but as a result the Front was virtually discredited, especially among university students. In the twelve years that followed, the Front did not issue a single statement on the political situation. During these years very few, if any, members of the National Front were jailed. Taher Ahmad Zadeh's imprisonment for seven years was due to the activities of his sons, one of whom was a Fedayeen leader (*Kayhan*, October 28, 1978).

The Shah ordered that repression be eased somewhat in 1977, which provided an opportunity for opposition organizations to resume their activities. Highly dependent on the United States, the Shah decided to institute some changes to stay in the good graces of President Carter, who had addressed the issue of human rights in Iran during his presidential campaign. In March, the Shah granted amnesty to 256 political prisoners; one month later, he condemned the use of torture and allowed the International Red Cross to visit political prisoners. In June, the leaders of the Rastakhiz party declared that they would welcome "free discussion" and constructive criticism. Most importantly, a law was passed specifying that those arrested for political activities could not be held for more than twenty-four hours without charge. In addition, such persons would have to be tried in civilian rather than military courts.

Although minor changes did take place, Iranian society still did not offer favorable conditions for the political opposition. Political organizations were not allowed to form or to mobilize support. Freedom of the press and of expression were nonexistent. When two journalists wrote a letter to Prime Minister Amuzegar protesting the lack of freedom of the press, they lost their jobs (*Zamimeh* 1978, no. 16:53). Free elections did not exist, nor was there any separation of powers within the government. Although physical torture was reduced in prisons, psychological punishments were frequently applied.[1] The government insisted that conditions in jails had improved and that torture was absent. Political prisoners, however, contested these assertions by going on hunger strikes (*Zamimeh* 1978, no. 14:18).

National Front activists, recognizing the dimensions of the economic crisis of 1977 and the vulnerability of the government, quickly took advantage of the very limited opportunity and began to organize for a second time to form a third National Front. Initially, approximately fifteen persons gathered to plan Front activities from scratch. A comparison with the situation of the Front in its heyday in the early 1950s reveals the weaknesses of the Front in the 1970s. The Front had flourished during the political conflicts of the 1950s, attained a position of power, and had access to the media. In 1977, they had no such resources. Nor did the political situation as yet permit open political opposition on a large scale. The Front had no specific, safe location in which members and supporters could gather to discuss political issues, communicate decisions, coordinate activities, and mobilize for collective action. Because they lacked such an infrastructure, Front leaders acted secretively in the early stages, thereby reducing their capacity for communication and mobilization. The Front's leaders had decreased considerably in number. By 1978, nine of the twenty founders of the original National Front, including Mosaddegh, had either died, abandoned politics, or left the country (*Ettelaat*, October 31, 1978). Of the remainder, only Karim Sanjabi, then head of the Front, was active. Bazargan, a member of the National Front during Mosaddegh's time, had formed the Freedom Movement and did not join the Front in 1977, although he cooperated with them.

Furthermore, the National Front remained concentrated in Tehran and exerted little influence in the rest of the country. Its networks had been dissolved during the years of repression and inactivity. Mobilization in Tehran alone, although significant, would not have been sufficient to mount a political challenge, especially against a regime that had proven itself capable of repression. A national network that could have been mobilized during political confrontation might have led to a consolidation of forces and neutralization of repression. Without a national network, however, the Front's capacity for national mobilization and confrontation was significantly reduced. In addition, even in Tehran the Front's primary network was restricted to a fraction of the bazaar, along with white-collar employees and professionals. Finally, the Front lagged behind the pace of the uprising by failing to call for the overthrow of the regime when the popular struggles in the streets generated shouts of Death to the Shah.

On June 12, 1977, three leaders of the then-outlawed National Front published a statement announcing "the demands of the Iranian people." Five months later, a third National Front was formally organized by three parties that had been banned by the regime, including the Iran party, Iran People's party, and the Society of Socialists. This third incarnation of the National Front was composed of lawyers, liberal intellectuals, professionals, and holders of medium-sized capital in the private sector. They invited other groups to organize and join them. The central demands of the National Front consisted of political changes and reforms. "The Shah should reign, not rule," they said, as was the arrangement during Mosaddegh's period. On July 21, 1978, the Front's Provisional Central Council proclaimed its basic principles: independence from all chains of imperialism, personal and social freedoms, and an independent foreign policy. The

Front condemned Iran's economic dependence, the imperialist exploitation of the country's resources, and foreign cultural domination. Instead, the Front proposed establishing a society free from dictatorship and foreign domination. Most members of the National Front would have been satisfied had the constitution been implemented as written. Their politics had not changed since the 1950s.

The Front had some allies in the private sector and the bazaar, specifically the Tehran bazaar. These were mostly holders of medium-sized capital who had long been dissatisfied with the government's capital-allocation policies, which favored big capital. They had been denied government grants, subsidies, and favors. In addition, they were excluded from the most profitable sectors of business and industry by the government's licensing policy, which protected big capital and monopolies by limiting competition. This group within the bazaar was directly mobilized by the SMGATB, which was very active in mobilizing the bazaar during the initial bazaar strikes. Leaders of this organization were also members of the National Front.

Outside the bazaar, the Front had some supporters and sympathizers who had little organization. Their supporters included a small group of students, some white-collar employees and professionals, some teachers, and a group of army officers.[2] Some of the officers distributed several statements against the Shah's regime; in some of their proclamations, they disclosed the names of twenty officers who were working as spies within the armed forces. When General Abbas Ghara-Baghi became the new joint chief of staff of the armed forces, replacing Azhari, officers who supported the National Front condemned the new chief of staff. They reiterated their support for the Front and Dr. Mosaddegh and announced their readiness to sacrifice themselves for the people.

Nonetheless, these supporters of the Front represented only fragments of classes or social strata. They did not even have the support of the vast majority of bazaaris. Their support was very limited among students and the young generation, who had little familiarity with the Front. Their ignorance was understandable because of the Front's capitulation to repression and retreat from politics after 1963. Significantly, there was no statement of support for the Front from any segment of the industrial working class. Because the National Front was tied to the capitalist class and represented its interests, the Front made no attempt to mobilize the working class, which played such a crucial role in the downfall of the regime. Regionally, backing for the National Front was very narrow. Only some educators in scattered regions such as Azerbaijan indicated support. For these reasons, the National Front was limited in its ability to mobilize the opposition.

Because the Front lacked a broad base of social support and a widespread network, it was obliged to cooperate with the clergy during the revolutionary conflicts. The Front supported and participated in mourning ceremonies. Significantly, in almost every mourning ceremony the National Front invited its backers to join the event only after it had first been announced by the clergy because the clerics were the ones who ran the mosques and their networks.

More importantly, the National Front failed to keep pace with the popular struggles and the escalation of conflicts that took place during the liberalization promised by Sharif-Emami's government at the end of August 1978. On September 4, bazaari supporters of the National Front, Maniyan and Lebaschi, organized the special prayer at the end of the fasting month of Ramadan. The Front and the Freedom Movement also participated in the event. The clergy led the prayer, of course, as it was a religious ceremony. After the prayer, the organizers announced that the event had concluded and asked participants to disperse (Lebaschi 1983, tape 3:4). The crowd refused to disperse, however, and instead began a march toward the center of Tehran. During this event, marchers numbering several hundred thousand shouted the radical slogan Death to the Shah. The large size of the demonstration reduced the risk of repression. With the resource of large numbers, the demonstrators moved one step ahead of the government by demanding revolution while the government was announcing mere reform. At this critical point, the Front hesitated to escalate its program and failed to call for the overthrow of the monarchy.

The Front did not, of course, accept the government of Sharif-Emami. Within two days after Sharif-Emami had been appointed, the National Front rejected his government, declaring that the only acceptable government was one whose members were free from any association with the past twenty-five years of dictatorship and imperialism. The Front reiterated its usual demands for reform, including the elimination of military trials for civilian indictments; an independent judiciary; release of all political prisoners; return of all exiles and others who had fled the country; freedom of association, thought, and the press; independent labor organizations; and dissolution of government labor unions and the Otagh-e Asnaf, or Chamber of Guilds, which controlled prices. Although Sharif-Emami had promised some of these same liberal reforms, the National Front rejected any compromise with him and held out instead for the chance to form their own government. At that time, however, the Shah was unwilling to invite them to participate in the government.

Despite rapidly escalating conflicts and ever more radical demonstrations, the National Front failed to call for the overthrow of the government. As late as November 1, Sanjabi, head of the National Front, still had not completely rejected the monarchy as an institution, though he expressed doubts about its future. He declared that the new government, which they hoped would succeed Sharif-Emami, could be either a republic or a monarchy as long as it was democratic. As Sanjabi himself admitted, the Front lagged behind the popular movement and failed to take the initiative in directing the opposition (*Kayhan*, November 1, 1978).

Eventually the leaders of the National Front, recognizing that conflict was mounting, abandoned their reformist position and adopted a revolutionary stance. In part, this shift was prompted by the growing strength of the anti-Shah movement. By autumn of 1978, industrial workers and white-collar employees had joined the opposition to the regime. The National Front's shift toward revolution was also partly in response to the killing of sixty-five students and injury of even more (M. J. 1979:65) by the army on the campus of Tehran University on November 4, an event broadcast on national television. In retaliation, students set fire to numerous government buildings and offices throughout Tehran the next day. That day, Sanjabi flew to Paris and met with Ayatollah Khomeini, who had remained intransigent in his opposition to the Shah. Khomeini pressured Sanjabi to change his stand and reject the monarch. At this meeting, Sanjabi signed a public declaration that the Shah's regime lacked any legal basis for violating Islamic laws; that the nationalist Islamic movement would not compromise with any form of government as long as the monarchy remained; and finally, that the government must be both democratic, that is, determined by popular vote, and based on Islamic rules. Sanjabi's declaration represented an explicit alliance with Khomeini's forces against the Shah.

Sanjabi's decision to link up with Khomeini led the Shah to move against the alliance, and he quickly dismissed Sharif-Emami and appointed a military government. Sanjabi and Dariush Forouhar were the two National Front leaders most in favor of joining with Khomeini.[3] On November 11, as they were about to hold a news conference, they were arrested. Despite repression, they refused to cooperate with the government, and within a month both men were released from prison. A few days later, Sanjabi was summoned by the head of the Savak and taken to the

Niavaran Palace, where he was asked by the Shah to accept the premiership. Sanjabi refused and informed the monarch that the only solution to the political crisis was for him to step down. Gholamhossein Sadighi, a university professor and former cabinet member under Mosaddegh, was then approached by the Shah. As rumors spread that he might accept the post, the National Front reiterated that no cooperation was possible with an illegal monarch and that Sadighi was no longer to be considered a member of the Front. Eventually, Shahpour Bakhtiar, who had spent more than five years in the Shah's jails, accepted the premiership. Bakhtiar immediately proclaimed freedom of the press; as a result, striking newspapers resumed publication after a walkout of sixty-two days. He also released from Savak prisons the last nine hundred political prisoners, most of whom were members of leftist organizations, including Masoud Rajavi, the leader of the Mojahedeen. Bakhtiar's acceptance of the premiership was extremely damaging to the public image of the National Front, which by then was calling for the overthrow of the monarch. As a consequence, Bakhtiar was immediately expelled from the Front.

By this time, it was clear that the Front had fallen behind Khomeini and the masses who had participated in major demonstrations following Sharif-Emami's appointment. During the premiership of Bakhtiar, one of their ex-allies, the Front might have been able to initiate independent action in the wake of dramatically reduced repression. But once again the Front failed to take the initiative. In early January 1979, the Front called for a national day of mourning for those killed in the previous week. When Ayatollah Khomeini announced that the mourning would be held on a later day, January 7, the Front called off its own mourning observance and instead declared that the day Khomeini had chosen would be the day of mourning.[4] On January 7, the Front held a ceremony to mark the anniversary of the death eleven years earlier of Takhti, a world champion wrestler whose death in 1968 was widely believed to have been at the hands of the Savak. Takhti had been a member of the National Front and immensely popular. Thousands of people, including Ayatollah Taleghani, turned out for the mourning ceremony at Takhti's grave. This event was perhaps the peak of the Front's mobilization during the revolutionary struggles of 1977–1979.

Although the National Front had some influence in the initial stages of the political events that led up to the revolution, they were unable to attain the revolution's leadership for several reasons. In the first place, they had bowed to repression in 1963 and abandoned politics thereafter. This policy alienated students and the universities, which had been an important source of backing for the Front. When the Front was revived in 1977, they were limited to a few regions, especially Tehran, and lacked any network for mobilization throughout much of the rest of the country. While the Front had some support in the bazaar and among white-collar employees and professionals, they had little backing from students and no support among industrial workers. Finally, the Front failed to keep pace with the popular struggles when they were needed to call for the overthrow of the Shah.

THE WRITERS' ASSOCIATION AND POETRY NIGHTS

While the National Front represented one constituency that vied for political power, other organizations were formed to promote certain changes in the social system. These groups included the Lawyers' Association, the Committee in Defense of Freedom and Human Rights in Iran, and the Writers' Association. These organizations were formed in 1977 after the Shah proclaimed reforms for political arrestees. The Writers' Association was the most influential of these groups and played some role in mobilizing students.

The Writers' Association had originally been formed in 1967 but was soon dissolved by the government, which arrested a number of its members. The new association planned to press for freedom of expression and the elimination of press censorship. Their first statement, in June 1977, was an open letter to the prime minister, signed by forty poets and writers, requesting official recognition of the Writers' Association. They received no response. Over the next weeks, the organization attracted more members, and in July, ninety-eight members repeated their demands in another open letter, which criticized censorship and asked for permission to publish their own independent journal. At its peak, the association numbered approximately two hundred intellectuals holding wide-ranging political ideologies. Among them were liberal intellectuals and poets who supported the National Front, religious writers, communist writers formerly affiliated with the Tudeh party, and independent socialists and Marxists. In the early stages, the liberals and reformists predominated, but gradually leftists came to exert greater influence. Saeed Soltanpour, the well-known Marxist poet and playwright, joined this organization the day after he was released from jail. He became the association's secretary and one of its most influential members. Several other well-known secular leftists, such as Ahmad Shamloo, Gholamhossein Sa'di, Manouchehr Hezar-Khani, and Homa Nategh, were among the elected officials and activists of the association.

Among the most important contributions of the association were sixteen poetry nights that resulted in political mobilization. Persian poetry, with its rich symbolism, has historically been a means of political expression under repressive situations. Revolutionary poetry played a particularly important part in the conflict against the monarchy, perhaps because the realm of imagination represented the only potentially liberated area of individual life. Revolutionary poetry composed by leftist members of the Writers' Association was easily memorized and transmitted, and remained the only unrestricted medium of expression in an otherwise highly repressive environment. The greatest impact of revolutionary poetry was upon university students and the young, who became allies of the Writers' Association. Eight to ten thousand enthusiastic college students, some carrying tape recorders, participated in the poetry nights held by the association in the fall of 1977.

The most dramatic event of the poetry nights occurred the evening Soltanpour was to speak. The organizers had sent out two thousand invitations, but ten thousand people showed up to hear the talk. The police prevented the rest from entering the university. There was a confrontation between thousands of these people and the police outside the doors. Fifty students who had been denied permission to enter the amphitheater were arrested. To protest this act of government repression, Soltanpour refused to give his scheduled speech on art and its influence on society and instead read one of his most revolutionary poems, written while he was incarcerated in a Savak jail. His reading generated great excitement. A massive overnight sit-in was spontaneously organized inside the amphitheater and just outside the door to protest the students' arrests. The building that held the amphitheater was surrounded all night and into the morning by police, who threatened more arrests if the demonstrators refused to disperse. Throughout the night, those inside sang revolutionary songs such as "Siahkal" and the International (Nategh 1982).[5] In the morning a message of solidarity was sent by workers from south Tehran and read to the audience. The protesters then left the amphitheater for a street demonstration during which several students were slain or injured in clashes with the police. Three days later students called for a national day of mourning. Tehran merchants quickly responded by closing down the entire bazaar.

That day more demonstrations took place and additional people were killed and injured (*Zamimeh* 1978, no. 8:21). These events, which took place in the fall of 1977, gave a significant boost to the opposition by resulting in the closure of the bazaar, an event unheard of in more than a decade.

In response, the government embarked upon a policy of repression toward the Writers' Association. It immediately put an end to the poetry nights and proceeded to intimidate some of its members. Following these conflicts, the Savak arrested two members, Professor Homa Nategh, a leftist historian at Tehran University, and Na'mat Mir-Zadeh, a well-known poet, and took them to the police station for questioning. After their release, they entered a taxi parked outside the police station, not knowing it belonged to the Savak. Nategh and Mir-Zadeh were driven to a distant suburb of Tehran where a waiting gang of agents beat them up and abandoned them. After the gang left, people who had witnessed the event from a safe distance took Nategh and Mir-Zadeh to a hospital. Both were badly injured, and Mir-Zadeh was unconscious for several days.

The prohibition of poetry nights blocked the Writers' Association's capacity for mobilization. Once it was no longer allowed to gather an audience together under one roof, it had little capacity to organize the opposition or broadcast repression by the government. The association survived, however, with a more radical leadership, which continued to issue statements against the government. With the intensification of the struggles, the leadership of the Writers' Association shifted to the Left, leading some twenty writers who opposed the new tendencies to break away from the association.[6] The vast majority, however, remained in the association, which kept informal ties with radical student groups in the universities.

The Writers' Association played a crucial role by attacking the government in the initial stage of the conflict when it appeared unassailable. Although at its inception the association was mainly concerned with issues of freedom of expression and elimination of censorship, it moved beyond them and ultimately presented a clear challenge to the regime. The poetry nights attracted thousands of university students who, in turn, became important vehicles of mobilization against the government later on. Yet the Writers' Association was at a disadvantage because it was not a political organization with disciplined members and supporters or with networks that could challenge the existing power structure. Its membership was confined to writers and poets, a small category of people, and concentrated largely in Tehran. These factors limited the association's capacity to develop networks and link up with broad segments of the population. Once repression put an end to the poetry nights, writers were unable to extend their influence to any great degree.

THE IRANIAN PEOPLE'S FEDAYEE GUERRILLAS

The repression of 1962 and 1963 led the revolutionary Left to form a number of guerrilla organizations to wage armed struggle against the government.[7] One of the most significant groups formed during this period was the Iranian People's Fedayee Guerrillas, known popularly as the Fedayeen. They were formed in the mid-1960s, and began their armed struggle in the 1970s. The founders were mainly young Marxist students who had broken away from the Tudeh party and the National Front.[8] From the beginning, two factions existed within the Fedayeen. One, led by Bizhan Jazani, emphasized political organizing. The other, headed by Masoud Ahmadzadeh and Amir Parviz Pouyan, advocated armed struggle. After much deliberation, the Fedayeen concluded that armed struggle was the only means to fight the Shah's regime. Pouyan stated their position as follows: "Given the circumstances that the people's revolutionary intellectuals lack all types of direct and firm relations with their masses, our situation is not like the example of fish living in the sea of the people's support. . . . Terror, suppression, and the absence of any democratic conditions have made the establishment of relations with our own people extremely difficult." He argued that helplessness and resignation pervaded the proletariat as a result of the absolute domination of the enemy, which forced workers to submit to bourgeois culture. To liberate the working class from the dominant culture and terminate its alienation, it was necessary to "shatter its illusion that it is powerless to destroy the enemy." This, he proposed, could be done only through armed struggle carried out by the proletarian vanguard (Pouyan 1975:31–35).

In 1971, in an attempt to implement a program based on their ideology, the Fedayeen sent a team of thirteen guerrillas, most of whom originally had been trained in Palestine, to the mountainous region of Gilan. They planned to spend one year establishing bases and forming links with the region's peasants, who had a history of radicalism and rebelliousness. Soon after entering the region, two Fedayeen sympathizers were arrested. The guerrillas attempted to liberate their comrades and prevent them from revealing information under torture. They attacked the gendarmerie of

Siahkal, but did not find their comrades. After killing three gendarmes and expropriating weapons and ammunition, they withdrew into the mountains.

The Shah's response to the raid was out of proportion to the threat it posed. He sent his brother at the head of a large army equipped with highly sophisticated weapons to destroy the handful of guerrillas. The army sealed off the entire region, checked every movement, and set the jungle on fire in many areas where penetration proved impossible. Finally, after three weeks of fighting that left thirty soldiers and two guerrillas dead, the regime announced the capture of the remaining eleven guerrillas. Ten were sent to face the firing squad, while Ali Akbar Farahani, the team's commander, died under torture. Immediately following the Siahkal incident, the government arrested fifty-one left-wing dissidents, none of whom was connected to the Fedayeen, and installed security guards in all the universities to control student political activities. More than one hundred thousand dollars was offered in reward to anyone providing information on guerrilla suspects. In the meantime, the Savak intensified its search for Fedayeen members. Partly because they were unable to eliminate the organization immediately, the Savak arrested and executed two prominent Marxist intellectuals, Khosrow Golsorkhi, a journalist and poet, and Karamat Daneshian, for "plotting to kidnap the royal family."

The Fedayeen's Marxist ideology and tactics of armed struggle made them a serious threat in the eyes of the regime, which dealt harshly with them. The Savak had 20,000 members and approximately 180,000 paid informers (*Time*, August 16, 1976) who diligently searched for members and sympathizers of the regime's political opponents, especially the Fedayeen and other guerrilla organizations. Whenever they discovered the whereabouts of any member of the Fedayeen, every attempt was made to arrest them alive so they could be displayed on television and, more importantly, provide further information about the organization. The Fedayeen organization, in turn, supplied guerrillas with cyanide pills to commit suicide if arrested. Fedayeen who were taken alive were subjected to the most brutal torture in the Savak prisons. Indeed, no group suffered as much torture or as many deaths as did the Fedayeen. Several Fedayeen leaders died under torture, including Behrouz Dehghani, Shahroukh Hedayati, and Ghafoor Hasanpoor-Asl. These gross violations of human rights in Iran led the Geneva-based International Commission of Jurists to report that such violations, including torture, had "taken place on an unprecedented scale."[9]

Despite repression, the Fedayeen carried out several operations, including political assassinations. Among their victims were Fateh Yazdi, a millionaire industrialist instrumental in the repression and death of many of his workers, and Nik-Tab, a Savak torturer. The organization was also responsible for attacking police headquarters and bombing American establishments and the Iran and American Society. Although these actions had little political impact, they attracted considerable support for the Fedayeen among the youth, especially college students. When the Fedayeen killed Farsiew, the chief military prosecutor who had ordered the execution of ten Fedayee guerrillas following the Siahkal incident, university students in Tehran poured into the streets shouting, "Farsiew, your death is welcome!"

Much of the Fedayeen's following came from the universities; yet even there, Fedayeen supporters were in the minority until the regime fell and even for a few months after the revolution. They received their strongest support in Tehran, Tabriz, Abadan, Shiraz, and in the region of the Caspian Sea. In October 1978, approximately five thousand Fedayeen supporters demonstrated on the university campus in Tabriz in solidarity with workers and peasants (*Kayhan*, October 9, 1978). Another rally held in the soccer field at Tehran University also drew five thousand students. Demonstrators shouted pro-Fedayeen slogans and displayed a picture of Khosrow Rouzbeh, a communist executed by the Shah in the 1950s. Statements of support from other organizations, including the Writers' Association, were read during the rally (*Kayhan*, October 26, 1978). At a demonstration of some two thousand Fedayeen supporters in Rasht, students carried pictures of martyred Fedayeen and shouted, "The only route for liberation is unity with the Fedayeen!"

The organization of the Fedayeen had certain structural weaknesses. The membership was relatively small and drawn primarily from the intelligentsia. In a sample of 125 Fedayeen who were killed in battle, under torture, or by execution, 60 percent were university students or college graduates. Physicians and engineers accounted for 10 percent, while teachers constituted 8 percent of the sample. Government employees were 7 percent of the sample, while only 10 percent were industrial workers. The uneven distribution of the Fedayeen's membership resulted from the timing of their formation, which was not conducive to attracting large numbers of students and workers or to establishing networks. Also, the period during which the Fedayeen was formed was a highly repressive time in which insignificant political actions such as distributing political leaflets were punished by seven to eight years of imprisonment. In 1975, when the regime's Rastakhiz party was founded, the Shah declared: "Those who believe in the Iranian Constitution, the Monarchical regime, and the principles of the White Revolution, must join the new party. Those who do not believe in these principles are traitors who must either go to prison or leave the country" (Ghotbi 1978:18). Such a repressive atmosphere had already prevailed and put an end to all political mobilization when the Fedayeen were organized. Thus, the Fedayeen had no public forum to state their programs and attained no recognition among the general population or the working class. Whereas the Tudeh party and the National Front had both flourished during periods of relaxed repression, the Fedayeen did not have that advantage.

Another related problem encountered by the Fedayeen in mobilizing was that they were concentrated in a few areas only, where they operated underground. As a result, their influence was largely limited to Tehran and several other major cities. Data on arrests and executions of Fedayeen members indicate that nearly 85 percent of them were located in the capital. A small number of operations were carried out outside of Tehran in other cities with universities.[10] In the twelve months prior to the Shah's ouster, the Fedayeen launched sixteen armed raids on the police, army, and the Savak, all of which took place in a few major cities, including Tehran, Mashhad, Tabriz, Qom, Sanandaj, and Zanjan (OIPFG 1978b). Seven attacks were carried out in Tehran alone. Finally, much of their armed struggle took place during periods of heightened oil revenues rather than during economic decline or crisis, which might have increased their chances to mobilize support.

By the early stages of the revolutionary conflict, the Fedayeen were already too weakened by relentless government repression to have much influence on political developments. From their initial confrontation in Siahkal until the downfall of the regime, 207 Fedayeen were killed in battle, under torture, or by execution. Between 1971 and 1975 alone, 120 were slain. In 1976, the government intensified its already fierce attack and destroyed 65 more guerrillas. Several of those killed in the summer of 1976, including Hamid Ashraf, were leading members of the organization. From 1977 to 1979, another 22 were killed. Although Sharif-Emami's government freed some jailed clerics and National Front members, it did not release any Fedayeen prisoners; on the contrary, still more leftist supporters and sympathizers were arrested. No other political organization suffered comparable losses prior to the revolution.

Government repression was not the only obstacle encountered by the

Fedayeen. Religious groups also occasionally hampered their mobilization and collective actions. On December 11, 1978, on Ashoura, an important Shia day of mourning, a group of religious protesters disrupted a demonstration in Tabriz of two thousand workers, teachers, and students. The religious protesters countered the proworker and anti-imperialist slogans of the demonstrators by shouting, "The only party is God's party; the only leader is Khomeini!" In Tehran, an Islamic group broke up a leftist demonstration (*Kayhan*, January 16, 1979). About two weeks before Ayatollah Khomeini returned to Iran, the Fedayeen sent him an open letter protesting these disruptive tactics by extremist religious groups (*Kayhan*, January 21, 1979).

The dynamics of political development did not favor the Fedayeen because the reforms of Sharif-Emami were not extended to communist organizations. These groups continued to be unable to initiate political activities openly or to mobilize. Only in the final weeks of the revolutionary conflicts when Bakhtiar came to power did the Fedayeen's position improve somewhat. Many of their leaders and members were released from prison, and others who had left the country returned. As political repression was reduced and an opportunity was provided for political activities, the Fedayeen were able to mobilize greater support. Their emphasis on social justice and equality, combined with their heroic struggles during years of repression, made them an organization that appealed to students and workers. On February 10, 1979, the eighth anniversary of the Siakhal incident, they held a demonstration at Tehran University that, according to the press, drew more than 50,000 participants. They received statements of support from several groups, including factory workers, the Air Force Cadets, communications employees, physicians, university students, faculty, and others (*Ayandegan*, February 11, 1979). Although a promonarchy speaker had charged on the radio that the Fedayeen were demanding a share of the revolutionary government, this was denied at the rally. Instead, the Fedayeen declared that the Revolutionary Council should be composed of millions of strikers. A few days after the revolution, the Fedayeen held another rally at Tehran University that drew more than 150,000 people (*Ayandegan*, February 24, 1979). Although power had already been transferred by then, this rally indicated that the Fedayeen had become a strong political force capable of mobilizing large numbers of supporters. Had the course of the revolutionary conflict lasted longer and required armed struggle to overthrow the monarchy, the Fedayeen might have been able to play a larger role in the revolution's outcome.

In sum, the Fedayeen were formed during the period following the repression and defeat of all political organizations. Repression greatly decreased the possibility of political activity. The Fedayeen's limited operation during these years did not enable them to establish a widespread network of members and sympathizers. Once the Fedayeen inaugurated armed struggle, the regime responded with still greater repressive measures. The Fedayeen suffered many losses in their confrontations with the army and were forced to move deeper underground, which made their activities even more difficult. As a consequence, by the time of the revolution the Fedayeen were in no position to direct the mobilization of the working classes and lacked a broad enough base of support to have much of an impact on the collapse of the monarchy. Even within the universities, their influence was not very great. Finally, as a Marxist organization opposed to capitalism and private property, the Fedayeen were incapable of gaining the confidence and allegiance of most bazaaris. In the absence of a strong working-class movement to lead the revolutionary opposition, an alliance between the leftist Fedayeen and bazaar merchants and shopkeepers would have been highly unlikely.

CONCLUSION

What factors account for the emergence in the 1970s of groups such as the National Front and the Writers' Association? One possible answer is that the way was paved by a combination of President Carter's stand on human rights and the Shah's liberalization policies. When these organizations began their activities, however, the Shah had not really liberalized the political system. As mentioned above, he released only approximately two hundred political prisoners and changed the trial procedure for political activists. This can scarcely be called liberalization. The Shah was not willing to implement any fundamental changes. In August of 1977, after a brief period of so-called liberalization, he declared, "Democracy is not a commodity to be imported into Iran; for us, only the Iranian meaning of democracy is practicable" (*Ettelaat*, August, 6, 1977). A few days later he stated, "Only by supporting the monarchy can people attain political freedom" (*Kayhan*, August 17, 1977). In a country where growing numbers of commodities such as meat, rice, grain, and most industrial goods, not to mention the Shah's own throne and rulership, were imported from abroad, the monarch opposed the importation of liberal democracy.

The Carter administration, which had not really pressured the Shah to liberalize, quickly took note of superficial changes and praised the monarch for his shift in policy. United States Ambassador William Sullivan called the above alterations in the legal system positive steps toward the betterment of human rights in Iran. On a state visit to the Shah in the final days of 1977, President Carter noted, "The cause of human rights is one that also is shared deeply by our people and by the leaders of our two nations" (1978:2221). The Carter administration, which had sold seven AWACS airplanes to the Shah, supported the monarch throughout the revolutionary conflict. Two days after the Shah's troops massacred several hundred people in Tehran on September 8, 1978, Carter telephoned him to reaffirm continued U.S. support. In a press conference a month later, Carter again voiced his strong support for the Shah's regime in the words quoted at the opening of this chapter. The Carter administration also gave full backing to the decision to install a military government on November 6. As late as December 12, President Carter reiterated his support for the Shah, accusing Ayatollah Khomeini of exacerbating the crisis by encouraging "bloodshed and violence." In all, little if any credit can be assigned to Carter's policies on human rights as a factor in generating opposition against the regime.

It was not Carter's pressure after he took office, but rather the Shah's interpretation of the United States government's policy that led the monarch to introduce minor changes in the legal system. The leaders of the National Front, aware of the severity of the internal crisis and that conditions were ripe for mobilization, took advantage of the opportunity provided by legal reforms and began organizing. None of the members of the organizations that opposed the regime had any illusions that the United States State Department would help gain their release from Savak prisons. Most intellectuals who belonged to these organizations were highly educated. They had defied the Shah on previous occasions and most also had firsthand knowledge of the Savak's heavy hand. They could testify that Carter's principles of human rights had long been a part of the Iranian constitution without having had any measurable effect. They had no choice but to operate under these constraints and take advantage of a very small opportunity for action. At the same time, those same conditions handicapped their efforts to mobilize for opposition.

The National Front was the first organization to mobilize against the government by issuing a number of statements that challenged dictatorship and imperialism. The Front advocated the establishment of a liberal democracy but lacked both the resources and networks needed to neutralize the government's repression. Thus, the Front increasingly turned to the mosques and to mourning ceremonies in order to mobilize against the government. They were forced to borrow preexisting networks to mobilize because repression made it extremely difficult to establish new ones. The Front's ability to mobilize increased when Sharif-Emami's government proclaimed liberalization and granted permission for opposition political parties to be formed. During this same decisive period, however, the Front lost control over the opposition leadership because they failed to keep pace with the rapid escalation of conflict, the entry of the working classes into the opposition movement, and popular calls for the Shah's overthrow during the major demonstrations of this period. Although the Front did not retain the leadership of the struggles, they remained a junior partner in the ruling bloc because many of their leaders had government experience and, more importantly, because the Front had ties to segments of the bazaar as well as to white-collar and professional employees. These factors enabled the Front to claim a share of power in the provisional government that followed the Shah's ouster.

The Fedayeen, on the other hand, failed to gain the leadership of the opposition movement for somewhat different reasons. They had been formed during a period of intense repression, which prevented them from publicizing their programs and from mobilizing. Their tactic of armed struggle led to further repression, forcing them deeper underground. This, in turn, reduced their ties to the working classes in whose interests they claimed to fight. Instead, they remained underground with limited networks and resources. Furthermore, they lacked an economic base for their operations. Their raids on banks to finance their activities resulted in greater sacrifice, because some of their members were killed or arrested during these attacks. Their advocacy of the overthrow of the monarchy and the establishment of a socialist state could not have been supported by bazaaris. Merchants and shopkeepers defend private property and social stratification as positive social institutions and do not see the abolition of private property as in their class interests. As discussed in chapter 4, bazaaris were the principal social class behind the opposition. Because the bazaaris did not back them, the Fedayeen could not gain the leadership in the struggle against the Shah. Had a strong, well-organized movement of the working classes existed, different results might have been expected. In the absence of such a working-class movement, the Fedayeen failed to gain hegemony over the opposition forces.

In sum, two organizations represented different constituencies and struggled for different outcomes. The National Front was tied to the bazaar and medium-sized capital, while the Fedayeen were tied to students and fought in the interests of the working classes. As a result, these two organizations never attempted to form a coalition. Both organizations operated underground for at least part of the time during their struggles against the regime. Hence, both lacked the resources and networks necessary to mobilize the opposition. A long period of repression prevented both organizations from mobilizing significant resources against the regime. Instead, the mobilization took place through the mosque, where a fraction of the clergy played a crucial role in the political conflicts.

Chapter 7

The Mosque and Islamic Forces

The heads of the community should guide and support the people who have found their own way, have recognized the enemy, and have revolted. In this sensitive period they should not, through their deviations, divert the people from their chosen path. Today the courageous people of Iran, finding their own route, have risen and put an end to the excuses of the excuse-makers; and God has never accepted any excuse. Do those who make excuses and do not break the seal of silence and sometimes recommend silence know what transformations are in the process of completion? (Ayatollah Khomeini's message to the people of Yazd, April 30, 1978, quoted in *Zamimeh* 1978, no. 14:2)

Conflicts between governments and members of the religious community in developing countries have often been generated by high levels of state intervention in capital accumulation and industrialization in the twentieth century. Third World governments rely heavily on external resources, especially Western technology and arms, thereby reducing their dependence on internal allies and supporters. The state's promotion of social change and the breakdown of the traditional coalition between the landed upper class and the clergy, combined with growing dependence on external allies, often adversely affects the clergy. These changes undermine the power and position of religious institutions. As a result, segments of the clergy may oppose the government. In times of conflict, coalitions may emerge between these clerics and secular movements that seek revolutionary transformation.

With the growing extraction of oil in the twentieth century, the government's resources expanded and Iran became increasingly tied to the world market. In addition, the coup d'etat of 1953 and the widening American involvement in Iran led to an alliance between Iran and the United States. The Iranian government became increasingly dependent on American arms, technology, and politics. Partly as a result of American pressure, the Shah initiated some reforms in the early 1960s that undermined the position of the clergy. This process intensified after the White Revolution of 1963, which was accompanied by rapid economic development, secularization, and repression. Although secularization and repression had a negative impact on the mosque and the clergy, they were far from eliminated. Instead, many Islamic clerics simply adapted to the new conditions and avoided politics altogether. A small segment of the clergy remained political and opposed the government, but was unable to mobilize the population against the government. Because most clergy were nonpolitical, mosques were used exclusively for religious practices. Consequently, they remained open and available as places for gatherings and religious ceremonies. The mosque was the only institution with a national network that was relatively autonomous of the state. The mosque was a resource with a safe, designated space to gather and communicate. As a result, by the time of the revolution, the mosque was the only option available for mobilization.

It should be mentioned at the outset that political mobilization did not begin in the mosque, nor was the clergy the group that initiated mobilization. The mosque became the center of mobilization when repression intensified and stifled opposition protests elsewhere. Mosques were ideal places to gather because they were relatively safe from violent attacks. In the initial stages, protesters had to pressure religious leaders to demand action because the preeminent religious figures, Marja'a Taghlid, the "source of emulation,"were nonpolitical and preferred to avoid collective action, especially in violent forms. When the preeminent religious leaders did become involved, they called for mourning ceremonies only and requested that the participants keep calm and avoid confrontation. The political faction of the clergy was small and not in a position of power or able to initiate large-scale mobilization. Most of the clerics in this faction supported Ayatollah Khomeini and, in the process of struggle, found active allies among bazaaris, students, and moderate politicians who were also active in the mosque and in the mobilization. The government's relaxation of repression during the brief rule of Sharif-Emami in the autumn of 1978 enhanced the capacity of these clerics to mobilize.

Ayatollah Khomeini was the leader and source of inspiration for the Islamic movement. He was one of the half-dozen Shiite Marja'a Taghlid, a position that gave wide publicity to his views. His significance, however, derived primarily from his vehement political stand against the Shah, which led to his exile in 1964. In early 1963, Khomeini called for the overthrow of the government, and he continued to take this stance throughout the 1970s. This action made Khomeini popular among segments of the population. He demanded freedom, social justice, and the elimination of imperialist influences in Iran. An Islamic society, in his view, would fulfill such demands and revive Islam, which had been undermined by Western decadence. While in exile, Khomeini kept in contact with his supporters and through them was able to issue political statements at a time when all opposition organizations were repressed. During the revolutionary struggles, he consistently rejected any compromise with the Shah. Thus, by the end of the revolutionary period, he had become the undisputed leader of the revolution.

Some scholars, including Arjomand, Green, and Skocpol, have portrayed the politics of Shia clergy as homogenous. As my analysis will indicate, during the major political crisis the clergy were never entirely united behind a single course of action. The divisions were particularly clear during the revolutionary conflicts. In the following analysis, I shall first examine the nature of clerical politics from 1950 to 1975 and then investigate the Islamic forces during the revolutionary period.

THE STATE AND THE CLERGY, 1950–1975

For the past several decades, Shia clergy have not been a politically homogeneous group.[1] Differing social and class backgrounds, education, and ties to various social groups all have influenced clerical politics. During the 1950s, the clergy were divided into a majority who were not active in politics and a politically active minority. Although none of the highest clergy, or Marja'a Taghlid, were directly involved in national politics, they ended up opposing Prime Minister Mosaddegh in favor of the Shah. The politically active clerical minority was subdivided into pro-Shah and pro-Mosaddegh factions.

Among those clerics who were politically active, most supported the nationalization of oil. However, the ensuing crisis and conflicts prompted divisions within their ranks. A minority continued to support Prime Minister Mosaddegh's National Front throughout the 1950s, including Ayatollahs Taleghani, Sayyed Abolfazl Zanjani, and Sayyed Hadi Milani. Others deserted to the royalist camp, notably Ayatollah Kashani, influential speaker of the Majles from 1952 to 1953 (*New York Times*, April 16, 1953). He had joined Mosaddegh's National Front and was active in the struggle to nationalize oil, but he later opposed the prime minister's request for emergency powers to resolve the country's crisis. Kashani argued that although Iranians had fought against Great Britain in order to improve their conditions, Mosaddegh actually worsened Iran's economic situation. In one meeting he asked the prime minister rhetorically, "Our economy is bankrupt, our villages are destroyed, our sons have become communists, and our schools have taken red colors. What are you doing?" (*Kayhan*, September 14, 1953). Regarding the Shah, Kashani told an Egyptian reporter, "Our king is different from [Egypt's King] Farouk. . . . The Iranian king is neither corrupt or greedy like Farouk, nor a dictatorial autocrat. The Shah is an educated and wise man" (*Ettelaat*, March 30, 1953).

Toward the end of 1952, in an attempt to obstruct the passage of Mosaddegh's policies, Kashani refused to attend and preside over the Majles. In early January 1953, when Mosaddegh requested an extension of his emergency powers in order to resolve the country's crisis, Kashani refused to go along, asserting that as long as he remained in the Majles he would prevent the passage of such bills. In February, the Shah was pressured by Mosaddegh to leave the country for a period of time, but Kashani intervened and prevented his departure. In April, Kashani refused to convene the Majles to pass the report of the Eight-Member Committee designed to curb the monarch's power, which liberals argued interfered unconstitutionally in all aspects of Iranian society.

During the crucial confrontation over the fate of parliament in 1953, Kashani opposed Mosaddegh's referendum, labeling it illegal and dictatorial. When the Majles recessed at the end of July to await the voting, he invited opposition politicians to anti-Mosaddegh meetings in his home. Two days before the voting, Kashani led the right-wing opposition in a call for a boycott of the referendum (*Ettelaat*, August 1, 1953). It is said that during the coup d'etat that followed he helped Ayatollah Behbahani organize gangs of hoodlums who, along with segments of the army, looted National Front headquarters, the homes of the prime minister's supporters, and even the house of Mosaddegh himself (Cottam 1979:154–156; Akhavi

1980:69). After the coup d'etat, Kashani praised General Zahedi, the new prime minister, for his willingness to sacrifice whatever was necessary to defend the country (*Kayhan*, October 2, 1953).

Ayatollah Behbahani also consistently opposed Mosaddegh and supported the royalist position. He, too, condemned Mosaddegh's referendum on the Majles and played an important part in the coup d'etat against the prime minister. While abroad, the Shah sent a telegram to Behbahani thanking him for the kindness the Iranian people had revealed toward him and the constitution. He also asked that the entire nation obey General Zahedi as his new prime minister. Ayatollah Behbahani responded by expressing his happiness over the Shah's health and saying he looked forward to the monarch's return (*Ettelaat*, August 22, 1953).

Ayatollah Khomeini was not politically active at the time, but disliked the National Front's disrespect for Islam. On one occasion, Mosaddegh's supporters had put a pair of glasses on a dog, taken it to the Majles, and named it "ayatollah." They then toured the dog through the streets. Speaking later of that event, Khomeini said that he had predicted, "Mosadegh will be slapped; and it was not long before he was slapped; had he survived, he would have slapped Islam" (Khomeini 1983, 15:15).

Nonactivist clergy also supported the Shah. They were led by the most preeminent Marja'a Taghlid in the country, Ayatollah Sayyed-Mohammad Hossein Boroujerdi. During the nationalization of oil, he and royalist members of the Majles held demonstrations in the Qom seminary, Madreseh-e Faizieh, rejecting nationalization as a violation of property and contrary to the laws of Islam (Nategh 1982). In July 1952, during the conflict between Mosaddegh and the Shah over control of the army, the conservative clerics of Qom sent their representative to Tehran to support the Shah (Nategh 1982). In the view of these clerics, Mosaddegh was moving the country toward communism. When the monarch left the country on August 16, 1953, Boroujerdi sent him a telegram that read, "Return because Shiism and Islam need you. You are the Shiite King." The Shah sent Ayatollah Boroujerdi a telegram from Rome, declaring his intention to return. Boroujerdi responded by sending the Shah another telegram, hoping the monarch's arrival would effect "religious progress, bring glory to Islam, and comfort to Moslems" (*Ettelaat*, August 25, 1953). Shortly after the coup d'etat on the religious holiday of Aid-e Ghadier, Ayatollah Boroujerdi telegrammed his congratulations to General Zahedi, wishing the new prime minister luck in the great responsibility he had accepted to serve Islam (*Ettelaat*, September 1, 1953).

The clergy's political position was strengthened after the ouster of Mosaddegh. They embarked upon an anti-Baha'i campaign, demanding that Baha'is be purged from government offices, their religious properties confiscated, and Baha'i preaching prohibited. For several weeks, the state-run radio ran a special daily program in which Mohammad Taghi Falsavi, an influential religious preacher, condemned Baha'is.[2] The army occupied the Baha'i center in Tehran, where General Batmanghelich, chief of staff of the armed forces, personally participated in the destruction of the center's dome.

THE WHITE REVOLUTION AND THE CLERGY

Relations between the state and the clergy changed in December 1959 when the Shah proposed land reform. Ayatollah Boroujerdi expressed dissatisfaction with the land reform bill drafted by the government, but he died in March 1961, before the proposed reform was enacted (McLahlan 1968:690). In May 1961, the Shah dissolved the Majles, which was dominated by landlords, and ordered the government to implement a series of reforms, including land reform. In October 1962, the government approved a law to form local councils throughout the country. The same law gave women the right to vote. It did not require voters or candidates to adhere to Islam, nor did it state that elected councillors must take their oath of office on the Koran (Bakhash 1984:24). Most clerics viewed the law as contrary to Islam. In support of their views they could point to the constitution of 1906, which prohibited any law that was against Islam. The clerics began to protest the law by sending telegrams and petitions to Prime Minister Asadollah Alam (served 1962–1964). The prime minister attempted to ignore the protests until November 1, when the clergy called for nationwide prayer and protest. In the early hours of that day, the government capitulated and contacted the religious leaders in Qom and Tehran, stating that the local councils law had been suspended (Bakhash 1984:25).

The government did not, however, do away with the land reform and women's franchise. In January 1963, the government held a national referendum to ratify what was later called the White Revolution. After the voting, the government claimed that the reforms had received the overwhelming support of the people.

The clergy's response to the reforms was divided. Unlike the conflicts of 1953, this time only a small clerical minority with ties to the government supported the Shah, including Ayatollah Mahdavi, Allamah Vahidi, and the Imam Jumah of Tehran (Akhavi 1980:103). Most of the clergy opposed the Shah's reforms, although they were divided on some of the issues. The majority opposed both land reform and the vote for women. In some areas, especially Azerbaijan, Isfahan, and Kerman, the clergy were large landholders who stood to lose under the proposed reforms. Land belonging to mosques and religious institutions was also slated to be confiscated. For some clerics, including Ayatollahs Shariat-Madari and Mohammad Reza Golpaygani, women's franchise was unacceptable, and they specifically asked the Shah to withdraw this proposed reform. Other clergy, including Ayatollahs Taleghani, Zanjani, and Mahallati Shirazi, adopted a radical position. They criticized the Shah's dictatorship and the capitulation laws and advocated justice for the poor (Akhavi 1980:101). As for Ayatollah Khomeini, he vehemently opposed the regime's attack on Islam and the clergy. He denounced the Shah's referendum as contrary to the interests of the Iranian nation. In early June 1963, religious ceremonies of the month of Muharram became highly political and often turned into political protests. The government, threatened by the politicization of the religious processions, arrested Ayatollah Khomeini and a number of other clerics on June 5. Within a few hours, protests erupted in Tehran, Qom, Mashhad, Isfahan, Shiraz, Tabriz, and Kashan. Harsh repression demobilized the protesters, enhancing the power of the government and the Shah. As a result, the loose alliance between the monarch and the clergy broke apart, an alliance that had existed since the Shah first came to power during World War II.

In the years that followed, the Shah introduced a number of policies designed to undermine the status and influence of the clergy and strengthen his own position. In the early 1960s, clerical students, known as *tullab*, and teachers at religious educational establishments received monthly stipends from the Sahm-e Imam, a clerical fund. These stipends amounted to between 300 and 400 rials per month, though they sometimes ran as high as 1,000 rials. Following bureaucratic reforms in 1964, the stipends were abolished and replaced by financial assistance from the newly created Endowments Organization (Sazman-e Owghaf). The funds available through this organization were far less than clerical students had formerly received from religious sources; in 1973, for example, the stipend was only 228 rials per month (Akhavi 1980:140). Many clerical students were hard-pressed to survive in the face of declining financial support. The Endowments Organization also oversaw the disposition of religious establishments. Land acquired by religious institutions through donations by individuals was placed under the control of the Endowments Organization. During the severe housing shortage of 1976, the Shah himself ordered that workers' housing projects be built on such land (*Kayhan*, February 15, 1977). In another instance, a ruined Tehran mosque with no income was turned into a large office building (Fischer 1980:115). The Endowments Organization also illegally appropriated and sold religious properties.

Partly as a result of these policies and partly because of growing secularization, the number of mosques, theological schools, and theology students declined rapidly. In 1965, according to official figures, there were 20,000 mosques in Iran. Ten years later, the Endowments Organization reported the existence of only 9,015 mosques. Between 1960 and 1975, Tehran lost nine out of a total of thirty-two Madrasehs, or theological schools (Akhavi 1980:129). The regime exercised its repressive apparatus to close the Madraseh-e Faizieh-e Qom, one of the country's most important clerical schools. The Hedayat Mosque and Hoseinieh-e Ershad were also shut down and several prominent clerics prohibited from giving sermons. In addition to pursuing secular, anticlerical policies, the Shah made a point of glorifying Persian identity and history at the expense of Shiite symbols. He abolished the traditional Islamic calendar, replacing it with one dating back more than two millennia, and he celebrated the twenty-five hundredth anniversary of Persian civilization in the early 1970s. The shift from an Islamic calendar to a secular one harking back to the Persian empire violated an established religious symbol and inevitably alienated clergy.

The Shah further threatened to undermine traditional practices by creating a Religious Corps in 1971, modeled on the Literacy Corps, to propagate Islam. The early graduates of this corps were trained in such diverse areas as political science, geography, theology, Arabic literature, social science, archaeology, and philosophy. The Religious Corps taught peasants that "true Islam" was distinct from the preaching of so-called black reactionary mullahs. By establishing a state-sponsored organization to propagate Islam, the Shah claimed to give equal weight within his White Revolution to progress and spirituality. The Shah's opponents charged that he was creating his own brand of Islam and clergy, and that the corps was designed to "nationalize religion" and undermine traditional spiritual leaders. Meanwhile, the Shah continued to claim that as a devout Moslem he received special assistance from God: "Without divine favor, my revolution would not have been possible. Without God's support, I would be a man like all the rest! And divine assistance will guarantee the continuation of our work!" (Hoveyda 1980:12). These claims further riled the monarch's clerical critics.

Finally, the clergy also faced the problem of growing secularization and the gradual decline of religious education. As the number of clerical schools declined, the number of students also declined. Conditions deteriorated to the point where "many religious students were attempting to complete secular high school at night, but many also merely drifted" away from clerical study (Fischer 1980:127). Clerics attacked the general secularization of Iranian society during the 1970s. Hojjat Al-Eslam Akbar Hamidzadeh, a prominent cleric, spoke of the drift away from religious values during a mourning ceremony for the Tabriz martyrs held at the Azerbaijani Mosque in the Tehran bazaar. He said, "It has been a while that we have been asleep. Materialistic concerns filled our beings so much, and worldly, oppressive appearances looked so God-like that we had forgotten about our mission, commitment, movement, and all the messages. But sleep, how long?" (*Zamimeh* 1978, no. 14:24). Ayatollah Khomeini also denounced cultural transformations. After the revolution, he declared that under the Shah "there was nothing left of Islam; there was only the name" (*Jumhuri Eslami*, December 25, 1982). "Our culture had been imported from the West. This culture penetrated all aspects of Iranian life, detaching people from Islam" (*Ettelaat* and *Jumhuri Eslami*, December 20, 1982).

During this period, different segments of the clergy adopted at least three different political positions. A minority always supported the Shah and received generous subsidies in return. According to Amirani, an executive of the national magazine *Khandanie-ha* who was placed on trial after the revolution, Prime Minister Hoveyda maintained a list of some fifteen thousand clerics on the Savak payroll (*Iranshahr*, December 24, 1982). Bakhtiar, the Shah's last prime minister, made a similar charge (Bakhtiar 1982:136). Although their claims may be exaggerated, it is clear that there were some clerics who cooperated with the government. Ayatollah Khomeini regularly attacked these pro-Shah clergy, charging that they had sold out to the royal court. He declared, "These clerics are against our movement and have tied our hands" (Khomeini 1979:196). Again he stated, "If people became aware of the principles of the Koran and learned about the important duty of the clergy and spiritual leaders of Islam, those who appear to be spiritual men and clerics in the royal court would be eliminated. If these dishonest, counterfeit clerics are excluded from society and no longer deceive the people, the ruthless system will never succeed in executing the awful plans of imperialists" (Khomeini 1976:182).

A second group of clergy, also a minority, opposed the Shah's social, economic, and international policies. Ayatollah Khomeini was the most well-known clergy of this faction. Some of the clerics of this faction had been supporters of Mosaddegh, including Ayatollahs Taleghani and Zanjani. The government's policy toward politically active clerics was to repress them. Two of the clerics, Ayatollahs Mohammad Reza Saeedi and Ghaffari, were killed by the Savak. By mid-1975, approximately seventy clerics were in jail or exile, including Ayatollahs Meshkini, Mahdavi-Kani, and Lahouti and Hojjat Al-Eslam Ali Akbar Hashemi-Rafsanjani. Ayatollah Tabataba'i Qomi was placed under house arrest for ten years. Although he was ill during the revolutionary conflicts, the government denied him access to a physician (*Zamimeh* 1978, no. 16:46). After Ayatollah Khomeini, the most well-known figures of this faction were Ayatollahs Taleghani and Montazeri. Ayatollah Taleghani was arrested several times after 1963 and spent several years in jail. He criticized the regime's lack of political freedom, inegalitarian economic policies, and the imperialistic exploitation of Iran by the United States. Taleghani was last arrested in 1975 for supporting the Islamic Mojahedeen, who fought for Islamic socialism. After spending two years in jail awaiting trial, he was sentenced to ten years' imprisonment. Ayatollah Montazeri was also imprisoned several times. He was last arrested while in exile in Kurdestan in 1975 and charged with opposing alcohol, listening to Iraqi radio, and supporting an Islamic government (*Kayhan*, November 4, 1978). He, too, was sentenced to ten years in prison.

Many clerical students supported this faction of the clergy, but were unable to garner much social support. On June 5, 1975, the twelfth anniversary of the uprising that followed Ayatollah Khomeini's arrest, more than one thousand clerical students took control of the Madraseh-e Faizieh-e Qom. They were joined by clerical students from the Madraseh-e Khan, an adjacent school. The rebels raised a red flag, symbol of Shia martyrdom, high enough to be seen throughout the city of Qom and broadcast tapes of Khomeini's fiery speeches against the Shah. When the uprising broke out, the government shut down the school's water and electricity. Police surrounded the school and attempted to rout the students with tear gas and high-pressure water hoses, but the protesters defended themselves with bricks and sticks. After three days, the rebellion was put down, but not before some students had been killed and many more injured.

Clerical response to the student revolt varied. Khomeini spoke out swiftly in support of the clerical students. He called it the "dawn of freedom and elimination of imperialism and its agents." His statement said that forty-five students had been killed and a larger number injured who had been denied admission to the hospitals.[3] Despite Khomeini's support, the majority of the clergy remained uninvolved. At one point during the uprising, the rebellious clerical students called upon Qom's important religious leaders for assistance but received no response. When the revolt was finally crushed, Ayatollahs Shariat-Madari and Sayyed Shahhab Aldin Marashi-Najafi publicly denied the government's charge that the clerical students had been communist agents, but they offered no explanation or defense of their actions.[4] Support for the Qom rebels was manifested in demonstrations by clerical students in Mashhad and university students in Tehran. In Mashhad, two clerics who had encouraged clerical students to protest were arrested along with some thirty student protesters. However, no support for the rebellious clerical students was offered by the general public anywhere in the country.

The third group of clerics was not politically active and comprised the vast, silent majority.[5] Their most important concern was to maintain the religious and cultural precepts of Islam. This faction was led by the Marja'a Taghlid, including Shariat-Madari, Marashi- Najafi, and Golpaygani.

THE FREEDOM MOVEMENT AND THE ISLAMIC MOJAHEDEEN

During the political liberalization and partial relaxation of repression in the early 1960s, a group of activists formed the Freedom Movement. The leadership of this group included Bazargan, who had served under Mosaddegh; Ayatollah Taleghani, one of a minority of clerics who remained loyal to Mosaddegh; and Ezzatollah Sahabi, another supporter of Mosaddegh. They joined the second National Front in the early 1960s and contributed to the mobilization of the opposition during that period. The Freedom Movement's platform stated, "We are Muslims, Iranians, constitutionalists, and Mossadeqists: Muslims because we refuse to divorce our principles from our politics; Iranians because we respect our national heritage; constitutionalists because we demand freedom of thought, expression, and association; Mossadeqists because we want national independence" (Abrahamian 1982:460). During the conflicts of 1962–1963, leaders of the Freedom Movement were imprisoned for some time and the organization was outlawed. Although the organization did not openly engage in political activities, its members kept their networks through religious events and meetings. The organization was fully revived in 1977 and played a role in the political mobilization against the government. Like the National Front, the Freedom Movement had some ties to professionals and white-collar employees. In addition, it also had ties to the mosque and was able to use mosques for political purposes. The Freedom Movement held a number of public meetings in mosques and a few of its leaders, such as Bazargan, gave talks and speeches during such events. A significant, but indirect, contribution of the Freedom Movement to the formation of other Islamic forces was the rise of the Islamic Mojahedeen, a radical organization that broke away from the Freedom Movement.

After the repression of 1963, when the Freedom Movement and other political organizations faced a severe political crisis, the Islamic Mojahedeen emerged from the Freedom Movement. In 1965 a group of graduates from Tehran University led by Mohammad Hanifnezhad formed secret discussion cells and studied the Algerian, Cuban, and Vietnamese revolutions, preparing themselves for political struggle. At the same time, they sent a few of their members to receive guerrilla training in Palestine. The opening of Hoseinieh-e Ershad, a religious center in Tehran, in the late 1960s and early 1970s provided a significant opportunity for the Mojahedeen to propagate their programs and recruit members. The lectures at Ershad given by Ali Shariati greatly helped the Mojahedeen to popularize a new interpretation of Islam. Initially, the government tolerated the Hoseinieh-e Ershad and Shariati's lectures, which criticized both traditional clerical Islam and Marxian philosophy. When it became clear, however, that Shariati advocated Islamic socialism and a classless society, the government closed down the Hoseinieh-e Ershad and imprisoned Shariati for eighteen months (Shariati 1979:119).

The Mojahedeen argued that true Islam was a fight against despotism and tyranny. They reinterpreted Islam in such a way as to be incompatible with capitalism. Private property in the means of production, according to the Mojahedeen, was the source of human exploitation. Those who owned the means of production exploited the workers. Just as there was only one God, Towheed, so should a just society also eliminate dualities and strive for unity and oneness. Like Shariati, the Mojahedeen advocated the establishment of a classless society.[6] They rejected the Islam of the clergy as conservative, although some clerics such as Hashemi-Rafsanjani were members of the organization and had been jailed for political activities. Although they were supported by Ayatollah Taleghani, the Mojahedeen never received the backing of Ayatollah Khomeini.

The Mojahedeen initiated armed struggle to overthrow the regime in August 1971, shortly after the Fedayeen had begun their armed conflict. They carried out a number of successful attacks against the regime but were soon paralyzed by the government's repression, in which most of their leadership and a large number of their members were arrested. The Mojahedeen survived the repression, however, and continued to be active until 1975, when a fraction of the new leadership, including Mojtaba Taleghani, son of Ayatollah Taleghani, adopted Maoism and severed their ties with religious groups. This action had an adverse effect on the Mojahedeen, who might otherwise have played a crucial role during the revolution. Although the original leaders of the Mojahedeen were not released from prison until the final days of the monarchy, Mojahedeen supporters participated in the revolutionary conflicts and fought for an Islamic Republic.

ISLAMIC OPPOSITION DURING THE REVOLUTIONARY PERIOD

In the mid-1970s, the government made no new attempt either to improve or further weaken the clergy's position in any new way. Hence, relations between the state and the clergy remained virtually unchanged. In 1977, however, the Amuzegar government stopped payment of several million dollars in clerical subsidies in an effort to reduce inflation. Despite the reduction of subsidies, the clergy continued to hold varied views of the regime during the revolutionary struggles as they had done earlier. A small fraction of the clergy still supported the Shah and, as a result, occasionally were subjected to popular expressions of anger. In two separate incidents in Dezful, large crowds attacked the homes of two progovernment clerics (*Payam-e Mojahed* 1978, nos. 53 and 54). In another incident, clerical students in Khoy rejected stipends from their teacher because of allegations that he supported the Shah (*Zamimeh* 1978, no. 16:80). In Ahvaz, where oil workers had actively opposed the government, people attacked a mosque in which a mourning ceremony was being held for the mother of the Ahvaz parliamentary representative (*Akhbar* 1978, no. 6).

The majority of the clergy remained nonpolitical. This nonactivist faction was led by the three Marja'a Taghlid in Qom who advocated the correct implementation of the constitution, rather than the formation of an Islamic Republic. In their view, the implementation of the constitution would suffice to eliminate anti-Islamic laws and practices. When asked in May

1978 about the need for an Islamic Republic, Ayatollah Shariat-Madari replied that such a society was their long-term goal; but that for the time being, the strict observance of the constitution would give people all that was necessary (*Kayhan*, November 2, 1978). Shariat-Madari repudiated acts such as burning down cinemas for he did not regard all movies as necessarily anti-Islamic. During Azhari's military government, in autumn 1978, government representatives met with the three Marja'a Taghlid in Qom, requesting them to ask people to cease their opposition to the government. The Marja'a Taghlid responded that they were willing to do so, provided the government implemented the constitution and respected Islam. They expressed the fear, however, that any such request would fall on deaf ears and go unheeded (Ladjevardi 1983, tape 2:2–3).

As the conflict against the Shah intensified throughout the late 1970s, many clerics who were not politically active condemned the regime's brutalities and demanded that the constitution be restored and observed. They stopped short, however, of advocating the overthrow of the monarch. Although they expressed concern over violations of Islamic precepts, they never demanded the establishment of an Islamic Republic. This nonactivist faction repudiated political protests, calling instead for calm and the observance of mourning ceremonies.[7] They consistently tried to avoid politicization of religious ceremonies. When the rebellious Qom clerical students were massacred in January 1978, Shariat-Madari rejected a popular request for a national strike, even though the Qom bazaar had struck independently. Ayatollah Khonsari advised Tehran bazaaris not to strike. When the Qom clerics gathered to discuss a strategy in response to the massacre, they failed to reach any agreement (The Freedom Movement [Abroad] 1978, 1:54). When the inhabitants of Tabriz on February 18, 1978, the fortieth day following the Qom massacre, clashed with police and burned government offices, Ayatollah Shariat-Madari condemned the protesters, calling their actions destructive.[8] Clerics in Tabriz followed his lead and denounced "anarchy" in their city. They requested the government to "make use of the guidance of the highest spiritual leaders so that the beloved Shiite Iran, a perfect model of Islam, is not harmed by a few anti-Islamic and anti-clerical elements. Let us follow the highest clerics to secure the independence of this country with all its holiness" (The Peoples' Mojahedeen 1979:11).

On March 30, a few days before the fortieth day marking the Tabriz massacre, the three Marja'a Taghlid from Qom called for a mourning procession and recommended calm, rejecting political slogans. In Qom, Hojjat

Al-Eslam Aba'i stated at the mourning ceremony, "Since there are corrupt elements who want to take advantage of the situation and provide excuses for the enemy, we urge the audience to avoid slogans during and after the ceremony. Those who disobey do not belong to us" (*Zamimeh* 1978, no. 14:24). The clerics were successful in preserving the mourning ceremony as a nonpolitical event. Between July and mid-August 1978, many protesters were killed in Isfahan, Shiraz, Mashhad, and Hamedan, but the three Marja'a Taghlid refrained from calling for mourning ceremonies. On August 14, they publicly condemned government "massacres" in these cities. They warned against "imperialists and enemies of Islam" who wished to misrepresent the popular struggles; it was better, they recommended, to pursue these struggles using a "choice of strategies that have greater results with the least damage."[9]

The contrast between Ayatollahs Shariat-Madari and Khomeini during the conflicts leading up to the revolution is instructive. In August 1978, when Sharif-Emami was appointed prime minister, Khomeini categorically rejected his government, while Shariat-Madari gave the new prime minister three months to prove that his government could meet the criteria of a just Islamic government. In October, Khomeini refused to meet or negotiate with Amini, an ex–prime minister, or any of the Shah's representatives. Two weeks later, Shariat-Madari met with Amini and later chose Pezeshkpour, a member of parliament, to negotiate with striking employees of Iran Air so that pilgrims could be flown to Mecca. When Khomeini asked for the sacrifice of more lives in the autumn, Shariat-Madari rejected attempts to obtain arms to use against the army, declaring instead that such an alternative should be chosen only when all avenues were blocked (*Kayhan*, October 29, 1978; *Ettelaat*, November 2, 1978). In December, when Khomeini called for "rivers of blood," Shariat-Madari warned that a jihad would be announced only if the government did not dismiss the existing parliament and call for new, genuinely free elections. In January 1979, Khomeini condemned the new government of Prime Minister Bakhtiar, but Shariat-Madari and Ayatollah Shirazi refrained from following suit.

The clerical community of Mashhad, another important religious center, adopted a course of action similar to that of Shariat-Madari and other nonpolitical clergy. As late as August 29, 1978, Mashhad clerics issued a statement that called for political changes but stopped short of abolishing the monarchy (*Kayhan*, August 30, 1978). Their statement contained the following demands:

1. The abolition of anti-Islamic laws
2. Freedom of expression for clergy and other social classes
3. Cancellation of the prohibition against religious preachers
4. Freedom for individuals jailed in defense of Islam
5. Return of all exiled religious leaders, especially Ayatollah Khomeini
6. Elimination of financial and tax pressures on the people
7. Punishment of those responsible for deaths during the previous eight months
8. Elimination of centers of immorality
9. Correspondence between the national culture, the Koran, and the ordinances of the Imams
10. Return to the Islamic calendar
11. Supervision of parliamentary elections by religious leaders and genuine representatives of the people
12. Cabinet members to be of the Shia faith
13. Dismissal of Baha'is from official and semiofficial positions
14. All rules passed by parliament to correspond to the principles of Shia Islam

Although the demands clearly call for greater clerical power, they make no mention of an Islamic Republic. Had a statement such as this been issued at the onset of the conflicts, it would have represented a direct attack against the regime. At this late stage, however, when the regime was already in retreat, this statement by Mashhad clerics did not represent a major challenge. In fact, these demands did not diverge significantly from the stated aims of Sharif-Emami's government.

The lack of initiative or strong challenge against the regime during the crucial revolutionary conflicts prompted Ayatollah Mohammad Sadooghi, a prominent cleric who supported Ayatollah Khomeini and headed the Tehran revolutionary courts after the Shah's downfall, to write to Ayatollah Hossein Khademi, spiritual leader of Isfahan, on the subject of the lack of clerical leadership. "People, especially the young, expect the clergy to lead, and the silence of the clergy in response to the people is contrary to their expectation. The recent silence of the clergy has been extremely costly to the clerical community. . . . The stronger the moves of the clerical community against the regime, the greater the result and optimism on the part of the people" (*Zamimeh* 1978, no. 20:29). In another letter, he pointed out the weakness of spontaneous leadership within the clerical community, which, in the absence of early, coordinated activities, could be eroded by non-Islamic elements (*Zamimeh* 1978, no. 20:33).

The passivity of the influential Qom Marja'a Taghlid, along with the Shah's efforts at reform in late summer 1978, led some Iranians to fear a compromise. Fears and rumors of clerical compromise ran so high that on August 28, two days after the Shah appointed Sharif-Emami as prime minister, Ayatollah Khomeini himself publicly rejected any move to reach a settlement with the monarch. He argued that the people were unanimous in desiring the ouster of the Pahlavi regime, and that to agree to anything less would be an eternal disgrace forever recorded in history (*Zamimeh* 1978, no. 19:2). Khomeini's intransigence prevented any compromise by clerical or National Front leaders with the Shah.

A third faction of the clergy consisted of highly political clerics who persisted in confronting the regime. Although they represented different points of view, most were followers of Ayatollah Khomeini. This faction was geographically concentrated in a few large cities and religious centers. To widen their networks they traveled frequently to different parts of the country, making contact with bazaaris, teachers, university students, and professionals. Their statements were designed to mobilize wide segments of the population by criticizing government policies that adversely affected various classes and interests. In fact, their rejection of the monarchy and advocacy of an Islamic Republic to a great extent derived from challenging the government's adverse policies toward the interests of various groups and classes, including workers and peasants. These clerics regularly condemned rising economic inequalities and the concentration of wealth in the hands of a few, the plundering of the nation's wealth, the Shah's dictatorial rule, the antiprofiteering campaign and arbitrary arrest of shopkeepers and merchants, usury, and growing moral decadence and use of alcohol. They claimed that an Islamic government would solve all these problems, but they never advocated theocracy.

Although the exact number of clergy within this faction is not known, the group was relatively small, given that the total number of clergy reached at least in the tens of thousands. The size of this faction can be judged in part by the number of clerics who signed political statements and petitions and called for a series of mourning ceremonies to commemorate massacres during the early months of the conflicts. Some 30 clerics from Isfahan signed a statement condemning the deaths of students in Qom

(Abouzar 1978, vol. 1, pt. 3:32). The Tabriz massacre was denounced in separate statements signed by 41 Qom clergy (*Zamimeh* 1978, no. 14:3), 56 clerics in Tehran (*Zamimeh* 1978, no. 14:20), and 40 clerics from Yazd (*Zamimeh* 1978, no. 16:8). When people were killed in Yazd during a mourning ceremony, 39 Qom clerics signed a condemnatory statement (*Zamimeh* 1978, no. 16:6), while in Tehran, 101 clergy called for mourning ceremonies (*Zamimeh* 1978, no. 16:19). The attack by police on the Tabriz clerical school in which many clerical students were wounded was condemned by 40 clerics (*Zamimeh* 1978, no. 18:40). As the mourning cycles continued, 77 clerics in Tehran called for another mourning ceremony on June 17 (*Zamimeh* 1978, no. 18:29).

The distribution of arrests indicates the relative concentration of this faction of the clergy. By mid-summer, some seventy of the best-known outspoken supporters of Khomeini had been arrested and exiled (Abouzar 1978, vol. 1, pt. 3:67; *Zamimeh* 1978, no. 18:27). They included Ayatollah Haj Morteza Pasandideh, brother of Ayatollah Khomeini; Ayatollahs Ali Asghar Dastgheib and Ali Mohammad Dastgheib from Shiraz; Ayatollahs Mohammad Taghi Alemi, Abdolrahim Rabbani Shirazi; Mousavi-Ardebili, and Hossein Nouri; and Hojjat Al-Eslams Sayyed Ali Khameneh'i, Akbar Hamidzadeh, Golsorkhi, Sayyed Hadi Khosrow-Shahi, Sayyed Ali Mousavi, Mehdi Rabbani Amlashi, Sayyed Ahmad Khorasani, and Hashemi-Rafsanjani (*Zamimeh* 1978, no. 18:27–28). For the most part, these radical clergy were located in a few religious centers and large cities. Data on clerical arrests during the first nine months of their protests indicate that roughly 25 percent were from Qom, 13 percent from Tehran, 7 percent each from Mashhad and Hamedan, 5 percent each from Isfahan and Semnan, 4 percent from Shiraz, 4 percent from Rezaieh, and the rest from other cities. The data show a high level of concentration: fully one-quarter of all arrests took place in the religious center of Qom, while an additional 45 percent occurred in seven other cities.[10] It is important to notice, however, that despite its concentration this clerical faction was more widely distributed than any other political organization, including the Freedom Movement and the National Front.

Given its small size and concentration, this clerical faction could not initiate political mobilization at will and had to wait for appropriate opportunities when the pressure of repression was reduced. The political conflicts of 1977 and the mobilization of the National Front, bazaaris, and students during the poetry nights provided favorable grounds. Among religious groups, it was not the clergy who initiated the mobilization, but rather the leaders of the Freedom Movement. Their first action was a call for a day of fasting and prayer to be held in early October 1977 at the Sahn-e Hazrat-e Abd Al-Azim, a holy place in Tehran. They urged the release of political prisoners and the return of Ayatollah Khomeini from Iraq, where he had been living in exile. Because of police deterrence only several hundred people took part in the event according to one of the participants, Dr. Yadollah Sahabi, a devout Moslem and member of the Freedom Movement. In response to this action, the next day the regime reiterated its charge that Ayatollah Khomeini was opposed to land reform and women's equality. This accusation was published in *Kayhan* newspaper but caused no public reaction, unlike a similar article, also critical of Khomeini, that was published a few months later and provoked a massive protest by Qom clerical students (*Payam-e Mojahed* 1977, no. 51). Neither the pro-Khomeini clergy nor clerical students reacted to the government. The only one who responded was Sahabi, who wrote a letter to *Kayhan*, which was not published, criticizing the paper for making false accusations.

Two weeks later one of Ayatollah Khomeini's sons died in Iraq. To commemorate his death, seventy-two clerics and a number of leaders of the Freedom Movement, the National Front, and the bazaar called for a mourning ceremony in Tehran on October 30, the seventh day after his death. The gathering was uneventful and no political statement was made, although a large number of people, especially bazaaris, attended. A few days later, a poetry gathering became politicized and led to the arrest of students and the closing of the Tehran bazaar. Subsequently, pro-Khomeini clerics in Qom held a mourning ceremony on December 2, the fortieth day after Khomeini's son's death. They turned this event into a political occasion and issued a public statement that contained the following demands:

1. Immediate return of Imam Khomeini to Iran
2. Release of political prisoners, especially Ayatollahs Taleghani and Ayatollah Montazeri
3. Release of students recently arrested at Tehran University and during other events in Tehran
4. Return of the Madraseh-e Faizieh-e Qom to the clergy
5. Return of buildings and schools forbidden to the clergy
6. Freedom of assembly, expression, and the press; elimination of the ban prohibiting certain clerics and religious leaders from making public sermons

7. Censorship of movie theaters, artistic festivals, and education that arouse sexual passion
8. Release of the "student library" at Tehran University
9. Permission for female university students to wear the veil; relaxation of anti-Islamic laws and condemnation of those who enact them
10. Prosecution of those who attacked a gathering in Karvansara Sangi, Karaj
11. Dissolution of the university guard and lifting of repression within universities; guarantee of an atmosphere conducive to learning
12. Improvement of the deplorable conditions of workers and peasants; revitalization of agriculture; economic independence from foreign powers and their internal lackeys, especially Jews and "Fergheh-e Zalleh" [Baha'is]
13. Cessation of political, economic, and military relations with the anti-Islamic government of Israel
14. Return to the Islamic calendar (Abouzar 1978, vol. 1, pt. 3:14)

Even though this statement did not call for the overthrow of the Shah, its authors were arrested by the Savak because they demanded broad political changes including the return of Ayatollah Khomeini, release of political prisoners, and improvement in conditions of workers and peasants. For the first time, these clerics had begun to voice concern over the conditions of the working classes. The government, of course, was not about to institute such major changes. In particular, the government opposed working-class mobilization and had long fought the leftists in order to prevent the working classes from acting collectively. Hence, the government proceeded with repression. Sheikh Sadegh Khalkhali, Abdolrahim Rabbani Shirazi, Maadi-Khah, and Hojjatie Kermani were arrested and exiled, while Ali Tehrani, a preacher, was later arrested for having spoken at a mourning ceremony in Mashhad. Unlike in previous years, however, the arrestees were exiled instead of being given long prison terms.

Shortly after the mourning ceremony for Khomeini's son, government newspapers again accused Khomeini of espousing reactionary political views on land reform and women's rights. Neither the clergy nor the leaders of the Freedom Movement responded to the government's charges. In Qom, clerical students attempted to organize an evening protest by meeting at the Great Mosque, but the meeting was canceled when some students were arrested earlier in the day. The detained students were released after two days (*Payam-e Mojahed* 1978, no. 53).

At this point Khomeini noted a lack of intitiative for mobilization on the part of clerics despite the rise of new opportunities and the mobilization of other groups, including the National Front, the Writers' Association, and students. On the last day of December 1978, Khomeini stated that there existed an opportunity in Iran to express problems. The clergy should take advantage of this opportunity. "Other parties have been writing and signing petitions, and we notice that nothing has happened to them. This is a unique opportunity that, if it is lost and this man's position is somewhat stabilized, he would cause serious damage that would hurt the clergy first" (Khomeini 1983, 1:265). Khomeini also urged intellectuals and the clergy to cooperate. He asked intellectuals to refrain from saying that the clergy were reactionary, and the clergy not to say that university people did not believe in God.

A few days later, on Women's Day in early January 1978, *Ettelaat* published another anti-Khomeini article, presenting him as opposing land reform and women's suffrage. Once again, the article generated no protest anywhere in the country except in Qom. This time, Qom clerical students boycotted their classes and visited the residences of major religious leaders, demanding that a strong stand be taken against the government's publication of the article. For two days, Qom clerical and high school students and Tehran University students went to the homes of influential ayatollahs, demanding unequivocal condemnation of the regime and government sanctions against the article's author (Abouzar 1978, vol. 1, pt. 3:26–32). Two days after the article was published, the Qom bazaar spontaneously closed down in protest against the regime and joined the demonstrators.

Although the Marja'a Taghlid and other religious leaders in Qom did condemn the article for insulting the clerical community, they could not agree on any action. While some suggested that students hold peaceful protests, others preferred that the Marja'a Taghlid act through bureaucratic channels to present their complaints to government authorities. Most seemed determined to avoid a repetition of the bloodshed that had accompanied the rebellion by clerical students at the Madraseh-e Faizieh in June 1975. By evening of the second day of protests against the *Ettelaat* article, many people had joined antigovernment demonstrations directed by clerical students. When protesters left the Great Mosque in Qom to hear a religious speaker they were attacked by police, who killed dozens and wounded and arrested many more. The next day more arrests took place. Ayatollah Nasar Makarem-e Shirazi and six other clerics were arrested in Qom and exiled. Arrests and exiles followed during subsequent rounds of mourning ceremonies. Shortly after the mourning ceremony marking the fortieth day after the death of the Qom martyrs, several other clerics were arrested and exiled. On March 23, in Firuz Abad-e Fars, Ayatollah Abdol-rahim Rabbani Shirazi's residence in exile was attacked by police, who arrested the inhabitants and sent him to Tehran (*Zamimeh* 1978, no. 14:26). A week later another cleric, Hojjat Al-Eslam Sayyed Mohammad Ahmadi, was arrested in Isfahan following a mourning ceremony and exiled to Kurdestan (*Zamimeh* 1978, no. 14:33). Many of the exiled clerics were relocated repeatedly to prevent them from reestablishing a following. Ali Tehrani, for example, was exiled from Mashhad to Chah Bahar, then to Sirjan, and finally to Mahabad. Ayatollah Khalkhali, who had been exiled from Qom to Rafsanjan, was moved to Lar, and then to Baneh in Kurdestan. Asad Ollah Madani was banished from Khorram Abad to Gonbad, then to Nour Abad, and finally to Boushehr. Fahim Kermani was exiled from Qom to Sirjan, to Saghez, and then to Mahabad in Kurdestan (*Zamimeh* 1978, no. 14:27–28).

The arrests of these highly political clerics weakened somewhat the organizational apparatus of the opposition, especially as the moderate clergy indicated no interest in escalating the conflicts. Nevertheless, the protests continued unabated. Popular collective action against the regime was often expressed spontaneously. Such actions were facilitated by the arrival in early August of the fasting month of Ramadan, which provided a great opportunity for gathering in mosques and praying at night. In this way, mosques became the starting places for antigovernment protests. On numerous occasions, people went to the mosque for evening prayers and, while returning home, attacked banks and government offices. Protests sometimes occurred despite requests for restraint by religious authorities. For example, in Yazd one cleric, Rashad Yazdi, finished his sermon by urging people to leave the mosque peacefully and refrain from shouting slogans. They ignored his request and demonstrated outside the mosque, where many were killed by police (*Zamimeh* 1978, no. 16:75). The spontaneous nature of many of these demonstrations was noted by Bazargan, later the first prime minister of the postrevolutionary provisional government. He expressed concern over their outcome and complained that religious and opposition leaders were unable to control many such incidents of collective action (*Kayhan International*, August 26, 1978).

Opposition continued to mount during Ramadan. When martial law was imposed in Isfahan and Shiraz, the bloodshed that resulted sparked still more protests. Bazaars in Tehran and several other cities closed down. When several hundred persons died in a fire at the Rex Cinema in Aba-

dan, people charged that the government had deliberately torched the theater and prevented firefighters from putting out the blaze in order to blame
the disaster on the religious opposition. As a result, protests and demonstrations were held in Abadan and other cities in Khuzestan during burials
between August 22 and 25.

To counteract the effect of Ramadan and prevent the spread of protests
to the oil fields and refineries, the main source of state revenues, the regime decided to soften the use of repression. Six days after the movie theater fire in Abadan, on August 26, the Shah replaced Prime Minister
Amuzegar with Sharif-Emami. Sharif-Emami announced that his most important task would be to establish communication with opposition groups.
Almost immediately, he contacted top religious leaders and liberal opposition organizations, reintroduced the Islamic calendar, and made some additional changes. In this way, Sharif-Emami attempted to appease both
religious leaders and the liberal opposition. These stated aims of reforms
and liberalization provided new opportunities for opposition. The reforms
only enhanced the position of pro-Khomeini clergy. During the first few
days of his government, Sharif-Emami released clerics who had been imprisoned for many years as well as clerics who had been exiled in the current protests. Almost all the clergy who were in prison were released
during this time. In addition, reduced repression allowed those living underground or afraid to express their political tendencies openly for fear of
repression to surface and take an active role in the mobilization. Finally,
some of the nonpolitical clerics now joined Khomeini's supporters, increasing the impact of this faction.

The temporary relaxation of repression led to a few large antigovernment rallies and demonstrations in some cities, with the most important
ones taking place in Tehran. The magnitude of participation swelled from
thirty or fifty thousand in the mourning ceremonies to at least several hundred thousand people. On September 4, Aid-e Fetr, a religious holiday
marking the end of Ramadan, bazaari supporters of the National Front,
Maniyan and Lebaschi, along with other groups, organized a prayer. Ayatollah Dr. Mohammad Mofatteh, a pro-Khomeini cleric, led the prayer procession. A large number of people participated. Although Maniyan had
promised the police that everyone would disperse after the prayer, the organizers could not control the crowd (Lebaschi 1983, tape 3:4). After the
prayer Dr. Mofatteh announced, "Our program has ended here" (Abouzar 1978, vol. 1, pt. 1:141). The crowd, however, began a spontaneous
march toward the center of the city. In the ensuing demonstration,

protesters shouted antigovernment slogans demanding that the Shah be overthrown. During this demonstration two clerics, Mohammad Javad Bahonar and Hadi Ghaffari, publicly announced their opposition to the Shah and the existing order (Abouzar 1978, vol. 1, pt. 1:141). Most importantly, as a result of this demonstration, pro-Khomeini clerics escalated the conflicts by going along with the marchers and directly confronting the Shah, leaving behind those moderate clergy who had wished to avoid politicization as well as the National Front, which had failed to call for the overthrow of the government. During the march, the pro-Khomeini clergy also took the initiative and called for a political protest for September 7.

On that day an even larger demonstration and march took place, despite the disapproval of some preeminent clerics. Slogans shouted during the march were more even more radical: "Say death to the Shah!" "Dictator, get lost!" "Traitor, shame on you; leave the reign!" "We are Islamic people; we do not want Shah! Khomeini is our leader!" During the march, people spontaneously changed the names of San'ati University and the Pahlavi crossroad to Khomeini, and the Shahyad Plaza to Shariati Plaza. This demonstration departed significantly from previous expressions of political opposition, which had taken the form of mourning ceremonies. The event had no religious importance, but was instead an explicit representation of opposition to the existing political order. It signaled a change of strategy from defensive protests against killings by the regime to an offensive attack on the Shah and his rule.

Thereafter, the position of the pro-Khomeini clergy improved until the monarchy was overthrown. Only a handful of clerics were arrested and only one was killed over the next few months, despite the imposition of martial law in twelve cities on September 8 and a military government two months later.[11] At the end of August, Ayatollahs Pasandideh and Naser Makarem-e Shirazi were released from exile, and in late October, Ayatollahs Taleghani and Montazeri were freed from prison. Six days later, bazaari supporters of the National Front called for a march to Taleghani's residence. Taleghani, a member of the National Front and a staunch supporter of Dr. Mosaddegh, had been jailed most recently for supporting the Islamic Mojahedeen who, like Taleghani himself, advocated Islamic socialism. A quarter of a million people marched to Taleghani's home to pay their respects. On November 4, Ayatollah Khomeini telegrammed Taleghani and Montazeri from Paris, asking them to lead the movement. This formal request was significant because Ayatollah Taleghani was not among the preeminent Marja'a Taghlid, and Khomeini never asked any of them to play such a role. Several weeks after his release, Ayatollah Tale-ghani called for demonstrations on the religious holidays of Tasoua and Ashoura, December 10 and 11, 1978. In Tehran, millions of people turned out in what were the largest demonstrations held to date. The slogans shouted by the crowd demanded primarily freedom and independence and included the following chants: "Death to imperialism and internal reactionaries!" "The Iranian people will release all political prisoners!" "Hail to the oil workers!" "The only party is God's party! The only leader is Khomeini!" "Hail to the toiling workers of the private and public sectors!" "Neither communism nor imperialism; only the Islamic Republic!" "The beauty of life is freedom! The blossoming of freedom is equality!" "The people demand the punishment of those who take their money out of Iran!"

By the end of the revolutionary conflict, the religious forces composed of pro-Khomeini clergy, the leaders of the Freedom Movement, bazaaris, university faculty, and lawyers had organized a council of two hundred people to coordinate all popular activities against the regime. This council gave commands to ten groups, who in turn carried them out through the mosques (*Kayhan*, January 21, 1979). With expanded personnel and organization, the Islamic forces were in an advantageous position to dictate policy and hasten the retreat of the regime, although each of these groups had different visions of what was to follow after the government's collapse.

COLLECTIVE ACTION AND RELIGIOUS PROTESTS

Before ending this chapter, we should examine the nature of the events of collective action. Available evidence indicates that in gatherings where political issues were involved, large numbers of people participated. This is understandable because the origins of the conflicts were complex (as discussed in previous chapters), even though demonstrators were using mosque networks and even calling their movement Islamic. For example, in the summer of 1978, the government decided to put on trial Ayatollah Taheri of Isfahan, who had been exiled without a court hearing. On the day Taheri returned to Isfahan to be tried, more than a hundred thousand people turned out to welcome him at the entrance to the city, even though Isfahan was under massive police and military control. Two days later, Taheri spoke at a religious ceremony that was attended by twenty thousand people, a relatively small number considering that it was a Friday, the

Islamic holy day, as well as a religious holiday. At Friday prayer the following week, Taheri spoke about Islamic government to a crowd of approximately forty thousand (Abouzar 1978, vol. 1, pt. 3:98). The vast difference in size of crowds on each occasion can be explained by the fact that the day of Taheri's return was seen by the people as a political victory over the government and consequently an occasion for celebration. In contrast, the Friday prayer, a religious occasion, drew fewer participants because it did not involve any political issues. The following week, when Taheri spoke about Islamic government, the meeting drew a larger crowd because it addressed a major political issue of the time. Similarly, during Sharif-Emami's premiership, the prayer of Aid-e Fetr, the end of Ramadan, held at Ghatarieh drew two hundred thousand people, according to *Kayhan*. As the participants initiated a march toward the center of Tehran, shouting anti-government slogans, over one million people joined the demonstrators.[12] Three days later, the purely political demonstration on September 7 drew many more people, despite the disapproval of some preeminent clerics who did not want the demonstration to be held. According to the same source that reported the September 4 event, this demonstration drew some four million people, although the date was neither a religious holiday nor a Friday (Abouzar 1978, vol. 1, pt. 1:160). On December 28, a rally was held in front of a hospital in the religious city of Mashhad to protest hooligans' attacks on patients. At the end of the rally, the crowd refused to abide by the requests of clergy, who tried to organize a collective prayer, but instead simply left the place (Fischer 1980:208).

Finally, it is important to mention the content of the slogans shouted during the major religious holidays and protests. Even during those protests that were largely organized through mosques, the slogans are indicative of the political nature of the conflict. Bazargan, first prime minister of the Islamic Republic, and his associates examined tapes recorded during major religious holidays and made the following analysis: the largest category of slogans was antidespotic, comprising about 38 percent; a second group of slogans, 31 percent, called for independence, freedom, and the formation of an Islamic Republic, although anti-American and anti-Soviet slogans were also included in this category; a third category consisting of 16 percent asserted the leadership of Ayatollah Khomeini; and finally, 15 percent of the slogans praised other leaders such as Ayatollahs Taleghani and Montazeri, both of whom were imprisoned by the Shah, and the martyrs of the Mojahedeen (Bazargan 1984:37–38). Bazargan's analysis also included a number of slogans that were not present during the revolutionary conflicts but were shouted by certain groups only after the Shah was ousted; these included: "Destruction of the proud rich!" "Support the deprived poor!" "Enforcement of Islamic laws!" "Exportation of the revolution and Islam!" "Leadership of the clergy and the Valayat-e Faghieh!" "Death to liberals!" "Death to unveiled women!" (Bazargan 1984:39–40).

My own analysis of the slogans during the final days of the monarchy indicates that the most important and widely shouted slogan was "Independence, Freedom, Islamic Government." It is interesting to note that during the early 1950s, bazaaris, workers, white-collar employees, and intellectuals had fought under the slogan "Independence and Freedom!" At that time, the opposition struggle for freedom and independence from imperialism was articulated by the nationalist movement led by Mosaddegh. In the late 1970s, "Islamic Government" was added to the the earlier slogan. To most Iranians, the new slogan, "Independence, Freedom, Islamic Government," promised independence from imperialism, civil liberties and political rights, and social justice based on Shia notions of egalitarianism. Although each group and class defined social justice differently, they had no doubts that the monarchy had not provided social justice.

AYATOLLAH KHOMEINI AND THE LEADERSHIP OF THE STRUGGLES

When Ayatollah Khomeini returned to Iran on February 1, 1979, after fourteen years of exile, millions lined the streets to demonstrate their support. Despite having been out of the country for almost fifteen years, Khomeini had become the single most important leader of the struggles against the Shah. He had achieved this position not because of his place in the religious hierarchy, although he was among the highest religious leaders, but because of his political stance against the regime. Khomeini began his political activities during the reforms of the early 1960s. At that time, he had just become an ayatollah and was not widely known. He was certainly not among the preeminent religious leaders, or the Marja'a Taghlid. His opposition to the Shah quickly gave him renown and soon made him one of the most important religious leaders. One of his earliest protests was a letter sent to Prime Minister Alam objecting to a decision to use books other than the Koran for administering oaths to local councils. Khomeini asserted that this decision was contrary to the constitution. Like the leadership of the National Front, Khomeini protested the government's referendum that approved land reform and women's suffrage. But unlike National Front leaders, Khomeini was not arrested, which provided him with an opportunity to continue opposing the government. A few weeks later, just before Persian New Year in March 1962, Ayatollah Khomeini called for mourning instead of celebration, "to awaken Moslems and the country to the dangers that are ahead" (Khomeini 1983, 1:27). In that message, Khomeini called for the overthrow of the "despotic government" that violated the constitution, so that a government that respected Islam and cared for the Iranian people could come to power. On the second day of the new year, clerical students who had organized a ceremony to commemorate the martyrdom of Imam Sadegh in the Madraseh-e Faizieh-e clerical school in Qom were attacked by the military and a number of students were killed and injured. Khomeini responded with a strongly worded statement that with this crime the ruling apparatus revealed its "Ghengis Khan-like nature. With this crime, the tyrannical regime guaranteed its own failure and destruction" (Khomeini 1983, 1:38). In the following months, Khomeini consistently opposed the Shah's regime, criticizing its reforms, its violation of Islam and the constitution, and its economic policies that adversely affected the bazaaris. His radical rejection of the government and unwillingness to compromise made him known and respected among some Iranians, especially a segment of the bazaar.

Khomeini's position on the Shah's reforms, particularly land reform, has not always been clearly understood. Although Khomeini consistently rejected women's franchise and equality, which he argued was a Baha'i principle (Khomeini 1983, 1:56), only once did he express opposition to land reform (Khomeini 1983, 1:13). His main concern was the position of the clergy and of Islam, which he considered synonymous. He maintained that the government's policies would strengthen the power of United States' imperialism, of Israel, and of Baha'is in Iran, all of which would, in his view, weaken Islam. Unlike other Marja'a Taghlid, Khomeini made statements that went beyond religious and clerical matters, moving toward establishing coalitions by taking up the causes of other groups. He expressed concern over the economic plight of bazaaris and the government's policies toward them (Khomeini 1983, 1:24). Khomeini condemned the growing economic penetration of the United States and Israel in Iran, the loss of Iranian markets, and bankruptcies among bazaaris and farmers (Khomeini 1983, 1:112).

Khomeini's outspoken criticism of the government led to his arrest in

June 1963. After release from jail, unlike all political leaders, who bowed to the repressions and kept silent, Khomeini continued his attacks on the government. As a result, the government exiled him to Turkey in 1964. Ironically, Khomeini's exile rendered him more invulnerable to repression. While in exile, first in Turkey, then in Iraq, and finally in France, Khomeini could not be intimidated. Thus, he continued to issue political statements and give speeches on political matters. In Iraq, Khomeini could meet with his followers who had gone on pilgrimages to the holy cities and give them messages to take back to Iran. Between November 1964, when he went into exile, until the fall of 1977, when the conflicts began, Khomeini sent at least ten major statements to the Iranian people, including an open letter to Prime Minister Hoveyda.[13] In addition, he sent a greater number of letters to the clergy and to Iranian students studying abroad.[14] Ayatollah Khomeini even gave money from religious contributions to the families of political prisoners arrested during the 1963 uprising and afterward. For example, he once sent two thousand tomans, a considerable amount at the time, to Shanehchi, a bazaari who was also a member of the National Front and who had been arrested in 1963 (Shanehchi, 1983, tape 3:15). During the revolutionary period, Khomeini quickly recognized the opportunity to mobilize for political opposition. Between the fall of 1977 and the end of his stay in Paris, Khomeini sent another forty-five messages to the Iranian people. In all these messages and statements, Khomeini mainly attacked the Shah's dictatorship, the government's violation of Islamic principles, the lack of freedom, and imperialist pillage of Iranian national resources. Khomeini refused to accept the inevitability of the existing situation and consistently called for the monarchy's overthrow.

Furthermore, he consistently maintained that an Islamic government would guarantee political freedom. While in Paris, he declared that even Marxists would be free to express themselves under the Islamic Republic. Women, too, would be free "to govern their fate and choose their activities." The dictatorial regime, he stated, reduced women to objects of consumption, while Islam was against such treatment of women (*Ayandegan*, January 17, 1979). Finally, Khomeini, who had sacrificed so much in his struggle against the Shah, did not claim to aspire to any political position. While in France he asserted that, as in the past, he would be a guide to the people (*Ayandegan*, January 10, 1979). These statements were confirmed by a number of bazaaris who met with him while he was in Paris (Lebaschi 1983, tape 3:15). Other bazaaris, who had met Khomeini prior to his exile, received positive impressions especially because, unlike other religious leaders, Khomeini was modest and did not seek rank, honor, power, or influence (Shanehchi 1983, tape 3:12). In combination, these factors made Khomeini the undisputed leader of the revolution.

In summary, the clergy were politically divided during the early 1950s, with most ending up opposing Mosaddegh and the National Front. The state's reform policies of 1962 and 1963 undermined the clergy's social, political, and economic position and kindled their opposition to the Shah's regime. But the clergy were unable to overthrow the government at that time, despite Ayatollah Khomeini's call to do so. After the repression that followed, the vast majority of clergy retreated from politics and limited their concern to religious issues. During this period a new organization, the Mojahedeen, emerged from the Freedom Movement and presented a new interpretation of Islam along socialist lines. Some clerics joined this organization, which benefited from the government's tolerance of the Hoseinieh-e Ershad in the early 1970s. The Mojahedeen were also weakened by repression and divisions, however, which for all practical purposes destroyed them by the time the revolutionary conflicts began.

During the revolutionary conflicts, the clergy were divided among themselves, with different factions taking divergent stands on political issues. The political faction interested in confronting the government was small and unable to mobilize the population against the government. As a result, the clergy were not the ones to initiate political mobilization. Instead, the conflicts of bazaaris and other social groups with the government provided an opportunity for clerical and religious opposition to mobilize. The clergy became significant because they controlled the mosques, and the mosques were the only safe places for gathering permitted by the government. The mosque became a key rallying place for people to express grievances and hold mourning ceremonies, which were not only religious occasions but also provided opportunities for political expression. Mosques across the country provided an extensive network for communication and mobilization. This network was used by opponents of the regime to gather, mobilize their resources, and broadcast the violence of the regime.

This mobilization eventually forced the government to reduce repression and introduce some reforms toward the end of the sumer of 1978. The reforms enhanced the position of the pro-Khomeini clergy while radicalizing the popular demonstrations and rallies. By the end of 1978, support for the Islamic movement had burgeoned dramatically. In the final days of the revolution, most people throughout the country, including bazaaris, industrial workers, white-collar employees and professionals, and students were calling for freedom, independence, and Islamic government. Ayatollah Khomeini's uncompromising policy toward the Shah and his promise of freedom for social and political groups and independence from imperialists and their internal associates made him the single most important leader of this revolution.

Part Three

Denouement

Chapter 8

The Final Collapse

Iran, because of the great leadership of the Shah, is an island of stability in one of the more troubled areas of the world. This is a great tribute to you, Your Majesty, and to the respect and admiration and love which your people give to you. (President Carter, toast to the Shah of Iran in Tehran, New Year's Eve, 1977; see Carter 1978:2221)

I commit myself to make up for past mistakes, to fight corruption and injustices, and to form a national government to carry out free elections. . . . I guarantee that after the military government, freedom and the constitution will be reimplemented. . . . Your revolutionary message has been heard. I am aware of everything you have given your lives for. (Shah of Iran, address to the nation, November 6, 1978)

In late August 1978, after several months of bazaari mobilization and the broadcasting of the government's violence through the mosque, the Shah was forced to initiate a series of reforms to be carried out by the new prime minister, Sharif-Emami. The promise of liberalization and reduced repression provided an opportunity for workers and white-collar employees to mobilize and engage in collective action. Some political prisoners were released, and media censorship was lifted, which enabled news of strikes and opposition statements to be broadcast. As a result, popular mobilization expanded, the scale of demonstrations grew, and collective action spread to smaller cities throughout the country. Initially, the government's response was to impose martial law in twelve major cities; then, as the conflicts intensified, the government began to organize hooligans, primarily recruited from rural areas, to attack demonstrators in the rest of the country. These actions did not succeed in quelling the popular collective actions, however, but instead further intensified demonstrations and politicized segments of the strikers. Hence, in early November the government abandoned the reforms Sharif-Emami had begun and embarked upon a course of repression, replacing him with a military government.

This new policy was doomed to failure because by November the vast majority of Iranians, including bazaaris, white-collar employees, and industrial workers, had mobilized and developed at least some degree of organization, solidarity structures, and networks to bring about social change. Although the social and historical roots of opposition to the monarchy can be traced back years, even decades, this was the first time since the downfall of Mosaddegh these major classes had mobilized for collective action.

The mobilization of bazaaris, industrial workers, and white-collar employees and the disruption of important social functions indicated the existence of broad-based opposition and provided a favorable basis for attacks on the regime. Encouraged by the scale of opposition to the government and victimized by hooligan attacks, students and the younger generation, led in part by clerics and bazaaris, throughout the country began organizing to counter government-sponsored assaults. This young generation constituted a sizable percentage of Iranian society, which was relatively young during the 1970s. In 1976, the mean age of the urban population was 22.9 years, and the median age was 18.7. Twenty-two percent of the population ranged in age from 15 to 24 years, most of whom were students whose concentration in colleges, universities, or high schools facilitated communication and collective action. In this transitional stage, students lacked direct family responsibilities, which made it easier for them to take risks. Most of them were concerned with growing social inequality and injustice, which also affected their own futures. In the last stage of the revolutionary conflicts, this social group bore much of the burden as students became the main victims of repressive violence and were killed in large numbers.

In the autumn of 1978, the younger generation, who had been subjected to arrest, injury, and death during the previous stages of the revolutionary conflicts, became increasingly organized and aggressive in attacking the government. In response to hooligan attacks, students formed neighborhood defense committees to assume the responsibility of protecting their communities. Soon they began attacking the government symbols of the armed forces and the Savak throughout the country. Eventually, the neighorhood committees took control of the functions of government and became the foundations for what has been called multiple sovereignties; that is, alternative, competing constituencies that assume a number of tasks, including imposing order, guarding property, controlling traffic, distributing necessary goods, and arresting suspicious persons.

Thus, the nature of the insurgents' response to repression shifted from holding mourning ceremonies protesting killings by the armed forces to launching daring attacks against the military. This transformation took place over a period of nearly one year. The repertoire of confrontation with the repressive forces shifted from purely defensive acts such as protecting individuals and property from hooligan attacks to offensive measures directed against the armed forces. Eventually, mounting attacks combined with growing divisions and defections weakened the regime's repressive apparatus, forced the Shah to leave the country, and left no alternative for the military commanders but to side with the opposition.

REFORMS AND INFORMAL REPRESSION

Sharif-Emami's proclamation of reform and reduced repression greatly expanded popular mobilization and collective action. Prior to Sharif-Emami's government, some seventy cities had experienced some form of collective action. By the end of his time in office, approximately two and one-half months later, roughly one hundred cities had been rocked by antigovernment collective action. The scale of these incidents mushroomed. Before Sharif-Emami's government, mourning ceremonies and demonstrations in large cities had drawn tens of thousands of people. In Tehran, for example, between thirty thousand and fifty thousand people took part in each of several mourning ceremonies. After Sharif-Emami took office, the number of participants swelled to at least the hundreds of thousands. The slogans shouted by demonstrators became openly political and pointedly anti-Shah. The government responded by imposing martial law in twelve major cities on September 8, when several hundred people were killed in Tehran.

Elsewhere, the regime employed hooligans to assault demonstrators and loot and burn shops. These hooligan attacks were supported by at least small numbers of the dominant class that backed the monarchy. On November 4, a group of the Shah's supporters in Tehran gathered at the house of Dr. Fallah, a member of the executive committee of the Iranian National Oil Company, to devise plans for hooligan attacks on different sections of the city. One of those present, Ali Reza'i, reportedly agreed to contribute two hundred million tomans toward the project (*Akhbar* 1978, no. 1).

Prior to Sharif-Emami's regime, only a few incidents involving hooligans had been reported.[1] But by November 5, when his rule ended, hooligan attacks, burning, and looting had extended to more than forty cities. Occasionally, the government used hooligans to demonstrate support for the Shah. On October 26, the Shah's birthday, hooligans organized progovernment demonstrations in cities throughout the country. Most of the time, however, hooligans were used to attack government opponents. The targets of attacks included people assembled for rallies and demonstrations, bazaaris and their shops, students, and sometimes even entire cities. The first such incident to receive wide publicity occurred on October 16, 1978, in the capital of the province of Kerman when slum dwellers and Gypsies attacked a gathering at a mosque. They set the mosque afire, killing twelve people and injuring hundreds. These hired thugs then proceeded to destroy and burn the city's business section. Municipal authorities did nothing to hinder the escalation of events, leading Jalali Naieni, a member of the Majles, to dispute the government's claim to have had no part in the hooligans' acts (*Kayhan*, October 23, 1978). Subsequent investigations by the Lawyers' Guild and the Iranian Human Rights Committee charged that these attacks were drawn up in the office of the governor of Kerman in the presence of Savak officials and the police (*Ettelaat*, October 31, 1978). In another incident, some one thousand villagers demonstrated in the streets of Khoy and stormed the city mosque, breaking windows and shouting slogans in favor of the regime.

Demonstrators were one of the main targets of attacks. On October 18, hooligans assaulted antigovernment demonstrators in Shahr-e Ray, a part of Tehran, injuring many persons. On October 29, in the Kurdish city of Mahabad, people celebrating the release of political prisoners were joined by residents of Miyandoab, a nearby city. Following the celebration, 150 cars and buses from Mahabad escorted their guests to the edge of town. On their way back they were attacked by thugs, who injured dozens and destroyed forty cars (*Kayhan*, October 29, 1978). In Ardekan Yazd and Shahr-e Kord, hooligans fought with participants at antigovernment rallies (*Kayhan*, October 29, 1978). In Sar-e Pol-e Zahab, hooligans and police opened fire on demonstrators, killing and wounding a number of them. In Sabzevar and Gonabad, several demonstrators were injured by thugs; while in Amol, hooligans killed or wounded more than twenty-five persons and set fire to numerous government buildings (*Kayhan*, October 30, 1978).

Students and teachers were also regular targets. On October 30, thugs set upon striking students in Bam and injured several. They smashed cars belonging to schools and the fire department as well as windows of the Rastakhiz party headquarters. Students were assailed in Khoy. Thugs assaulted a high school teacher in Klardasht after a demonstration, leading students to boycott classes (*Kayhan*, November 2, 1978). Thugs in Dezful demolished the court building to prevent an impartial investigation of a complaint brought by educators against known organizers of hooligans (*Kayhan*, October 29, 1978). Shops and bazaars were another target of attack. In Asad Abad in the province of Hamedan, thugs sacked shops and pharmacies (*Kayhan*, October 26, 1978). In Shah Abad-e Gharb, hooligans looted shops and the city mosque (*Ettelaat*, October 29, 1978). In Zanjan, hooligans assaulted the bazaar sentinel and set fire to the court building while the family of the head of the court was inside. Their lives were saved with great sacrifice despite police refusal to help, but all the court files were destroyed.

Hooligans occasionally attacked entire cities and destroyed considerable property, especially in the bazaars. Such actions paralyzed and disrupted the functioning of the cities as well as demobilizing the opposition, if only for temporary periods. On the evening of October 28, thugs attacked the city of Kermanshah, burning and looting shops and houses, including the homes of teachers and educators (*Kayhan*, October 29, 1978). More than half a million tomans were stolen. Supported by government forces, the hooligans killed five people and injured forty-two, seven of whom were firefighters attempting to put out a fire. In Rezaieh, villagers were told that landlords opposing the government wanted to take away their land. In protest, angry villagers attacked and looted shops, forcing the city to close down. On October 31, rumors of hooligan attacks led several cities to close down, and thousands fled to the mountains. Such events completely demobilized the opposition. In an effort to forestall violence and bloodshed in the Kurdish city of Paveh, the men decided to withdraw, leaving the women and children in the city. Two thousand hooligans hired by Salar

Jaf, the city's parliamentary representative, invaded and destroyed the city, killing eighteen persons and wounding fifty others (*Kayhan*, November 1, 1978). In separate incidents, a total of twenty-nine antigovernment demonstrators in Paveh, Yazd, Soma-Sara, and Sar-e Pol-e Zahab were killed by hooligans. Thugs looted shops and houses in Sar-e Pol-e Zahab, another Kurdish city, and invaded Sanandaj with the intention of setting the city on fire (*Kayhan*, October 31, 1978). That same day, hooligans sacked shops and set fire to houses in Bam. Similar attacks were reported on the same day in Kamiaran, Shah Abad-e Gharb, and Miyandoab (*Kayhan*, October 31, 1978). In Khorram Abad, hooligans attacked and injured several people in the street. At the same time, police arrested several young men, stripped and beat them publicly, and finally released them without their clothes (*Kayhan*, October 29, 1978). On November 2 in Babol, hooligans set fire to many government and private buildings, factories, and movie theaters. The city burned for twenty-four hours while police stood by and did nothing to interrupt the hooligans (*Ettelaat*, November 2, 1978). Similar events were reported in Hamedan, Azar Shahr, Oghlid, Shahpour, Marand, Dareh Shahr, Ghorveh, Ravar, Behshahr, and Garmsar (*Ettelaat*, November 2, 1978).

THE PEOPLE RESPOND

The promise of reforms by Sharif-Emami had signaled the government's retreat and the possibility of social change. After several years of inaction, people were finally able to mobilize, create solidarity structures, and force some concessions during the brief periods of reduced repression. The abrupt imposition of martial law and burgeoning hooligan attacks, however, contradicted the government's claim of reforms and social change. The government's tactic of using hooligans was critical in organizing student defense groups. In response to hooligan attacks, students and the younger generation became more aggressive against the government and soon formed neighborhood defense groups to ward off such assaults.

Toward the end of Sharif-Emami's government, as hooligan attacks became more frequent, violent actions directed against the regime proliferated. Previously, people had been the victims of government attack with a few exceptions such as the events in Tabriz. Now they started to attack back. On October 20, residents of Hamedan pulled down the Shah's statue and set fire to the building housing the Rastakhiz party. Four days later, city police were accused of raping Mahin Ardekani, a high school student who subsequently committed suicide (*Kayhan*, October 24, 1978). Two of her high school friends were also reportedly raped by police officers. As the news spread, violent protests erupted throughout the city, and Hamedan was transformed into a panorama of blood and fire. Residents erected barricades and set fire to government buildings. The city burned for several days until it came to resemble an ancient ruin. The army was called in and massacred many protesters.

In separate incidents, large parts of Gorgan and Boroujerd were also gutted by fire (*Kayhan*, October 24, 1978). Inhabitants of Rasht stormed the headquarters of the Savak and the Rastakhiz party on October 25. The next day, a secret policeman was slain and several officers injured in Khorram Abad (*Kayhan*, October 28, 1978). Residents of Ardekan Fars organized a huge demonstration on October 29 that alarmed the mayor into seeking refuge in the gendarmerie headquarters (*Kayhan*, October 29, 1978). In Lar, people descended upon the house of a police detective and demolished it. In Yazd and Malayer, the Chamber of Guilds was attacked and all the files destroyed (*Kayhan*, October 29, 1978). The next day, a high-ranking Savak official was shot and wounded in the Kurdish city of Mahabad (*Kayhan*, October 30, 1978).

The most militant action of this period occurred in Amol, a city near the Caspian Sea in the province of Mazandran, which had a leftist tradition. The inhabitants of Amol took the protection of the city into their own hands on October 31 and arrested and disarmed several persons with pro-government leaflets, charging them with setting fire to the bazaar; three of those arrested were Savak agents. Students quickly organized to patrol the highways leading into the city. They checked each car, looking for suspicious individuals. Rumors spread that a people's republic had been established in Amol. The inhabitants denied this, stating that they were merely protecting shops and houses from assault by slum dwellers incited by the gendarmerie (*Tehran Journal*, November 1, 1978; *Ettelaat*, November 2, 1978). According to reports, the government told people in five nearby villages that the Amol demonstrators were former landlords who wanted to confiscate their land. Some one thousand villagers gathered to attack the city. Upon arriving, the villagers realized that thousands of citizens had assembled to repulse the attack, and they rapidly withdrew (*Kayhan*, November 2, 1978).

Five thousand persons organized themselves on October 31 to defend the Kurdish city of Sanandaj against an invasion by hooligans, whom they successfully drove off. Twenty-five thousand people then held a rally protesting the invasion (*Ettelaat*, October 31, 1978). That same evening in Kashan, the inhabitants armed themselves in defense against thugs; while in the Kurdish city of Baneh, residents stayed up all night, checking traffic to foil hooligans. They were joined by villagers who came to the city to help in its defense (*Kayhan*, November 1, 1978).

The police academy in Isfahan was set on fire on November 3. In Mahabad the next day, to forestall possible hooligan attacks, residents detained six suspicious individuals who reportedly were from the nearby city of Kermanshah (*Ettelaat*, November 4, 1978). That same day, protests erupted in Zanjan against the arrest of four persons who had demonstrated against hooligans. They were released, but one bore marks of having been tortured with lighted cigarettes. When his brother went to the police station to file a complaint, the police suspended him by the wrists and tore out his moustache (*Kayhan*, November 4, 1978). On November 4, students at Jondi Shahpour University in Ahvaz undertook to secure the university and their dormitories against hooligan attacks. That day, the army massacred a number of students at Tehran University. The next day, in retaliation, students tore down the Shah's statue on the university campus and burned hundreds of government buildings and banks throughout the city, while police did nothing to stop them. It was later asserted by many that the regime permitted the protesters to do as they wished in order to create an excuse to impose martial law.

THE IMPOSITION OF THE MILITARY GOVERNMENT

On November 6, the Shah reversed his policy of reform, appointed a military government headed by General Azhari, and imposed martial law throughout the country. The military succeeded in temporarily breaking most, but not all of the strikes. Some workers in major factories remained on strike, while others, like the oil workers in the south, returned to work in order to form a national organization to coordinate their strikes and prevent strikers from going back to work. Even more significant was the indefinite shutdown of bazaars in major cities to protest the imposition of martial law and the military. Neighborhood self-defense groups, formed in many cities to fight off hooligans, aggressively struck back at the armed forces (*Ettelaat*, October 4, 1978).

During the first weeks of the military government, sporadic attacks erupted against highly visible symbols of the regime such as statues and government buildings. In Arak, after a protest march that drew one hundred thousand people, a group of marchers tore down the Shah's statue in the city park. The police arrived and shot to death more than forty people and injured sixty (*Akhbar* 1978, no. 8). The police then assaulted Shir Khorshid Hospital to prevent people from donating blood for the wounded. The next day, hooligans invaded three nearby villages—Sanjan, Ghijan, and Grahrou—whose residents had participated in the Arak protests. In the clashes that followed, between twelve and seventeen hooligans were killed (*Hambastegi* 1978, no. 6).

Residents of Behshahr in the province of Mazanderan near the Caspian Sea held a large rally on November 12, and the next day briefly seized control of their city (*Akhbar* 1978, no. 3). When police in Songhor defaced pictures of Ayatollah Khomeini on November 16, students retaliated by setting fire to the city hall and attacking the homes of police and Savak agents. The same day, residents of Zanjan paid tribute to local martyrs on the seventh day following their deaths. As they were leaving the cemetery, they were assailed by police. Returning to the city, the crowd pulled down a statue of the queen and set it afire. They then toppled the Shah's statue and smashed it with sledgehammers. In Shoushtar, a portion of city hall was blown up on November 27.

Statues of the Shah were pulled down in Najaf Abad on December 11. That same day, residents of Isfahan also tore down statues of the Shah and his father. They then went on a rampage, attacking a police station and burning movie theaters, banks, supermarkets, and stores that sold alcohol. The crowd attempted to burn down the Savak headquarters as well, but succeeded only in removing the door before being driven off by police; 48 people were killed and 130 injured in the incident. In Yazd, 200 people used cables and a truck to topple the Shah's statue and drag it around the city. Residents of Langeroud pulled down statues of the Shah on December 25. On December 30, the people of Sari set fire to the government newspaper's offices and printing presses. They also burned the governor's office, the Culture and Arts building, and the Consumer Protection Agency. Finally, they torched the home of Baghban, a hooligan leader (*Hambastegi* 1979, no. 9).

Other incidents were designed to capture weapons from the police and the army. In mid-November, groups of students in Amol armed themselves with bows and poisoned arrows, which they used to attack soldiers and seize their weapons (*Akhbar* 1978, no. 1). Residents of Gonabad gathered on November 21 to hear an antigovernment speech. When an armed soldier began to speak in support of the regime, he was quickly silenced by the crowd, which disarmed him and then negotiated the exchange of his weapon for the release of local political prisoners (*Akhbar* 1978, no. 3). In Isfahan, a group of people in one neighborhood mounted an antigovernment rally on November 22. Suddenly, a gendarme arrived and fired in the direction of the protesters, who retaliated by throwing stones and Molotov cocktails. The officer fell to the ground and was set upon by demonstrators, who wounded him in the head and confiscated his weapon before disappearing. Shortly thereafter, General Naji arrived and promised a reward of ten thousand tomans for information regarding the missing weapon. When no information was forthcoming, he arrested all the shopkeepers in the neighborhood in retaliation (*Akhbar* 1978, no. 5). In Dezful, residents gathered on rooftops with bags of sand, which they dropped as military and police officers passed by; the fallen officers were then jumped and their guns expropriated (*Akhbar* 1978, no. 6). In Isfahan people disarmed three police officers at the end of November and vandalized the house of an American (*Akhbar* 1978, no. 6).

During this stage, numerous collective actions were directed specifically against agents of state repression, with the result that many military personnel and police officers were assassinated. This represented a major change from the earlier period of mourning ceremonies when demonstrators were the victims of violence. Three soldiers in Isfahan were killed with a hand grenade on November 16. In another incident, a group of demonstrators chased a sergeant, who took refuge in a nearby house; the demonstrators followed, killed him, and took his gun. During a religious holiday in Nishabour on November 19, people gathered in a mosque to organize an antigovernment rally and were attacked by some twenty hooligans backed up by police, who killed two protesters. In retaliation, two policemen were shot and killed (*Akhbar* 1978, no. 2). In Kerman, members of two Islamic guerrilla organizations, Badr and Malek-e Ashtar, shot the deputy chief of police, whom they accused of complicity in the mosque attack (*Akhbar* 1978, no. 4). Police in Rafsanjan killed two people at a gathering on November 22 to welcome newly released political prisoners. Six days later, in retaliation, Sarvan Haidary, deputy chief of police, was assassinated by an Islamic guerrilla group (*Akhbar* 1978, no. 9). In Dezful, seven military personnel were killed by a hand grenade on November 24. A few days later, ten more people were killed, some of whom were soldiers. In Ahvaz, residents slew two policemen who had opened fire and killed a six-year-old girl during antigovernment demonstrations sparked by the imposition of the military government (*Hambastegi* 1978, no. 1). In the same city on December 8, several policemen were killed and their weapons taken (*Akhbar* 1978, no. 8). In Amol, an army sergeant was slain during a demonstration (*Hambastegi* 1978, no. 4). In Zanjan, following an attack on a women's bathhouse by armed guards using tear gas, people killed four guards and at least twelve military personnel (*Akhbar* 1978, no. 9). In Darab, three police officers were killed. An army officer, a corporal, and a policeman were slain in Tehran on December 26 (*Akhbar* 1978, no. 9). Also in Tehran, several motorcycle riders killed three army officers who had earlier opened fire on oil refinery workers. A few days later in Hamedan, Major Kazrouni, the commander of a police station, was murdered (*Akhbar* 1979, no. 10). An army officer who had been involved in the attack on the Kerman mosque had his foot blown off in a bomb attack on December 27 (*Akhbar* 1979, no. 10). At the end of December, a clash broke out in Qom between residents and the armed forces; one army officer was killed and five soldiers wounded. People then stormed the home of a police officer, who fled; they destroyed his belongings and put the remains on display. When the army continued killing people the next day, an army commander and a soldier were slain (*Akhbar* 1979, no. 11). In Nahavand, nearby villagers rushed to defend people from a police massacre. Their arrival in overwhelming numbers frightened the police, who called in helicopter reinforcements from Hamedan (*Akhbar* 1979, no. 11).

Individual policemen were not the only targets of attack. In some cases, police stations were assaulted by armed groups. A police station in Mahabad was stormed on December 3, and several police officers were killed and injured. The next day, the Fedayeen assaulted Police Station No. 2 in Tehran, killing several officers. Political prisoners in the Kurdish city of Sanandaj staged a fight among themselves on December 24. When police arrived to quell the disturbance, the inmates turned on them and quickly disarmed them. The prisoners then broke into the ammunition storage, expropriated additional weapons, and set fire to the prison. Five inmates were killed along with sixteen policemen, while four hundred prisoners managed to escape. Residents of Torbat Haidarieh, helped by nearby villagers, attacked police headquarters on December 30. They succeeded in disarming the police, releasing the prisoners, and tearing down the Shah's statue. In the process, twelve people lost their lives and twenty-five more were injured (*Hambastegi* 1979, no. 9). In Mashhad, a crowd attacked the police headquarters on January 1 and burned a government building housing the National Resistance Force. They also seized the Hyatt Hotel, expropriated its assets for religious purposes, and decided to convert the hotel into a hospital (*Akhbar* 1979, no. 10).

During this period, people continued to defend themselves from government-organized thugs and to punish hooligan attacks. Thugs invaded Ardestan on December 14; residents defended their city and forced the invaders to flee (*Akhbar* 1978, no. 7). In Mashhad, people pursued hooligans brought in from Ghochan and Shirvan, set fire to their cars, and captured one of them. He revealed that they were promised one hundred tomans for agitating, but had been given only ninety (*Hambastegi* 1978, no. 4). In the Tabriz bazaar, hooligans initiated a progovernment demonstration, which was quickly broken up by residents of the city. A number of the hooligans were injured and taken to the hospital, where they later expressed regret for their actions (*Hambastegi* 1978, no. 4). In Shiraz, an army officer who had organized hooligans was killed along with two of his relatives (*Hambastegi* 1978, no. 4). In Tabriz on December 18, inhabitants seized a hooligan, who confessed that he and others were paid nine hundred tomans each for their activities (*Hambastegi* 1978, no. 5). In Malayer, a crowd awaiting the arrival of Ayatollah Madani on December 26 was set upon by hooligans, two of whom were severely beaten in the melee. That night, a butcher who had led the hooligans was shot and killed (*Akhbar* 1979, no. 11). In Baft, the homes of eleven teachers were torched by hooligans on December 29. In retaliation, an army officer was killed and two others wounded. In Yasooj the governor, accompanied by a number of government supporters, went to the village of Dehdasht to hire hooligans; they were beaten up by the villagers and forced to flee (*Hambastegi* 1979, no. 9).

Two hundred thugs stormed the Great Mosque in Rezaieh during services on December 14 and tried to set it on fire. Those inside defended the mosque and forced the thugs to retreat after breaking a window. An hour later, police and army units attacked the mosque and opened fire. Twelve people were killed, six of whom were military personnel, while thirteen others were injured. The crowd then demolished two banks and set fire to several others. By the end of the day, the police and army were forced to withdraw, leaving the city under the control of its residents (*Hambastegi* 1978, no. 6). Shortly thereafter, five hundred armed Kurds attacked the army garrison in retaliation for the attack on the residents of Rezaieh. One report indicated that many soldiers fled, while General Varham, governor of the province of Western Azerbaijan, escaped to Tehran (*Akhbar* 1978, no. 9). In Isfahan, police opened fire on a group of people gathered at the

Mesri Mosque. The officers were then attacked from behind. One police-man was killed with a shovel and four others with Molotov cocktails (*Akhbar* 1978, no. 5). Residents of Bojnourd decided to turn over control of their city to young people on December 31. This plan was thwarted by army and police forces who launched a nighttime assault against people gathered in the mosque (*Hambastegi* 1979, no. 9).

Savak agents also came under attack. In mid-November, residents of Kashan went to the cemetery, where they exhumed and burned the body of Ata-Pour, father of a Savak deputy. The chief of the Savak in Ker-manshah was shot and badly wounded on December 9; he was later taken to a London hospital for treatment (*Akhbar* 1978, no. 7). In Sari, capital of the province of Mazandran, the chief of the Savak published the names of all Savak agents in the city and then committed suicide. People searched for the agents, who were forced into hiding. In Tehran on December 21, a Savak agent stationed on a rooftop during a demonstration killed a pro-tester; other demonstrators rushed to the top of the building and threw him to his death (*Hambastegi* 1978, no. 6). In Ahvaz, an American deputy of the oil company was assassinated on December 23, and the car of another oil official was set afire. The same day, two other oil company employees who were allegedly working for the Savak were assassinated (*Hambastegi* 1978, no. 6). A Savak employee in Isfahan was badly beaten on December 25 and later died in the hospital (*Akhbar* 1979, no. 11). On December 27, Tehran demonstrators became suspicious of a Mercedes Benz equipped with a mobile radio. When they approached, the driver emerged from the automobile and opened fire, killing three demonstrators. His car was set afire, but he managed to escape in an army ambulance. In his haste, he dropped some papers that identified him as Colonel Zibaie, an alleged Savak torturer and prosecutor. The crowd hastened to apprehend him at his home, but he was not to be found. They confiscated three automatic machine guns, a number of communication devices, and leaflets con-taining false statements. Beneath his house was a 150-meter underground tunnel that led to another house. The tunnel had several torture cells con-taining human bones (*Kayhan*, January 6, 1979). The crowd vandalized the house, destroying its luxurious furnishings, cutting up the rugs, and set-ting fire to the building (*Akhbar* 1979, no. 9).

Scattered demonstrations in Kennedy and Eisenhower streets in Tehran on December 30 were broken up by the army. The demonstrators regath-ered in Esmaiel Samani Alley and continued to shout anti-Shah slogans. Suddenly, Mrs. Vejdani, wife of a Savak agent, emerged from one of the houses and began shooting at the demonstrators. They immediately assaulted the house and broke down the door, but Mrs. Vejdani escaped. Soldiers were summoned once again to disperse the crowd. Ten minutes later, Mr. Vejdani arrived and went to a neighboring house that belonged to Haj Said Javadi, a well-known writer and dissident who was away from home in hiding. Vejdani insulted Mrs. Javadi, who returned the insults. He then left to confront a group of demonstrators who were shouting, "Savaki! Savaki!" Vejdani fired upon them, killing two people and wounding several others. The crowd responded by throwing stones. Vejdani managed to kill three more and injure several others before being felled by a stone. The protesters then jumped on him, stoning and kicking him to death (*Hambastegi* 1979, no. 9).

On some occasions, groups of protesters challenged the army in direct confrontations. In Mashhad on December 30, protesters marched to the governor's palace, where employees had been engaged in a four-day sit-in. When the marchers arrived at noon, they were confronted by four army tanks and five truckloads of soldiers. Shouting "Military brother, why do you kill us?" the protesters rushed the tanks, preventing them from maneuvering rapidly. Religious leaders climbed onto the tanks to address the crowd. At this point, the soldiers laid aside their arms and mingled with the protesters in a friendly manner. Soon three more tanks and five additional truckloads of soldiers arrived and bore down upon the demonstrators, who anticipated a similar cordial response. This time, however, the tanks opened fire, killing a number of people, including twelve who were run over, and wounding many others. In retaliation, the demonstrators hurled Molotov cocktails, killing Colonel Kalali, commander of the artillery unit. They then stormed three police stations and confiscated arms and ammunition. They also rushed the women's prison, blasting open the door and freeing the inmates. Some protesters broke into the Army Cooperative Store, expropriated goods, and delivered them to Imam Reza Hospital. Around mid-afternoon, three Savak officials opened fire on people gathered outside the Cinema Shahr Farang. When their supply of bullets was exhausted, they were set upon by the crowd, captured, and immediately hanged in the street. Their bodies were taken to the same plaza where Colonel Kalali's body was being kept. Later in the evening, a crowd detained two armed Savak officers who carried copies of the Koran, upon which they swore that they had not been involved in any killings. When eyewitnesses countered that the officers had indeed fired on demonstrators, they were summarily executed and their bodies taken to Statue Plaza, where they were strung up on a tree (*Hambastegi* 1979, no. 9). The crowd burned several buildings, including government offices, buildings housing the Iran and American Society and the Iran and British Society, and the homes of several American military advisors (*Akhbar* 1979, no. 10). During these events, hundreds of people were slain and two thousand wounded. In retaliation, a major and three soldiers were killed.

One city came under complete control of the people at the end of December 1978. In a funeral procession, residents of Tobat Haidarieh arrested an armed man, who confessed that he was a Savak agent who had planned to fire at the police from the crowd to provoke a response. He was immediately killed by the crowd. A few days later, as a group of protesters was pulling down the Shah's statue, several people were killed and injured by the police. The next day the inhabitants of Torbat Haidarieh, aided by armed villagers, surrounded and attacked the police station. After several hours of fighting in which twelve people were killed, they forced the police to evacuate the station and take refuge in the army barracks. By December 30, the city had come under the people's control. Torbat Haidarieh became an important center for the provision and sale of arms and amunition for the province of Khorasan (*Kayhan*, January 1, 1980).

THE FINAL RETREAT AND THE RISE OF DUAL SOVEREIGNTY

In early December, oil workers went on strike, declaring their opposition to the monarchy and support for Ayatalloh Khomeini. Soon workers in all major industries and white-collar employees followed and disrupted all production and services. At the same time, popular attacks against the armed forces and hooligans intensified, forcing the Shah to reverse himself yet again and, for what would be the last time, attempt a reformist policy. On January 2, 1979, Bakhtiar was confirmed by the Majles as prime minister. Although he was able to attract several large, favorable rallies in a few major cities such as Tehran and Shiraz, popular attacks against the regime did not cease but became more widespread and daring than ever because the government's retreat and proclamation of reform and reduced repression allowed more open opposition and the strengthening of solidarity structures. In the two short weeks between the new prime minister's inauguration and the Shah's departure, the repertoire of collective action changed markedly. The Shah's departure was a major event and caused popular attacks to intensify and the repressive apparatus to retreat, especially once Bakhtiar dissolved the Savak. In addition to burning statues and government buildings, crowds stepped up assaults against high-ranking government officials and members of the Savak, the police, and the military. Most important, young people, often organized by the clergy, took control of many cities, forming governments of their own and generating dual sovereignty.

Attacks against government officials increased. A popular uprising in Hormozgan on January 5 forced the governor to take refuge in the naval headquarters. A member of the Majles was assassinated in Tehran on January 28. The Tehran residence of Mirzaie, another member of the Majles, was set on fire on February 4. People also continued to strike back aggressively against government-paid hooligans. On January 17, two hundred people were wounded by hooligans, three of whom were then killed. Two days later in Boroujerd, hooligan attacks injured many people; in retaliation, several hooligans were slain. Residents of Kazroun and Ghasr Shirin took up weapons on January 30 to defend themselves against hooligan attacks. Five thousand armed people from Firuz Abad and the nearby Ghashgha'i tribe gathered on February 9 to proclaim their readiness to embark on a jihad if Khomeini issued the order.

Government buildings and statues of the Shah were assailed as symbols of the regime. On January 3, residents of Kermanshah burned the ruins of the governor's palace, which had been demolished earlier. In Rafsanjan, a crowd toppled the Shah's statue on January 8, and in Sirjan another statue of the Shah was pulled down two days later. A crowd in Kerman killed a former air force officer on January 14 and tore down three statues of the Shah and his father. When the Shah left the country on January 16, his departure was interpreted as a significant victory, and people celebrated by demolishing his statues in numerous cities, including Amol, Shahr-e Ray, Shahy, Babol, Babolsar, Bandar Abbas, Zanjan, Karaj, Saveh, Khorram Abad, Tabriz, Masjed Soleyman, Shahroud, Lahijan, and in the Baharestan Plaza in Tehran. In response, the government itself gave orders that the Shah's statues be pulled down to prevent people from destroying them in other cities, including Dezful, Hamedan, Shahsavar, Gorgan, Abadeh, Rasht, Chalous, Andimeshk, Kashan, and Sari.

People stepped up their assaults on Savak officials and their headquarters. On the same day Bakhtiar received his vote of confidence, people assaulted the Savak building in Firuz Abad-e Fars; under fire, they gained entrance to the building and located the underground tunnels containing political prisoners, whom they promptly liberated (*Kayhan*, January 2, 1978). In a similar attack on Savak headquarters in Masjed Soleyman, many people were killed and wounded in an unsuccessful attempt to take over the building. They succeeded several days later, and the building was demolished. A Savak officer was killed in Isfahan on January 12, while in Sardasht, the house of a Savak employee was set afire. In Abadeh, the Savak headquarters was seized by a crowd on January 16. The next day, people set fire to the Savak building in Arak. In Tehran on January 18, a Savak office that had been evacuated the previous day was taken over by the opposition after several days of shooting. Two days later, the Savak headquarters in Kermanshah was evacuated to prevent attacks. The Savak office in Nahavand was dissolved on January 22, and Savak personnel left town. The next day, residents of Astara set fire to the local Savak headquarters. In Shiraz, a Savak colonel and two other officers were slain.

The police and their headquarters continued to be targets of attack as well. Residents of Kurdkooy killed a gendarme and wounded two others during a funeral on January 2 (*Hambastegi* 1979, no. 10). In Isfahan on January 14, two police officers were fatally wounded. The Fedayeen killed the Tabriz police chief and injured two of his guards on January 15. On January 28, a policeman in Gorgan was slain during a funeral; while in Hamedan, a policeman and a sergeant in the army were killed. The chief of police of Kerman was shot dead on January 31. Gendarmerie stations in rural areas of Shahsavar began evacuations in mid-January. Later that month, the police station in Shahr-e Ray was also evacuated. Three of the seven police headquarters in Tabriz were evacuated on January 18 in order to strengthen their defenses. In Semnan, police headquarters and the Savak office were evacuated on January 23. In Tehran, the Fedayeen stormed a gendarmerie station, killing several officers. In Sanandaj, a police station was assaulted on January 29 and one officer killed. On February 10, seven police stations in Tehran were taken over by civilians, while in Varamin many people were killed attempting to capture the police headquarters.

The military was also a target of attack. In a clash between residents of Lar and the army on January 4, three persons died, including an army sergeant. In Tehran, two army officers were shot in front of Tehran University on January 9. The following day in Jiroft, people torched the house of a member of the military. In Kazroun, military personnel grew so alarmed that they evacuated their homes and took refuge in the army barracks (*Kayhan*, January 15, 1979). They were reassured by the people of the city, who invited them to return to their residences. In retaliation for hooligan attacks on Tehran's San'ati University, the Fedayeen assaulted a military truck on January 26, wounding eight soldiers. On February 7, Colonel Shakouri, an important military commander, was gunned down.

By this time, the strikes and bazaar shutdowns had totally paralyzed production, distribution, and services. In this context, popular assaults on the military intensified. The rebellion had assumed a national character, and the government would have had to kill a massive number of people in order to demobilize the insurgents. The Shah's appointment of Bakhtiar and his own departure from the country had precisely the opposite effect and instead intensified mobilization and attacks against the government.

As the official forces of the government began to retreat because of the Shah's departure and popular attacks, young people assumed the responsibility of patrolling their cities, generating multiple sovereignties. Residents of Ardabil seized control of their city on January 9. In Shehmirzad, government lands were divided up by the people among themselves. On January 10, three hundred young men in Shiraz took over directing traffic and guarding neighborhoods at night. Their assistance was welcomed by police (*Kayhan*, January 10, 1979). Ramsar youth assumed a number of police functions on January 11. In Yazd, young people wearing special uniforms took control of the city on those days when demonstrations were to take place. Young people also took charge in Khorramshahr, Kermanshah, Noshahr, Khorram Abad, Rasht, Kangavar, Saghez, Gonbad Kavous, Khomein, Dameghan, and Amol. In Amol, they arrested four masked men who had injured an educator while robbing his home. The men were incarcerated in a people's jail and scheduled for trial in a people's court (*Kayhan*, January 20, 1979). In Tehran, thousands of students and young people organized neighborhood committees throughout the city to stand watch at night. Three thousand youths performed this task in south Tehran (*Kayhan*, February 5, 1979).

During the final two days of the uprising, many people were killed in clashes with the military. Statistics from thirty-eight Tehran hospitals show that over 650 people were killed and more than 2,700 others were injured by the armed forces. Elsewhere, more than 300 persons died during the same period (*Kayhan*, February 12, 1979).

Some politicians who heard the voice of the revolution began to resign. Jalal Tehrani, head of the Council of the Monarchy appointed to carry out the Shah's duties in his absence, resigned on January 22, declaring that the council—which had been selected by the monarch—was illegal. The

Savak's second-in-command defected to Ayatollah Khomeini. Bakhtiar announced on January 24 that he would be willing to change the system of government if proper elections were held. By February 4, some forty parliamentary representatives had resigned and another forty had either fled the country or gone into hiding for fear of retaliation (*Kayhan*, February 3 and 4, 1979). That same day, the mayor of Tehran resigned and employees in the prime minister's office struck against the government. The next day, Bazargan was appointed by Khomeini to preside over a provisional government. Sharif-Emami left the country on February 8 amid nationwide demonstrations supporting Bazargan as the new prime minister.

THE COLLAPSE OF THE ARMED FORCES

As the armed forces were regularly employed to repress what had become a national struggle, they became subject to mounting attacks by popular forces as well as to internal disintegration. Insubordination and desertion in the armed forces began in the autumn of 1978 and assumed crisis proportions by mid-January 1979 with the departure of the Shah, to whom the army was ultimately accountable. Most of the defections occurred among enlisted men in the early stages, but they later spread to low-ranking officers. During these final days, the United States government was instrumental in persuading military commanders to proclaim their neutrality, thereby preventing the total disintegration of the army, which had been an American construct and was the basis for American support.

On a number of occasions, soldiers and junior officers fired upon their commanders or notorious officials rather than shoot protesters.[2] Sometimes individual soldiers or police even committed suicide in the face of orders to kill civilians.[3] A deputy chief of police in Tabriz committed suicide on January 11. The penalty for insubordination in most cases was summary execution. Opposition sources reported that one hundred soldiers in Tehran as well as naval personnel in Ahvaz were executed for insubordination during the last week of November (*Akhbar* 1978, no. 4). In Kerman, four soldiers who refused to open fire on demonstrators on October 16 were ordered executed by their commander (*Akhbar* 1978, no. 9). Three soldiers refused to fire on demonstrators in Behshahr on November 13; they were shot by their commanding officer for insubordination. Seven other soldiers who were present at the incident defected to the side of the demonstrators (*Akhbar* 1978, no. 3). Three soldiers, later labeled "destructives" disguised in uniforms, attacked a military patrol in the streets of Tabriz in mid-September. They killed six military personnel and a civilian and wounded several others before two of the attackers were slain (*Ettelaat*, September 16, 1978). Three soldiers in Lavizan Garrison opened fire on a number of officers on December 11, killing dozens and wounding more than fifty (*Akhbar* 1978, no. 7). Toward the end of the revolutionary conflicts the armed forces eventually became so unreliable that the army reportedly circulated an order prohibiting the issuing of weapons to lieutenants and corporals, whether enlisted or regular career personnel, because they were considered untrustworthy.

On December 19, Sotvan Ghadranian, an army officer in Ahvaz whose term of duty had ended, invited a group of officers to say good-bye. He pulled out his gun, intending to shoot them, but his weapon failed to work. He was executed in the garrison (*Akhbar* 1978, no. 8). A few days later in Mashhad, a colonel and a sergeant joined demonstrators, but both were slain by another colonel, who was in turn killed by the crowd (*Akhbar* 1979, no. 10).

Divisions among the military continued and intensified. On at least one occasion a high-ranking officer expressed solidarity with demonstrators. Colonel Amir Ahmadi, deputy military commander of Tabriz, joined a group of demonstrators on December 18, declaring that he would rather commit suicide than obey orders to shoot civilians. The protesters embraced him, while 150 soldiers under his command set aside their weapons and mingled with the crowd. The demonstrators climbed onto tanks and continued their protests until evening (*Hambastegi* 1978, no. 5). When the unit was ordered back to the garrison, another troop of soldiers arrived and opened fire, killing seven demonstrators and wounding four others (*Akhbar* 1978, no. 8).

In late November, a group of army officers and soldiers formed the Revolutionary and Liberation Army. They claimed that most of those who defected from the regular army during this time joined their organization. This group tried unsuccessfully to assassinate General Khosrowdad in early December; three of their members were slain in the attack. They mounted several assaults in Saveh on December 12 that resulted in the deaths of a number of policemen. Many soldiers and air force cadets were arrested for insubordination, only to escape from their garrisons. Five hundred soldiers escaped from a Mashhad garrison on December 5 to join those opposed to the regime (M. J. 1979:84). On December 11, 300 more soldiers imprisoned in the air force garrison and 150 from the Jay garrison escaped (M. J. 1979:89). A clandestine army report indicated that by December 7—exactly one month after the military government had been installed—a total of 5,434 army personnel, mostly low-ranking enlisted men, had defected from thirty-one garrisons. Meanwhile in Mashhad and Yazd, young men cut their hair short to make it difficult for the government to identify defecting soldiers (*Akhbar* 1978, no. 7). Near the end of December, 600 soldiers escaped from the Kazroun garrison. Two were captured and sentenced to death. The following day, the commander requested all officers to witness the execution of the two defectors. When he gave the order to the firing squad, they turned their guns on the assembled officers and commanders, killing many of them (*Akhbar* 1978, no. 9).

Groups within the military spoke out to condemn the regime with growing frequency. Soldiers from the Isfahan artillary unit publicly declared on December 5 that when they accepted their commissions they had sworn to defend the nation and its people, not kill civilians. They announced their refusal to support a regime engaged in massacring its own citizens and pledged instead to support Ayatollah Khomeini. To those still deceived by the Shah, they issued a warning that soon the regime's associates would be put on trial. A group of soldiers and officers from various units within the military published a statement in mid-December declaring that they had thrown their support to Khomeini and would no longer serve in the Shah's army. When General Ghara-Baghi succeeded General Azhari as chief of staff of the armed forces at the end of December, both were condemned by supporters of the National Front within the military. The latter hailed Dr. Mosaddegh and vowed to follow the leadership of Ayatollah Khomeini.

When Bakhtiar replaced the military government and the Shah announced he would go abroad for a vacation, the armed forces became even more unreliable. Acts of insubordination took place on a massive scale. According to General Ghara-Baghi, the daily rate of desertion from the army was approximately one thousand soldiers and grew progressively higher (1984:138). The day before the Shah left the country, military trucks in Tehran for the first time displayed pictures of Ayatollah Khomeini. In Hamedan, twenty-eight hundred air force cadets went on a hunger strike in protest against the government. Three days later, their number had grown to six thousand. Air force officers and sergeants joined the hunger strike on January 17. The Ahvaz garrison split into two factions, with some supporting the Shah and others in favor of Khomeini. Many of the Khomeini supporters were arrested, including Faroukh Nia, one of their leaders. Two hundred naval officers at the Bandar Pahlavi Naval Base went on strike on January 18 to express their solidarity with the revolution. Three days later, conscripts at the base joined their officers in a hunger strike. In Tehran, twenty-three hundred military personnel were arrested on January 18 at two air force bases. One thousand air force officers, cadets, and sergeants in Bandar Abbas demonstrated to express their solidarity with the popular struggles. They demanded the removal of Savak agents who had been relocated to their base from all over the country (*Kayhan*, January 21, 1979). Finally, they expressed support for members of the air force on hunger strikes in Hamedan and Dezful.

In Tehran, a group of air force officers, sergeants, and cadets, along with their families, demonstrated on January 24 and shouted revolutionary slogans. That same day, demonstrators elsewhere rallied in support of Khomeini, including four hundred air force cadets and sergeants in Isfahan and several thousand air force cadets and sergeants in Shiraz and Boushehr. Demonstrating air force cadets were arrested in Isfahan on January 27; eight hundred more cadets were later arrested in Boushehr. Five thousand officers and sergeants at the Shiraz Air Force Base demonstrated on January 30 in support of the constitution. The army was called in and arrested many of the military demonstrators. In Bandar Abbas, officers of the Shah's Immortal Guard were dispatched on January 30 to put down striking air force personnel. Air force cadets and military personnel in Behbahan demonstrated against the government on February 3, as did Qom air force cadets the next day. In the Kurdish city of Sar Pol-e Zahab, a group of military personnel announced their support for the revolution. On February 4, the military governor of Tehran legalized political demonstrations. Some high-ranking military personnel responded to decreased repression by publicly declaring their loyalty to Ayatollah Khomeini.

The final two days of the regime were marked by widespread violence and bloodshed. The Immortal Guard attacked striking air force cadets in Tehran on February 10, killing many of them. The news of this incident quickly spread throughout the city. In response, guerrilla organizations, notably the Fedayeen, assaulted the Immortal Guard, rescued the cadets, and expropriated many weapons from the garrisons. Two army units dispatched from Ghazvin to assist the Immortal Guard were stopped in Karaj when people destroyed a bridge and surrounded the stranded soldiers. One hundred tanks were sent from Kermanshah to Tehran as reinforcements for the Immortal Guard. Once the tanks reached Hamedan, they were immobilized by tens of thousands of people who blocked the road.

The tank soldiers did not attempt to force a path through the crowds, but instead announced their solidarity with the people (*Kayhan*, February 11, 1979). Many weapons and ammunition were captured by the opposition in these events.

The resistance of the Immortal Guard was the last significant attempt to preserve the monarchy. With their collapse on February 10, sizable segments of the navy announced their solidarity with the popular struggles. That day, many pro-Shah army commanders fled their garrisons throughout the country for fear of people's attacks. Crowds attacked the Eshrat Abad garrison on February 10 and confiscated many weapons. Radio and television stations were taken over by the opposition forces. Prisons were stormed, and political prisoners were released along with many other inmates. Three thousand prisoners were released from the Ghasr Prison alone (*Kayhan*, February 12, 1979). In Rasht, the Savak headquarters was stormed and nine Savak employees were killed. In Azar Shahr, nineteen police officers were slain by the opposition. In Shiraz, air force officers joined armed civilians in assaulting and capturing three police headquarters, while the city's two other police stations were evacuated. In these attacks, weapons and ammunition were seized.

The high council of the armed forces met on the morning of February 11 to discuss the situation and make a decision regarding the position of the armed forces. General Ghara-Baghi, chief of staff of the armed forces, summarized the overall situation as follows:

Two nights ago clashes occurred between air force cadets at Doushan Tappeh and the Immortal Guard. About 8:30 yesterday morning supporters of the cadets entered the garrison, broke the door of the ammunition storage and recovered some arms; the cadets also armed themselves against the Guard. . . . The army and the commander of martial law were unable to help the air force against the rebels. . . . With regard to the police, I should say that yesterday afternoon some of their stations were evacuated and are now occupied by the opposition; some of their personnel are now at the Vanak gendarmerie garrison. . . . The army's munition factory came under fire by the opposition, and the commander of the army and the commander of martial law were unable to send help to defend the guard against the intruders. . . . I ordered General Atabaki to send some personnel with helicopters to defend the factory, but he was unsuccessful. (Ghara-Baghi 1984:447)

Other commanders then reported on the situation of their units, indicating how the popular mobilization and struggles paralyzed the armed forces. General Naser Moghaddam, deputy prime minister and head of the Savak, informed the council that the Savak was no longer providing information and, indeed, had been dissolved, and its personnel were wandering around the country. In Tehran and most other cities, people were attacking, looting, and burning Savak buildings (Ghara-Baghi 1984:449). General Abdolali Badre'i, commander of the army, noted that all available army personnel had been placed at the disposal of the commander of martial law and that no additional personnel were available to assist elsewhere. The day before, he had asked the army in Ghazvin to send a unit to Tehran, but the opposition blocked the road at Karvansara Sangi and prevented the troops from proceeding. That night thirty tanks were dispatched to Doushn Tappeh to aid the air force, but the road was blocked by the people in Tehran Pars; many of the tanks were set on fire and only a few were able to return to the garrison (Ghara-Baghi 1984:451). Badre'i concluded, "As a result of unfavorable events in recent days, the army is in such a situation that it is incapable of doing anything" (Ghara-Baghi 1984:452).

General Mohaghgheghi, commander of the gendarmerie, reported to the council that the previous evening some soldiers had escaped from the Vanak garrison as police officers were taking refuge there. The gendarmerie headquarters had been surrounded for several days, and gendarmes were forced to go to their offices dressed in civilian clothes. The training office was surrounded by demonstrators who threatened to attack the building. Mohaghgheghi requested assistance from the army and the martial law commander, but neither had any additional personnel to spare.

General Amini, head of army intelligence, reported that the police headquarters in the Sepah Plaza had just been set on fire by opposition forces. He added that the previous evening, soldiers had escaped from some of the garrisons where the situation was critical, and disorder ruled everywhere. Rioters had surrounded most of the garrisons and were demonstrating; clashes had broken out at the Eshrat-Abad garrison (Ghara-Baghi 1984:457). General Houshang Hatam, deputy chief of staff of the armed forces, declared that the army was not in a position to do anything. He noted that Prime Minister Bakhtiar was planning to call for the formation of an Islamic Republic and that people had demonstrated that they supported both a republic and Ayatollah Khomeini. The Shah was not going to return to the country. He stated his opinion that the armed forces should announce solidarity with the opposition and stop "killing our brothers" (Ghara-Baghi 1984:460). General Naser Firouzmand and General Abdol-majid Ma'somi, deputy minister of war, agreed, declaring that the army should express its solidarity in order to put an end to fruitless bloodshed (Ghara-Baghi 1984:461). Eventually, following two and one-half hours of discussion, the heads of the armed forces voted to announce political neutrality and support for the demands of the Iranian people, stating, "To prevent disorder and further bloodshed, the army proclaims neutrality in the current political conflicts and has ordered all units to return to their garrisons. The Iranian army has always supported and will support the noble and patriotic people of Iran and their demands" (Ghara-Baghi 1984:464–465).

CONCLUSION

The disintegration of the armed forces resulted from a combination of a number of factors: the mobilization of bazaaris, workers and white-collar employees; the disruption of the country's trade, production, distribution, and services; and the popular struggles and attacks on the regime. In addition, the structure of the army had weaknesses of its own. It was accountable only to the Shah himself, who had the entire army under his personal control. Finally, more than 90 percent of the four hundred thousand army personnel were conscripts who served for only eighteen months; they remained closely tied to the civilian population and became unreliable instruments during periods of massive conflicts.

The critical factor was the formation of the broad national coalition and disruption of the social order, which engendered instability within the military and paralyzed the armed forces. By autumn 1978, and especially with the advent of the military government, the spiral of conflict had accelerated to such an extent that virtually the entire nation had risen against the monarch. The scope of collective action expanded to the point where enormous numbers of people would have had to be killed in order to maintain the Shah's rule. Another factor was the formation of self-defense groups by students and the younger generation to fight off hooligans in many cities. These groups aggressively struck back at the armed forces and, indeed, had some success. The weaknesses in the army's structure also played a part in its disintegration. Many garrisons in large urban areas were located within city limits; consequently, soldiers had some contact with the civilian population. They could not help but notice the high level of mobilization and disruption of essential services, such as electricity, trade, gasoline, post offices, and transportation. Increasing unrest may have indicated not only the possibility of defiance and opposition, but also the probability of success. These factors certainly encouraged insubordination and desertion within the military.

The military came in close contact with the people and events in early November 1978. As demonstrations mounted along with rallies, strikes, and bazaar shutdowns, the Shah reversed his reformist policy and appointed a military government. As the armed forces assumed immediate political responsibility and came into direct contact with the massive disruptions and struggles, instability within the military mounted. Military personnel were only thinly dispersed throughout the country to repress the population, making soldiers increasingly unreliable and insubordinate. Many conscripts and low-ranking officers began deserting the garrisons. In several garrisons, soldiers and low-ranking officers organized small cells and launched armed attacks against their commanding officers. As a result of such actions, several high-ranking officers were killed, leading the army to prohibit issuing weapons to lieutenants and corporals. After only two months, the regime replaced the military government with a civilian prime minister, Bakhtiar, an ex-member of the National Front who promised greater reforms. Ultimately, the Shah's departure in mid-January signaled the regime's total collapse. This was claimed as a victory by the people and, consequently, the number of desertions grew rapidly. Groups of low-ranking officers expressed their support for the revolution.

During the final days, the United States was instrumental in persuading the Shah to leave the country and encouraging the chiefs of the armed forces to remain neutral. This action by the United States came about precisely because the Carter administration and its Western allies realized that even a military regime could no longer rule Iran. The Shah's departure shattered the cohesion of the army, which had been loyal and accountable to the monarch alone. In the last days of the regime, overwhelming popular assaults against the buildings, personnel, and munitions of the armed forces, combined with growing defections, rendered the military incapable of carrying out orders. Eventually, the council of the armed forces proclaimed its neutrality and withdrew to the garrisons. Thus came to an end the institution of the monarchy and a throne that had reigned for twenty-five hundred years. In its place an Islamic Republic was established, to which we now turn.

Chapter 9

Conflicts within the Islamic Republic

In these days after the revolution when all social strata should cooperate to reconstruct the country . . . strike after strike, sit-in after
sit-in, march after march, and lies after lies are prevailing attempts
to weaken the government with deceit and rumors. Those who incite others to strike and sit in to weaken the government are opponents of our movement and supporters of foreigners. (Ayatollah
Khomeini, *Kayhan*, August 8, 1979)

Revolutions result from the protracted struggles of broad coalitions of
classes and groups with disparate interests, different capacities for action,
and different resources. Depending on the nature of the new state that is
then established, certain sets of conflicts may be resolved, while others
may persist. Similarly, revolutionary coalitions may hold up or may disin-
tegrate once the previous regime has been overthrown. If the coalitions do
break down, new rounds of mobilization and collective action may result.
The narrower the coalition that heads a postrevolutionary regime, the
greater the likelihood and intensity of new conflicts. The nature of the new
conflicts will derive, once again, from interests, organization and solidarity
for action, and opportunity for mobilization. Once again, the success of
the new actors and challengers will depend on their ability to mobilize
resources, form coalitions, consolidate opposition forces and classes,
and disrupt the social structure. Without consolidation, repression may

demobilize and even eliminate the new contenders. Demobilizing the challengers facilitates control by the new power holders, who may rule without their former partners, relying on coercion rather than coalition. Although a wide coalition is essential to overthrow a regime, a narrower coalition buttressed by a strong repressive apparatus may be sufficient to keep it in power.

Unlike other theorists of the Iranian revolution, such as Arjomand and Skocpol, who argued that an underlying ideational consensus among all Iranians brought about the ouster of the Shah and thus predicated an end to conflict with the establishment of the Islamic Republic, the analysis that has been presented here predicts that conflicts will continue at least until demobilization sets in. The new government faced a severe economic crisis, with millions unemployed, factories lying idle, and prices rising. In addition, the deeply divided coalition of liberals and clergy that composed the new government was enmeshed in a number of conflicts that prolonged the crisis. From 1977 to 1979, conflicts of interests and divisions were subordinated in order to combat the Shah's regime. The removal of the monarchy precipitated new divisions. These factors, combined with the temporary collapse of the armed forces and the Savak, provided an opportunity for various classes and groups to mobilize in order to pursue their separate interests. At that time, events such as the hostage crisis, the American embargo, and the war with Iraq generated nationalism and redirected the internal conflicts outward, mitigating their intensity.

A number of groups and classes, including national minorities, segments of the peasantry, large groups of industrial workers, segments of bazaaris, intellectuals, and the vast majority of students, mobilized for social change. Their collective actions can be explained in terms of their interests, organizations, solidarity structures, and opportunities for mobilization. With the collapse of the monarchy and the weakness of the new government, national minorities, especially Kurds, saw an opportunity to gain autonomy. As landlords fled the countryside, peasants organized and pressed for better agricultural policies. In some parts of the country they seized land and urged land reform. With the exodus of hundreds of industrialists and over ten thousand managers, industrial workers organized in separate factories to control large enterprises, alter industrial relations, and improve their economic circumstances. Segments of bazaaris mobilized to defend their interests against adverse state policies and intervention. Students and intellectuals organized to press for greater political freedom, civil liberties, and radical social change.

Although broad segments of the population opposed the new state, they failed to consolidate their resources and act against a single target at the same time. Significantly, they had lost control of the mosque, which had been an important base of their mobilization against the monarchy. In addition, they were now pursuing disparate interests, some of which were incompatible with one another. Schisms within the opposition groups, along with the clergy's enhanced ability to control the population through the establishment of a large Revolutionary Guard, insured the survival of the new regime. In the following analysis, I shall examine some of these conflicts, focusing primarily on the initial two years of the Islamic Republic, during which the clergy successfully ousted liberals from the government and consolidated their power.

STATE STRUCTURE AND THE ESTABLISHMENT OF THE ISLAMIC REPUBLIC

Ayatollah Khomeini, the undisputed leader of the revolution, appointed Bazargan, an engineer, supporter of Mosaddegh, and devout Moslem, to form a provisional government and revolutionary council. Even before the monarchy collapsed, Bazargan selected the Revolutionary Council, whose membership changed a number of times in the first few months after the revolution. The first council was composed of five clerics; eight intellectuals and political activists, mostly from the Freedom Movement including Bazargan himself; two bazaaris; and two army generals (Bazargan 1983b:25). The task of the council was to oversee the work of the government. The provisional government was headed by Bazargan, as prime minister (February–November 1979), and his cabinet, made up primarily of leaders of the Freedom Movement and the National Front. The distribution of the cabinet members was as follows: eleven from the Freedom Movement, eight from the National Front, four from the Islamic Association of Engineers, and three independents (Bazargan 1983b:38–39). Although no cleric held a ministerial post, four clergy served as deputies to different ministries.

The provisional government accomplished little in the way of social change. Two of its main accomplishments were to carry out a referendum to approve the establishment of an Islamic Republic and to expropriate wealth belonging to a number of industrialists. The referendum was held on March 30–31, 1979, to decide whether the government should be a monarchy or an Islamic Republic. Voters could respond by indicating either yes or no. A number of political organizations boycotted the referendum, claiming it was "anti-democratic" because it did not give voters any real choice as the people had already overthrown the monarchy. Nevertheless, the vast majority—20,406,591 out of 22,800,000 eligible voters—voted in favor of an Islamic Republic. A few months later, in July, the Bazargan government nationalized the industrial assets of fifty-one of the wealthiest businessmen, many of whom had already fled the country (*Kayhan*, July 7, 1979).

The provisional government lasted for nine months and resigned in protest against "interferences" that made it impossible to continue to operate. Bazargan had made similar charges before on numerous occasions, but he did not actually quit until the students took over the American Embassy in November 1979. Khomeini then asked the Revolutionary Council to take charge of the operation of the government until the new Majles was elected in May 1980. The council was at that time composed of six clerics, including Ayatollahs Dr. Sayyed Mohammad Beheshti, Mahdavi-Kani, Mousavi-Ardebili, Dr. Mohammad Javad Bahonar and Hojjat Al-Eslams Hashemi-Rafsanjani and Khameneh'i; and seven nonclerics, including Abolhasan Bani-Sadr, Dr. Abbas Shaybani, Sadegh Ghotb-Zadeh, Dr. Yadollah Sahabi, Ali Akbar Moienfar, Sadr, and Bazargan himself.

Although the clergy did not predominate within the government's formal structure, they controlled the nongovernmental organizations such as the Komitehs—the committees—and the armed Revolutionary Guard. These organizations had been formed soon after the monarchy's collapse to bring the country under control and were to have been either dissolved or incorporated into the government. On February 28, 1979, Khomeini stated that as soon as the government was in full control of the cities, the Komitehs should relinquish their power to the government and avoid interfering in government affairs (1983, 5:120). Popular criticism of the Komitehs and the Revolutionary Guards reached a peak after two Marxist sons of Ayatollah Taleghani were arrested for no apparent reason. In protest, Taleghani closed his office and vanished for a few days after securing the release of his sons. Large demonstrations protesting the arrests were organized by leftist groups. Finally, Khomeini asked Taleghani to return to public life, which he did. A few days later, Ayatollah Mahdavi-Kani, supreme commander of the Central Komiteh, announced that the Guard would be incorporated into the police after its unfit elements had been purged (*New York Times*, April 25, 1979). Neither the Komitehs nor the

Guard were dissolved, however. The Revolutionary Guard became a strong force and played an important role in future conflicts. Unlike the army, which was composed largely of conscripts who could prove unreliable under certain conditions, the Guard was staffed by full-time, permanent personnel who had joined voluntarily, some for economic reasons, others out of fundamental commitment to the Islamic Republic. Despite Bazargan's constant criticism and complaints that they represented the "Rule of Revenge," they survived and formed an important base of power for the clergy organized in the Islamic Republican party (IRP).

On July 3, an Assembly of Experts was elected; 10,735,240 voters elected seventy-five members to represent the entire country. The decision to limit the number of representatives gave rise to controversy and criticism. Government authorities justified the limit of seventy-five members on the grounds that provisional, disorderly conditions prevailing within the country did not permit prolonged debate and that the national interest required a rapid end to such conditions (Interior Minister Y. Sahabi, *Ettelaat*, June 16, 1979). Opponents countered that restricting the assembly would reduce popular participation and prepare the way for the "monopolization" of power. They also attacked the way in which assembly seats had been allocated. Religious minorities, excluding Baha'is (who were considered heretics), totaled less than 500,000 and had been given four seats, roughly one seat for every 125,000 people. In contrast, the remaining 35.5 million people had been allocated seventy-one seats, or an average of one seat for every 500,000 people. Despite criticism, the Bazargan government proceeded with the plan.

After the elections, several organizations charged that voting had been marred by numerous irregularities. The critics included Ayatollah Mahallati of Shiraz (*Kayhan*, August 9, 1979), the Society of Merchants and Shopkeepers of Mashhad (*Kayhan*, August 16, 1979), the Society of the Clergy in Mashhad, the Fedayeen, five Islamic political organizations including the Mojahedeen (*Kayhan*, August 9, 1979), and the Moslem People's Republican party, established in Azerbaijan and supported by Ayatollah Shariat-Madari (*Kayhan*, August 11, 1979). Despite their protests, the election as a whole was declared valid, although votes from ten polls in Tehran were thrown out. In August 1979, seventy-four of the seventy-five duly elected members held their first meeting. The sole dissenter was Dr. Abdolrahman Ghasemlou, the Kurdish representative, who boycotted the assembly to protest the army's bombing of Paveh, a Kurdish city (*Kayhan*, August 9, 1979).

The Assembly of Experts drafted a new constitution, which was approved by popular referendum in December 1979. The constitution proclaimed that the Islamic government was to be based on religious authority, and that it would provide conditions under which all citizens could grow toward perfection. Articles 107–110 gave absolute power to the supreme religious leader, Valayat-e Faghieh, who could ultimately veto all government decisions and was authorized to dismiss the president. Many political organizations and leaders criticized this clause of the constitution, which was not part of the original draft prepared by Bazargan and his associates but was inserted later. Critics of the new constitution included Ayatollah Taleghani, who had received the highest number of votes for the Assembly of Experts that drafted the constitution. Before the new document was approved, Taleghani expressed misgivings that "the standard and level of (Islamic) Constitution would be much inferior to the one we had 70 years ago" (Irfani 1983:199; Shanehchi 1983, tape 2:23).

While the new constitution was being debated, hostages were taken at the American Embassy. The hostage crisis was effectively used to rally popular support for the government and promote unity. Much of the controversy was deflected away from the constitution and directed instead toward the United States, thus facilitating the ratification of the constitution.

The 1979 Constitution of the Islamic Republic of Iran did support certain democratic and egalitarian principles. "Regarding the character of this great movement, the Constitution guarantees help to abolish any kind of ideological, social, or economic despotism and provide the way to break the system of despotism by entrusting the fate of the people to their own hands. . . . The Constitution provides for such participation by all circles in decision-making in determining the fate of all persons in society in order to perfect every person" (Introduction). The constitution emphasized that the economy of the Islamic Republic should prevent foreign domination, "uproot poverty and impoverishment and fulfill growing human needs, while preserving its independence." In addition, the Islamic Republic should secure basic needs such as "housing, nourishment, clothing, hygiene, medical care, education, and vocational training and establishing a suitable environment for all to start a family" (chap. 4, principle 43). The constitution permitted the formation of political parties, groups, and political and professional associations, as well as independent labor organizations (chap. 3, principle 26). The constitution also called for the establishment of industrial and agricultural councils composed of representatives of workers, villagers, and managers to operate productive units (chap. 7, principle

104). These aspects of the constitution directly reflected the demands of the various groups and classes that fought against the monarchy.

The next step was to choose a president. Rivalry among political groups intensified. Serious candidates included Bani-Sadr, who represented liberals; Hasan Habibi, representing the Islamic Republican party (IRP), which advocated fundamentalism and was dominated by the fraction of the clergy who acted in the name of Ayatollah Khomeini; and Masoud Rajavi, the leader of the Mojahedeen, which advocated Islamic socialism and a classless society. The Fedayeen and other Marxist groups did not believe in God or Islam, and their members were thus barred by the constitution from becoming president. Both groups announced that they would support Rajavi, as did the Kurdish Democratic party. Such support would have constituted many votes for the Mojahedeen. Ayatollah Khomeini intervened, however, declaring Rajavi ineligible because the Mojahedeen had refused to approve the constitution on the grounds that granting highest power to a supreme clergy or body of clerics was undemocratic and contradicted other aspects of the constitution. In the presidential election held in January 1980, Bani-Sadr received 75 percent of the fourteen million votes cast, while the IRP candidate received only half a million, or approximately 3.5 percent.

The final stage in the formation of the Islamic Republic was the election of representatives to the Majles. As a prelude to the election, the IRP, joined by liberals led by Bani-Sadr, launched attacks upon the universities, which had become centers of antigovernment activity. These attacks resulted in bloodshed and deaths of students and the closure of the universities. With the universities eliminated, the IRP turned against political opponents and favored conducting the elections in two stages. Those who received an absolute majority in the first round would be elected. A second election would then be held for the remaining positions, with those candidates who got the highest number of votes entering the Majles. Opposition organizations charged that the purpose of a two-stage election process was to eliminate smaller parties and political organizations. To discover the popular response to the proposed election procedure, President Bani-Sadr's office conducted a poll in seven locations, including the Tehran bazaar. Of 1,359 people polled, 43.1 percent opposed two-stage elections, 22.1 percent favored them, 27.5 percent were undecided, and approximately 7 percent had no opinion (*Kayhan*, March 13, 1980). Despite widespread criticism, the elections were carried out in two stages. The outcome was extremely favorable to the clergy. Clerics were elected to 45.4 percent of the seats, although not all of them were representatives of the IRP (Public Relations 1983:199). Overall, the IRP claimed roughly 130 of 241 seats (Zabih 1982:66–67; *New York Times* May 29, 1980). Liberals won approximately 40 seats, while the remainder went to independents and small political groups. No leftist representatives were elected to the Majles.

After the elections, many political leaders and organizations charged that irregularities had taken place. One such critic was Ayatollah Pasandideh, elder brother of Ayatollah Khomeini. In a cable to President Bani-Sadr he charged, "People were made to vote for the IRP candidates through the use of deception, intimidation . . . mass imprisonment and murder. . . . I am grieved to declare that at no period (in history) acts such as these have been witnessed. People did not expect the Islamic government to act in this manner" (*Kayhan*, March 19, 1980; Irfani 1983:198).

The new Majles was deeply divided. Liberal representatives emphasized political freedom, civil liberties, and economic growth. Bazargan, main leader of the liberals in the Majles, had already indicated he was not interested in fundamentally reorganizing the social structure once the monarchy had been eliminated. For example, the head of the Central Bank under Bazargan announced that the lives and property of capitalists who had fled would be guaranteed if they brought their capital back into the country (*Kayhan*, May 5, 1979). In the early days of the provisional government, noting the growing demands of the people for social change, Bazargan complained, "We asked for rain; we got a flood." Although the clerical faction advocated the rule of Islam and of ideologues, they disagreed on many social and economic issues. In fact, Majles representatives were divided into radicals, who emphasized egalitarianism, and conservatives, who opposed fundamental change. These conflicts led Fuad Karimi, head of the Economic Committee, to complain, "There is a strong minority in the Majles who opposes any bill or law intended to serve the oppressed on the grounds that such bills are 'non-Islamic' or 'anti-Islamic.'"

In the midst of these conflicts, Ayatollah Khomeini kept emphasizing unity and constantly attempted to instill support for the government; when advice and threats did not work, Khomeini used his power to resolve the issues. He repeatedly insisted that the Islamic government would recognize and grant freedom to all political groups. He maintained that even the law of Valayat-e Faghieh, which gave absolute power to the highest religious leader, was not intended to establish dictatorship, but rather to prevent its occurrence (1983, 10:29). When mosque attendance declined shortly after the revolution, Khomeini called upon the nation, especially intellectuals and students, to participate and fill the mosques to prevent defeat and insure the revolution's victory (1983, 7:58; 12:148, 218).

Most importantly, Khomeini shifted the emphasis in his public statements from freedom and independence, which had been prominent themes prior to the Shah's overthrow, to serving the interests of the *mostazafin*, the oppressed and the deprived. This shift took Khomeini further to the Left than any established Iranian politician in the twentieth century, including Mosaddegh. He declared that the feast of the oppressed is when the oppressors are eliminated (1983, 9:246). Khomeini stated that God had determined to clean the earth of the oppressors and put the oppressed in power. Islam had come for this purpose (1983, 6:71). Khomeini also declared that the poor should be elevated and the rich brought down so that they would live like brothers (1983, 5:237). Islam wants people to have both a spiritual and a material life (Khomeini 1983, 5:127). Shortly after the revolution, he ordered that the assets of the Pahlavi dynasty be appropriated and used for housing and work for the poor and oppressed (1983, 5:127). Khomeini himself opened an account and asked people to contribute money to build housing for the poor. Finally, he ordered the provisional government to provide free water and electricity for the poor who had been deprived by the monarchy (1983, 5:120). Khomeini was well aware of the conflicts and warned, "If we cannot reduce economic polarization and reduce the inequalities between the rich and the poor, and if consequently people get disappointed in Islam, nothing can prevent the resulting explosion; and we will all be destroyed" (1983, 10:50). Only once did Khomeini claim that the revolution was for Islam, not for "the stomach," meaning material things (1983, 13:143). Khomeini's promises of freedom and social justice in the interests of the poor and oppressed gained support for the Islamic regime from some segments of every social class, especially the urban poor.

Despite Ayatollah Khomeini's pleas to support the Islamic regime, the continuing crisis, combined with conflicts within the ruling coalition and the government's inability to satisfy people's demands, reduced popular participation in formal political affairs. The number of voters who participated in succeeding elections illustrates this point. In the referendum of March 1979, 20,406,591 people voted out of a total of 22,800,000. In the elections for the Assembly of Experts in July, the number decreased by one-half to 10,735,240. In December, 15,688,407 people voted to approve the constitution. In January 1980, 14,146,622 people voted in the presidential elections. By March 1980, only 10,833,843 people voted to elect representatives to the Majles (*Kayhan Havaee*, March 25, 1984). This figure was less than one-half of the eligible voters. As participation in formal politics declined, segments of the population mobilized for collective action to bring about change. Let us now briefly examine the conflicts of such groups and classes.

AUTONOMY MOVEMENTS

The national minorities had benefited little from the development policies of the Persian monarchy. State capital-allocation policies did not favor most national minorities mobilized as the collapse of the repressive apparatus of lacked independent educational institutions in their own languages. Sharing common interests and concentrated in specific geographical regions, national minorites mobilized as the collapse of the repressive apparatus of the old regime provided an opportunity for collective action. Shortly after the revolution, movements demanding self-rule within the Islamic Republic emerged in Kurdestan, the Turkoman region, and among the Arab minority in Khuzestan. Both the Kurdish and Turkoman movements were strongly influenced by socialists, who advocated fundamental changes. Hence, a conflict of interest existed between these movements and both the liberal and clerical factions of the government. Self-rule would have challenged the central government's authority and might have set a precedent for other regions of the country. Although autonomy for these national minorities was favored by some religious leaders, including Ayatollah Taleghani, the government eventually rejected their demands. In the confrontations that ensued, the Turkoman and Arab movements were quickly suppressed. The Kurdish struggles, largest and longest of the three, have continued up to the present day.

After the defeat of the Autonomous Republic of Kurdestan in 1946, the Shah implemented policies designed to subjugate and subordinate the Kurdish people. Teaching of the Kurdish language was banned in the schools of Kurdestan, and students were even prohibited from wearing traditional Kurdish clothing to school. At the same time, the government built several large army garrisons in Kurdestan to ensure control over the region. The available structural indices reveal the nature of the uneven development that characterized Iran under the Shah's regime. The average household expenditure in the central state of Tehran was 1.4 times greater than that in Kurdestan. The estimated rate of literacy for Tehran in 1973 was 76 percent, while literacy in the rest of the country stood at 38 percent. In contrast, literacy was only 22.3 percent in Kurdestan, which ranked above only Ilam, with a rate of 21.5 percent. Similarly, the number of students attending universities was significantly lower in Kurdestan than in the rest of the country. For the Farsi-speaking region in 1976, this figure was three per thousand, while for Kurdestan, it was one per thousand. Kurdestan had the lowest rate of industrial development in the nation and possessed neither private nor state-sponsored industrial development. The size of the industrial work force in the Farsi-speaking region was twenty-one per thousand in 1976, while in Kurdestan it was ten per thousand. Financial and banking growth was also lower in Kurdestan compared to other regions.

During the revolution, Kurds were very active in the conflicts. After the revolution they were the first national minority to press for autonomy, and they actively supported other minorities engaged in similar struggles. Their demands included the following: (1) internal autonomy for Kurdestan, which would continue to follow the Iranian government's policies in foreign relations, economy and commerce, and defense; (2) formation of an independent Kurdish parliament by means of free elections to manage Kurdestan's economic, political, and cultural affairs; (3) recognition of the Kurdish language as the official language of Kurdestan; (4) insistence that the government allocate funds to help eradicate Kurdestan's economic backwardness, which resulted from national oppression; (5) democratic freedoms of expression, association, religion, and the press throughout Iran; and (6) Kurdish representatives should play a role in the central government. Ayatollah Taleghani traveled to Kurdestan and declared that the grievances of the Kurdish people were just and that the government should help develop the region.

In the early stages, the new government vacillated and even promised autonomy to the Kurds. In a few rounds of armed conflicts, the Kurds made impressive military gains. As the country's army was reorganized, however, and the Revolutionary Guards were formed and strengthened, the government refused to agree to the Kurdish demands. Government authorities asserted that to show any weakness in Kurdestan would encourage other national minorities to demand similar rights. Clashes erupted shortly after the revolution and continued in many parts of Kurdestan between Kurds and government forces. In August 1979, Ayatollah Khomeini ordered the army to attack Kurds in Paveh, whom he called "corrupt rebels." The army dispatched tanks and cannons, and massive bloodshed resulted. Both sides took numerous hostages: the government announced the arrests of one hundred members of the Kurdish Democratic party and the Fedayeen, while the Kurds claimed to have taken many military prisoners. During the first few days of fighting, the government declared that three hundred rebels had been killed. Ayatollah Khalkhali, who was in charge of the troops sent to crush the rebellion, ordered the execution of nine Kurdish rebels in Paveh (*Kayhan*, August 21, 1979). In addition to these clashes in Paveh, other major uprisings took place throughout Kurdestan, notably in Sanandaj, Mahabad, Naghadeh, and Marivan. Many people were killed and injured in these cities. The government outlawed the Kurdish Democratic party and the Koomeleh, a Kurdish leftist political organization that was especially strong in southern Kurdestan. Nevertheless, some ten thousand armed Kurdish guerrillas have continued to wage war against government forces in the mountains of Kurdestan. For a few years after the revolution, rebel Kurdish forces held many parts of rural Kurdestan and many small towns under their control.

From the beginning, the Kurds were supported by the Fedayeen, who joined them in armed confrontation with the government. The Fedayeen were recognized as one of the partners in the Kurdish conflict. They participated in the formal negotiations with the government held in Kurdestan shortly after the revolution, which broke off because of the government's refusal to agree to Kurdish demands. A Fedayeen physician, Rashvand Sardari, who had been dispached from Tehran to treat wounded Kurdish rebels and Fedayeen guerrillas, was arrested and executed. The Mojahedeen also backed the Kurds' right to autonomy, but consistently advised them to refrain from confronting the government. After the ouster of President Bani-Sadr in 1981, the Mojahedeen also established guerrilla bases in Kurdestan to carry out armed attacks on government forces.

Autonomy was demanded by the Turkoman people as well. The Turkoman minority, like the Kurds, had been adversely affected during the decades of Iran's economic development. As agriculture became increasingly commercialized, the Turkoman region became fully integrated into the national and international economy. Turkoman land, located near the Caspian Sea, receives abundant rainfall and is agriculturally very productive. But much of the land had been expropriated by the royal family and their associates, depriving the Turkomans of their land.

Five days after the revolution, a group of Turkoman intellectuals who were also members of the Fedayeen formed the Political and Cultural Headquarters of the Turkoman People. This organization soon gained the support of the vast majority of the Turkoman people, who participated in their rallies and marches. The organization demanded (1) free elections to form revolutionary councils that would advance the cause of laborers in cities and the countryside; (2) redistribution by peasant councils to landless peasants of land held by the Pahlavi family and other expropriators; (3) cancellation of debts to banks and government institutions incurred by workers, peasants, artisans, and low-ranking white-collar employees; (4) lifting of all national and cultural restrictions on the Turkoman people and self-determination in Turkoman cultural, religious, and national affairs; (5) formation of a people's army to protect the country and punish Savak agents and members of the previous regime; and (6) condemnation of any monopoly of power and support of demands by national minorities for self-determination (*Ettelaat*, April 4, 1979).

Several clashes took place between government forces and Turkoman rebels. In March 1979, Turkoman guerrillas in Gonbad Kavous, with the assistance of the Fedayeen, captured the police station, taking eighteen hostages (*Ettelaat*, March 27, 1979). In other incidents, eighty-five people were killed. After several days of clashes, the government asked Ayatollah Taleghani to intervene; his mediation restored calm. At the request of Turkoman leaders, Taleghani visited Gonbad Kavous to investigate their grievances. A second round of conflicts began a year later when the Political and Cultural Headquarters of the Turkoman People in Gonbad Kavous arranged to commemorate the anniversary of the Fedayeen Siahkal conflict of 1971. Although the mayor of Gonbad Kavous issued a permit for the demonstration, the evening before the demonstration the Revolutionary Guard arrested four Turkoman leaders: Toomaj, Makhtoum, Vahedi, and Jorjani, all of whom were also members of the Fedayeen. The next day, as thousands of people joined in the demonstration, the Guard intervened, claiming that a conspiracy had been discovered. Violence broke out when a Turkoman cigarette vendor was killed by the Guard. Armed clashes persisted for several days, and more people were slain on both sides. Ayatollah Khalkhali was dispatched to the region to reassert government control and immediately arrested many Turkoman activists. A few days later, the bodies of the four leaders were found beneath a highway bridge near the city of Bojnourd (*Kayhan*, February 24, 1980). Three days later, twenty-three other Turkoman leaders and activists were murdered in Gonbad (*Kayhan*, February 27, 1980).

Like the Kurds, the Turkoman people were supported in their quest for autonomy by the Fedayeen, which had a small cell in Gonbad Kavous at the beginning of the rebellion. When clashes erupted over Turkoman autonomy, the Fedayeen sent additional reinforcements to the region. The Turkoman also received assistance from the Kurds, who supplied nurses and physicians to treat those wounded in the clashes. In one incident, nine doctors and nurses traveling to Gonbad Kavous to assist Turkoman rebels were killed in a car accident (*Ettelaat*, March 31, 1979).

A third group to demand self-rule was the Arab minority of Khuzestan, which after the revolution formed a group called the Political Organization of the Arab People of Khuzestan to promote regional autonomy from the national government. In April 1979, more than 100,000 Arabs in Khorramshar demonstrated in support of Ayatollah Shobare Khaghani, their religious leader, who opposed the government, and they demanded local autonomy, but not independence (*New York Times*, April 28, 1979; *Kayhan*, April 28, 1979). Khaghani declared that the legal rights of all peoples should be recognized and that the government should not discriminate against anyone, regardless of whether they were Fars, Turks, Balouchs, or Kurds (*Kayhan*, April 24, 1979). Arabs also organized demonstrations in Ahvaz to press for autonomy. The government was no more inclined to grant autonomy to Arab peoples than to Kurdish or Turkoman autonomy-seekers. In May, several demonstrations and rallies led to violence. Government militias searched the house of Ayatollah Khaghani and claimed to have discovered concealed weapons (*Ettelaat*, July 16, 1979). Shortly afterward, the government reported that seven people, including two government militiamen, were killed in Khorramshar in clashes in a mosque. Ayatollah Khaghani protested the incident at the mosque, but was taken by the government to Qom (*Kayhan*, July 21, 1979). The official explanation of his departure was offered by General Madani, governor of Khuzestan, who said that Khaghani had left to prevent any harm from coming to him.

All these minorities had participated in the revolutionary conflicts that led to the monarch's overthrow. Individually or even in combination they could not have overthrown the government, but in alliance with the rest of the country they helped oust the government that had failed to serve their interests. However, they did not have support from broad segments of the population for their goals of autonomy. As a result, the government succeeded in repressing these movements.

THE PEASANTRY

The peasantry were divided during most of the revolutionary conflicts, with one segment supporting the monarch and another opposing him. After the monarchy was overthrown, peasants in many parts of the country engaged in greater political activity. The flight of landlords from the countryside created a political vacuum in which control over the peasantry was reduced, providing an opportunity for mobilization. In addition, peasants in urban areas who had become radicalized during the revolution migrated back to their villages and organized for collective action. Finally, the opening of the political arena, reduced repression, and the growth of leftist political organizations advocating land reform contributed to peasant insurgency.

In the Turkoman region a combination of land concentration in the hands of big landlords and a high percentage of the proletariat among the rural population generated a high level of collective action. The Turkoman region had the highest concentration of land in the entire country: 19 percent of the land was controlled by a mere .26 percent of the landowners. Most of the landlords were not Turkoman, however. The Shah's brother, Gholamreza, and his sister, Shams Pahlavi, each owned thousands of acres in the Turkoman region of Gonbad Kavous, as did top army officials and Persian associates of the royal court. In addition, the royal family claimed the entire Golestan Jangal, a large forest near Galikash, for their private hunting range, thus preventing its use by people in the region. The Turkoman area also had the highest rate of proletarianization in the nation. According to the 1976 census, more than 50 percent of the rural population in Gonbad Kavous worked for wages.

As many landlords associated with the previous regime fled the country in the final months of the revolutionary conflicts, peasants adversely affected by economic inequality reclaimed some of their ancestral land. They organized land seizures beginning in villages with a tradition of rebellion, until several villages had come under peasant control. Soon after the establishment of the Islamic Republic, fifteen thousand Turkoman peasants marched through the streets of Gonbad demanding return of their lands, democratic land reform, a ban on imported agricultural goods, government support for fishermen and rug-weavers in the region, cancellation of bank debts and interest payments on loans, and autonomy for the

Turkoman region. Land expropriations proceeded rapidly, and within a few months four hundred newly formed peasant councils had seized land throughout the region. The councils, assisted by the Political and Cultural Headquarters of the Turkoman People and the Fedayeen, were grouped into twenty-five larger unions, which met regularly to discuss local problems. Because the expropriated land often consisted of enormous tracts, the decision was made by the councils to cultivate them collectively.

In other areas where land concentration was high, peasants soon followed suit and regained their lands. In the northern states of Kurdestan, Khorasan, and Mazanderan, peasants formed councils and expropriated large expanses of land. In hundreds of villages they fought with proprietors over land ownership. In parts of Kurdestan where the Shah's land reform had never been introduced landlords fought back, organizing their own committees and arming themselves with the support of right-wing Barzani tribal leaders and Ghiadeh Moveghat (*Kayhan*, May 9, 1979). In skirmishes between landlords and Kurdish peasants, many people were slain. When peasants in Khorasan organized councils and initiated land seizures, landlords mobilized and clashed with peasants.

As peasant demands for land redistribution mounted, a call for land reform was incorporated into the new constitution. The first Majles even passed a land reform bill, and Reza Isfahani, a top official in the Ministry of Agriculture, drew up plans to implement the reform. Committees composed of seven persons, known as Komiteh-e Haft-Nafareh, were formed throughout the country to distribute land. Land reform was criticized by landlords and some prominent religious leaders, such as Ayatollah Golpaygani, on the grounds it was non-Islamic. Ayatollah Khomeini ordered the reforms stopped until a clear decision was reached. Undaunted, the peasantry continued to press for reform. In one gathering of Turkoman peasants, those who opposed land reform were condemned as "feudals" (*Ettelatt*, May 11, 1981). A number of secular and religious groups, including members of the Islamic Association of Mosques in Tabriz, also demanded the implementation of land reform (*Ettelaat*, May 10, 1981). Eventually, after debating for several years, the Guardian Council rejected land reform, stating that it was non-Islamic (*Jumhuri Eslami*, January 19, 1983). A compromise was finally reached permitting local authorities to decide whether peasants' grievances against landlords warranted transfer of land.

To date, land reform as a matter of principle has not been approved. The distribution of rural land remains highly unequal. Even in the Turkoman region, where peasants succeeded in keeping some of the expropriated lands, distribution is uneven. Half the arable land still belongs to big landlords, while 90,000 peasant families remain without land (*Ettelaat*, April 17, 1983). In Khorasan, out of a rural population of 1.2 million, between 700,000 and 800,000 need land (*Ettelaat*, October 24, 1982). Everywhere, big landlords still hold the land best suited for cultivation (*Ettelaat*, June 14, 1983). Some big landlords whose land was expropriated after the revolution returned to their estates and regained control over their property (*Ettelaat*, June 21, 1983, January 26, 1983; *Kayhan*, February 9, 1983). According to Mohammad Hoseini-Nia, member of parliament from Roudsar, "a 'green light' has been given to many who went abroad during the revolutionary conflicts and are now returning" (*Ettelaat*, May 26, 1984).

Continued inequities in land distribution has led to the resumption of urban migration by peasants. Seven villages near the city of Abhar were totally vacated through migration (*Kayhan*, December 6, 1983). In 1982, five thousand families migrated to urban areas from the province of Hamedan (*Kayhan*, July 20, 1983). One member of the Majles noted that in Malayer, 100 of 345 villages were vacated in the years following the revolution (*Kayhan*, July 28, 1984). Partly as the result of migration, the population of large cities has expanded dramatically. Tehran, for example, grew from four million inhabitants in 1979 to seven million in 1981. According to one study, approximately fifteen hundred people moved to Tehran every day (*Kayhan*, January 5, 1984). Dr. Najafi, deputy governor of Tehran for political affairs, noted that the following factors were responsible for increased peasant migration: (1) inadequate rural income in comparison to large cities; (2) inadequate living conditions; (3) high prices and shortages of basic goods in rural areas; (4) shortages of agricultural necessities such as water and machinery; (5) persistent problems of land ownership; (6) absence of a law authorizing the formation of representative peasant councils; (7) the impossibility of preventing peasants from squatting on urban land; (8) uneven government expenditures in urban and rural areas; (9) inadequate credit allocated for agriculture; and (10) the uneconomical nature of agricultural production (*Ettelaat*, May 23, 1981).

THE UNIVERSITIES

Under the monarchy, universities were centers of continual dissent and opposition against the regime. From 1977 to 1979, Ayatollah Khomeini and his clerical supporters repeatedly praised the struggles of students and intellectuals against the Shah's regime. After the revolution, however, university students became a prime target of the Islamic cultural revolution. Once in power, the new regime denounced the anti-Islamic nature of universities under the Shah (*Jumhuri Eslami*, December 16, 1982), in particular the prevalence of anti-Islamic slogans in universities and that women could not wear the chador on campus for fear of ridicule.[1]

After the revolution, a temporary reduction of repression provided an opportunity for activists to initiate political campaigns in the universities. Leftist political organizations, especially the Fedayeen and the Mojahedeen, stepped up their activities in universities and received growing support. Supporters of leftist political organizations set up offices in the universities and gained the support of the major part of the faculty. Soon the universities became centers of advocacy for political freedom, support for worker and peasant councils, and autonomy of national minorities. When, in March 1979, women were ordered by some religious leaders to wear the traditional chador, or veil, they organized rallies and protests through Tehran University, forcing the government to partially rescind the order, making it merely advisable instead of obligatory.

As universities became centers of opposition activities, supporters of the IRP were reduced to a minority. In autumn 1979, when university students held free elections, two-thirds of those elected were supporters of the clergy-backed Islamic Republican party (IRP), while only one-third of the votes went to candidates affiliated with all leftist groups combined. The balance of forces changed abruptly, however, and a few months later in another election, the proportion was reversed: two-thirds of those elected were leftists, while only one-third were supporters of the IRP. During the following months, the influence of IRP supporters declined to the point where they were no longer active in the universities.[2]

These changes revealed a dramatic shift in allegiance within the younger generation, which had initially supported Ayatollah Khomeini. As university students gradually moved toward more radical positions, the government grew increasingly unwilling to tolerate their views. The regime charged that universities were centers for the transmission of imperialist culture and influence and fostered opposition groups "tied to the East and the West." After the universities were closed down, Ayatollah Khomeini declared, "Universities were bastions of communists, and they were war rooms for communists" (*Christian Science Monitor*, December 19, 1980). Government officials accused the Mojahedeen and the Fedayeen of using university resources to attack Islam and the Islamic Republic. According to the government, the forces of Islam had been weakened due to their activities (*Jumhuri Eslami*, December 23, 1982).

The rise and expansion of the Left within the universities united the liberal and clerical factions of the regime. Liberals, then led by President Bani-Sadr, joined the clerical attack on universities. Although student resistance was widespread, campus organizations were unable to defend themselves for a long period. Following the deaths of a number of student protesters, student opposition was crushed. In April 1980, the government ordered the closure of universities across the country. In an unprecedented move, the government kept the universities closed for two years. When they were reopened, Ayatollah Khomeini announced that only those students without affiliations with either eastern or western ideologies would be permitted entrance (*Ettelaat*, August 28, 1982). Thousands of students were expelled, and political criteria are still applied to all incoming students. Some thirty-five hundred faculty, or one-half of the teaching staff, who were considered leftist or antigovernment were fired. Thousands of university graduates with leftist politics who were employed as high school teachers were also purged. Mohammed Ali Raja'i once recalled that during his period as minister of education twenty thousand teachers were expelled (Bakhash 1984:112). According to an opposition report, after Bani-Sadr was ousted in June 1981, several hundred of these teachers and a larger number of students were either killed in armed struggle or executed for opposing the government (*Mojahed*, appendix to no. 261, September 6, 1985).

THE RISE OF WORKERS' COUNCILS

Workers' mobilization and collective action after the revolution was determined by a number of factors. The economic crisis continued and gave rise to inflation, which adversely affected the working class. The new government was unable to overcome the crisis and respond to the demands of workers. In addition, the temporary collapse of the army and the Savak and the departure of many owners and thousands of managers provided a favorable opportunity for workers to mobilize and act collectively. At the same time, however, other factors reduced workers' capacity for collective action. The continuing crisis resulted in constantly rising unemployment, compelling workers to become more passive in order to keep their jobs. In the first year of the revolution, at least 590 large factories employing between ten and one thousand workers were left idle. Unemployment was even higher in construction and other sectors. Rising unemployment weakened workers' solidarity by removing them from the workplace, which had brought them together and provided conditions for mobilization. A second factor involved organizational weaknesses and lack of a national workers' organization. Part of the problem was the limited period of time during which workers were allowed to organize, because a few months after the revolution all such activities were banned. The organizational problem was exacerbated by political divisions among activist workers. One segment of workers supported the IRP, convinced that it would serve the interests of the working classes and the oppressed. Those workers who did not support the IRP were divided among themselves. A very small fraction chose to support Bani-Sadr during his conflict with the IRP, primarily as a tactical means of opposing the IRP. Most of the rest supported the various leftist organizations that mushroomed after the revolution and attempted to influence working-class politics. These organizations, including the factions of the Fedayeen, the Mojahedeen, the Workers' Path, the Maoist Paykar, the Tudeh party, Union of Communists, Union of Socialist Workers, and Toilers' party, added to existing divisions because they did not have a single program and regularly opposed each other. Finally, the formation of the Revolutionary Guard enabled the government to repress the dissident leadership of the workers' movement. The Guard established an organization called the Basieg, or mobilization, which opened branches in a number of factories (Bayat 1983). These full-time guards were used to recruit workers for the war with Iraq and to control the workers.

Despite adverse conditions, workers in many factories mobilized and struggled to improve their conditions. Workers' collective action surfaced over issues of unemployment, economic conflicts, changes in labor laws, and the formation of independent labor organizations. Virtually every factory was the scene of intense conflicts between workers and employers, management, and the government. During the first two years of the Islamic Republic, workers engaged in hundreds of strikes, sit-ins, marches, hostage-takings, and factory takeovers. A government report indicated that industry was operating at only 58 percent of capacity and maintained that 40 percent of the waste resulted from industrial disputes (Bayat 1983).

Immediately following the revolution, Ayatollah Khomeini asked workers and other groups to end their strikes and resume work; continued strikes and marches, he argued, would only weaken the Islamic regime and benefit the enemies of the revolution (*Kayhan*, February 14, 1979). Within three days, all the factories in the country reportedly reopened (*Kayhan*, February 17, 1979). Conditions persisted unchanged, however, generating conflicts that soon led workers to resume collective action to change their situation. During the first year of the Islamic Republic, intense conflicts and collective actions broke out every day, leading Ayatollah Khomeini to issue repeated condemnations, such as that quoted at the outset of this chapter.

Unemployment caused concern among workers who could not find jobs after the revolution. They organized rallies, marches, and sit-ins to obtain jobs or unemployment compensation. Initially, only a few thousand unemployed workers participated in these collective events, a small fraction of the millions estimated to be out of work.[3] In March 1979, two thousand unemployed workers held a sit-in at the Ministry of Labor and began a hunger strike on the Persian New Year. When the government promised to consider their grievances, the workers ended their strike. In large cities such as Tabriz, Shiraz, Isfahan, Abadan, and Sanandaj, unemployed workers demonstrated and joined sit-ins to draw government attention to their plight. In Tehran, several thousand unemployed workers marched several times to the Ministries of Labor and Justice, as well as to Ayatollah Taleghani's home. They shouted slogans such as "Workers' wages must be paid! Workers should not be dismissed!" "Enough talk! It's time to act!" "Promises don't make bread!" "The arm of the worker is the pillar of the revolution!" "Workers' unemployment is the greatest sin!" Workers demanded jobs and a special treasury to help the unemployed (*Ettelaat*, April 9 and 11, 1979). In April, more than fifty people representing unemployed workers throughout the country met in Tehran to discuss solutions to their problems. The representative from Tehran charged that more than two months had passed since the group had contacted the minister of labor, but nothing had been done. The Abadan representative noted that fourteen thousand unemployed workers had elected seven representatives to meet with officials, but they were attacked by "misled" youth. According to the representative from Shiraz, the Shah's regime would not have been overthrown without oil workers' strikes. "Now we, the workers, want unemployment compensation; why should workers who brought about the revolution extend their hands for charity?" (*Kayhan*, April 26, 1979). On the first May Day celebration to be observed since the 1953 coup d'etat, thousands of unemployed workers marched. Eventually, on May 22, the Ministry of Labor announced a program to provide loans to unemployed workers (*Kayhan,* May 22, 1979). Nevertheless, inadequate funds and rising unemployment led workers to continue their collective action for employment.

A second issue of importance to workers was organizational independence and control of factories. During the final months of the revolutionary conflict, when workers struck against the government, a group of militant workers emerged to gain the leadership of most of the working class. With the support of the rank and file in many large factories, these leaders pressed for worker control after the revolution and demanded worker participation in decision making in large industries. In some large establishments, especially where owners or managers had fled the country, workers formed councils and assumed control over factory affairs. The councils called for the nationalization of all industries "dependent on imperialism." Among the first to form councils were oil workers and employees of the machine-tool and tractor companies in Tabriz. The Oil Workers' Council demanded an improvement in their economic conditions and participation in decisions regarding production and distribution. They also called for the dismissal of officials who had acted against the "interests of the people" during the previous regime. Their pressure led to the resignation of ten members of the company's executive board (*Kayhan,* April 20, 1979). In April 1979, Hasan Nazih, chief executive of the company, announced the dismissal of four hundred high-paid oil officials who had opposed the people during the revolution. Others, who had been dismissed by the previous regime, were recalled to work (*Kayhan,* April 29, 1979). The company also allocated one day's oil revenues to improving workers' economic conditions.

The formation of workers' councils in factories was so widespread in the early days of the new regime that Ayatollah Beheshti, head of the Supreme Court and powerful leader of the IRP, advised employers, "If factories could be better organized with councils, they should be accepted. . . . It is not possible to run a factory with bayonets" (*Kayhan,* April 29, 1979). His notion of workers' councils differed from that of the workers, however, because he suggested that such councils be composed of workers, management, and owners of industry. Nevertheless, recognition of some workers' rights in decision making was an important victory for workers. In a large May Day rally, Beheshti reaffirmed the Islamic Republic's commitment to workers' participation in decision making (*Kayhan,* May 2, 1979). Councils were even formed in the army by soldiers as well as among white-collar government employees, although soldiers' councils were quickly rejected and dissolved, forcing them underground.

The leadership of workers' councils was highly politicized and clearly influenced by leftist organizations. On May Day 1979, they organized a march independently of the IRP and included such groups as the Chamber of Labor, or Khaneh-e Kargar, the Joint Syndicate of Oil Workers, the Organization of Unemployed and Dismissed Workers, the Independent Teachers' Guild, the Fedayeen, the National Democratic Front, the Association for the Liberation of Women, the Association for the Unity of Women, Pishgam University Students, and many others. Their demands included the nationalization of factories, banks, and all assets belonging to foreign corporations; expropriation of all land belonging to associates of the royal court and turning it over to peasant councils; dissolution of antilabor laws and labor syndicates belonging to the previous government; and support for the autonomy movements of national minorities. Finally, they demanded that the new constitution should support the toiling masses (*Kayhan*, May 2, 1979). The leadership of the workers' councils also organized political meetings to discuss social issues beyond the factory. Shortly before the election of the Assembly of Experts, a group of council leaders gathered in the Chamber of Labor to examine the draft of the new constitution. They demanded that the government pay more attention to workers' conditions. One council leader declared that workers would be comfortable only when imperialism, dependent capitalism, and autocracy were destroyed. He also stated that labor representatives must be recognized through labor councils that genuinely represented workers. Finally, he affirmed that workers would participate in the upcoming election even though the Assembly of Experts could not fulfill their demands (*Kayhan*, July 31, 1979). A week later, representatives of the Tehran syndicate also met at the Chamber of Labor and objected to decisions taken by the Ministry of Labor, which, they declared, was not truly representative of workers. They complained that others made decisions for workers, and they reiterated the need for unity and organization within workers' syndicates (*Kayhan*, August 7, 1979).

Leftist organizations attempted to strengthen workers' councils as a basis for improving workers' capacity for action to fundamentally transform the social structure. Hence, workers' councils presented a threat to the government and as such were opposed by both the liberal and clerical factions of the government. Both factions of the government instead favored private property and the right of the owners to realize profits. The new constitution also recognized the owners' right to possession and profit. A clear conflict of interest existed, which the government was determined to resolve in the interest of law and order.

As a result, workers' councils came under government attack. The government charged that interference by councils in management reduced efficiency. On May 21, 1979, Prime Minister Bazargan announced that, due to provocations by counterrevolutionaries and illogical expectations of segments of workers, some factories and road and construction enterprises still could not work efficiently. Bazargan stated, "The resumption of work in these firms is not meant to serve the profits of the employers but to deal with unemployment, which is the main social problem." Finally, the prime minister maintained that strikes and interference in management created disorder and could no longer be tolerated. "The instigators will be severely pursued by the authorities" (Bazargan 1983a:37). Bazargan asserted that workers' councils should be dissolved. He complained that white-collar employees in government offices made exorbitant demands in terms of salaries and benefits, interfered in decision making and contributed to disorder, and were unable to work as efficiently as they had done under the non-Islamic government of the Shah (1983a:158, 185, 265). In June 1979, the government arrested three of the oil workers' leaders who had headed the strike committees during the revolution (*Kar* no. 16, June 21, 1979). Oil workers in Ahvaz protested the arrests by organizing a sit-in. The government refused to back down and several weeks later dismissed a dozen leftist employees who had been active in promoting workers' councils, which were dissolved as well.

In reaction to workers' activities, the government passed a bill punishing strike organizers in factories with prison terms of two to ten years (*Ettelaat*, June 24, 1979). Despite government opposition, workers' strikes and collective actions continued. In March 1980, Ayatollah Khomeini banned all strikes, but walkouts, sit-ins, and rallies persisted. President Bani-Sadr also favored dismantling workers' councils, maintaining that intervention by the councils in management decisions disrupted production. During the summer of 1980, the Komiteh dismantled the councils and purged large numbers of their members and activists from the factories. In some cases, bloody confrontations erupted between the Revolutionary Guard and workers, who lost these battles (Bayat 1983). The dismantling of the workers' councils in 1980 reduced the number of strikes the following year to less than one-half of what they had been before.[4]

Repression succeeded in eliminating the workers' councils for a number of reasons. First, a segment of the working class cooperated with the government and opposed the councils, thereby reducing the capacity of workers to act collectively against repression. A more important factor was the absence of a national organization to mobilize and coordinate workers' actions. Nor did workers have the means by which to broadcast the repressive measures taken against them. They no longer had strong ties to the mosque that might have enabled them to use mosques for such purposes. Ayatollah Taleghani, who strongly supported the councils, had died, and the mosques were controlled by the tiny group of clergy who were part of the government. The universities, which had been staunch allies of workers, had already been repressed and closed. Consequently, workers could not use that avenue for support. Finally, bazaaris, who had supported workers during the antimonarchy struggles, were not interested in advancing the cause of workers who demanded interference in owners' affairs. Some bazaaris owned factories outside of the bazaar and consequently did not favor workers' councils. As a result, repression and the government's attack on workers' councils succeeded because they did not result in an escalation of conflict or the formation of alliances to support workers' resistance. After the ouster of President Bani-Sadr, according to opposition sources, more than two hundred leaders and activists of the workers' councils who were involved in leftist organizations were executed or slain in armed confrontations (*Mojahed*, appendix to no. 261, September 6, 1985).

As an alternative to independent workers' councils, the IRP promoted the formation of Islamic Associations as vehicles for strengthening the position of the ruling clergy within the working class. Mohammad Kamalee, a member of the Labor Committee in the Majles, noted, "As long as workers' councils act to defend class interests, they cannot be allowed to operate in an Islamic society. Order in an Islamic society is based on guardianship, rather than on consultation" (*Iran Times*, May 21, 1982). He suggested that workers' councils should use appropriate government channels to express their concerns about social and political issues. Tavakoli, the minister of labor, also referred to "guardianship" in opposing workers' councils: "Islam does not recognize class struggle; rather, it believes in class harmony" (*Jumhuri Eslami*, February 10, 1981). According to guidelines prepared by the Ministry of Labor, members of Islamic Associations, who would be elected by employees, were to be committed to the principle of clerical leadership and have no connection with parties and organizations opposing the government. These associations were to encourage a spirit of cooperation between employees to advance the affairs of the unit, detect problems, and provide better working conditions in order to increase factory productivity (*Kayhan*, October 12, 15, 20, and 22, 1983). The deputy labor minister stated that cooperation between Islamic Associations and management in productive units would prevent the growth of counterrevolution and "unfavorable elements" (*Ettelaat*, November 1, 1983). At one point some officials, including Tavakoli, even opposed the formation of Islamic Associations and dismantled those that did not have employers' consent. However, he did promise to allow associations to be formed once new laws were passed (*Jumhuri Eslami*, February 19, 1981).

A new set of labor laws proposed by the Ministry of Labor was met by harsh criticism from organized workers (*Jumhuri Eslami*, November 15, 1982). Members of the Chamber of Labor charged that under the new law Islamic Associations were even weaker than workers' syndicates had been during the Shah's reign. They repeatedly demanded strong, independent labor organizations with officials chosen by workers and rejected the presence of government and employer representatives in labor organizations. Partly as a result of their protests, the labor minister was forced to resign. Those workers still organized and active in Islamic Associations continued to demand radical changes. When the new labor minister drew up a new labor law, representatives of the Islamic Associations were invited to a three-day seminar to discuss the proposed statute. They ultimately rejected it, complaining, "The new labor law ignores the future of workers and leaves employers' hands free for ever greater exploitation of workers." The representatives demanded that Islamic Associations be allowed to participate in decisions regarding hiring and dismissal of workers, planning for production and distribution, and setting wages and prices (*Kayhan*, March 5, 1983). There has been no evidence that any of these demands have been accepted by the government.

Without collective power and independent organizations, workers' conditions did not improve. Workers continued to complain about rising inflation, the absence of health insurance, the rising cost of housing, and the lack of labor organizations in their enterprises (*Ettelaat*, April 30, 1984). Despite high inflation, the government resisted wage increases, maintaining that they would only compound inflation and be counterproductive.[5] Workers objected to the government's proposal to replace profit sharing with a program of extra wages contingent upon increased productivity (*Kayhan* and *Ettelaat*, September 15, 1982). In many factories, however, workers' share of profits were not paid because employers claimed that they had not made any profits for several years. In addition to wages, workers also complained about the dissolution of workers' councils and syndicates, job insecurity, dismissals, factory closings, lack of health insurance, and long working hours. Despite the ban on walkouts, each year several strikes erupted over these issues, and workers occasionally were able to win some concessions.[6]

In the aftermath of the violent conflicts of June 1981, when most organizations were repressed, the Islamic Associations also fell into neglect. By 1982, only eighty of three hundred Islamic Associations survived, and many of these remained inactive (*Ettelaat*, October 6, 1983). The continued presence of leftist and secular elements, however, led the government to renew its encouragement of the activities of Islamic Associations. Prime Minister Hossein Mousavi (1981–) told a group of members of Islamic Associations that the enemies of the revolution continually attempted to generate conflicts in factories. Islamic Associations should continue to operate in order to prevent such deviations "because, as the result of 50 years of the Pahlavi regime, people have been kept away from Islam" (*Kayhan*, March 12, 1983). On May Day 1985, the minister of labor declared that the best way to prevent the influence of elements opposed to the government was to strengthen the Islamic Associations (*Kayhan*, May 1, 1985).

BAZAARIS AND THE ISLAMIC REPUBLIC

Unlike their early mobilization against the monarchy, bazaaris were slow to act collectively against the Islamic Republic. Also, in contrast to their backing of other groups who opposed the monarchy, bazaaris did not support the mobilization of other classes and groups against the Islamic government. At first, bazaaris appeared to be united in their support for the clergy. When Ayatollah Khomeini called for donations to build housing for the poor, bazaaris everywhere were quick to contribute. Maniyan, representative of the SMGATB, praised the bazaar's response to Khomeini's request (*Kayhan*, April 23, 1979). When autonomy-seeking Kurds and government troops clashed, bazaars shut down in protest against the Kurds (*Kayhan*, August 20, 1979).

Bazaaris' initial support for the new regime can be explained by several factors. First, the provisional government was composed of liberal groups from the Freedom Movement and the National Front, which had supported Mosaddegh. Because both groups were liberal and nationalist, they were supported by bazaaris. In addition, the provisional government pursued policies that served bazaari interests. An early act of the government was to dissolve the Chamber of Guilds, which had overseen price controls and the antiprofiteering campaign. The government also destroyed more than one hundred thousand files on shopkeepers and merchants who had violated the price controls under the monarchy (*Kayhan*, August 4, 1979). Furthermore, the nationalization of industries held by major industrialists who had been associated with the previous government opened the way for the growth of medium and small capitalists in the bazaar by potentially expanding their resources and markets. All these factors had a positive impact on bazaaris, who therefore gave their early support to the new government.

A number of significant developments, however, eventually led bazaaris to mobilize for collective action. One was the growing attempt by the IRP to take power away from liberals, whom most bazaaris considered their allies. In addition, the clerical faction of the government supported and enforced the resumption of price controls. Still another development was the formation of an alliance between the IRP and one segment of bazaaris, which enabled them to benefit economically while excluding the rest of the bazaaris.

Nevertheless, bazaari mobilization was weakened by a number of factors. In the first place, the new economic division within the bazaar was more significant than previous divisions had been. Although the IRP was supported by only one segment of the bazaar, this support was greater than the Shah had had. The resulting division undermined bazaari solidarity and reduced their capacity for collective action. Second, bazaaris had borrowed and used mosque networks for mobilizing and opposing the monarchy. After the revolution, however, Khomeini and the IRP controlled this channel, and bazaaris were unable to reactivate this network for mobilization. Finally, the IRP confronted opposition within the bazaar by escalating its repression to an unprecedented level and executing a few of the leading organizers of the bazaar. Repression thus succeeded in defeating bazaari opposition.

Soon after the revolution, the clerical faction of the regime launched a campaign to strengthen the IRP's position among bazaaris and attempt to bring the bazaar under IRP control. Sayyed Taghi Khamoushi, a bazaari member of parliament and supporter of the IRP, declared, "After the revolution it was felt that, politically, the bazaar had to come under the control of the Hezb-Ollah."[7] The IRP's policies brought about significant changes in the organization and leadership of the bazaar. Ayatollah Khomeini ordered the formation of a treasury, headed by a cleric and two bazaaris, to assist merchant guilds by extending interest-free loans to "needy" shopkeepers and merchants (*Ettelaat*, March 29, 1979). Another agency, the

Imam's Committee for Guild Affairs,[8] was organized to guide and regulate economic activities of the guilds, select and supervise guild leaders, and prevent violations and "infiltration by counter-revolutionaries and their conspiracies."[9] In this way, highly committed supporters of Khomeini and the IRP came to occupy all positions of power within the guilds. In turn, the guilds were given the important responsibility of granting and revoking licenses, as well as receiving goods—including all imports—from the Ministry of Commerce and redistributing them to bazaar outlets.

As a result, one segment of the bazaar with important connections was able to prosper. Several clerics who served as government officials complained that, after the revolution, wealth tended to concentrate in the hands of a few merchants and shopkeepers.[10] Other government officials publicly pointed to ties between wealthy bazaaris and powerful members of the government.[11] Karimi, a Majles representative from Ahvaz, charged that while Khamoushi headed the Imam's Committee for Guild Affairs, he allocated and monopolized the most profitable imports among his friends and relatives; they engaged in numerous, highly profitable dealings, compiling huge fortunes that harmed the public and the government. Karimi also charged that, as guild head, Khamoushi acted arbitrarily in administering punishment or not to individuals in the guilds (*Kayhan*, April 14, 1983). According to Sahabi, head of the Majles Planning and Budget Committee, in the two years following the revolution the Tehran bazaar enjoyed the highest rate of profit in the country's history (*Kayhan*, April 7, 1981). He claimed that some importers charged the public four times the wholesale costs of goods (*Kayhan*, May 3, 1981). Referring to the Iran-Iraq war, Hasan-Zadeh and a few other members of the parliament charged, "Unfortunately, the Ministry of Commerce has been converted into the Ministry of the Bazaar and bazaar capitalists have been taking advantage of the war situation to make millions of tomans" (*Ettelaat*, May 7, 1983; *Iranshahr*, May 27, 1983). Other prominent officials of the regime made similar statements, including Hashemi-Rafsanjani, speaker of the parliament, and Prime Minister Mousavi (*Kayhan*, March 5, 1983; *Iranshahr*, July 18, 1983).

At the same time that some bazaaris were accumulating vast amounts of wealth, popular outrage was mounting against rising consumer prices and profiteering. Attempts were made to form a grassroots organization to prevent profiteering, and a number of spontaneous collective actions were directed against shopkeepers (*Kayhan*, August 4, 1979, January 30, 1980). In Tehran, more than three thousand women attacked fruit stores in one neighborhood and closed down the shops. They then marched through the streets shouting, "Death to profiteers!" (*Kayhan*, May 29, 1980). In Tabriz, rioters attacked shopkeepers shouting, "Capitalists should be destroyed! Islam is victorious! Workers are victorious! Profiteers should be executed!" (*Kayhan*, August 12, 1979). Retailers often responded that they did not set prices; they themselves bought goods at high prices and were forced to sell them at higher rates (*Kayhan*, March 30, 1980).

In the midst of this popular discontent, Revolutionary Committees organized by IRP clerics inaugurated a series of actions that adversely affected segments of the bazaar. The Revolutionary Committees attacked moneylenders, who had long benefited from lending money. A number of wealthy moneylenders in different parts of the country were arrested, and a special court was formed to investigate grievances against them. In Isfahan, for example, one hundred moneylenders were put on trial (*Kayhan*, July 23, 1979). In another move, radical Islamic clerics bolstered by public pressure succeeded in incorporating a measure into the new constitution that nationalized foreign trade and obtained Majles approval for it. Although this measure was not put into practice during the early years of the Islamic Republic, it was regarded by big merchants as a distinct threat to their businesses.[12] In addition, the government set limits on rug exports, which had become an important means of circumventing restrictions on foreign exchange. This new policy also jeopardized both artisans and merchants throughout the entire rug industry, which, according to officials, supported some five million people nationwide (*Kayhan*, August 6, 1984). In 1972, Iran exported fourteen thousand tons of rugs. Ten years later, rug exports totaled little more than one thousand tons (*Kayhan*, June 4, 1984). Some rug artisans reportedly emigrated to other countries in the region and, with the help of big Iranian exporters operating abroad, have continued to manufacture and export rugs.

At the same time, the government jeopardized small shopkeepers by instituting rationing to insure the availability of basic foodstuffs at stable prices.[13] The Islamic Association of the Bazaar criticized the government's commerce policies, charging unfair competition from cooperatives and from the government's distribution of basic goods to the public. These policies, the association claimed, severely squeezed the bazaar distribution system.[14] Most important, public outcry against inflation soon led the Revolutionary Committees to establish special courts to control prices and punish violators. These courts had the approval and cooperation of the Imam's Committee for Guild Affairs. The Revolutionary Committees established a Headquarters for Combating Profiteering across from the entrance into the Tehran bazaar (*Kayhan*, July 25, 1979). Sanctions against shopkeepers included monetary fines and public flogging (*Kayhan*, January 30, 1980). In rare cases, violators were jailed or exiled for short periods of time.

As a result of these policies bazaari politics diversified. The Imam's Committee for Guild Affairs, controlled by supporters of the IRP, continued to back the clergy by circulating petitions, organizing rallies, and participating in demonstrations. In contrast, other organizations, including the SMGATB, opposed clerical policies. The SMGATB, which was tied to the liberal National Front, was strengthened after the revolution, and its members stepped up their participation in National Front activities (*Ettelaat*, October 17, 1979). Bazaari participation in the opposition was denounced by one member of the Majles and leader of the clergy-dominated IRP: "Rich, monopolistic bazaaris and moneylenders who sucked the blood of the people are continuing these practices today while hiding behind political organizations such as the National Front" (*Ettelaat*, July 6, 1981). Another bazaar organization, the Society of Islamic Associations of the Bazaar, was established and supported Bazargan's Freedom Movement against the IRP. Still less well-off shopkeepers who favored the Islamic Mojahedeen formed the Traders' Towhidi Guild and joined the above-mentioned organizations to back the liberals, who were led by President Bani-Sadr in 1980–1981.

In a succession of conflicts between liberals and the IRP, bazaar organizations mobilized for collective action. On November 7, 1980, Ayatollah Hadi Ghoddusi, revolutionary prosecutor of the Islamic Republic, ordered the arrest of Ghotb-Zadeh, who was from a merchant family and had been foreign minister under Bani-Sadr. A large segment of the bazaar opposed the IRP's attack on liberals and organized protests on behalf of Ghotb-Zadeh, gathering thirty thousand signatures on a petition pressing for his release. Four days later, amid growing bazaar opposition, Ayatollah Ghoddusi ordered that Ghotb-Zadeh be released.[15] A few days later, disturbed by these political developments, Ayatollah Khomeini denounced those bazaaris who had supported Ghotb-Zadeh (Bakhash 1984:148). Khomeini declared that "a deceived group" gathered in Qom, the center of clergy and Islam, and demanded the clergy's expulsion from politics; they want "absolute freedom" so that the Fedayeen and other groups that did not believe in Islam could say and write whatever they liked. He added that if the bazaars in Qom and Tehran favored such plans, it would be a great calamity; and if they opposed such plans, why did they not say anything? (Khomeini 1983, 13:170). In all previous periods, he noted, anytime there was a political problem for Islam and the religious leaders, closure of the bazaar for half a day was sufficient to solve the problem (Khomeini 1983, 13:279).

Despite Khomeini's statements, the conflicts between liberals, the bazaar, and the IRP continued in the following months. Shortly after Ghotb-Zadeh was released, Ahmad Salamatian, the liberal Majles representative from Isfahan, spoke in Mashhad to condemn clerical repression. After supporters of the IRP disrupted his talk, bazaaris in Mashhad protested by striking the next day. The clergy called for action, charging that a conspiracy was underway to discredit them and force them out of politics. According to the foreign press, the clergy then forced bazaaris in five major cities to close their shops to show solidarity with the clergy (*Christian Science Monitor*, December 8, 1980). In Tehran, a group of pro-IRP bazaaris led by Khamoushi marched to the office of *Ettelaat*, where they read a strong statement supporting the clergy.[16] In Isfahan, Ayatollah Taheri, Khomeini's representative, organized a large rally on a Friday to demand the dismissal of Isfahan's representative to the Majles. Two days later the Isfahan bazaar, oldest and largest national center for Persian handicraft, responded by closing down for two days to support their parliamentary representative, who came from a well-known bazaar family. This action outraged Ayatollah Taheri, who reacted to the mounting conflicts by leaving the city in protest against alleged insults against Islam and the Valayat-e Faghieh, the supreme cleric (*Ettelaat*, December 16, 1980).

The conflicts quickly intensified. The SMGATB decided to take the initiative. In January 1981, Lebaschi, a member of the National Front and leader of the SMGATB, publicly declared that Prime Minister Mohammad Ali Raja'i's (1980–1981) cabinet, which represented the IRP and the clerical faction, lacked the political and economic experience to solve the nation's problems. Lebaschi announced that the bazaar would attempt to bring down the government (*Ettelaat*, January 4, 1981). This was an extremely bold statement to make against the IRP by an individual as well as an organization, both of which had been important in mobilizing bazaaris since the 1940s and had supported the clergy throughout the revolution. Lebaschi's statement signaled the deepening conflict between segments of the bazaar and the IRP. A few days later, Khameneh'i and several other people invited Lebaschi to an IRP member's residence to discuss the conflict. Lebaschi was told that the bazaar had always been allied with the clergy and that he should not cause divisions. They told him that they all should be united. According to Lebaschi they said, "If you have some business, you should choose a few people, and the prime minister will also choose a few people to work together and observe the prime minister's office to solve the problems." Lebaschi refused to cooperate and instead questioned the prime minister's competence to solve the country's problems (Lebaschi 1983, tape 3:18).

Early in March, the Imam's Committee for Guild Affairs called upon the bazaar to close down to protest President Bani-Sadr's criticisms and attacks upon the IRP at Tehran University. In turn, Bani-Sadr asked merchants and shopkeepers to keep their shops open and not contribute unnecessarily to the tensions. On the morning of the announced shutdown, *Ettelaat* reported that some Tehran bazaars were closed, others remained opened, and still other merchants tended their shops behind closed doors, indicating a preference for carrying out business (March 8, 1981). *Enghelab-e Eslami*, Bani-Sadr's newspaper, reported that bazaars were open throughout most of the country except where "hooligans" forced them to close down (March 8, 1981). The next day, the *London Times* reported that in Qom, fundamentalists showed their support for the clergy by marching to the residences of preeminent clerics, but they failed to close down the bazaar (March 9, 1981).

A shift in allegiance had occurred. Later that month, the SMGATB announced that, to support the president, the bazaar would close for two hours. Bani-Sadr thanked them, but asked that bazaaris continue their economic activities in order to benefit the economy. He pledged to continue his efforts to fight against "law-breaking and disorder" and to make possible the rule of law (*Enghelab-e Eslami*, March 17, 1981).

In another round of conflicts, the IRP faction of the government arrested Dr. Reza Sadr, the executive of *Mizan* newspaper, which belonged to the Freedom Movement headed by Bazargan, all of whom opposed the IRP. A special investigative court set Sadr's bail at five million rials. The Society of Islamic Associations of the Bazaar intervened on his behalf and provided funds for his release. The society threatened to condemn the authorities if they refused the money and chose instead to make a political issue of his arrest (*Kayhan*, April 19, 1981). Eighteen Islamic Associations of the Bazaar signed a petition supporting Dr. Sadr and denouncing the abuse of laws regulating the press. In response, the special prosecutor's office announced that twenty thousand signatures of bazaaris and Islamic Associations of the Bazaar had been gathered on petitions backing Sadr's arrest (*Kayhan*, April 19, 1981).

By June 1981, it was clear that the earlier coalition between the bazaar and the clergy within the IRP had broken down. According to the opposition, segments of the bazaar supported the liberals against the clergy, including the SMGATB, the Society of Islamic Associations, and the Traders' Towhidi Guild, which backed the Mojahedeen. As a result, the IRP intensified its actions against the bazaar by escalating repression of bazaaris to an unprecedented scale. The data on sanctions and executions meted out to shopkeepers and merchants after President Bani-Sadr's ouster is revealing. On June 21, the day before Bani-Sadr was dismissed, Zehtabchi, a bazaari activist, member of the Traders' Towhidi Guild, and supporter of the Mojahedeen, was executed for "counterrevolutionary" activities (*Ettelaat*, June 22, 1981). Three weeks later, two more bazaaris— Karim Dastmalchi, a leading member of the SMGATB, and Ahmad Javaherian, a supporter of the Mojahedeen—were also executed after being charged with "rebellion in the Moslem bazaar leading to its closing" (*Kayhan* and *Ettelaat*, July 12, 1981). Following the arrests of additional shopkeepers and merchants, several others fled the country, including Lebaschi, a member of the National Front; Shanehchi; and Ebrahim Mazandrani, a supporter of the Mojahedeen. According to the Mojahedeen, in the wake of these conflicts between IRP clerics and opposition groups more than one hundred shopkeepers, artisans and merchants were executed or killed in armed confrontations throughout the country.[17]

The IRP further intensified its attacks on the bazaar through a campaign against profiteering. Toward the end of June 1981, a few days before Bani-Sadr was replaced, the Majles discussed prices, profiteering, and speculation, unanimously concluding, "There must be a determined and revolutionary struggle against these corrupt acts committed against the people and against Islam" (*Kayhan*, June 20, 1981). Nazem-Zadeh, a cleric in charge of the special court prosecuting price violations, asked people to report profiteers to his office in the same way that counterrevolutionaries were exposed. Within a short time, the number of fines against shopkeepers increased dramatically. Between November 1980 and April 1982, twenty-five thousand shopkeepers and merchants were fined, jailed, flogged, or exiled. Although the terms of imprisonment and exile were usually not long, sizable monetary fines were levied.[18] Government officials also threatened to execute those speculators and profiteers who withheld goods from the market or raised prices out of political motives to cause general dissatisfaction.[19]

POLITICAL CONFLICTS

The collapse of the Shah's repressive forces and the consequent reduction of repression after his downfall provided an opportunity for various political organizations to mobilize. The political atmosphere remained relatively open for a few months, during which numerous political organizations rapidly emerged with their own publications and programs. Soon, however, the IRP, along with the Komiteh and their armed guards, began to limit the activities of such groups and restrict their political mobilization. At the same time, political freedom quickly became one of the most important popular demands after the overthrow of the monarchy. A poll conducted by *Kayhan* during the presidential elections less than one year after the revolution indicated that the vast majority of voters had two principal demands for the government: to put the economy back to work and to provide political freedom for the people (*Kayhan*, January 27, 1980).

Political organizations that opposed the new government had only limited amounts of time and resources before they were all eliminated. Individually, none of these groups possessed sufficient resources to challenge the regime. Most of them had mobilized through the mosque prior to the revolution, but could no longer use that option because the IRP now controlled the mosques and Khomeini appointed the leaders of the Friday prayers. However, in combination they could have been a significant political force. Even at the beginning of 1979, long before each group had mobilized fully, it was clear that in combination these forces could be very substantial. For example, in March 1979, on the anniversary of Mosaddegh's death, one million people demonstrated, representing the National Front, the Freedom Movement, and a number of leftist organizations, notably the Fedayeen and the Mojahedeen (*Ayandegan*, March 5, 1979).

These opposition groups, however, did not consolidate their forces into a single bloc during the critical stages of the conflicts. In addition to divisions among organizations that emerged and grew after the 1979 revolution, divisions and fragmentation characterized those organizations that had fought against the monarchy. For example, the Fedayeen grew very rapidly after the revolution, but soon split into four organizations and factions, with the largest two known as the Majority and the Minority.

Similarly, the National Front was characterized by factionalism and was divided into two organizations. Even the split did not end the factionalism in the Front. More importantly, ideological differences that were insignificant during the anti-Shah mobilization gained greater importance in the post-revolutionary conflicts and prevented formation of broad coalitions and consolidation of the opposition into a single bloc. One of the main factors that prevented the formation of a coalition was that these organizations were tied to different social groups and therefore pursued different interests. The National Front was tied to the bazaar and medium-sized capital, while various factions of the Fedayeen, Mojahedeen, and smaller leftist organizations were interested in mobilizing the working classes and promoting their interests. These latter groups were all divided among themselves, with each presenting a different analysis of the nature of the state and proposing different political programs. These differences prevented the consolidation of their forces.

The separate mobilization of various groups and organizations in the two years after the overthrow of the monarchy was sufficient, however, to threaten the IRP and the clergy's involvement in politics. In response, the IRP used various measures to prevent mobilization by these groups. In the end, they were all repressed after the IRP ousted President Bani-Sadr from power. As a result, in slightly more than two years after the downfall of the monarchy, all political organizations were outlawed and forced underground, including the National Front, the Writers' Association, the Lawyers' Association, the Mojahedeen, and all secular leftist organizations ranging from the Minority faction of the Fedayeen, which opposed the new government, to the Tudeh party, which supported it. Each of these organizations held numerous separate actions, but they never joined forces. I shall briefly mention some of the issues of conflict and the measures taken to prevent mobilization by the opposition.

As each organization continued to mobilize, dissemination of news and declarations became crucial. Thus, from early on, political conflicts focused on censorship and repression in the government media, which was under liberal control. Two weeks after the revolution, eighty lawyers in Tehran held a news conference at which they protested censorship in general and censorship imposed against Marxists in particular. They argued that the revolution did not belong to any specific social class alone and that Marxists had a right to free expression and action (*Kayhan*, February 24, 1979). Shortly thereafter, government radio and television censored part of an interview with Ayatollah Taleghani. A group of journalists published a statement demanding an explanation of why censorship had been imposed.

mid-April 1979, the governor of the province of Fars resigned because media coverage of his talk on Mosaddegh was censored. Sayed Hossein Khomeini, grandson of Ayatollah Khomeini, criticized censorship in radio and television, declaring that no intelligent person could work with Ghotb-Zadeh, then director of the national radio and television. The Writers' Association condemned all forms of censorship and restrictions on publishing and teaching.

Soon radical and non-Islamic bookstores and newspapers became targets of attacks. For example, three workers in a bookstore near Tehran University were stabbed (*Ettelaat*, April 18, 1979). Other attacks were directed toward bookstores throughout the country, and non- Islamic books and literature were torn apart and burned. The Ata'i bookstore in Isfahan was bombed and completely demolished (*Kayhan*, July 24, 1979). In Tabriz, assaults on bookstores brought a denunciation from the governor of Eastern Azerbaijan (*Kayhan*, May 8, 1979). Non-Islamic newspapers were also attacked. When Ayatollah Khomeini expressed dissatisfaction with a report in *Ayandegan* national newspaper of his interview with *Le Monde*, a group of demonstrators attacked it. The next day the newspaper published a blank section containing only a single editorial, which asserted that the report on Khomeini's interview had been accurate and that both President Bani-Sadr, who had acted as translator, and the French reporter could corroborate the newspaper's report. Despite this defense, *Ayandegan* was banned. *Kayhan* came under fire a few days later, prompting writers and editors to refuse to work. A group of Islamic workers took over the newspaper and resumed publication without the writers, who were eventually dismissed. The next day, in a meeting with the Islamic employees of the newspaper, Ayatollah Khomeini endorsed their action (*Kayhan*, May 16, 1979). Newspaper vendors alleged that they were attacked by people demanding that they cease selling leftist newspapers (*Kayhan*, May 12, 1979). Even the National Front complained that they had great difficulty in distributing newspapers and other materials because of hooligan attacks (*Kayhan*, July 25, 1979). A new government bill that would ban several newspapers was denounced by the Writers' Association on the grounds that "approval of the new rules constituted an attack on the freedom of expression" (*Kayhan*, July 16, 1979). In August 1979, the government banned ten newspapers that allegedly were affiliated with the Shah's regime. A week later, more than twenty additional leftist and liberal newspapers were banned because they did not follow Islam and the revolution (*Kayhan*, August 20 and 21, 1979).

Offices and headquarters of activist groups were also attacked. At Azarabadgan University in Tabriz, an armed group stormed the offices of the Pishgam University Students, supporters of the Fedayeen. The assault was condemned by the president of the university (*Kayhan*, August 20, 1979). Soon Pishgam students and Fedayeen headquarters were assaulted throughout the country. In Tehran, a group of IRP supporters burned bookstores in Dehkadeh Street in Tehran and then attacked the nearby Fedayeen headquarters (*Kayhan*, August 14, 1979).

Rallies and marches became object of attacks. For example, a rally at Tehran University of the National Democratic Front led by Matin-Daftari, Mosaddegh's grandson, was attacked and disrupted. The Front sent an open letter to Prime Minister Bazargan demanding an explanation of how his regime intended to deal with such flagrant violations of individual and social freedoms (*Kayhan*, June 23, 1981). Matin-Daftari went underground after writing another open letter to Khomeini, criticizing repression. The Writers' Association announced a new round of poetry nights to be held from October 24 to November 3, 1979. The main objectives of the poetry nights were to "defend freedom of thought and speech, and oppose absolutely any censorship of writing." Officials of the association claimed they were not affiliated with any political party and planned to address critical analytical issues and avoid politics. They noted that officials in the Bazargan regime had been contacted and expressed interest in the plan. The association representatives warned, however, that the poetry nights would be held only if the government guaranteed the safety and security of the meetings; otherwise, they would be cancelled, and public opinion could be the judge of where blame should be assigned (*Ettelaat*, October 17, 1979). In the end, the poetry nights were never held.

In one instance, club-wielders attacked a gathering in a mosque in Hamedan, Bani-Sadr's hometown, during a talk by Ayatollah Mohammad Taghi Alemi, who spoke against the IRP. According to the report, the assailants broke the windows of the mosque and injured a number of people, some of whom had to be hospitalized (*Enghelab-e Eslami*, January 26, 1981). Ayatollah Alemi charged that the IRP had been behind the attack.

As a result of clashes between club-wielders and political groups, more than one hundred demonstrators were killed during this period. The intensification of attacks on demonstrators led Ayatollah Khomeini's son to speak against club-wielders: "No issue can be resolved with clubs except to the shame of the Islamic Republic; our people strongly oppose the use of clubs, and it should be fought against" (*Kayhan*, April 13, 1981). A'zam

Taleghani, daughter of Ayatollah Taleghani and a member of the Majles, criticized illegal arrests and assaults on political gatherings, charging that such actions gravely endangered the new regime. She recalled that when her two brothers were arbitrarily arrested shortly after the Shah's downfall, her father had believed that such illegal arrests constituted a threat to the revolution (*Ettelaat*, May 10 and 11, 1981).

With the intensification of conflicts in 1981, the government banned all gatherings and the Revolutionary Guard stepped up its arrests of members of the Mojahedeen, Fedayeen, and other leftist organizations. Opposition groups charged that thousands had been arrested and that torture was prevalent in prison. The clergy denied those charges and appointed a committee to inspect the jails. In April 1981, this committee concluded that torture was not currently used in prisons and that if it had been present earlier, it was abolished six months earlier. Besharat Jahromi, a member of the Majles, claimed to have investigated 3,620 complaints in eight prisons and concluded that charges of torture were unfounded. He noted that the prisoners did not complain about their treatment (*Kayhan*, April 12, 1981). Ayatollah Mousavi-Ardebili, the chief justice, visited political prisons in Tabriz and declared that among 1,500 prisoners there were no signs of torture; he, too, claimed that prisoners had made no complaints (*Ettelaat*, May 9, 1981). Yet allegations of torture persisted.

By this time liberals, led by President Bani-Sadr, had entered the conflict against the IRP. Bani-Sadr had collaborated with the clergy to establish the Islamic Republic and was one of seven individuals who drafted Principle 110 of the constitution granting supreme political power to the clergy (*Enghelab-e Eslami*, January 16, 1980). As his own power came under increasing restriction, however, he began to voice criticism of the clergy within the IRP, who, he claimed, "wanted to establish the government of clubs at any cost" (*Enghelab-e Eslami*, March 9, 1980). Bani-Sadr also criticized the government media for censoring even his statements (*Enghelab-e Eslami*, March 10, 1981). "The radio and television have become just like the media of the previous regime" (*Enghelab-e Eslami*, March 11, 1981). IRP leaders responded that most cabinet posts and powerful government positions were held by nonclerics and that only a few cabinet positions and important posts were occupied by clergy. They charged that imperialism was actively involved in discrediting the clergy. Ayatollah Beheshti, head of the Supreme Court, rejected charges that all social problems were the clergy's fault, hinting that perhaps the many accusations against the clergy were indicative of a conspiracy against them (*Jumhuri Eslami*, November 22, 1980).

Beginning in the fall of 1980, conflicts between political liberals and the IRP mounted. Opponents of the clergy demonstrated in Mashhad and ripped up pictures of Ayatollah Montazeri. Elsewhere, President Bani-Sadr's supporters rallied against the clergy. Clerics were criticized in Isfahan, where Ayatollah Taheri, Khomeini's representative, left Isfahan to protest disrespect for the Valayat-e Faghieh (*Ettelaat*, December 16, 1980). Even in Qom the clergy were apparently threatened by those who opposed the IRP. Ayatollah Sane'i, for example, noted that during Bani-Sadr's presidency even the people of Qom occasionally insulted him and other clerics (*Jumhuri Eslami*, February 2, 1983).

On March 5, 1981, a rally was held at Tehran University to commemorate Mosaddegh's death. While President Bani-Sadr spoke a group of people stormed the crowd, attempting to disrupt the rally. Mojahedeen militia present at the rally arrested dozens of assailants and confiscated their identification cards, which they submitted to the president. The cards revealed most of the attackers to be members of the Revolutionary Guard and the IRP (*Enghelab-e Eslami*, March 7 and 8, 1981). Bani-Sadr displayed the cards to the assembled audience and live television cameras, which broadcast the incident throughout the country. The action infuriated the clergy, who charged that Bani-Sadr had abused his authority, allied himself with the Mojahedeen, and sought to monopolize power. A similar attack took place in Isfahan when Bazargan spoke in a mosque to commemorate Mosaddegh's death (*Enghelab-e Eslami*, March 7, 1981). To defuse the issue, Ayatollah Khomeini ordered both the president and leading clerics to avoid making public statements as long as the war with Iraq continued.

Nevertheless, conflicts continued. On May 2, the prosecutor of the revolution filed suit against *Enghelab-e Eslami*, Bani-Sadr's newspaper, and *Mizan*, published by ex-Prime Minister Bazargan. Both papers were charged with making false statements (*Ettelaat*, May 2, 1981). On June 5, anniversary of the 1963 uprising, the clergy organized a large march and denounced both "internal and external enemies" who were determined to weaken their power. They proposed that those who ridiculed Islamic ideologues—i.e., the clergy—be deprived of their wives and property and put to death. Under no circumstances, they insisted, would nonideologues be permitted to attain leadership positions in the country (*Enghelab-e Eslami*, June 6, 1981). Three days later, Ayatollah Khomeini stated that the day he felt a threat against Islam, he would cut off the hands of those who threatened Islam. He warned that there were groups that were planning to close the bazaar. Such groups were composed of capitalists who wanted to cause rebellion and incite sedition, actions that meant standing against Islam and the prophet. Finally, he ordered the Revolutionary Guard and the military to do their duty and prevent unauthorized rallies and demonstrations (Khomeini 1983, 14:270–271).

Five days later, Ayatollah Khomeini dismissed President Bani-Sadr from his position as commander of the armed forces. Three days afterward, 120 of the 217 sitting members of the Majles signed a bill agreeing to debate Bani-Sadr's lack of merit. On June 21, 1981, the Majles approved the president's dismissal by a vote of 177 votes in favor, 12 abstentions, and only a single vote against his removal. Some forty of Bani-Sadr's supporters boycotted the session. Bani-Sadr had already gone underground because, as the Majles was dominated by the IRP, he had foreseen the result of their voting.

During these conflicts, various opposition organizations were divided in their politics. The Tudeh party threw its support behind the clergy, regarding them as egalitarian and anti-imperialist. The Fedayeen, after expanding rapidly following the revolution, split as noted above; the main organizations were known as the Majority and the Minority. The Majority faction implicitly supported the clergy against President Bani-Sadr, claiming that the clergy represented the petty bourgeoisie and were anti-imperialist. They argued that Bani-Sadr represented the bourgeoisie and wanted to reestablish ties with the West and with imperialism and had no interest in changing the social structure in the interests of the working classes. In contrast, the Minority faction condemned the clergy and liberals alike as representatives of the bourgeoisie opposing fundamental changes that served the interests of the working classes. Other leftist organizations such as Paykar, Workers' Path, and the Fedayee Guerrillas led by Dehghani also opposed both the clergy and the liberals. These leftist organizations did not support Bani-Sadr because they reasoned that as president he had been instrumental in directing government actions against dissenters. He had opposed the Turkoman autonomy movement and had ordered the army to crush Kurdish rebels seeking autonomy. Bani-Sadr led the attack against university students and had been instrumental in the closing of the universities. He had opposed workers' councils and called upon workers to cease interfering with management decisions. Consequently, none of these organizations rushed to Bani-Sadr's support when he came under attack.

The National Front was also beset by internal factionalism and was split into two main factions. The leftist faction, the Society of Socialists, criticized the Front for turning to the right; they left the Front to join the National Democratic Front (NDF), led by Matin-Daftari. Both the National Front and the NDF opposed the IRP, but made no attempt to join forces. The National Front explicitly threw its support behind Bani- Sadr. Similarly, various professional and intellectual organizations such as the Writers' Association and the Lawyers' Association opposed clerical rule, but only some supported Bani-Sadr.

The most important organization to explicitly support Bani-Sadr was the Mojahedeen. Immediately following the revolution, the Mojahedeen participated in the referendum of the Islamic Republic and supported its formation. Masoud Rajavi, leader of the Mojahedeen who had been imprisoned for several years under the Shah, endorsed the merger of political and clerical powers (*Kayhan*, April 28, 1979). Soon, however, the Mojahedeen declared that the clergy's interpretation of Islam was reactionary. True Islam, according to the Mojahedeen, advocated a classless society. They declared that the greatest threat to the revolution was the clergy's suppression of political and civil rights. As conflicts intensified between Bani-Sadr and the clergy, Mojahedeen supporters and militia throughout the country demonstrated in favor of the president. On the day Bani-Sadr was dismissed, the Mojahedeen, followed by a few other leftist groups, organized a large demonstration in Tehran during which many people were killed. The government claimed that 14 Revolutionary Guards were also slain by the demonstrators.

The next day the government executed 23 political prisoners, including Saeed Soltanpour, secretary of the Writers' Association and a leading member of the Minority faction of the Fedayeen (*Ettelaat*, June 22, 1981). A few days later a bomb exploded at the IRP headquarters, killing a number of IRP leaders, including Ayatollah Beheshti, first secretary of the IRP. Soon the violence escalated as the government responded with more executions. Over the next few months, the Mojahedeen assassinated many prominent high-ranking members of the government who had opposed the Shah, including Raja'i, president of the Islamic Republic and a political prisoner under the Shah; Prime Minister Mohammad Javad Bahonar, who served in 1981; Hasan Ayat, a member of parliament; and Ayatollah Haj Sayyed Abdolhasan Dastgheib, a high-ranking religious leader in Shiraz. For its part, the government killed well-known leftists who had fought against the Shah's regime: Shokrollah Paknejad, a socialist and one of the founders of the NDF; Mosa Khiabani, a leader of the Mojahedeen; and Mohsen Fazel, a leading member of the Paykar, a Maoist group. The government escalated the wave of executions. For example, on September 19, 1981, 149 persons were executed; a week later, 110 persons were executed on a single day (Bakhash 1984:220). "We cannot practice forgiveness or leniency," the revolutionary prosecutor general, Hossein Mousavi-Tabrizi, said, "when faced with so many people" (Bakhash 1984:221). On November 6, 1982, a government official revealed that some 2,000 persons had been executed since February 11, 1979, when the Shah's regime collapsed (*Jumhuri Eslami*, November 6, 1982). Although this figure included pro-Shah supporters, most of those executed belonged to leftist political organizations, primarily the Mojahedeen, the Fedayeen, and Kurdish groups. According to lists compiled by the Mojahedeen, between summer of 1981 and summer of 1985, approximately 12,000 persons were either executed by the regime or killed in armed struggle. These figures indicate that the average age of those slain was twenty-three years and that more than 3,700 were students (*Mojahed*, appendix to no. 261, September 6, 1985).

Given the scale of the conflict, government authorities stressed the need for vigilance against opponents of the regime. Ayatollah Mousavi-Ardebili, chief justice of the Islamic Republic, stated, "We still have people in the bureaucracies who, if left alone, would violate the rules and damage the revolution. . . . We have these people in all social strata, in the bazaar, bureaucracies, the private sector, everywhere" (*Ettelaat*, August 3, 1983).

THE IRP AND CLERICAL DIVISIONS

The IRP's victory and the establishment of a theocratic state should not obscure the major political disagreements that existed among the clergy throughout the revolution and into the postrevolutionary period. With the advent of the new regime, major political and ideological disagreements surfaced among the clergy regarding the composition of the Islamic Republic and the clergy's role in the new government. This should not have been unexpected because, as mentioned previously, the clergy had never constituted a homogenous social category. By approximately three years after the revolution, the IRP had eliminated its clerical and liberal opponents. Conflicts and disagreements intensified within the IRP, however, leading Khomeini to dissolve it. Let us now briefly examine those conflicts.

Almost immediately upon assuming power, the new government launched a campaign against clerics who had supported the Shah or cooperated with the Savak. Special courts were formed to hear testimony about clerical cooperation with the previous regime. Within a few months, more than one hundred clerics had been defrocked; others lost their property and were exiled or imprisoned, and a few were even executed.[20] According to the authorities, those clerics who promised to cease their opposition to the revolution and the people were not punished (Ayatollah Beheshti, *Kayhan*, May 27, 1981).

The main divisions existed among those who favored either theocracy, Islamic socialism, or parliamentary democracy. Ayatollah Khomeini was the main figure advocating theocracy, although no mention of this had been made during the conflicts against the Shah. In a theocratic state, according to Khomeini, sovereignty would rest in God alone. At the apex of the government would be the Valayat-e Faghieh, a position occupied by the supreme cleric.[21] Separation of governmental powers would be eliminated. Because laws had already been revealed by the Prophet and the Imams, parliament would merely set the agenda for the ministries. In Khomeini's view, an Islamic Republic in which clergy lacked the power to enforce Islamic laws would be meaningless and eventually degenerate. Hence, the establishment of clerical rule was essential.

A different point of view was expressed by Ayatollah Shariat-Madari, a Marja'a Taghlid from Qom. He endorsed a system similar to parliamentary democracy with civil liberties that would allow people to choose their representatives to rule the country. He opposed direct political participation by high-ranking clerical leaders, though lower-echelon clergy with the knowledge and expertise could participate if popularly elected (*Kayhan*, August 31, 1979). During the referendum for the Islamic constitution, he argued that Shia religious doctrine had no provision for a Valayat-e Faghieh, or supreme clerical leader, as advocated by Khomeini. Shariat-Madari contended that the constitutional provisions establishing the Valayat-e Faghieh contradicted other provisions granting sovereignty to the people.

A group of clerics and lay Moslems who opposed the IRP founded an independent political party, the Moslem People's Republican party, arguing that a one-party system might lead to party dictatorship, which would be worse than personal dictatorship (*Kayhan*, May 6, 1979). Although Shariat-Madari was not active in the Moslem People's Republican party, he supported them implicitly. Some IRP clerics opposed the existence of an alternative Islamic party. Ayatollah Khalkhali argued that such a party would create confusion among Moslems and provide a platform for attacks against the Islamic government by former supporters of the Shah, Savak agents, and other counterrevolutionaries. He suggested that Shariat-

Madari voluntarily dissolve the independent party (*Ettelaat*, May 2, 1979). When Khalkhali's criticisms were published in *Ettelaat* they triggered protests in Tehran, Qom, and other cities. In Tabriz, bazaaris and government employees who supported Shariat-Madari shut down the city and organized large demonstrations, while in Mashhad the clerical school closed down in protest (*Kayhan*, April 24, 1979). In Tehran, some bazaaris and Azerbaijanis held a rally on Shariat-Madari's behalf, calling for independent economic development, political freedom, and elimination of exploitation. Eventually, Ayatollah Khalkhali apologized.

The Moslem People's Republican party was strong in Tabriz, Shariat-Madari's hometown, and also had some following among bazaaris in Tehran. In Tabriz, the Moslem People's Republican party was popular among bazaaris and had armed some of its members. Before President Bani-Sadr was removed from office, the Revolutionary Guard attacked the party's headquarters, leading to violent clashes and deaths and to the dissolution of the party. In 1982, the IRP began to attack Shariat-Madari directly. They organized several rallies and demonstrations against him. According to Mohammad Khoieniha, who had led students in the hostage taking at the American Embassy, embassy documents indicated that Shariat-Madari had cooperated with the Shah and the Savak for some thirty years (*Jumhuri Eslami*, April 29, 1982, and April 24). Mousavi-Tabrizi, the revolutionary prosecutor general, charged that following the death of Ayatollah Boroujerdi, most high-ranking religious leaders had favored Ayatollah Mohsen Hakim as the Marja'a Taghlid for the entire Shiite community; instead, "Ayatollah Shariat-Madari was imposed on the community by a bunch of paid chaghookesh [knife-wielding hooligans], assisted by lies and charges fabricated against Ayatollah Hakim and attacks against people" (*Jumhuri Eslami*, April 26, 1982). As a result of these charges, Shariat-Madari was stripped of his title of Marja'a Taghlid, "source of emulation," and placed under house arrest until his death in 1985. After Shariat-Madari was put under house arrest, Ghotb-Zadeh was arrested for conspiring against the Islamic Republic. The government provided evidence linking him to Shariat-Madari, and Ghotb-Zadeh was executed.

Ayatollah Taleghani, who acknowledged Khomeini's leadership, represented yet another perspective on Islamic society. He envisioned a socialistic Islam with emphasis on popular democracy and community control over politics.[22] He called for elected city and state councils along with workers' representatives. Taleghani also sympathized with the aspirations of national minorities to determine their own destiny. A few weeks after the revolution, he traveled to Kurdestan to express his sympathy for Kurds, a group he believed had been overlooked by the previous regime. He condemned the lack of industrialization in Kurdestan and promised to assist in the region's economic development. He urged Kurds to form independent councils to run their local affairs (*Kayhan*, April 21, 1979). When his two sons, both Marxists, were arrested by the clerical Revolutionary Committee, Taleghani protested by closing his Tehran office and withdrawing from public life for a few days. In response to popular outcry and Ayatollah Khomeini's personal request, he reappeared in public to urge the formation of city and regional councils to run the country. He was the head of the Revolutionary Council and received the most votes in Tehran to the Assembly of Experts, convened to formulate the constitution of the Islamic Republic. Yet he participated only a few times in each, boycotting both organizations. Regarding the Assembly of Experts, he expressed fears that the new constitution might be inferior to the previous constitution written seventy-five years earlier.

In his last public speech, Taleghani reiterated that the only solution to Iran's problems was to give people responsibility for governing themselves through councils. Those in power opposed the formation of councils, he suggested, because they feared losing their position. He stressed the importance of being accountable to the electorate, saying, "Some of our friends might criticize me and ask why I say such things in these places. We have to say these things here because these people have elected us; we have to talk to them about their pain and problems." Taleghani ended his talk on a wishful note, expressing the hope that "all of us become alert, accept responsibility . . . put aside sectarianism, opportunism, and ideological domination. And may God forbid autocracy under the cover of religion. Let us join our voices with the people and the suffering masses" (*Ettelaat*, September 9, 1979). Ayatollah Taleghani died three days later, under conditions that some claim to have been suspicious.[23]

Clerical divisions were especially evident during the conflict between the IRP and President Bani-Sadr. These divisions were so intense that Ayatollah Khomeini issued repeated warnings to dissenting clerics in Tehran, Qom, and Mashhad clerical schools to "give up their satanic acts." He threatened to summon them to court if they did not (*Kayhan*, April 16, 1981). A few days later, the Revolutionary Guard in Qom repeated the warning and asked people to tell them about any dissenters (*Kayhan*, April 20, 1981). The Qom Revolutionary Court asked people to identify those clerics who had cooperated with imperialism and with opponents of the Islamic Republic (*Kayhan*, May 14, 1981). Ayatollah Beheshti, head of the Supreme Court and the IRP, warned that those who reneged on promises not to oppose the revolution and the people would be punished for any objectionable actions committed either before or after the revolution (*Kayhan*, May 27, 1981).

Some clerics supported the National Front and President Bani-Sadr, while others supported the Mojahedeen, but none of them possessed their own independent organizations through which to act. Sayed Hossein Khomeini, grandson of Ayatollah Khomeini, suggested that 90 percent of all clerics actually sided with President Bani-Sadr but were powerless to act because they stood outside the political arena.[24] A minority of these clerics did openly oppose the IRP, backing instead the liberal Bani-Sadr and others. Sheikh Ali Tehrani, a student of Khomeini and brother-in-law of the current Iranian president, publicly endorsed Bani-Sadr and encouraged people to demand the dissolution of the IRP, "the party of club-wielders" (*Enghelab-e Eslami*, March 9, 1981). After Bani-Sadr's ouster, Tehrani was forced underground and eventually fled to Iraq. Ayatollah Alemi accused Bani-Sadr's opponents of conspiring to monopolize power and repress all opposition (*Mojahed* no. 125, June 17, 1981). While Alemi was giving a sermon in his mosque in Hamedan, IRP supporters attacked the mosque, breaking windows and injuring several people (*Enghelab-e Eslami*, January 26, 1981). After the fall of Bani-Sadr, Ayatollah Alemi fled the country. Ayatollah Lahouti, a member of the first Islamic Majles and onetime head of the Revolutionary Guard, also supported the president and objected to the clerical "monopoly of power" (*Iran Times*, December 12, 1980). Mohammad Al As-hagh, a faculty member of the Qom seminary, opposed the IRP; as a result, his classes were disrupted by party supporters.[25] Both Ayatollah Tabataba'i Qomi and his son, Mahmoud Qomi, were defrocked because they rejected the principle of a Valayat-e Faghieh (*Kayhan*, June 23, 1981). Ayatollah Zanjani refused nomination to run for election to the Assembly of Experts, choosing instead to cooperate with the National Front (*Kayhan*, May 8, 1979). In an open letter (in possession of the author) he condemned virtually every aspect of clerical rule, especially the IRP's practice of "monopolizing" power.

A few other clerics who opposed the IRP backed the leftist Mojahedeen. One, Jalal Ganjeh'i, member of the Qom seminary faculty, criticized the IRP for monopolizing power; he objected to the elimination of stipends for clerical students who opposed the ruling clerical party. He was finally forced to flee to Paris. According to opposition Mojahedeen, ten other clerics and clerical students were executed or killed in armed conflicts after the ouster of Bani- Sadr.[26]

After the elimination of its opponents, divisions erupted within the IRP. The IRP, which had been formed after the revolution, did not have a basic constitution until 1983 when the party's first and only congress was held. Divisions that had existed after the removal of the liberals were intensified during the following years. In a broad sense, the party had two major factions. One faction advocated greater egalitarianism through land reform, nationalization of foreign trade, and substantial state control of the economy. The other faction, which included elements of the bazaar, opposed these measures. The continuing economic crisis and the war with Iraq magnified these divisions, leading Khomeini to warn everyone several times to maintain unity and avoid criticizing the government. Nevertheless, disagreements and divisions continued to such an extent that in many cities the party was unable to function and, for all practical purposes, closed down. Eventually in 1987, after repeated warnings, Khomeini ordered the dissolution of the party that had played such a crucial role in the establishment of the Islamic Republic.

CONCLUSION

The evidence presented above illustrates that social conflicts did not cease with the establishment of the Islamic Republic. Conflicting interests and continuing crisis, combined with the collapse of the Shah's repressive forces and divisions within the new Islamic government, provided a temporary opportunity for mobilization and collective action. This mobilization suffered from weaknesses, however. In the first place, no social group, except the clergy organized through the IRP, could mobilize through the mosque, which had provided a safe place during the revolutionary conflicts for gathering and communication and a national network for coordinating collective action. In addition, after the collapse of the monarchy, each group and class experienced divisions and fragmentation, with segments of each supporting the IRP, the liberals, or the leftists. More importantly, unlike the prerevolutionary mobilization, contending groups and classes did not consolidate their forces against a single target at the same time because each of them had different, and sometimes contradictory, objectives.

When the national minorities mobilized for autonomy, bazaaris did not join their struggles. Students and the Fedayeen were the only groups who actively supported the national minorities. When universities came under attack, bazaaris and liberal organizations approved of the assault because students had shifted to the Left. When workers were attacked, students could offer little assistance because they had already been partially demobilized by the closure of the universities. Most bazaaris opposed workers' control and workers' councils because they were tied to the Left and challenged private property and rights. By the time bazaaris began mobilizing and came under attack, other groups and classes had either been demobilized or did not have an interest in joining their struggles. As a result, repression against one social group or class did not invoke new protests by other groups, which might have led to the escalation of conflict and, consequently, neutralized repression.

Divisions and lack of consolidation also pervaded political organizations. The Fedayeen and the National Front had split into factions and remained apart from each other. The Freedom Movement, which had led the provisional government, did not join the National Front in actively supporting Bani-Sadr in the final days of his presidency. The Tudeh party and the Majority faction of the Fedayeen did not back Bani-Sadr because they considered him pro-Western. Similarly, other lefist organizations did not support Bani-Sadr, claiming that he was not interested in changing the social order in the interests of the working class. The only major organization that supported Bani-Sadr and joined him in a coalition against the clergy was the Mojahedeen. In response to this coalition, the IRP and the Komitehs escalated repression by arresting and executing their opponents. The Mojahedeen's response was similar: use of armed attacks against the IRP leaders and the Revolutionary Guard. Violence and repression quickly put an end to all popular mobilization and collective action.

The IRP succeeded in seizing power for a number of reasons. First, divisions within the opposition and the failure to consolidate greatly benefited the IRP. Second, the IRP had the support of segments of the working class, white-collar employees, and bazaaris during at least the first several months after the overthrow of the monarchy. More significant was Ayatollah Khomeini's support for the IRP. Khomeini clearly recognized the nature of the social conflicts, the polarization of society, and potential explosions; therefore, he promised social justice and equality to the oppressed and the poor. The promise of fundamental change enabled the IRP, through its mosque networks and such newly acquired resources as the Mostazafin Foundation (formerly the Pahlavi Foundation), to mobilize segments of the urban poor and recent urban migrants on their behalf and incorporate them into the Revolutionary Guard. Finally, the IRP's control of the armed Revolutionary Guard was fundamentally crucial for their victory. The IRP turned the Revolutionary Guard into a permanent organization with strongly committed personnel, which made it more reliable and efficient than an army based on conscripts.

In the initial stages of the formation of the Islamic Republic, the IRP in coalition with liberals used the Revolutionary Guard to prevent or weaken the mobilization of leftists, workers, students, and national minorities. Once those tasks were at least partially accomplished, the IRP, using its extensive resources eliminated its liberal opponents, who were divided between Bani-Sadr, the National Front, and the Freedom Movement. For several years, the various factions of the IRP were held together partly by Khomeini's authority and partly by the threat of the Mojahedeen and the Kurds, who waged armed struggle against the government. Eventually, the IRP was itself dissolved by Khomeini because of internal divisions and conflicts.

In sum, the evidence presented above indicates that divisions among all major social groups and classes pervaded Iranian society after the overthrow of the monarchy. This evidence confirms the conclusion that ideological consensus was lacking on fundamental issues in the Islamic Republic, even within the IRP. Although the major groups and classes had coalesced against the Shah and supported the formation of an Islamic Republic, they later clashed on major social and political issues once their short-run goal of overthrowing the monarchy was achieved. This conclusion refutes any suggestion that a single, overarching ideology was responsible for the overthrow of the monarchy. Rather, the data support the analysis presented in this research, which emphasizes the significance of classes, differently located in the social structure and characterized by diverse interests, resources, solidarity structures, and opportunities for mobilization and collective action.

Chapter 10

Conclusion

In the preceding chapters, a structural analysis was presented of the factors and conflicts leading up to the overthrow of the Iranian monarchy in 1979 and the establishment of a theocracy in 1981. The investigation indicated the weaknesses of current theories and explanations of the revolution. As the evidence and analysis demonstrated, neither rapid modernization per se, nor an emerging disjunction between economic and political development and the rise of a new middle class, nor uprooted populations instigated the conflicts that brought down the monarchy. Rather, the stage was set for conflict by the high level of state intervention in capital accumulation, the undermining of the market mechanism, and the adverse impact of these factors on major social groups and classes. A revolutionary situation was generated by the mobilization and disruption of the social structure by bazaaris, industrial workers, and white-collar employees in response to the government's adverse development and accumulation policies. These same classes had previously opposed the monarchy in the conflicts of the 1950s and bazaaris had opposed the monarch again in the 1960s, long before the period of rapid modernization and economic development. The slogans of freedom and independence shouted during the 1979 revolution were identical to the slogans shouted in the 1950s. Their origins cannot be attributed to the rise of a new middle class during the 1970s.

The leading role among the social groups and classes in the earlier conflicts as well as those that culminated in the monarchy's ouster was played, not by the new middle class or by white-collar employees, but by bazaaris, who were neither a new class emerging from modern economic development, nor a class that had been uprooted or had experienced anomie as a result of modernization. In the period under investigation, bazaaris undertook the highest number of collective actions of any of these classes. In the 1950s, bazaaris had been adversely affected by a major economic crisis, which caused widespread bankruptcies in the bazaars. Their mobilization was facilitated by the liberalization of the political sphere, which enabled them to form their independent organization, and by divisions within the dominant class, which allowed the formation of coalitions. In the conflicts of the early 1950s, bazaaris mobilized in support of Mosaddegh and the National Front against the royalists, despite most clergy's support for the latter. Bazaaris in major cities also participated in the anti-government protests of 1962 and 1963, once again before the period of rapid economic development, which according to some analysts raised expectations and created a new middle class. Their mobilization occurred again during an economic crisis and a temporary liberalization of the political system. They participated in the protests because of the adverse impact of the government's economic policies. In the conflicts from 1977 to 1979, bazaaris mobilized in the context of an economic crisis, slight changes in the legal sphere, and adverse government economic policies, rather than in response to rapid social change, anomie, or rising expectations. They were able to use their trading networks, independent economic resources, and ties to the mosque to mobilize for collective action. Their resources enabled them to continue bazaar shutdowns for long periods of time and thus play an important role in the revolutionary conflicts.

Unlike bazaaris, the working classes exhibited less capacity for collective action. They were severely restricted by state repression, geographical dispersion, and a highly dependent economic position. Oil workers, who consistently played a leading role in political confrontations, were the major exception. Their concentration in high numbers in Khuzestan enabled them to act collectively with great impact during the nationalization of oil in the early 1950s. Other industrial workers followed the lead of oil workers in their collective actions. Workers exerted an influence upon political events until the coup d'etat that deposed Mosaddegh. From 1978 to 1979, oil workers' strikes and collective action by other industrial workers were crucial in intensifying the state's economic and political crisis. It should be kept in mind, however, that the foundation for actions by industrial workers was established through bazaaris' persistent struggles, which forced the Shah to initiate reforms and thereby provided an opportunity for workers to mobilize.

The evidence presented in the preceding chapters demonstrates that the collective actions of white-collar employees and professionals were less frequent and less crucial than those of either bazaaris or industrial workers during the past several decades. This undermines the argument of those analysts who would emphasize the significance of the rise of the new middle class and its contribution to the political conflicts. Although the new middle class produced a number of political leaders who were active in the struggles, by and large the class itself lacked the necessary capacity for collective action. With the exception of teachers, the new middle class followed the actions of others in the political conflicts. In the 1950s, white-collar employees and professionals were unable to initiate independent collective action and acted only during periods of national holidays and celebrations or major crises. In fact, with the exception of teachers, who organized a nationwide strike in 1961, white-collar employees initiated no independent collective action during the decades that are the focus of this study. In the revolutionary conflict of the late 1970s, except for the upper echelon of the bureaucracy, which supported the government, most white-collar employees and professionals initiated their mobilization after bazaaris and industrial workers. Unlike bazaaris, white-collar employees were dispersed throughout the major cities and were economically dependent on the state. Unlike industrial workers, they occupied a comparatively privileged economic position and suffered relatively little from direct repression. These factors, in addition to their lack of autonomous organizations, reduced the capacity of white-collar employees and professionals to act collectively.

The evidence and analysis presented in this research also contradict theories that explain the mobilization and collective actions of the Iranian revolution in terms of the social movement model. Proponents of the social movement model place their emphasis on traditional urban communities, belief systems, an encompassing ideological consensus, or the erosion of the monarchy's legitimacy. The available data demonstrate that the actors in the revolution did not constitute communities, but represented instead a coalition of classes and groups with disparate interests, resources, and solidarity structures. The divergences in the timing of their actions and their demands clearly reveal the absence of community. Antigovernment forces mobilized through the mosque not because of ideological consensus, but because government repression had left no other option. The continuation of conflicts after the establishment of the Islamic Republic is evidence that contradictory interests and contending classes characterized the Iranian revolutionary conflicts. An analysis based on the erosion of the monarchy's legitimacy does not explain the rise of the conflicts and the revolution in 1979. The mere absence of conflict in the late 1960s or early 1970s cannot be counted as evidence that the Shah's rule was legitimate. Illegitimate regimes can repress conflicts and remain in power for long periods of time. The fact that all the major classes had opposed the monarchy from at least the early 1950s points to the deeper roots of the conflict. Also, the government's ban on and elimination of all political organizations and the independent trade unions testifies to the weaknesses of the regime, not to its legitimacy. In addition, the importance of external intervention in returning the monarchy to power in 1953 severely weakens any claim to legitimacy the monarch might have had among the major classes and political contenders.

SUMMARY OF THE ANALYSIS

My analysis indicates that the Iranian revolution can best be explained by a structural theory of the state, combined with the resource mobilization theory of collective action. The argument can be briefly summarized as follows. With increased oil revenues, and especially following the reforms of the early 1960s, the state expanded its intervention in capital allocation and accumulation, which reached a peak in the mid-1970s. As oil revenues grew, the state became the nation's largest capitalist, banker, industrialist, and employer, owning the most important sources of wealth. With expanded resources, the state greatly influenced the allocation of capital and, consequently, the economic development of the country. In addition, the state heightened its regulatory activities, ever increasing its control over the market. As a result, the high level of state intervention in capital allocation and accumulation undermined the abstract, impersonal market forces and the "invisible hand." Thus, state intervention politicized the accumulation process, preparing the conditions for the politicization of class conflict. Furthermore, as the state grew increasingly reliant upon oil revenues, the economy became more dependent on the world market, and both grew ever more susceptible to crisis and fluctuations in the world market. Consequently, a combination of a high level of state intervention in accumulation and growing dependence rendered the state vulnerable to crisis, challenge, and attack.

At the same time, high state intervention in capital accumulation contradicted any claim that the government's economic policies were independent of the interests of the upper class. In other words, the high level of state intervention in accumulation visibly demonstrated that the government served particular, rather than general or societal, interests. The state systematically served the interests of big capital linked to multinational corporations and the upper-echelon bureaucrats at the expense of other classes. Although small, this upper class appropriated the lion's share of the national wealth. The government's capital allocation policies consistently favored big capital, which received interest-free loans or cheap credit, tax holidays, and favorable conditions for investment. Industrialists and large importers were the main beneficiaries of the government's accumulation policies and were allowed to form the relatively autonomous Chamber of Industry and Commerce. Medium and small capital did not receive the same sorts of economic resources, nor were they permitted to form independent organizations of their own. Industrial workers were severely repressed as the result of state intervention in capital accumulation; they were prevented from forming autonomous organizations and from using the strike as a bargaining tool. Agriculture and rural areas were neglected by the government, leading to deteriorating conditions for the country's peasantry. The state's capital allocation policies ignored areas such as Kurdestan and gave rise to uneven development and wider regional inequalities. The overall result of state intervention in capital accumulation was rising disparities among social classes, between urban and rural areas, and among regions.

The immediate factors that set the stage for the conflicts of 1977 to 1979 were rising inflation, reduced government oil revenues, and an economic crisis precipitated by the government's attempt to bring the economy under control. Uneven development of the oil sector led to a crisis of revenue absorption, high inflation, and speculation. The massive influx of oil wealth was not matched by a rise in the availability of commodities, with the result that the economy was unable to absorb the increased revenues. The demand-pull inflation was exacerbated by declining agricultural production, rising urbanization, and the government's high expenditures. Then, in the mid-1970s, the world demand for oil dropped, causing a fiscal crisis for the government, which needed additional capital to complete its ambitious projects. To resolve the problem, the government pursued a contradictory policy. On the one hand, it began borrowing funds from abroad, while initiating price controls and an antiprofiteering campaign on the other. These policies did not remedy the problem, however. Finally, unable to pursue its policies further, the government effected a recession, which brought about an economic crisis in 1977 and set the stage for social conflict.

The government's attempts to check inflation through price controls and the antiprofiteering campaign violated the established rights and interests of bazaaris and generated a new set of conflicts. These government policies politicized previously nonpolitical bazaaris and united various elements of this group against the state. Bazaari mobilization provided an important base for opposition and ultimately for the revolution.

Mobilization and Revolution

By 1977, the regime's policies had adversely affected major social groups and classes including bazaaris, industrial workers, white-collar employees, and professionals. The mobilization and collective actions of these classes and their coalition were responsible for the overthrow of the monarchy. These classes had different sets of conflicts and resources for mobilization and, as a result, the nature and timing of their actions varied. The variables that determined their collective actions included interest, organization and solidarity structures, and opportunity for action. These variables had been determinants of the mobilization and collective actions of these classes for several decades prior to the revolution.

Despite the traditionalism of segments of the bazaar, bazaaris' collective actions can best be explained in terms of the variables we have specified. During the economic crisis and political opening of the early 1950s, bazaaris formed an independent organization and supported Dr. Mosaddegh because he advocated nationalist economic policies, which served bazaari interests, and a liberal political system. While most clerics backed the royalists, bazaaris overwhelmingly supported Mosaddegh. In the early 1960s, a combination of a severe economic crisis and a brief liberalization provided an opportunity for political activities and led to bazaari mobilization. Bazaari interests had been adversely affected by the economic crisis and by the government's credit policies and taxation scheme. Bazaaris supported the second National Front, which was formed during this period. The National Front was soon repressed, however, and all of its leaders and most

Front activists were imprisoned before the June 1963 uprising. The government also arrested a number of bazaari activists and drove many others underground. Thus, the repression severely weakened bazaaris' capacity for mobilization and collective action. Clerical opposition to the regime provided bazaaris with an opportunity to oppose the government, especially because Ayatollah Khomeini, unlike other religious leaders, openly condemned the government's policies toward the bazaar. Once again, repression succeeded in defeating the opposition, in part because industrial workers and white-collar employees did not join in the antigovernment protests.

Although segments of the bazaar were economically squeezed during the early 1970s, the oil boom of 1973 provided an opportunity for many bazaaris to take advantage of favorable economic conditions. The bazaar still controlled more than two-thirds of the domestic trade and more than one-third of the foreign trade and was in an advantageous position to benefit from the economic boom. Accordingly, bazaaris throughout the country took no action when Ayatollah Khomeini called for support for rebellious clerical students in Qom in June 1975, even though many students were arrested, some were injured, and a few were killed.

Bazaari mobilization and collective actions during the 1977–1979 period were in response to the government's violations of their established rights and interests. The government's accumulation policies had systematically benefited the modern industrial and commercial sectors over the bazaar and thus generated a strong basis for conflict. In response to rising prices, the government intervened in the market mechanism in August 1975 and attempted to control inflation through price controls and an antiprofiteering campaign. A decline in oil revenues the following year prompted the government to increase bazaar taxes, thereby generating additional adverse conditions for bazaaris. Despite prevailing economic adversity, bazaaris' capacity for mobilization had been weakened by several factors in the 1960s and 1970s. The merchants' guild was controlled by the government and possessed no autonomy. The SMGA had been repressed and was virtually nonexistent. Moreover, bazaaris' politics had differentiated in the years following the reforms of the 1960s. A tiny minority of big merchants who had greatly benefited from the oil boom supported the government. Other successful bazaaris had left the bazaar for larger operations and better opportunities outside the confines of the bazaar. Those who opposed the government were not unified; various segments supported different organizations such as the National Front, the Freedom Movement, and the Mojahedeen. Religious bazaaris who paid religious taxes were likewise characterized by divergent orientations. The upper echelon paid their taxes to Ayatollahs Shariat-Madari, Khonsari, and Kho'i, while some middle- and lower-echelon shopkeepers paid taxes to Ayatollah Khomeini. These religious leaders pursued different political aims. Finally, the vast majority of bazaaris had become nonpolitical during the years of repression.

The government's antiprofiteering campaign provided the impetus for mobilization in the bazaar. However, given organizational weaknesses, bazaaris had to wait for favorable opportunities to mobilize and act collectively. In 1977, a change in the laws governing trials encouraged the mobilization of bazaari activists who had supported Mosaddegh. Initially, they acted to support students and university faculty. As mobilization continued, it became increasingly clear that repression would not permit the opposition to gather and organize safely. In January 1978, the massacre of clerical students and others in Qom provided an opportunity for bazaaris to mobilize through the mosque. The mosque was the only organization that had maintained relative autonomy from the state. Mosques were safe locations for gathering, communication, broadcasting the government's repression, and organizing the opposition nationally through the mosque network. In the early stages, however, bazaaris had to pressure the nonpolitical preeminent religious leaders to call for mourning ceremonies and refocus the mosque networks to broadcast violence by the government. Finally, bazaari mobilization was also facilitated by their spatial concentration in urban bazaars; their extensive trading networks; specialized trading in single items, which generated a strong basis for common interest vis-à-vis their opponents; and their independent economic resources.

Bazaari mobilization, shop closures, and participation in mourning cycles held in the mosques forced the government to retreat from its policy of repression and to promise liberalization and reforms. At the end of August 1978, the Shah appointed Sharif-Emami to carry out the reforms. Sharif-Emami declared that his government's mission was "national reconciliation," and he initiated some reforms in order to put an end to the political conflicts.

The promise of reforms provided an opportunity for industrial workers and white-collar employees to mobilize and act collectively. During the political liberalization of the 1940s, most workers, who were organized by the Tudeh party, had engaged in various events of collective action against the monarchy and the British. During the nationalization of oil and the confrontation between Mosaddegh and the royalists, industrial workers, led by oil workers, had played a crucial role in support of Mosaddegh. White-collar employees also supported the prime minister against the monarch. Later, during the uprising of 1963 led by the clergy, neither of these classes took advantage of the opportunity to mobilize. Their inaction can perhaps be explained by various factors such as the lack of independent organizations; repression of the Tudeh party; the government's new policy of profit sharing, which had gone into effect in some factories before the uprising; and support among workers for land reform. Independent labor organizations had been repressed and workers' strikes banned as a result of state intervention in capital accumulation. Workers' organizations and their capacity for collective action had been weakened by government policies. Labor unions were confined to single factories, and workers did not have nationwide or industrywide unions. Moreover, most of these organizations were government-controlled and possessed no autonomy. Similarly, white-collar employees and professionals did not have any formal organization of their own.

Within a few days of the proclamation of liberalization by Sharif-Emami and the reduction of repression, industrial workers, followed by white-collar employees, used their informal networks in workplaces and began to strike. Workers' concentration in large factories facilitated their mobilization. Ignored by the promised reforms and adversely affected by repression and rising inflation these classes demanded better wages, salaries, and improved work conditions. Industrial workers had not taken part in the earlier cycles of mourning ceremonies attended by bazaaris. Their strikes were independent of bazaaris' political protests and closures and were not even coordinated with each other. In addition, the initial demands made by workers and white-collar employees were economic and job-related, rather than political.

At first, the government responded to some strikers' demands, and, as a result, segments of strikers went back to work. Most workers and white-collar employees remained on strike, however, because they demanded greater concessions from the government. Toward the end of Sharif-Emami's government, some strikers began pressing for political changes as well as economic improvements. For example, they demanded the lifting of martial law that had been imposed on twelve major cities, the dissolution of the Savak, and the release of all political prisoners. A number of factors facilitated the strikers' politicization. The media had gained relative freedom by this time and could report most of the strikes and their demands. In this way, the sizable dimensions of the strikes were publicized, revealing the ineffectiveness of repression. For government repression to have been effective, it would have to have been applied on a massive scale. At the same time, reduced repression allowed the strikers to develop their organizational capabilities and solidarity structures. These factors enabled some strikers to escalate their conflicts in the political sphere. Because most of the strikers were employed by the government, the likelihood of their politicization was further increased.

The Shah's response to the growing politicization was to reverse his promise of liberalization and resort to military repression. He dismissed Sharif-Emami and appointed a military government. The armed forces were rapidly dispatched to all parts of the country, where they occupied major installations and strategic locations. Most, but not all, strikers were forced back to work. In response, bazaaris in major cities began an indefinite strike. Oil workers in the south returned to workplaces in order to form a national organization to coordinate their struggles and prevent strikers from going back to work. In less than four weeks, oil workers were back on strike, determined to bring down the monarchy. They defied the government and declared that they supported Ayatollah Khomeini because of his struggles against imperialism and dictatorship. Oil workers were in a very sensitive position because they controlled the main source of the government's revenues. In addition, a strike by oil workers disrupted transportation and all other industries as well. Thus, oil workers' strikes had an enormous impact: they deepened the state's fiscal crisis, disrupted production, and facilitated the overthrow of the monarchy. Workers in other sectors, along with white-collar employees throughout the country, soon followed suit. They organized strike committees in their workplaces, resumed their walkouts, and paralyzed the entire production system and services. With bazaaris, these groups threw their support behind Ayatollah Khomeini as the leader of their "anti-imperialist, anti-despotic" struggles, generating dual sovereignty. The formation of an explicit coalition among bazaaris, industrial workers, white-collar employees, and professionals that disrupted production, distribution, trade, and services created a revolutionary situation.

A number of factors quickly led to the collapse of the armed forces. Widespread signs of insubordination appeared within the armed forces during military rule in November 1978. During this period, the army was spread thinly throughout the country in order to repress the vast majority of the population who actively opposed the government. In response to the massive disruption and opposition they witnessed nation-wide, conscripts, who constituted more than 90 percent of the army, and low-ranking officers began deserting and defecting. At the same time, neighborhood committees, which had been formed by students and the younger generation to protect their communities from hooligan attacks, aggressively attacked the armed forces as they were in the process of disintegrating. The Shah's departure in January 1979 and Bakhtiar's reforms further enhanced the insurgents' capacity to attack the government and the military, and the military was further demoralized when the Shah left as they had been accountable to him alone. Defections and desertions increased. In the final days of the revolution, popular actions and insubordination from within completely paralyzed the military, forcing the chiefs of staff to declare neutrality.

Leadership Organizations

Secular political organizations, which had been supported by most social groups and classes during the 1950s, were drastically weakened by the government's repression and were not in a position to gain the leadership of the collective actions during the 1977–1979 period. The Tudeh party was virtually nonexistent during the revolutionary protests. The Fedayeen, which emerged as a revolutionary alternative during the 1960s and 1970s, were severely repressed both because of their Marxist ideology and because of their tactic of armed struggle. Their armed struggles were not timed in such a way as to result in mobilization because of the economic boom in the early 1970s. Unlike the Tudeh party and the National Front, which grew rapidly during periods of political liberalization and reduced repression, the Fedayeen could not gain recognition and support because, by the mid-1960s, repression had eliminated the possibility of open political discourse. Consequently, their resources and networks were too limited to influence political developments before the revolution. The Fedayeen had no ties to bazaaris because they rejected private property, and they were able to establish only a few links with industrial workers. Nor did the dynamics of political conflict favor the Fedayeen. Fedayeen leaders were not released from prison under Sharif-Emami's reforms. They were finally freed during Bakhtiar's government and thus were unable to influence events until the final two days of the revolution.

The National Front, which had the backing of large segments of the country in the early 1950s, was weakened by government repression after the coup d'etat of 1953. In the early 1960s during a period of temporary political liberalization, the second National Front emerged and was able to gain the support of most bazaaris and university students. But Bakhtiar's speech sharply criticizing the Amini government led to the repression of the National Front prior to the uprising of June 1963. Upon their release from prison, Front leaders prevented university students from holding a demonstration against the government. Thereafter, the Front lost the backing of the students, an important base of their support. The following year, some of the leaders attempted to form a third National Front but were all arrested. They were released from prison after signing commitments not to participate in opposition politics.

In the absence of any political activities, the Front lost its networks, supporters, and resources. As a result, during the revolutionary struggles the National Front did not have a strong, organized position from which to influence political developments to any significant extent, although they opposed the government earlier than other organizations. In addition to lacking a national network, the Front had no communication channels nor a safe, designated place to organize and mobilize the opposition. Moreover, the leaders of the National Front were not prepared to take radical action when political conflicts escalated. The Front failed in its bid for leadership, most notably when large, popular demonstrations during Sharif-Emami's reforms escalated the conflict against the monarchy by calling for the Shah's overthrow. Given this organizational context as well as the failure of the National Front to call for the ouster of the monarchy, the central leadership fell to the Islamic forces and a fraction of the clergy led by Ayatollah Khomeini.

Although this fraction of the clergy came to power through a complicated process, there had been no indication during the prerevolutionary period, as Bazargan has stated, that they wanted to rule the country. The Shah's regime had undermined the clergy's position after the 1963 reforms. But the erosion of clerical authority was insufficient to generate strong, popular mobilization against the government. Ayatollah Khomeini's call for the overthrow of the government in early 1963 did not lead to the ouster of the monarchy, partly because industrial workers, white-collar employees, and students, not to mention the peasantry, did not participate in the struggles. The movement was repressed, and Khomeini was exiled. In the following years, pro-Khomeini clerics, who constituted a small minority of the clergy, were unable to mount an opposition against the government. Whenever they attempted to organize the opposition, they were arrested, imprisoned, or exiled.

Bazaari mobilization provided an opportunity for this antigovernment faction of the clergy to oppose the regime. This mobilization pressured the three leading clerics in Qom to use the mosque networks to broadcast the government's violence and repression by calling for mourning ceremonies. Several cycles of mourning ceremonies during which people protested government repression were coordinated nationally. Mosques provided safe places for gathering, communicating, expressing shared grievances, and coordinating protests and opposition, all of which strengthened the position of pro-Khomeini clerics. As a result of this mobilization, the Shah initiated the reforms of August 1978 by appointing Sharif-Emami. His reforms enhanced the position of the radical clergy by releasing all imprisoned clerics and allowing those who had been exiled during the mourning cycles to return. In addition, liberalization and reduced repression, combined with the intensification of the popular struggles, politicized some of the nonpolitical clerics. Significantly, when Death to the Shah became the main slogan of demonstrators during this period, this faction of the clergy, unlike the National Front, escalated its slogans and called for the monarchy's ouster.

Through their mosque network, this faction of the clergy advocated political freedom, independence, and social justice throughout the revolutionary conflicts. They attacked the Shah's "despotic" rule, foreign domination, especially by the United States, and moral decay. They condemned the government's antiprofiteering campaign against bazaaris. They supported the rights and freedom of university students and condemned government repression and attacks on colleges. Unlike the National Front, they called for changes in the conditions of workers and peasants and asserted that an Islamic republic would provide social justice and serve the interests of the poor and the oppressed.

Ayatollah Khomeini, head of this faction of the clergy, became the supreme leader of the revolution because he had taken an uncompromising stand against the Shah's regime since March 1963, when he called for the overthrow of the government. In exile, Khomeini continued to attack the government during a period when the National Front and all other political leaders bowed to repression and remained silent and inactive. He sent messages to the Iranian people and to his supporters abroad. Ironically, exile provided him with a favorable position from which to continue his opposition to the regime. He continually criticized the pillage of the national resources by imperialists and their internal associates. Throughout his messages, Khomeini attacked the Shah's dictatorship, the lack of freedom and civil liberties, and the violation of the Iranian constitution. He condemned the government's immorality and disrespect for Islam and the clergy. He promised that an Islamic government would guarantee political freedom and independence from imperialism.

As our theory predicted, conflicts continued after the revolution with the establishment of the Islamic Republic. Factors responsible for the continuation of conflict included the continued economic crisis, divisions within the new government between liberals and the IRP, the temporary collapse of the repressive forces, and the mobilization of various groups and classes to advance their interests and gain what they had demanded during the revolutionary conflicts. During this period, however, these actors were disadvantaged by their lack of access to the mosque as a channel through which to mobilize because the IRP brushed aside its clerical opponents and took control of this network. The media, which had gained independence during the governments of Sharif-Emami and Bakhtiar, came increasingly under IRP control and refused to broadcast the views and demands of different groups and classes. The Komitehs soon expanded and transformed the Revolutionary Guard into a permanent organization that, unlike the army, was staffed by hundreds of thousands of permanently employed individuals who were more reliable than conscripts and were used to block the mobilization of groups and classes. Finally, divisions erupted within every social class and among political organizations, preventing the formation of coalitions and the consolidation of opposition. Liberal and leftist political organizations were sharply divided among themselves and did not attempt to join forces. More importantly, the major social classes and groups that had fought against the monarchy did not consolidate their opposition because of divergent interests. For example, bazaaris initially supported the government because it was under the control of liberals; they did not support the struggles of national minorities, workers' councils, and university students because of the leftist tendencies among these classes and groups. As a result, these groups and classes were repressed and partially demobilized. Later, when liberals and bazaaris came under attack, these classes did not join the struggles, in part because they had been partially demobilized by the closure of the universities, the dismantling of the workers' councils, and purges of their members. Unlike the struggles against the monarchy, repression did not lead to the escalation of conflicts and the eventual failure of repressive forces. In the absence of consolidation, the IRP was able to defeat its opponents. Finally, the IRP was itself dissolved by Khomeini in an attempt to suppress the divisions and the conflicts.

Before concluding, it is appropriate to consider briefly the structural conditions of the Islamic Republic today. A novel consequence of the establishment of the Islamic Republic has been the growing integration of both the state and the mosque into the economy. Mosques and financial institutions work together closely to determine capital allocation. Mosques maintain extended financial profiles of private individuals and firms, which are used by clergy to direct banks on matters of credit and capital allocation. In this way, mosques have become directly integrated into economic structures and capital accumulation. More significantly, state intervention in capital allocation and accumulation has expanded even further, undermining the market mechanism. By the second year after the revolution, all banks and large private industries had been nationalized, and 70 percent of all industries were state-owned. At the same time, the economy remained highly dependent on the world market, although political dependence was eliminated, at least in the initial years. Economic dependence rendered the state and society susceptible to international economic crises.

Although the campaign against profiteers continued in the years following Bani-Sadr's ouster, its intensity was reduced. As a result of pressures by bazaaris influential in the government, Borhani, a young cleric who served as deputy of the special court investigating price controls, was dismissed. He had been known for his hard-line approach to "profiteering." He was charged with having made politically motivated decisions, and thus he was pressured to resign (*Iranshahr*, March 4, 1983). This change signaled a softer approach toward the bazaar. The latest evidence indicates that at least a fraction of the bazaar has prospered tremendously in the past few years, despite the continuation of economic crisis, the war, and price controls. As late as 1986, five thousand bazaaris made substantial profits (*Kayhan*, August 25, 1987). Thus, the Islamic Republic may have already established a lasting alliance with merchant capital in the bazaar.

It is conceivable, however, that the radical faction of the clergy, some of whom were organized in the IRP, may organize and launch attacks against growing merchant wealth and the landed upper class. They may attempt to institute land reform, nationalize foreign trade, and exert greater controls on the private sector, all of which they failed to do over the past several years. With access to the mosque and the media, the radicals may even be able to mobilize popular support for their policies. This in turn may provide an opportunity for various groups and classes to mobilize and press for social change.

Should state intervention in capital allocation and accumulation remain high, however, and a permanent, visible alliance develop between the state and large capital, within the bazaar, and against other classes and interests, the Islamic Republic, like many other Third World states, will become structurally vulnerable to challenge and attack. This will occur partly because the state will inevitably become the target of attack, given its limitation of the market mechanism, which would have otherwise confined the social conflicts to the private sphere and the civil society. Under conditions of economic polarization, the absence of formal democracy would increase the state's vulnerability. In addition, the state will become the target of attack because it has excluded major factions of the revolutionary coalition that brought the regime to power. In other words, the coalition may have become too narrow. This does not necessarily imply that adversely affected groups and classes would be able to mobilize sufficient resources to challenge the government. In the absence of major divisions within the government, the opposition would be unable to use the mosque as the basis for mobilization because this organization no longer has any autonomy from the state. The option of mobilizing through political parties and autonomous organizations, as occurred in the 1950s, no longer exists. Without autonomous organizations, sustained mobilization by the opposition would be severely restricted. Opponents could, of course, attempt to develop alternative organizations and repertoires of mobilization. Under the current circumstances, however, these would be extremely difficult undertakings. As a result, at least in the short run, opponents may be unable to develop the resources and solidarity structures necessary to mount a consolidated opposition against the regime, as occurred in the 1977–1979 conflicts.

In conclusion, the structural theory I have employed in this reseach has proven extremely useful in explaining the Iranian revolution. If this theory can illuminate the complicated and perplexing case of Iran, it should be applicable to other examples of political conflict and revolutionary struggles in other Third World countries. Sociological analysis of such conflicts should focus on state intervention in capital accumulation and its impact upon various social groups and classes, capacity for collective action, solidarity structures, options for mobilization, opportunity structures, and likelihood of coalition formation. I believe that these variables, rather than rapid modernization, anomie, rising expectations, or ideological consensus, shed greater light on the Iranian revolution and should form the core of sociological theories of collective action and revolution.

Notes

CHAPTER 1: EXPLANATIONS OF THE REVOLUTION

1. For a more complete discussion and critique of these theories, see Tilly 1978; Aya 1979; and Goldstone 1980.

2. Since I have reviewed this literature more extensively elsewhere, I will only briefly summarize them here. See Parsa 1988.

3. On the New Deal, see Schlesinger 1958; Leuchtangburg 1963.

4. On the Russian economic development, see Crisp 1976; Carson 1959; Lyashchenko 1949.

CHAPTER 2: THE POLITICS OF POWER

1. I shall rely primarily upon the work of Abrahamian, Halliday, Keddie, Cottam, and Bharier.

2. Wilber 1975:143. Most of the items were very important, including wheat, rice, dried fruits, fisheries' products, cotton, carpets, motor vehicles, matches, alcoholic beverages, and petroleum products.

3. Abrahamian 1982:151. Bharier, examining the data for 1947, states that small industry in Tehran might have suffered a drastic decline from twenty years earlier (1971:174).

4. United Nations, February 1953:40–41. These workers were employed in textile, sugar refining, tobacco, chemicals, cement, and several other sectors.

5. Overseas Consultants 1949, 3:227. This source notes that 25 percent of the inhabitants of Tehran obtain their living through some kind of retailing of goods.

6. *Kayhan,* July 22, 1952. The number of casualties might be an exaggerated figure.

7. United Press reporter in Tehran, quoted in Jami 1976:611.

8. Jami 1976:617. Supporters of the National Front shouted, "Mosaddegh is victorious!" while supporters of the Tudeh party shouted, "The people are victorious!"

9. The State Department denied the allegation on January 22, 1960 (Alexander and Nanes 1980:313–315).

10. Hooglund (1982) emphasized the political dimension of the Shah's decision for land reform; A. Tabari (1983) stressed the developmental aspect of the reforms.

11. President Carter's stand on human rights in Iran is discussed in greater detail in chapter 6.

CHAPTER 3: STATE ACCUMULATION POLICIES

1. *Kayhan,* January 3, 1977, gives a figure of 3.11 percent; my figures are calculated from BMI 1976:57 and BMI 1977:152.

2. According to Ladjevardian (1982), most of the nine thousand individuals who belonged to the chamber of commerce were industrialists, while a minority were importers of foreign goods.

3. Calculated from data in BMI 1976 and SCI 1976a.

4. Instead of at least cautioning against such a policy, the International Bank for Reconstruction and Development in 1974 advised the government: "Iran should not consider itself vulnerable to fluctuations in world supplies and prices if it adopts a logical long-term import policy. . . . Iran can, in addition, import many agricultural products at a lower cost than it would take to produce them locally. . . . Imports could thus serve to reduce consumer prices" (Burn and Dumont 1978:15).

5. The mean number of inhabitants was 4.8 for urban and 5.2 for rural households.

6. This statement was made by Rohani in *Ettelaat,* November 8, 1977.

7. *Ettelaat,* June 25, August 24 and 27, 1977. Because of several confrontations between shantytown dwellers and government authorities, the Shah ordered an end to the demolitions.

8. The data was compiled from a report published by the Statistical Center of Iran (SCI) 1977b.

9. Unfortunately, the source combines the two provinces of Khuzestan and Boyer Ahmad, making it impossible to assess the distribution of expenditures for each separately.

CHAPTER 4: THE BAZAAR

1. Bazaaris frequently make exaggerated estimates of the size of the central bazaar. The Tehran census of 1980 indicates that the covered bazaar had close to twenty thousand shops and workshops (SCI 1981b:223).

2. This estimate of the number of moneylenders is for the mid-1960s (Benedick 1964:66).

3. Arjomand (1981; 1986) spoke of a historical alliance between bazaaris and clergy. Skocpol (1982) also maintained that bazaaris always follow the lead of the clergy.

4. See the chapter on the clergy for more details.

5. There was little or no participation by university students, industrial workers, white-collar employees, or professionals in these events.

6. Although the following sources reported attacks on open shops, it is possible that such actions were carried out by progovernment hooligans: *Ettelaat*, June 6, 1963; *Christian Science Monitor*, June 6, 1963; *New York Times*, June 9, 1963.

7. These figures are taken from a written statement, in the possession of the author, by the Madraseh-e Faizieh-e Qom.

8. In personal communications with the author, several bazaaris from Tehran and Tabriz affirmed that during the initial stages of the oil boom the economic condition of merchants and shopkeepers in most sectors began to improve.

9. Unfortunately, the national census does not provide information regarding the total number of artisans, which includes self-employed in manufacturing and small producers employing only a few workers.

10. Among the most successful merchants who left the bazaar were Farman-farmanian, Vahabzadeh, Khayyami, Ladjevardi, Haddad, Mofid, Reza'i, Barkhordar, Moghaddam, Ghasemiyeh, and Shah-Vali.

11. In a statement issued during the summer of 1978, rug dealers in the Tehran bazaar condemned this minority, whom they labeled sellouts (Organization of Iranian Moslem Students 1978:62).

12. *Zamimeh* 1978, no. 16:31. The words "Tehran Bazaar," missing from the original name of the organization, were added perhaps because the commercial sector outside the Tehran bazaar, very small in the 1950s, had expanded by the 1970s to

the point where the new organization had to be more specific in identifying its members.

13. The leading supporters of Khomeini in the bazaar included Khamoushi, Pour-Ostad, Amani, Shafi'i, and Asgar-Oladi. The hard-core, activist segment of this group consisted of approximately thirty bazaaris who worked closely with the clergy to coordinate strikes during the final days of the monarchy.

14. Some of these arrests were reported in various issues of the *Zamimeh*.

15. Interviews with a number of bazaaris have confirmed this point.

16. Lebaschi 1983, tape 3:15. Lebaschi states that in his two meetings with Khomeini in Paris he received no impression that Khomeini had any political aspirations to rule Iran.

CHAPTER 5: AUTUMN ALLIES

1. SCI 1981a:16. A 1977 survey indicates that large factories employed approximately 404,000 workers. This survey, however, excluded the rug industry.

2. Eghbal became prime minister on April 4, and the government lifted the martial law on the same day (*Ettelaat*, April 4, 1957).

3. *Ettelaat* (May 8, 1961 reported that the executive committee of the Tehran Workers' Syndicates had issued a statement in support of teachers. In addition, syndicates of shoemakers, tailors, restaurateurs, sugar refiners, bakers, and shirtmakers also issued statements in support of teachers.

4. *Le Monde Diplomatique* 1975, quoted in Halliday 1979:190 and in Ghotbi 1978:32. At that time, a rial was worth approximately 1.4 cents.

5. On November 23, tractor employees in Tabriz held a demonstration in the factory yard; twelve workers were arrested by the army, while the remainder were prevented from entering the factory.

6. A *Le Monde* report of November 16, 1978, stated about workers in Abadan: "The workers we meet use the same words. Who has given them instructions to strike? No one in particular. Everyone agrees. There is really no organization" (quoted in Turner 1980:279 and *MERIP Reports*, March–April 1979:19).

7. Quoted in Abrahamian 1979:3.

8. On the issues of resignation and torture, see *Hambastegi* 1978, no. 8.

9. Early in February, seven hundred workers of the General Factory, which had been closed for forty-five days, held a sit-in to demand the reinstatement of two hundred dismissed workers and payment of over one hundred thousand dollars in workers' cooperative investments. Workers took hostage three officials of the factory and succeeded in forcing the company's executive to resign. With the support of several hundred university students who joined the sit-in, the workers took control of the operation of the factory (*Kayhan*, February 11, 1979).

CHAPTER 6: THE SECULAR CONTENDERS

1. In the spring of 1978, a mother of a political prisoner who was able to visit some of the political prisoners stated that psychological torture, such as sleep deprivation, was practiced in prisons and in fact drove one of the political prisoners to insanity (Abouzar 1978, 1:44–45).

2. Bank employees who backed the Front formed a committee to raise money for striking workers and white-collar employees. Some educators in Tehran organized the Society of Teachers, which was allied with the National Front; near the end of the revolutionary conflict, they met to coordinate teachers' struggles.

3. Forouhar spent eleven years in Savak jails after 1953.

4. The government agreed to the national day of mourning called by the National Front.

5. Siahkal is the place where the Fedayeen first launched their armed struggle.

6. These writers were led by Shams Al-e Ahmad, and Rahmat Allah Moghaddam (Nategh 1982).

7. In the 1960s, two political organizations with revolutionary ideologies emerged: the Organization of the Iranian People's Fedayee Guerrillas and the People's Mojahedeen Organization of Iran. In later years, other guerrilla organizations with Marxist and Islamic ideologies were formed, but they never gained the strength and attention of the Fedayeen and the Mojahedeen. Because the Mojahedeen were religious, we will consider them in the next chapter.

8. Many of them were sons of leaders of the National Front, including Masoud Ahmadzadeh, Mohsen Shanehchi, and Shaygan.

9. According to one report, the "repertory of tortures includes not only electric shock and beatings, but also the insertion of bottles in the rectum, hanging weights from testicles, rape, and such apparatus as a helmet that, worn over the head of the victim, magnifies his own screams." Most experts cited Iran as one of the two worst violators of human rights (*Time*, August 16, 1976).

10. Examples include Mashhad, Tabriz, Ghazvin, Karaj, Shiraz, Isfahan, and a few cities in the province of Mazanderan.

CHAPTER 7: THE MOSQUE AND ISLAMIC FORCES

1. The clergy had differentiated politically during the Constitutional Revolution from 1905 to 1911. Although most had supported the constitution in the beginning, they diverged to the point that by the end of this period a number of ayatollahs, led by Sheikh Fazlollah Nouri, a highly respected cleric, opposed the constitutionalists.

2. International protests and pressure evidently prevented the regime from fully carrying out its anti-Baha'i campaign, which was eventually halted.

3. Leaflet in the possession of author. The statement has also been published in Khomeini 1983, 1:215.

4. This information came from a statement issued by the Freedom Movement (abroad) in 1975.

5. Statement by Ahmad Khomeini, son of Ayatollah Khomeini (*Ettelaat*, September 23, 1979).

6. Various issues of *Mojahed* in 1981, particularly no. 106, January 20, 1981.

7. See various statements in *Zamimeh*.

8. See statement by Mousavi-Tabrizi, prosecutor of the Islamic Republic, in *Jumhuri Eslami*, April 26, 1982.

9. Their statement was published by the Organization of Iranian Moslem Students (1978:60–61).

10. Arrests are not a complete indication of the distribution of radical clergy, for many doubtless avoided arrest by moving underground. Living clandestinely, however, would have limited their effectiveness in mobilizing the opposition.

11. M. J. 1979:82. Ashouri was killed in Boushehr by the military on December 4, 1978.

12. Abouzar 1978, vol. 1, pt. 1:141. This source claims that by the end at least three million people were participating in the protest.

13. These are all included in the various volumes of Khomeini's collection, published by the government of Iran.

14. In the early 1970s, Khomeini wrote a book advocating the establishment of an Islamic Republic. The contents of this book, however, and the nature of such a government were not widely known among Iranians because government repression prevented publication of the book in Iran. According to Khomeini, such a government would guarantee independence, freedom, and social justice. In an Islamic society, the ruler must possess two characteristics: first, he must be knowledgeable about the laws, and second, he must be just. Islamic laws were just and would protect the oppressed and the hungry. In this book, Khomeini argues for a theocratic state (Khomeini 1979).

CHAPTER 8: THE FINAL COLLAPSE

1. The reported cases include an attack on bazaaris and leaders of the National Front at Karvansara Sangi; an assault on two members of the Writers' Association

who were in Lahijan to make speeches; an attack on university students who were mountain-climbing near Tehran.

2. During a massacre by army troops of Tehran demonstrators on September 8, one soldier refused to fire upon protesters as ordered; instead, he shot his commanding officer. On October 26, a soldier shot and killed the chief of police of Jahrom and seriously wounded the military governor. Two soldiers in Mashhad were killed by their officer for insubordination on December 3. That same day, a soldier was ordered to open fire on a group of people; when he instead turned his gun on the colonel who had given the order, he was quickly shot by the officer. Another soldier, Mohsen Mobasher, shot and wounded the governor of Hamedan and one of his bodyguards on December 12. The next day, the army opened fire on a group of people listening to a sermon in Shoushtar; more than thirty were killed. One soldier, who was angered by the incident, tossed his gun into the crowd and tried to run away but was shot and killed by a policeman. On December 14, two soldiers joined demonstrators in Rezaieh; one of them killed a major and two policemen and was in turn slain. In Mashhad, a sergeant shot and wounded a cleric on December 17 and was in turn killed by a policeman. On December 30, 150 soldiers who were ordered to open fire on protesters in Mashhad turned their weapons over to the demonstrators and joined the protest. An air force cadet fired on his commanding officer and the deputy commander on January 11, but failed to kill them. On January 12, a soldier who refused to open fire on demonstrators in Rasht was killed by his commander (see M. J. 1979, and various issues of *Akhbar, Hamba-stegi,* and *Ettelaat.*

3. On November 11, a religious holiday, the army opened fire on a group of peaceful demonstrators leaving a mosque in Khorramshahr. Nineteen people were killed, including two military men who committed suicide rather than shoot the demonstrators. A few days later in the same city, army troops again fired into a crowd of demonstrators, killing a baby in her mother's arms. One soldier who witnessed the event shot and killed a sergeant, another soldier, and then himself. In Tehran during the funeral on December 27 of Dr. Nejat-Ollahy, a university professor, one soldier killed his commanding officer and then committed suicide.

CHAPTER 9: CONFLICTS WITHIN THE ISLAMIC REPUBLIC

1. Speaker of the Majles, Hojjat Al-Eslam Hashemi-Rafsanjani (*Jumhuri Eslami,* October 30, 1982).

2. Professor Homa Nategh presented this data from the College of Literature at

Tehran University and claimed that the pattern was similar in all other colleges. See *Jahan* no. 1, January 1982 under Nategh 1982.

3. A government report cited in *Ettelaat*, April 15, 1979.

4. In 1979–1980, there were 366 strikes and sit-ins. The number declined to 180 in 1980–1981, and to 82 in 1981–1982 (Bayat 1987:108).

5. Statement by Kamal Ganjeh'i, a high-level official of the Ministry of Labor (*Kayhan*, January 3, 1984; *Ettelaat*, January 4, 1984).

6. One walkout occurred over a plan to retire or dismiss ten thousand workers at an Isfahan steel mill. These workers struck and were soon joined by an equal number of workers who demanded health insurance. The government quickly moved to investigate the grievances by establishing a committee composed of officials from the Ministries of Interior, Labor, Information, and Mines and Metal, along with the governor of the province of Isfahan. The officials claimed that leftist political organizations had been involved in agitating against the government. Nevertheless, the authorities agreed to the strikers' demands, justifying their decision as a measure to gain the confidence of 90 percent of the workers, whom they claimed were Islamic (*Ettelaat*, April 14, 1985).

7. See Khamoushi's defense in the Majles, in *Kayhan*, April 14, 1983. Hezb-Ollah means God's party and in Iran refers to the Islamic Republican party.

8. Imam means leader and here refers to Ayatollah Khomeini.

9. Saeed Amani, a bazaari and member of the Supervisory Council of Guild Affairs, provided this information in an interview with the IRP newspaper, *Jumhuri Eslami*, August 16, 1982.

10. Khatami, Khomeini's representative in Azerbaijan, claimed that in the three or four years following the revolution, some people accumulated more capital than during the previous forty years (*Ettelaat*, April 12, 1983). Harandi, a member of the Majles, charged that some merchants sold goods costing four hundred to five hundred tomans for fifteen thousand to sixteen thousand tomans, and thus made millions of tomans a year (*Ettelaat*, April 26, 1983). Hasan-Zadeh, another member of the Majles, claimed that in taking advantage of the war, some bazaaris have made millions of tomans (*Kayhan*, May 7, 1983). Dr. Yadollah Sahabi, also a member of the Majles, made a similar charge in 1980.

11. Borhani, a cleric and deputy of the special courts, suggested in an interview that big speculators and profiteers had supporters who protected them and prevented the courts from acting against them (*Ettelaat*, December 22 and 25, 1982).

12. Following several years of debate, the powerful Guardian Council rejected the bill nationalizing foreign trade as non-Islamic, although both the constitution and the Majles had approved it. At present, importers of most goods must allocate

30 percent of their imports to the government for distribution by cooperatives on the basis of rationing.

13. Rationed items include butter, cooking oil, sugar, tea, rice, chicken, meat, and eggs.

14. *Ettelaat*, September 19, 1984. Ayatollah Montazeri also criticized government interference in commerce (*Kayhan*, July 30 and August 29, 1984).

15. *Ettelaat*, November 12, 1980. Ladjevardi, Tehran's public prosecutor, stated in a 1983 interview, "The pressures had come from liberals, and because we do not want more tensions in our society, we decided to release Ghotb-Zadeh for the time being."

16. This group of bazaaris called themselves "Followers of the Imam's Line"; they supported Ayatollah Khomeini and condemned the liberal criticism of clerics in many cities, especially in Mashhad. They also criticized *Enghelab-e Eslami* and *Mizan* newspapers published by Bani-Sadr and Bazargan, respectively (*Ettelaat*, December 2, 1980).

17. See *Mojahed*, appendix to no. 261, September 6, 1985. This figure is especially high when considered in light of the fact that after the revolution only three major capitalists associated with the Shah were executed.

18. In August 1981, Nazem-Zadeh reported that in the preceding ten months, more than eight thousand merchants and shopkeepers had been fined, jailed, or exiled for profiteering (*Ettelaat*, August 23, 1981). In April 1982, he stated that in the previous eighteen months, his office had arrested and punished twenty-five thousand shopkeepers and merchants (*Iran Times*, April 23, 1982). Fines ran as high as several hundreds of thousands of tomans and in some cases two million tomans (*Ettelaat*, July 7, and December 1, 1981).

19. See a statement by Sane'i, a cleric and prosecutor, in *Kayhan*, July 18, 1983; another official made a similar remark in *Ettelaat*, July 21, 1983. Thus far, there have been no reports of any executions of profiteers.

20. For example, a cleric who was a faculty member of the Mashhad seminary was executed for longtime spying for the Savak (*Ettelaat*, April 23, 1979). Another cleric was executed in Hamedan on charges of supporting the Shah (*Ettelaat*, April 19, 1979).

21. Ayatollah Khomeini discussed the need for a Faghieh in an Islamic government in his book *Islamic Government* (Tehran: Entesharat-e Amir Kabir, 1971. Reprint, 1979).

22. Ayatollah Taleghani told the Cuban delegation in Iran that Moslems shared with Marxists the negation of imperialism and exploitation; they differed over the issue of creation (*Ettelaat*, August 6, 1979).

23. Shanehchi, chief aid to Ayatollah Taleghani in 1978–1979, has expressed suspicion over Taleghani's death (Shanehchi 1983, tape 2:27).

24. *Enghelab-e Eslami*, March 16, 1981. Jalal Ganjeh'i made a similar statement in an interview with *Le Monde* on February 23, 1983; however, this figure seems inflated.

25. He protested hooligan attacks in a letter to Bani-Sadr (*Enghelab-e Eslami*, March 14, 1981).

26. The Mojahedeen published the names of the following clerics: Mazhari, Ashouri, Abas Hoseini, Ali Shirvani, Mesbah, Malek-Alreghabi, Mohades, Mir Nour Elahi, Ahmadi, and Emami (*Mojahed*, appendix to no. 261, September 6, 1985). Sunni clerical leaders opposed the government's policies toward national minorities seeking independence. Ayatollahs Khaghani of Khuzestan, Ezzoddin Hoseini of Kurdestan, and Arzanesh of the Turkoman region all defended local autonomy, but without success.

References

BOOKS AND ARTICLES IN ENGLISH AND FARSI

Abouzar. 1978. *Asnad va Tasaviri as Enghelab-e Khalgh-e Mosalman-e Iran.* Vol. 1, Parts 1 and 3. Tehran: Abouzar.

Abrahamian, E. 1968. "The Crowd in Iranian Politics." *Past and Present* 41:184–210.

———. 1981. "The Strengths and Weaknesses of the Labor Movement in Iran, 1941–1953." In *Modern Iran: The Dialectics of Continuity and Change,* edited by M. Bonnine and N. Keddie. Albany: State University of New York Press.

———. 1982. *Iran Between Two Revolutions.* Princeton: Princeton University Press.

Akhavi, S. 1980. *Religion and Politics in Contemporary Iran.* Albany: State University of New York Press.

Alexander, Y., and A. Nanes, eds. 1980. *The United States and Iran: A Documentary History.* Frederick, Md.: University Publications of America.

Arjomand, S. 1981. "Shi'ite Islam and the Revolution in Iran." *Government and Opposition* 16:293–316.

———. 1986. "Iran's Islamic Revolution in Comparative Perspective." *World Politics* 38:383–414.

————. 1988. *The Turban for the Crown: The Islamic Revolution in Iran*. New York: Oxford University Press.

Ashraf, A., and A. Banuazizi. 1985. "The State, Classes and Modes of Mobilization in the Iranian Revolution." *State, Culture and Society* 1:3–40.

Aya, R. 1979. "Theories of Revolution: Contrasting Models of Collective Violence." *Theory and Society* 8:39–99.

Bakhash, S. 1984. *The Reign of the Ayatollahs: Iran and the Islamic Revolution*. New York: Basic Books.

Bakhtiar, S. 1982. *Yekrangi*. Paris: Albion Michel.

Bank Markazi Iran (BMI). various years. *Bank Markazi of Iran: Annual Report and Balance Sheet*. Tehran: BMI.

Bashiriyeh, H. 1984. *The State and Revolution in Iran, 1962–1982*. New York: St. Martin's Press.

Bayat, A. 1983. "Workers' Control After the Revolution." *MERIP Reports* 13 (3): 19–34.

————. 1987. *Workers and Revolution in Iran*. London: Zed.

Bazargan, M. 1983a. *Moshkelat va Masael-e Avvalin Sal-e Enghelab*. Tehran: The Freedom Movement.

————. 1983b. *Shora-ye Enghelab Va Dolat-e Movaghat*. Tehran: The Freedom Movement.

————. 1984. *Enghelab-e Iran Dar Du Harkat*. Tehran: Mazaheri.

Benedick, R. 1964. *Industrial Finance in Iran: A Study of Financial Practice in an Underdeveloped Economy*. Harvard University, Graduate School of Business Administration, Division of Research. Boston.

Bharier, J. 1971. *Economic Development in Iran, 1900–1970*. London: Oxford University Press.

Biderman, J. 1983. "The Development of Capitalism in Nicaragua: A Political Economic History." *Latin American Perspectives* 10 (7): 7–32.

Binder, L. 1962. *Iran: Political Development in a Changing Society*. Berkeley and Los Angeles: University of California Press.

Blair, J. 1976. *The Control of Oil*. New York: Vintage Books.

BMI. *See* Bank Markazi Iran

Burn, T., and R. Dumont. 1978. "Imperial Pretensions and Agricultural Dependence." *MERIP Reports* 8 (8): 15–20.

Carson, G., Jr. 1959. "The State and Economic Development: Russia, 1880–1939." In *The State and Economic Growth*, edited by H. Aitken. New York: Social Science Research Council.

Carter, J. 1978. *Public Papers of the Presidents of the United States: Jimmy Carter, 1977*. Washington, D.C.: GPO.

Cottam, R. 1979. *Nationalism in Iran*. Pittsburgh: University of Pittsburgh Press.

Crisp, O. 1976. *Studies in the Russian Economy Before 1914.* New York: Macmillan.

Deutsch, K. 1961. "Social Mobilization and Political Development." *American Political Science Review* 50:493–514.

Fischer, M. 1980. *Iran: From Religious Dispute to Revolution.* Cambridge: Harvard University Press.

The Freedom Movement. 1983. *Safehati As Tarikh-e Mo'aser-e Iran.* Tehran: The Freedom Movement.

The Freedom Movement (abroad). 1978. *Dar Bareh-e Ghiam-e Hammaseh Afarinan-e Qom Va Tabriz Va Digar Shahr Haye Iran.* 3 vols.

Gamson, W. 1975. *The Strategy of Social Protest.* Homewood, Ill.: Dorsey Press.

Ghara-Baghi, A. 1984. *Haghayegh Dar Bare-he Bohran-e Iran.* Paris: Sohail.

Ghoreyshi, A., and C. Elahi. 1976. "Social Mobilization and Participation in Iran." In *Iran: Past, Present, and Future,* edited by J. Jacqz. New York: Aspen Institute for Humanistic Studies.

Ghotbi, A. (T. Jalil). 1978. *Workers Say No to the Shah: Labour Law and Strikes in Iran.* London: CRTURI (Campaign for the Restoration of Trade Union Rights in Iran).

Goldstone, J. 1980. "Theories of Revolution: The Third Generation." *World Politics* 32:425–453.

———. 1986. *Revolutions: Theoretical, Comparative, and Historical Studies.* San Diego: Harcourt Brace Jovanovich.

Graham, R. 1979. *Iran: The Illusion of Power.* New York: St. Martin's Press.

Green, J. 1980. "Pseudoparticipation and Counter-Mobilization: Roots of the Iranian Revolution." *Iranian Studies* 13:31–53.

———. 1986. "Countermobilization in the Iranian Revolution." In *Revolutions: Theoretical, Comparative, and Historical Studies,* edited by J. Goldstone. San Diego: Harcourt Brace Jovanovich.

Halliday, F. 1978a. "The Economic Contradiction." *MERIP Reports* 8 (6): 9–19.

———. 1978b. "Trade Unions and the Working Class Opposition." *MERIP Reports* 8 (8): 7–13.

———. 1979. *Iran: Dictatorship and Development.* New York: Penguin Books.

Hezar-Kani, M. 1982. "The Only Obstacle is Khomeini Himself." *MERIP Reports* 12 (3): 33–34.

Hirsch, J. 1978. "The State Apparatus and Social Reproduction: Elements of a Theory of the Bourgeois State." In *State and Capital: A Marxist Debate,* edited by J. Holloway and S. Picciotto. Austin: University of Texas Press.

Hooglund, E. 1981. "Iran's Agricultural Inheritance." *MERIP Reports,* 11 (7): 15–20.

———. 1982. *Land and Revolution in Iran, 1962–1980.* Austin: University of Texas Press.

Hoveyda, F. 1980. *The Fall of the Shah.* London: Weidenfeld and Nicolson.

Huntington, S. 1968. *Political Order in Changing Societies*. New Haven: Yale University Press.

International Labor Office. 1972. "Employment and Income Policies in Iran." Geneva.

Iranian Oil Worker. 1980. "How We Organized the Strike that Paralyzed Shah's Regime." In *Oil and Class Struggle*, edited by Petter Nore and Terisa Turner. London: Zed.

Irfani, S. 1983. *Revolutionary Islam in Iran: Popular Liberation or Religious Dictatorship?* London: Zed.

Issawi, C. 1978. "The Iranian Economy 1925–75: Fifty Years of Economic Development." In *Iran Under the Pahlavis*, edited by G. Lenczowski. Stanford: Hoover Institution Press.

Ivanov, M. n.d. *Tarikh-e Novin-e Iran*. Stockholm: Tudeh Publication.

Jabbari, A., and R. Olson. 1981. *Iran: Essays on a Revolution in the Making*. Lexington, Ky.: Mazda.

Jami [pseud.]. 1976. *Gozashteh Cheragh-e Rah-e Ayandeh Ast*. Paris: Jami.

Jazani, B. 1979. *Tarh-e Jame-eh Shenasi Va Mabani-e Strategy-e Jonbesh-e Enghelabi-e Khalgh-e Iran*. Tehran: Maziar.

Johnson, C. 1966. *Revolutionary Change*. Boston: Little, Brown.

Kambakhsh, A. 1972 and 1974. *Nazari Be Jonbeshe Kargari Va Komonisti Dar Iran*. 2 vols. Stockholm: Tudeh Publication.

Katouzian, H. 1978. "Oil versus Agriculture: A Case of Dual Resource Depletion in Iran." *Journal of Peasant Studies* 5:347–369.

———. 1981. *The Political Economy of Iran*. New York: New York University Press.

Kazemi, F. 1980. *Poverty and Revolution in Iran*. New York: New York University Press.

Keddie, N. 1981. *Roots of Revolution: An Interpretive History of Modern Iran*. New Haven: Yale University Press.

———. 1983. "The Iranian Revolutions in Comparative Perspective." *American Historical Review* 88:579–598.

Khomeini, R. 1976. *Avay-e Enghelab*. United States: Moslem Student Association.

———. 1979. *Hokomat-e Eslami*. Tehran: Amir Kabir.

———. 1983. *Sahifeh-e Nour*. 16 vols. Tehran: Ministry of Guidance.

Klare, M. 1979. *Arms and the Shah*. Institute for Policy Studies Bulletin 43 (8). Washington, D.C.

Korpi, W. 1974. "Conflict, Power, and Relative Deprivation." *American Political Science Review* 68:1567–1578.

Lambton, A. 1969. *The Persian Land Reform*. Oxford: Clarendon Press.

Leuchtangberg, W. 1963. *Franklin D. Roosevelt and the New Deal, 1932–1940.* New York: Harper and Row.

Lyashchenko, P. 1949. *A History of the National Economy of Russia to the 1917 Revolution.* New York: Macmillan.

M. J. [pseud.]. 1979. *Vaghaye-a Enghelab-e Iran.* Tehran.

McCarthy, J., and M. Zald. 1977. "Resource Mobilization and Social Movements: A Partial Theory." *American Journal of Sociology* 82:1212–1241.

McLahlan, K. 1968. "Land Reform in Iran." In *The Cambridge History of Iran: The Land of Iran.* Edited by W. Fisher. Vol. 1, Cambridge: Cambridge University Press.

Moaddel, M. 1986. "The Shi'i Ulama and the State in Iran." *Theory and Society* 15: 519–556.

Momayezi, N. 1986. "Economic Correlates of Political Violence: The Case of Iran." *Middle East Journal* 40:68–81.

Moore, B. 1978. *Injustice: The Social Basis of Obedience and Revolt.* Armonk, N.Y.: M. E. Sharpe.

Morris, A. 1985. *The Origins of the Civil Rights Movement: Black Communities Organizing for Change.* New York: Free Press.

Nategh, H. 1982. "The Clergy and Democratic Freedoms." *Jahan,* January, March, and April, nos. 1, 3, and 4.

Overseas Consultants. 1949. *Report on Seven Year Development Plan for the Plan Organization of the Imperial Government of Iran.* Vol. 3. New York: Overseas Consultants, Inc.

Paige, J. 1975. *Agrarian Revolution: Social Movements and Export Agriculture in the Underdeveloped World.* New York: Free Press.

Parsa, M. 1985. "Economic Development and Political Transformation: A Comparative Analysis of the United States, Russia, Nicaragua, and Iran." *Theory and Society* 14:623–675.

———. 1988. "Theories of Collective Action and the Iranian Revolution." *Sociological Forum* 3:44–71.

Pesaran, H. 1976. "Income Distribution and its Major Determinants in Iran." In *Iran: Past, Present, and Future,* edited by J. Jacqz. New York: Aspen Institute for Humanistic Studies.

Pouyan, A. 1975. *On the Necessity of Armed Struggle.* New York: SCIPS (Support Committee for the Iranian People's Struggle).

The Public Relations of the Islamic Consultative Assembly. 1983. *Ashna'i Ba Majles-e Shora-ye Eslami.* Tehran: Islamic Consultative Assembly.

Ravasani, S. 1978. *Iran.* Stuttgart: Alektor Verlag.

Saikal, A. 1980. *The Rise and Fall of the Shah.* Princeton: Princeton University Press.

Schlesinger, A., Jr. 1958. *The Coming of the New Deal*. Boston: Houghton Mifflin.

Schwartz, M. 1976. *Radical Protest and Social Structure: The Southern Farmers' Alliance and Cotton Tenancy, 1880–1890*. New York: Academic Press.

SCI. *See* Statistical Center of Iran

Shaji'i, Z. 1965. *Namayandegan-e Majles-e Shora-ye Melli dar Bisto-yek Doreh-e Ghanoon Gozari*. Tehran: Tehran University Press.

Shariati, A. 1979. *On the Sociology of Islam*. Berkeley, Calif.: Mizan Press.

Sick, G. 1985. *All Fall Down*. New York: Random House.

Skocpol, T. 1979. *States and Social Revolutions: A Comparative Analysis of France, Russia, and China*. Cambridge: Cambridge University Press.

———. 1982. "Rentier State and Shi'a Islam in the Iranian Revolution." *Theory and Society* 11:265–283.

Smelser, N. 1962. *Theory of Collective Behavior*. New York: Free Press.

———. 1966. "Mechanisms of Change and Adjustment to Change." In *Political Development and Social Change*, edited by J. Finkle and R. Gable. New York: John Wiley.

Statistical Center of Iran (SCI). 1956. *National Census of Population and Housing*. Tehran: SCI.

———. 1966a. *National Census of Population and Housing*. Tehran: SCI.

———. 1966b. *Statistical Yearbook*. Tehran: SCI.

———. 1976a. *National Census of Population and Housing*. Tehran: SCI.

———. 1976b. *Netayej-e Amar Giri-e As Bank Hay-e Keshvar*. Tehran: SCI.

———. 1976c. *Tehran Census*. Tehran: SCI.

———. 1977a. *Statistical Yearbook*. Tehran: SCI.

———. 1977b. *Fehrest-e Nam Va Neshan-e Kar Gah Haye Bozorg-e Sanati 2534*. Tehran: SCI.

———. 1980. *Netayej-e Amar Giri-e Keshavarzi-e Rousta'i 1354*. Tehran: SCI.

———. 1981a. *Amar-e Kargah Haye Bozorg-e Sanati 1355*. Tehran: SCI.

———. 1981b. *Tehran Census*. Tehran: SCI.

Stempel, J. 1981. *Inside the Iranian Revolution*. Bloomington: Indiana University Press.

Tabari, A. 1983. "Land, Politics, and Capital Accumulation." *MERIP Reports* 13 (3): 26–30.

Tabari, E. 1977. *Jame'eh Iran Dar Doran-e Reza Shah*. Stockholm: Tudeh Publication.

Tehranian, M. 1980. "Communication and Revolution in Iran: The Passing of a Paradigm." *Iranian Studies* 13:5–30.

Tilly, C. 1978. *From Mobilization to Revolution*. Reading, Mass.: Addison-Wesley.

———. 1986. *The Contentious French: Four Centuries of Popular Struggle*. Cambridge: Harvard University Press, Belknap Press.

Tilly, C., L. Tilly, and R. Tilly. 1975. *The Rebellious Century, 1830–1930*. Cambridge: Harvard University Press.

Turner, T. 1980. "Iranian Oilworkers in the 1978–79 Revolution." In *Oil and Class Struggle*, edited by Petter Nore and Terisa Turner. London: Zed.

United Nations. 1953. *Review of Economic Conditions in the Middle East 1951–52*. Supplement to World Economic Report. New York: UN.

Vakil, F. 1976. "Iran's Basic Macroeconomic Problems: A 20-Year Horizon." In *Iran: Past, Present, and Future*, edited by J. Jacqz. New York: Aspen Institute for Humanistic Studies.

Walton, T. 1980. "Economic Development and Revolutionary Upheavals in Iran." *Cambridge Journal of Economics* 4:271–292.

Wilber, D. 1975. *Riza Shah Pahlavi: The Resurrection and Reconstruction of Iran*. New York: Exposition Press.

Wilkinson, P. 1971. *Social Movement*. New York: Praeger.

Zabih, S. 1982. *Iran Since the Revolution*. Baltimore: Johns Hopkins University Press.

NEWSPAPERS AND PAMPHLETS

Akhbar-e Jonbesh-e Eslami. A series of newsletters published by the Freedom Movement in 1978 and 1979.

Ayandegan. A national newspaper.

Enghelab-e Eslami. A national newspaper published by Bani-Sadr and his supporters.

Ettelaat. A national newspaper.

Guilds. A newsletter published in Tehran in 1979 by bazaar shopkeepers.

Hambastegi. A series of newsletters published by the National Organization of the Iranian Universities, the Writers' Association, and the Committee for Defense of Political Prisoners in 1978 and 1979.

Iranshahr. A newspaper published in the United States.

Iran Times. A newspaper published in the United States.

Jumhuri Eslami. A national newspaper published by the Islamic Republican party.

Kar. Weekly publication of the Organization of the Iranian People's Fedayee Guerrillas (Fedayeen).

Kayhan. A national newspaper.

Kayhan International and *Kayhan Havaee*. *Kayhan* newspaper for Iranians abroad.

Mizan. A newspaper published by the The Freedom Movement.

Mojahed. Newspaper published by the People's Mojahedeen Organization of Iran.

Oil Workers' Newsletter. 1979.

OIPFG. *See* The Organization of the Iranian People's Fedayee Guerrillas

Organization of Iranian Moslem Students. 1978. *Some of the Statements Published in Iran During July–August 1978*. Wilmette, Illinois.

The Organization of the Iranian People's Fedayee Guerrillas (OIPFG). 1979a. *Gozareshatie as Mobarezat-e Kharej as Mahtoodeh*.

―――. 1978b. *Pareh-ie as Ealamieh Hay-e Sazman-e Cherikhay-e Fedayee-e Khalgh-e Iran*.

Payam-e Mojahed. Official organ of the Freedom Movement published in the United States.

The People's Mojahedeen Organization of Iran. 1979. *Tahlile Jonbesh-e Khalgh-e Ghahraman-e Tabriz*. Tehran.

Rastakhiz. A national newspaper.

Tehran Economist. A journal published in Tehran.

Tehran Journal. The English edition of *Ettelaat* newspaper.

Zamimeh-e Khabar Nameh. 1978. A collection of newsletters published by the National Front (abroad).

Zobe-Ahan: Tahlily Bar E'atesab-e Mehr Mahe 1357. 1978. Pamphlet written by an anonymous group of steel mill employees.

ARCHIVAL MATERIAL

In addition to a number of my own interviews with bazaaris and members of various political organizations, I have used the following interviews conducted by Dr. H. Ladjevardi at the Middle Eastern Studies Center, Harvard University. Tape recordings can be found in the Iranian Oral History Collection, Houghton Library, Harvard University.

Lebaschi, A. 1983 (February 28)
Ladjevardi, G. 1983 (January 29)
Ladjevardian, A. 1982 (October 11)
Shanehchi, M. 1983 (March 4)

Index

Abadan, 55, 76, 182; oil refinery
strike, 134, 135, 158, 159–160;
protests, 111, 114, 269; theater fire
in, 55, 113, 210–211
Aba'i, Hojjat Al-Eslam, 202–203
Aghajari, 133, 136, 158, 159
Agricultural and Industrial Bank, 34
agricultural sector, 49, 68, 128, 250;
and development, 35–36, 71–75;
and mechanization, 73–74; and
productivity, 71–72, 74–75; and
reform, 39–40, 42; and state
intervention, 21–22, 68
Ahmadzadeh, Masoud, 180
Ahvaz, 76, 102, 241; oil workers, 157,
159; protests, 112, 114, 117, 201,
232–233, 235, 262; strikes, 145, 146,
147
AID, 49
Akhavan family, 70
Ala, Hossein, 134
Alam, Asadollah, 194, 215
Alemi, Ayatollah Mohammad Taghi,
206, 286, 295
alliances, 24, 25
Amini, Ali, 49 140, 170, 203, 246
Amirani, Mr., 197
Amlashi, Hojjat Al-Eslam Sayyed
Mehdi Rabbani, 206
Amnesty International, 54

Amol, 240; protests, 117, 152, 229,
231, 233
Amuzegar, Jamshid, 55, 84, 113, 211
Anglo-Iranian Oil Company, 40–41,
132, 133–134
Anglo-Persian Agreement, 33
Ansari, Houshang, 52, 158
Arab tribes: autonomy and, 258, 262;
oil industry and, 132–133
Arak, 116, 117, 154, 239
Ardabil, 116, 117, 240
Ardekani, Mahin, 229
Ardj factory, 143, 154
Arjomand, Said, 8, 9–10, 128, 250
armed forces. *See* military
arms sales, 51–52, 186
army, 40, 45, 47, 230; Pahlavi regime,
1–2, 37; and repression, 308–309.
See also military
arrests, 138, 143, 179, 180, 181, 200,
217, 252, 260, 287; of bazaaris, 103,
111, 112, 114, 282; of clergy, 195,
198, 206, 208, 209–210, 293; of
Khomeini, 50, 195, 216–217;
military, 242–243, 244; National
Front, 170–171, 175–176; protests
against, 97–98, 99, 230; of students,
111, 150, 208
Arsanjani, Hassan, 49
artisans, 39, 53, 106

335